The Origins of the Modern European
State System, 1494–1618

THE MODERN EUROPEAN STATE SYSTEM

THE ORIGINS OF
THE MODERN EUROPEAN STATE SYSTEM
1494–1618

A long-running staple of the Longman History list has been the distinguished and highly successful trio of books by Derek McKay and H.M. Scott (1648–1815), Roy Bridge and Roger Bullen (1814–1914), and Graham Ross (1915–1945) on the development of the European state system and the rise and fall of the European great powers. The original sequence is now being rewritten, expanded and extended to cover the whole span of modern European history from the late fifteenth century to the present day. The five volumes (each self-sufficient and useable separately) will be published under the series title *The Modern European State System*. Here, M.S. Anderson's entirely new introductory volume, *The Origins of the Modern European State System, 1494–1618*, inaugurates the enterprise in fine style.

The Origins of the Modern European State System, 1494–1618

M.S. Anderson

LONGMAN
London and New York

Addison Wesley Longman Limited
Edinburgh Gate,
Harlow
Essex CM20 2JE
United Kingdom
and Associated Companies throughout the world.

*Published in the United States of America
by Addison Wesley Longman, New York.*

First published 1998

ISBN 0 582 22945 6 CSD
ISBN 0 582 22944 8 PPR

British Library Cataloguing in Publication Data

A catalogue entry for this title is available from the British Library

Library of Congress Cataloging-in-Publication Data

Anderson, M. S. (Matthew Smith)
The origins of the modern European state system, 1494–1618 / M.S. Anderson.
p.   cm.
Includes bibliographical references and index.
ISBN 0-582-22945-6 (CSD). – ISBN 0-582-22944-8 (PPR)
1. Europe–History–1492–1648. 2. State, The–Origin. I. Title.
D231.A53 1998
940.2'1–dc21   97-31324
                                          CIP

Set by 7 in 10/12 New Baskerville
Produced by Longman Singapore Publishers (Pte) Ltd.
Printed in Singapore

Contents

List of Maps

Acknowledgements

It would have been impossible to write this book without the help of several great libraries. I have drawn upon the resources of the British Library, more heavily upon those of the British Library of Political and Economic Science, the library of my old college, the London School of Economics, and most heavily of all upon those of the London Library. To all of them I must express my thanks. I have also benefited greatly from the comments made on an earlier draft by Professor M.J. Rodriguez-Salgado and Dr Hamish Scott. I have not followed all their suggestions; but this does not lessen my gratitude for the time and care they gave to reading and improving what I had written. It goes without saying that for any defects that still remain I alone am responsible.

M. S. Anderson

CHAPTER ONE

The Instruments of International Relations: Armies and Navies

War: part of the natural order

It is appropriate that any account of international relations in Europe between those two traditional historical signposts, the French invasion of Italy in 1494 and the beginning of the Thirty Years War in 1618, should begin with a consideration of war and its implications. Throughout this period armed struggle, potential or actual, was the most important and enduring influence on the relationships between the European states. Personal rivalries between monarchs, conflicting dynastic claims, the workings of a still embryonic balance of power, generated conflicts to which religious antagonisms, between Christians and Muslims, later between Catholics and Protestants, added a more emotional dimension. War to men of that age was a natural condition, as natural as peace and perhaps more so. Martin Luther's often-quoted remark that it was 'as necessary as eating, drinking, or any other business' expressed a viewpoint from which few would have seriously dissented; and the voice of these few was a weak and ineffective one which rulers and their ministers could safely ignore. Erasmus might attack the aggressiveness and territorial ambitions of rulers.[1] Anabaptists might put forward their own brand of Christian pacifism. None of this made any practical difference. War, it seemed, had always existed and always would.

It could also be seen not merely as natural and inevitable but as in many ways and for much of society beneficial. The long-standing belief that it was the salutary punishment decreed by God for the transgressions of sinful mankind, and therefore part of the divine scheme

---

1. See the quotations from him in M.S. Anderson, *The Growth of Modern Diplomacy* (London, 1993), p. 209.

1

of things, had deep roots. So had the assumption, even more ancient and destined to be even more lasting, that enduring peace inevitably led to weakness and degeneration in any society, that it stifled energies and promoted an ignoble desire for material comfort at the expense of nobler ambitions. A people in this position, wrote an Elizabethan commentator, would 'wax rotten in idleness', while another had no doubt that 'Warre is the remedy for a State surfeited with peace, it is a medicine for Commonwealths sicke of too much ease and tranquil-litie'.[2] Such attitudes were to persist, unchanged in essentials, until the cataclysm of 1914.

Moreover, in an age with nothing approaching modern police forces crime, disorder, riot, discontent of any kind which might erupt in violence, were a continual threat. A war which swept, often forc-ibly, the unemployed, the vagrant, the starving and the criminal into the army, and sent them off to fight and die comfortably far from home, very often seemed to the respectable a valuable social safety-valve. Foreign war might well be the best of all guarantees of domes-tic peace.[3] At the very end of this period an English preacher could still see it as a welcome opportunity 'to cleanse the city and rid the country of as much as may be of those straggling vagrants, loytering fellowes and lewd livers . . . which doe so swarme among us';[4] and feelings of this kind were also to survive for centuries to come. Queen Elizabeth herself told a French ambassador in the 1590s that the Eng-lish soldiers then in France 'were but thieves and ought to hang'.[5] Of more strictly political weight was the argument that foreign war pro-vided an essential safety-valve for aggressive energies which otherwise would find a potentially disastrous outlet in factional struggles at home. The existence almost everywhere of a noble and gentry class trained and fit for little but fighting lent force to this claim. It was put most persuasively during the wars of religion in France from the 1560s onwards, in which soldiers returned from fighting in Italy or on France's north-eastern frontier played an important part; and it is not surprising to find a veteran French professional soldier then as-serting, in terms which many contemporaries would have agreed with, that 'A great estate replenished with warlike people, ought still

2. P.A. Jorgensen, *Shakespeare's Military World* (Berkeley/Los Angeles, 1956), pp. 172, 189.

3. J.R. Hale, 'Sixteenth-century explanations of war and violence', *Past and Present* 51 (May 1971), 21, conveniently assembles a number of contemporary expressions of this very widespread idea.

4. Idem, 'Incitement to violence? English divines on the theme of war, 1578 to 1631', in his *Renaissance War Studies* (London, 1983), p. 498.

5. Jorgensen, *Shakespeare's Military World*, p. 145.

to have some foreine warre wherewith to keep it occupied, lest being at quiet they (*sic*) convert their weapons against each other'. In the same vein a Venetian writer in 1589 could argue that Spain then enjoyed domestic tranquillity because she was so deeply involved in foreign wars 'that thought or the actual deeds of war occupy the Spaniards and their own country enjoys perfect peace: the evil humours have been driven elsewhere'. Even in Elizabethan England the government sometimes used the conscription of men to fight abroad as a means of averting possible unrest at home.[6]

Again, belief in the supreme importance of honour, the pervasive emphasis on personal glory and prestige, the persistence of a legacy of chivalric attitudes, meant that to rulers and nobilities alike war was often welcome as an opportunity to achieve these intangible but deeply important objectives. Frequently it was embarked on with what now seems almost criminal light-heartedness, without any clear idea of how it was to be paid for or what it might reasonably hope to achieve. At the very summit of society, to command successfully on the field of battle gave a monarch prestige as nothing else could. The young Henry VIII of England was perhaps the most obvious of a number of rulers who showed themselves very conscious of this fact; and the two who dominated the first half of the sixteenth century in western Europe, Francis I of France and the Emperor Charles V, were both at times prominent on the battlefield. There were certainly kings with different attitudes. Ferdinand VII of Aragon, Henry VII of England and Louis XII of France played little active military role (though this seemed unusual, perhaps even a little suspect, to their contemporaries). Philip II of Spain was only twice in his life, as a young man, even distantly involved in military operations, and never commanded on the battlefield. Nevertheless the ideal of the ruler who vindicated his territorial or dynastic claims by war, and if possible by personal leadership in the field, remained a powerful one. After all, the Church had for centuries taught that a just war was fully permissible; and arguments could always be found to maintain the justice of almost any conflict, even between Christians. War against the infidel, it went without saying, was not merely permissible but highly praiseworthy.

Further down the social scale the nobility and gentry in every European state often found war a field of opportunity, a source of personal gratification and material gain. To a class essentially military in

---

6. Ibid., p. 181; G. Botero, *The Reason of State*, trans. P.J. and D.P. Waley (London, 1956), p. 77; C.G. Cruickshank, *Elizabeth's Army* (Oxford, 1946), pp. 9–10.

origin it was a natural and welcome outlet for their energies; and here too the lure of fame and personal reputation was often important. To the minor nobility and gentry in particular, seldom wealthy, usually poorly educated and in any case contemptuous of sedentary civilian occupations, war could mean profit, even riches. Booty, best of all a really important prisoner able to pay a large ransom, could be a very welcome windfall to some poor squire or provincial noble. To the great bulk of society, to the tradesman, the artisan, the peasant, glory or profit hardly entered into the picture. But here also the assumption of the inevitability of war was complete. Like a hard winter or a poor harvest it was something very unwelcome but at the same time unavoidable. There might well be grumbling, even serious discontent, over some particular demand made or loss suffered as a result of some particular conflict. A new tax or an interruption of some established trading link might provoke serious opposition. But rejection of war as such, any idea that it could be banished from human life, struck no significant responsive chord at any level of society.

The lack of clear definitions

War was still, by the standards of the present day, very badly delimited. It was strikingly lacking in the clear definitions we now take for granted. It was possible, even normal, for there to be quite serious fighting between the subjects of two states without any formal declaration of war; and constant low-level hostilities of this kind were greatly encouraged by the fact that almost all frontiers were still very badly and vaguely defined. Indeed the modern idea of a frontier, a line precisely drawn and clearly demarcated, did not as yet exist. For generations to come frontiers were to remain badly defined zones, usually criss-crossed by traditional jurisdictions and privileges of many kinds, so that individuals or institutions subject to one ruler might assert rights to collect dues or taxes from the subjects of another.

Such a situation was almost inevitable in an age when maps were rare and the few that existed were extremely rudimentary. Without adequate maps men were still, in a sense, blind, unable to envisage frontiers in any large-scale or strategic way. Until the treaties of Madrid in 1526 and Cambrai in 1529, for example, it was hardly possible to speak at all of a frontier in any meaningful sense between France and the Low Countries. Such vagueness helped to make possible local conflicts, often on a considerable scale, even while the rulers on each side of these very vaguely defined boundaries remained at least technically at peace. In eastern and east–central Europe, where geographical divisions between states were even less well defined and the control of rulers over their subjects, especially on the periphery of their territories, was even less effective than in the west, this situation was still more marked. An outstanding example is the boundary area in Hungary and Croatia between the Ottoman Empire and the territories of the Austrian Habsburgs. Even after the Turkish conquest of most of Hungary in the 1520s and 1530s many Hungarian nobles kept up claims to rights of various kinds over their former lands – to levy feudal dues there or even to live on them tax-free for limited periods – and these were to play for generations to come a role in Habsburg–Ottoman negotiations.[7] The second half of the sixteenth century saw the frontier between the two powers become relatively stable; but it was hardly better defined. Yet conflict of this kind, however frequent and destructive, did not by itself mean formal war. The Treaty of Sitva-Torok in 1606 began an unprecedentedly long period of official peace between Habsburgs and Ottomans; but even after this much frontier raiding went on, with a tacit understanding that this did not amount to war if the forces involved on each side were of less than a certain size.[8]

There were other ways in which the dividing line between war and peace, so clear to modern eyes, could be blurred. A government might allow or encourage its subjects to attack the forces and territory of another, quite openly and on a large scale, or even use its own army and navy in this way, without any formal declaration of hostilities. War of this unofficial but sometimes serious kind became particularly important in the later decades of the sixteenth century as the power of Spain reached its zenith. The desire of other states to resist its growth, combined with their hesitations about challenging the greatest power in Europe, meant that this sort of underhand or semi-official war played for some years a very significant role. Thus in 1572 a French army commanded by a Huguenot leader, the Sieur de Genlis, attempted without any declaration of war (and with notable lack of success) to raise the Spanish siege of Mons in the southern Netherlands. In the same way a French fleet took a leading part in the unsuccessful Portuguese attack on the Azores, now Spanish-held, in 1582, while three years later Drake raided destructively Spanish settlements

---

7. P.F. Sugar, *Southeastern Europe under Ottoman Rule, 1354–1804* (Seattle/London, 1977), p. 91.

8. G.E. Rothenberg, *The Austrian Military Border in Croatia, 1522–1747* (Urbana, Ill., 1960), p. 65.

in the Caribbean, without either France or England having declared war on Philip II. At sea particularly the situation was confused and chaotic. The very widespread issue to privateers (who were often hard to distinguish from pirates) of letters of marque which gave them at least some claim to legitimacy did much to blur the dividing line between peace and war. The use, often on a large scale, of privately owned ships to supplement the small navies which were usually all that governments could afford, meant that even when war had been declared a naval expedition might be a private enterprise rather than an official act of hostility. Nor were the rights of neutrals any more clearly defined than the distinction between peace and war. In particular it was widely argued that a belligerent state had the right, in attacking its enemy, to move its forces across the territory of a neutral provided that it paid compensation for any damage these might do on their march (the so-called right of *transitus innoxius*). This alleged right was often resisted by the neutral states concerned, and belligerent ones tended to avoid unnecessary use of it; but it remained none the less a significant element in the structure of international relations. In a whole series of ways, therefore, war during this period lacked the clear definitions and precise dividing lines that it has since acquired.

War: seldom decisive

War, then, was endemic in sixteenth-century Europe. Yet of all the many struggles that mark the age, remarkably few ended in decisive victory for one of the combatants if these were at all evenly matched. Sweeping territorial gains, spectacular conquests, were very hard to achieve, at least in the western half of the continent. (The one great example of such conquests, those of the Ottomans in the Balkans and Hungary, was achieved at the expense of opponents militarily much weaker and often socially deeply divided.) For this situation there were several explanations; but one is of overriding importance. War was expensive and becoming more so. Though rulers spent money on other things – on their courts and palaces, on their civilian administrative machines, on gifts to favoured ministers and generals, even on the diplomatic services that were slowly taking shape – the costs of present wars and the debts incurred to pay for past ones were incomparably the greatest drain on their finances. Yet no government, not even that of Spain as she began to draw great resources from her American possessions in the later decades of the century, could sustain a long struggle on a large scale without crippling financial difficulties. Louis XII of France, as he planned a new assault on Italy in the first years of the century, was told by one of his chief commanders, a very experienced Italian, that for success in such an undertaking three things were needed: 'money, more money, and yet more money'. This was the voice of realism. But no ruler, however grandiose his ambitions, was ever rich enough to achieve great and lasting conquests in the face of determined opposition. (Philip II's acquisition of Portugal in 1580 was the nearest any ruler came to such an achievement; but he had a genuine claim to the vacant Portuguese throne and did not have to overcome sustained resistance.)

All governments were faced continually by deeply intractable financial difficulties, which generated what one historian has called 'a perpetual spiral of indigence and inefficiency'.[9] This meant that though they might win striking temporary success it was almost impossible for them to crush permanently a powerful enemy. Shortage of money often made it impossible to follow up effectively even the greatest victory in the field. An army, essentially made up of mercenaries and often recruited by dubious means, might waste away very quickly in the moment of triumph if there were no money to pay it. The crushing defeat of the French by the forces of Charles V at Pavia in 1525 could not be followed up, for this reason, by any effort to invade France; indeed, the imperial commanders were forced to risk a battle at all largely because their army was already threatening to disintegrate because it had been so long unpaid. A generation later the equally spectacular overthrow of a French army by a Spanish one at St Quentin in 1557 had no lasting result because Philip II lacked the hard cash which alone could hold the victorious force together. His correspondence after the battle, and that of the Duke of Savoy who commanded the Spanish army, is a litany of complaints about the lack of money and even of food. It was very often taken for granted that a commander, usually himself a great aristocrat, would contribute from his own pocket to the cost of his army: a campaign normally cost a general money. Thus the Duke of Alba, who led the Spanish army which conquered Portugal in 1580, claimed to have spent 80,000 ducats in the process, while part of the cost of the Spanish armada of 1588 was met by its commander, the Duke of Medina-Sidonia, and the Earl of Essex spent £14,000 on the English force which campaigned unsuccessfully under his leadership in Normandy in 1592.

An unpaid army might simply, in effect, go on strike, refusing to

9. I.A.A. Thompson, *War and Government in Habsburg Spain, 1560–1620* (London, 1976), p. 67.

obey orders or to move until it was paid at least part of what it was owed. The history of the Spanish effort to suppress the Netherlands revolt from the 1570s onwards is punctuated by repeated examples of 'industrial action' of this kind; while in the 1590s, it has been argued, 'it was the military mutiny that was the characteristic popular revolt of the decade'.[10] Mutiny could have very important political results. Philip II's hopes of intervening decisively on the Catholic side in the last critical years of the wars of religion in France, for example, were stultified partly by the unreliability of his forces in the southern Netherlands. Soldiers with grievances over pay might force their commanders into actions which were unwise and even disastrous. Thus in 1522 discontented Swiss mercenaries helped to compel the French army of which they were an important part to fight the imperialists at Bicocca in northern Italy and suffer a serious defeat. Most serious of all, unpaid and hungry soldiers might pillage, maltreat and even massacre civilians with unpredictable but potentially very serious political results. Spain's armies on the whole held together longer, throughout the century, than those of her enemies before they mutinied or melted away for lack of pay: this was a major source of her remarkable military success. But the sack of Antwerp by a mutinous Spanish army in November 1576, in which more than 7,000 civilians were killed, was the most spectacular of all examples of the potentially devastating results of leaving soldiers for long periods without what they were owed. It created a short-lived possibility of united action by all seventeen Netherlands provinces to expel Spanish influence and force the withdrawal of all Spanish troops. If realized, this would have affected deeply the whole fabric of international relations for generations to come. Almost simultaneously a much less well-known incident in the Baltic lands made the same point less spectacularly. In 1574 German mercenaries, disgruntled by the failure of their employer, John III of Sweden, to pay their wages, forced the king to hand over to them as security for what was owed three fortresses in Estonia, which the Swedes were then trying to conquer. When he could not produce the sum due they responded by surrendering these to the Danish forces they had been hired to fight.[11]

10. G. Parker, *The Army of Flanders and the Spanish Road, 1567–1659* (Cambridge, 1972), Pt ii, ch. VIII. Parker calculates that there were at least 45 mutinies in the Spanish forces in The Netherlands during the long struggle of 1567–1609, many of which lasted for a year or more. See also I.A.A. Thompson, 'The impact of war', in P. Clark, ed., *The European Crisis of the 1590s* (London, 1985), p. 275.

11. See below, p. 267; M. Roberts, *The Early Vasas: A History of Sweden, 1523–1611* (Cambridge, 1968), p. 256; F. Tallett, *War and Society in Early Modern Europe, 1494–1715* (London, 1992), p. 172.

Inability to pay an army could therefore be very dangerous. Yet the cost of waging war was growing. The short-lived conflict of 1546–47 in which Charles V defeated the Protestant princes of Germany cost about two million florins. In the years 1552–53, however, the struggle of the emperor and his son, the later Philip II, against France cost at least twice as much each year; and by the 1590s the war Spain was fighting in the Netherlands was draining her of some nine million annually (the size of the armies involved was about the same in each case).[12]

Currency inflation does a good deal to explain these growing costs; but they were also in large part the result of changes in military technology. The most important of these was the fact that major fortresses and strategically important cities were now more and more protected by new-style fortifications – walls thick enough to resist artillery fire, bastions which made the fire of the defenders more effective, wide moats and ditches and increasingly elaborate outworks of different kinds. These were expensive to build, often enormously so. They were also, if resolutely defended, difficult and very expensive to capture. More and more war in much of Europe, most strikingly in the Netherlands and the frontier area between France and the Holy Roman Empire, tended to become as the century went on a matter of sieges. This meant that the rapid movement of armies became more and more difficult and quick and easy conquests impossible.

The resistance of even a minor fortress could sometimes impede decisively the advance of an army and make ineffective an entire campaign. In 1532 the little fortified town of Güns, by holding out for three weeks against a great Turkish force, prevented the advance on Vienna, only twelve leagues away, which the Sultan Suleiman the Magnificent had planned. A quarter of a century later, after the Spaniards had won their crushing victory at St Quentin, the town, which was neither large nor very well fortified, held out long enough to prevent their reaping any real advantage from it and to give time for shortage of money and supplies to undermine their army. These are outstanding and often-quoted illustrations of the point; but there are plenty of others. In 1536, for example, France had already benefited in the same way from the much less well-known defence of the small fortified town of Péronne. By resisting for a month an invasion which seemed for a moment to threaten Paris itself, it stultified the entire plan of campaign of the imperial army. Eight years later an equally secondary fortress, Saint-Dizier, held up another invading imperial force for over six weeks with important strategic results.

---

12. Parker, *The Army of Flanders*, p. 134fn.

The capture of a large and well-defended fortress could be even more prolonged and costly. The successful Turkish siege of Rhodes in 1522 lasted for six months and the unsuccessful one of Malta in 1565 for more than three. Famagusta, the main Venetian stronghold in Cyprus, fell to Turkish attack in 1571 only after holding out for eleven months. The great siege of Antwerp by the Duke of Parma in 1584–85, though it recovered the city for Philip II, went on for thirteen months, and the unsuccessful one of Amiens by a French army under Henry IV in 1597 for six. The capture of Ostend, another eventual Spanish success, took three years, 1601–04. Operations of this kind tied down large forces for long periods and were correspondingly expensive. Accurate figures are impossible to calculate; but at the end of this period the long (over a year) siege of the Huguenot stronghold of La Rochelle by the forces of Louis XIII in 1627–28 may well have cost some 40 million livres, a gigantic sum for that age.[13] A really unsuccessful siege could be more disastrous than almost any defeat on the battlefield. When Charles V besieged Metz in 1552–53 (beginning the siege, against the advice of his generals, much too late in the year) the commander of the French garrison, the Duc de Guise, claimed that of the 60,000 men with whom the emperor began this disastrous enterprise, he had when he abandoned it only 12,000 left. The figures are unreliable; but there is no doubt that the losses were enormous. Two decades later the long siege of Haarlem, in the first stages of the Dutch revolt, cost the besieging Spanish army 12,000 men.

The expense of fighting a war was in any case growing for other reasons. French experts in the 1630s calculated that by then a soldier, because of the universal adoption of firearms and the use of increasing quantities of artillery, cost five times as much to arm and maintain as he had a century earlier: even if allowance is made for currency inflation during the period, this was a sharp increase.[14] The major monarchies of western Europe, those of Spain, France and England, all borrowed heavily to finance the unprecedentedly expensive cycle of wars they fought in 1585–1604; and the resulting indebtedness underlies many of the difficulties all three were to encounter during the decades that followed.[15] Heavy costs, the growing importance of siege warfare and of defensive as opposed to offensive strategies, the difficulty of holding together unpaid or

13. C. Tilly, *The Contentious French* (Cambridge, Mass./London, 1988), p. 87.

14. P. Contamine, ed., *Histoire militaire de la France*, (Paris, 1992), i, p. 343.

15. This point is developed in C.S.R. Russell, 'Monarchies, wars and estates in England, France and Spain, c.1580–1640', *Legislative Studies Quarterly* vii, No. 2 (May 1982).

irregularly paid armies – all these meant that in western Europe at least decisive victory in war and rapid or easy conquests were impossible to achieve. Rulers and commanders were often very reluctant to admit this fact; but it was a fact none the less.

Armies and recruiting

War in this period saw no Napoleonic-style offensive successes partly because armies were relatively small and did not grow much, at least from the 1550s onwards. Large forces, even if they could be raised in the first place, were so difficult to pay, supply and move that hardly any army in the field ever exceeded 35,000–40,000 men. Perhaps 30,000–40,000 were mustered for the French invasion of Italy in 1494. At Pavia the victorious imperial forces numbered no more than 20,000–25,000 and the French 25,000–30,000. The contending French and imperial armies in the Picardy campaign of 1543–44 each had about 30,000 men; and Henry II of France may have had about 38,000 available for that of 1552. In 1557 Philip II put about 40,000 in the field for the St Quentin campaign (including 7,000 English auxiliaries). The most successful sustained military operation of the century, the reconquest for Spain by the Duke of Parma of much of the Netherlands in the decade before his death in 1592, was achieved with a field force of less, sometimes much less, than 20,000. In 1610 Henry IV, for his projected war with Spain, planned to raise forces of 54,000 men; but of these only 30,000 were to form his main army in the field.[16] The total numbers theoretically at the disposal of major rulers were sometimes much larger and certainly grew during the century. Charles V may have mobilized something like 150,000 men throughout his widespread dominions in 1552. Sully, the chief minister of Henry IV, dreamed of raising 190,000 for the coming struggle with Spain in 1610 (though this included the forces to be supplied by France's putative allies). Philip IV of Spain claimed in 1625 to have 300,000 men at his command. But nothing approaching these numbers was ever assembled as a single coherent force. Even the greatest battles of the age were fought by relatively small armies.

Nor was there any fundamental change either in the weapons which the soldier carried or in the tactics he used on the battlefield.

---

16. Many of these figures are taken from J.A. Lynn, 'The pattern of army growth, 1445–1945', and S. Adams, 'Tactics or politics? "The military revolution" and the Habsburg hegemony, 1525–1648', both in J.A. Lynn, ed., *Tools of War: Instruments, Ideas and Institutions of Warfare, 1445–1871* (Urbana/Chicago, 1990).

By the beginning of the sixteenth century the arquebus had developed to a point at which effective small arms fire was possible: a Spanish army defeated a French one at Cerignola in southern Italy in 1503 by arquebus fire from a strong fortified position; and the later development of the musket made it even clearer that hand firearms were now an essential element in any fighting force. The proportion of 'shot' to pikemen grew steadily as the century went on, from one to five in its first years to one to two or even one to one. Charles V is alleged to have said that 'the outcome of my wars was decided by the matches of my arquebusiers'. However, pikemen in substantial numbers were always essential to protect the musketeer as he loaded and reloaded his still clumsy weapon: not until the development of the bayonet at the end of the seventeenth century was this position to change. The proportion of cavalry to infantry, again, declined steadily in all armies, at least in western Europe, as the sixteenth century progressed; though the decline of traditional heavy cavalry was offset in a number of armies by a growing use of lighter and more mobile mounted troops. But this also was a gradual rather than a revolutionary process, one of the most obvious signs of the ebbing away of traditional chivalric attitudes and their replacement by a professionalism which could not afford such luxuries.

The ways in which armies were raised also changed little in essentials during this period. The normal picture was that of a small, permanent force, supplemented in wartime by larger numbers of men persuaded or forced to become soldiers, and by mercenaries. Such an army might also be backed by a substantial militia; but this was usually poorly trained and equipped and always reluctant to fight outside its own immediate area. No state could face the cost of maintaining a large standing army in peacetime; and hardly any produced enough recruits of acceptable quality in all the different branches – heavy and light cavalry, musketeers and pikemen – that were needed to make up an effective one. Standing armies were therefore small.

In England which, protected by the sea, could afford to remain a bulwark of military conservatism, the garrisons of Calais (until its loss in 1558) and Berwick-on-Tweed, and a small number of royal yeomen, were the only such force available. In France there was a *gendarmerie* of heavy cavalry supplemented by royal household troops, the Scots and Swiss guards; but these again were relatively few in number, and the slowly declining importance of cavalry meant some lessening of their practical usefulness. An effort in 1534 to supplement them by the creation of seven 'legions' of 6,000 men each to be recruited in frontier areas was ambitious but unsuccessful. It was intended that they should be mustered twice a year and each have a nucleus which was permanently under arms; but this had little lasting effect. By 1558 they had already lost so much importance that an effort was made, again without success, to revive them. After 1568 they are heard of no more.[17] Nor were forces based on the surviving feudal obligations of nobles and landowners now of any real military use. In France levies of this kind, the *ban* and *arrière-ban*, were still frequently summoned during the first half of the century. But this was done to the accompaniment of a stream of complaints that they were too poorly equipped and trained to be worth much. By the 1560s a summons of the *arrière-ban* yielded only 2,000–3,000 men; and in 1579 the ancient post of its captain-general was suppressed.[18] Even in Russia a quasi-feudal cavalry force, recruited from landowners and their dependants, was supplemented in 1550 by the creation of new elite units of *streltsy* (musketeers) recruited from non-privileged commoners. Their strength grew rapidly, from an original 3,000 to 18,000–20,000 by the end of the century. Here too, in what to western eyes was still an exotic and non-European country, the need for disciplined professional soldiers trained in the use of firearms was impossible to ignore.[19] Similar forces were established in the grand duchy of Lithuania in 1551 and in Poland in 1562.

Since standing professional forces were necessarily small, and traditional feudal ones more and more a shadow of what they had once been, governments were forced in time of war to raise recruits as best they could from the populations under their control. This could yield substantial numbers of men. Well over 100,000 were recruited in England and Wales for service abroad in 1585–1602 – a high figure for what was still a small and unmilitary state.[20] But for almost all the men who joined up in this way the army was an occupation of last resort. Hardly anyone became a soldier if there were any practicable alternative; and the better the economic conditions and the higher the wages, the smaller was the incentive to enlist, particularly as the soldier's pay, even assuming that he received it promptly and in full, usually failed completely to keep pace with the price inflation that marked much of the century. The wages of an infantryman in Venetian service, fixed in 1509, did not increase for the rest of the century, while those of a Spanish one remained unchanged for 100

17. *Histoire militaire de la France*, i, pp. 250–1, 312.
18. Ibid., pp. 306–9.
19. J.H.L. Keep, *Soldiers of the Tsar: Army and Society in Russia, 1462–1874* (Oxford, 1985), pp. 60ff.
20. Cruickshank, *Elizabeth's Army*, p. 137.

years after they were fixed in 1534. The poverty of much of Castile, arid and unproductive, and the resulting relative ease of obtaining good recruits there, do much to explain the remarkable military achievements of Spain during the sixteenth century. But over most of western Europe the quality of such recruits, as has been seen, was poor. Many of the men concerned were criminals. From 1569 onwards the Spanish government, for example, regularly obtained recruits in Catalonia, the most lawless part of Spain, by the grant of amnesty to convicted bandits in return for a specified period of army service. Many were coerced into service, as when in 1592 an edict in the duchy of Piedmont ordered all men without a recognized trade or some means of support to join the army or leave the country within eight days.[21] And quite apart from their moral character, reluctant levies, resistant to discipline and often poorly trained, were unlikely to make good soldiers. The difficulty of recruiting men of the right quality stimulated a growing official propaganda, through use of the printing-press and sermons, in favour of war and military preparedness;[22] but the effect of this must have been very limited.

Militias were in general a secondary and muted element in the picture. In some countries they did not exist on more than a regional scale. In Spain a series of proposals to create a national force of this kind had had some effect by the end of this period only in some coastal areas – Galicia, parts of Catalonia, Andalusia and Valencia. In France also, though some urban militias could be considerable (Amiens by the end of the sixteenth century could raise a force of 3,000 men from its citizens), only one or two exposed frontier areas – the Boulonnais in the north-east and Béarn in the Pyrenees – had local militias of peasants serving under their seigneurs. In the Netherlands the Union of Utrecht, which in 1579 united much of the northern provinces in resistance to Philip II, provided for the registration of all men between the ages of eighteen and 60 as an essential step towards the creation of a militia; but this again had little effect. Some militias could be numerically impressive. In England Henry VIII and his ministers kept under arms throughout the summer of 1545, when French invasion threatened, as many as 120,000 men, a gigantic force for so small a country, while the menace of Spanish attack in 1588 called forth a great effort which was almost equalled in 1596–97 and 1599.[23]

21. Thompson, *War and Government*, p. 117; A. de Saluces, *Histoire militaire du Piémont* (Turin, 1818), i, p. 176.

22. J.A. Hale, 'War and public opinion in the fifteenth and sixteenth centuries', *Past and Present* 22 (July 1962), 24–6.

23. L. Boynton, *The Elizabethan Militia, 1558–1638* (London/Toronto, 1967), ch. V.

But inadequate arms and training, and infrequent and slipshod musters, often meant that the military value of militias, where they existed, was very limited. Everywhere there was resistance to the costs, in time and effort as well as money, which an effective system inevitably involved. Probably the best-organized and most reliable forces of this kind were to be found by the end of the sixteenth century in northern Italy, in the Venetian republic and perhaps Piedmont. But here as much as anywhere else was to be seen another basic limitation of all militias – the deep unwillingness of their members to serve anywhere outside their own immediate locality. This reluctance was very understandable. Any militiaman away from home for long was likely soon to be haunted by visions of crops spoiling or a business decaying from lack of attention; and this meant that he was likely to be of little use outside a very restricted area. One observer in the early seventeenth century complained that the countrymen of the Venetian territories were 'like farmyard dogs, fearless of death in the yard, fleeing at the least alarm outside it'.[24] The remark had relevance everywhere.

All this meant that mercenaries made up a large part of virtually every sixteenth-century army. They had some important advantages and were normally the first choice of any government that had to raise an army quickly. They could always be obtained, even at short notice, by any state, and retained as long as it could pay them. Within a month of the outbreak of war with the Ottoman Empire in 1570, for example, Venice received 46 different offers to raise substantial mercenary forces of between 1,000 and 5,000 men, as well as others for smaller numbers.[25] Mercenaries were normally better trained and armed than hastily raised domestic levies. They were usually willing (with the important exception of the Swiss, who refused to fight each other) to do battle with any opponent, untroubled by considerations of nationality or even religion, though the intensified religious antagonisms of the later sixteenth century did produce some heart-searching on the latter point. 'Soldiers go where they are paid the most', said a Spanish grandee in 1632, 'without taking into account either religion or the prince concerned'.[26] This summed up a position which had held good for generations. Their employers were as a rule equally undiscriminating. As early as 1482 the Neapolitan army fighting Venice

24. M.E. Mallett and J.R. Hale, *The Military Organization of a Renaissance State: Venice, c.1400 to 1617* (Cambridge, 1984), p. 364.

25. Ibid., p. 322.

26. R.A. Stradling, *The Spanish Monarchy and Irish Mercenaries: The Wild Geese in Spain, 1618–68* (Dublin, 1994), p. 15.

in the so-called 'War of Ferrara' included even Turkish mercenaries. However, the disadvantages of forces of this kind were also considerable. They were expensive; and as has been seen, unpaid mercenaries could produce political as well as military disaster. Since they often had no ties of any kind with the populations among whom they fought they were more likely than native levies to plunder and maltreat civilians, though here much depended on the regularity with which they were paid and the degree of discipline that particular commanders could impose.

None the less, they were used by all governments, and often on a large scale. In the early decades of the sixteenth century the reputation of Swiss mercenaries was at its height. They saw themselves, and were widely seen by others, as the best soldiers in Europe; and though they served many masters they formed in particular an important element in the French armies that struggled for control of Italy during these years. (The first agreement for the use of Swiss mercenaries by a French king was signed by Louis XI with some of the cantons in 1474.) From the 1520s, as the vulnerability of massed formations of Swiss pikemen to artillery and firearms became increasingly clear, their relative importance declined sharply. Simultaneously, that of German mercenaries, *Landsknechts* (infantry) and *Reiters* (cavalry), grew. Germany remained throughout the sixteenth century the greatest reservoir of hired professional soldiers, one on which rulers all over Europe drew heavily. Francis I of France, for example, recruited 23,000 *Landsknechts* for his invasion of Italy in 1515, while his son, Henry II, decided in 1557 to take German cavalry into his service, since its tactics were more up to date than those of the somewhat tradition-bound French cavalry. Large numbers of Italians also, particularly from certain areas – the Romagna, the Marches and Umbria – figured prominently in many armies, while by the later decades of the century Scots were playing a significant role in northern Europe. But mercenaries were drawn from a wide range of sources. Venice, for example, recruited them not merely in other parts of Italy and in Switzerland but also in Corsica, Dalmatia and Albania.

The provision of mercenary soldiers was an established and recognized trade. Military entrepreneurs raised men, usually after signing a contract with some employer, and organized, armed and equipped them as well as leading them in battle. Often such an entrepreneur even received a retaining fee in peacetime from his employer in return for an undertaking to raise a specified force on the outbreak of war. Some became wealthy by plying this trade and might, if of humble birth (as a good many were), acquire noble status. Others were ruined by the failure of their employers to pay what they owed, or by being taken prisoner in battle and forced to pay a heavy ransom.[27] The raising of armies by such methods was one of several illustrations of the fact that governments, often with relatively little administrative machinery at their disposal, could fight wars only by devolving to private enterprise many functions which they could not themselves perform, or could perform only less efficiently.

Artillery and fortifications

The greatest single factor making for change in sixteenth-century warfare was the growing importance of artillery. The potentialities of cannon, especially in siege warfare, and the need they created for a new type of fortification, were clear long before the French irruption into Italy in 1494. In the last throes of the Hundred Years War guns had been decisive in capturing the remaining English fortresses in Normandy and Guienne: in a single campaigning season in 1449 the siege-train of Charles VII had forced the surrender of 60 English-held castles.[28] In 1453 cannon had achieved their most spectacular success hitherto when the great bombards of Mehmet II smashed in the walls of Constantinople the breach through which the Turks entered and took the imperial city. Three years later the same sultan is said to have used 200 guns, an immense number for that age, in his unsuccessful siege of Belgrade. In the 1470s both Louis XI and Duke Charles the Bold of Burgundy made considerable use of artillery;[29] and by the end of the fifteenth century the siege-engines of the Middle Ages had been completely abandoned (the last use of the trebuchet, the most important of them, appears to have been at the unsuccessful Turkish siege of Rhodes in 1480). Castile, much the greatest of the Spanish kingdoms, was employing only four professional artillerymen in 1479: six years later it had 91, while the mere sixteen guns which made up its artillery train in 1480 had grown to 162 by 1508.[30]

27. F. Redlich, *The German Military Enterpriser and his Workforce*, 2 vols (Wiesbaden, 1964–5), remains the classical discussion of this aspect of early modern warfare.

28. S. Pepper and N.A. Adams, *Firearms and Fortifications: Military Architecture and Siege Warfare in Sixteenth-Century Siena* (Chicago/London, 1986), p. 8.

29. See e.g. E. Perroy, 'L'artillerie de Louis XI dans la campagne d'Artois', *Revue du Nord* XXVI (1943), 171–96, 293–315.

30. J.N. Hillgarth, *The Spanish Kingdoms, 1250–1516* (Oxford, 1978), ii, p. 377; A. Hess, *The Forgotten Frontier. A History of the Sixteenth-Century Ibero–African Frontier* (Chicago/London, 1978), p. 20.

Louis XI of France had forty *cannoniers* in 1469: Francis I in 1541 had 275. Even in the remote and backward grand duchy of Muscovy mobile artillery had appeared by the mid-fifteenth century, while a cannon-foundry existed in Moscow by 1488.[31]

Early artillery and the way in which it was used were still far from being standardized or in any real sense scientific. The guns differed so much in quality and performance even when of a similar pattern, and gunpowder was still so variable in quality, that gunnery was still 'an uncertain business with a certain grimy glamour and a tangible aura of mystery about it'.[32] The common practice of giving individual guns names of their own (Pope Pius II named one after his mother) reflected their uniqueness and variability; and a good gunner was made by experience rather than by any kind of training. The loud noise made by artillery, and the fact that it exemplified brute physical violence more spectacularly than any other weapon, added to the mystique which still to some extent surrounded it: this perhaps underlay its use, which seems to have begun in the 1520s, in salutes and public celebrations. This aspect of its history culminated in the ceremonial entry of Prince Philip (later Philip II of Spain) to Antwerp in 1549, when he found 1,000 guns arrayed outside the gate through which he rode into the city.[33] Rulers gave and received cannon as presents, even as wedding presents, another sign that they were still, at least in the early sixteenth century, status symbols and valuable curiosities (they often bore the personal arms of the nobleman or commander for whom they had been cast) as much as routine weapons of war.[34]

By mid-century this situation was changing markedly. Cannon were more numerous, less expensive and easier to obtain. Large quantities of cheap cast-iron guns from northern Europe – England, the Netherlands, Sweden and Germany – were from the 1540s radically changing the situation. Equally important, artillery now fired cast-iron balls, cheaply mass-produced, in place of the stone ones often used in the past, which could be made properly only by skilled

31. P. Contamine, 'Les industries de guerre dans la France de la Renaissance: l'exemple de l'artillerie', *Revue Historique* 271 (1984), 278; G. Alef, 'Muscovite military reforms in the second half of the fifteenth century', *Forschungen zur Osteuropäischen Geschichte* 18 (1973), 78–81.

32. J.F. Guilmartin, *Gunpowder and Galleys: Changing Technology and Mediterranean Warfare at Sea in the Sixteenth Century* (Cambridge, 1974), p. 174.

33. S.T. Bindoff, 'The greatness of Antwerp', *New Cambridge Modern History*, ii (Cambridge, 1958), 61.

34. J.R. Hale, 'Gunpowder and the Renaissance: an essay in the history of ideas', in *From the Renaissance to the Counter-Reformation: Essays in Honour of Garrett Mattingly*, ed. C.H. Carter (London, 1966), pp. 128–31.

stone-cutters. This transformation was already well under way by the end of the fifteenth century, at least in the more advanced parts of western Europe. In France, where stone balls were still widely used in the 1480s, they were obsolete by 1500. The effects of these changes were striking. In 1494 Charles VIII had at his disposal five *bandes* with a total of 150 guns. It was these, a number no other Christian ruler of the age could match, that largely underlay his deceptively easy first successes in Italy. Fifty years later a group of fifteen fortresses on the north-eastern frontier of France alone mounted between them 279 artillery pieces. A generation later still the spoils divided between the victors after the Christian naval triumph at Lepanto in 1571 included 390 captured Turkish guns. By 1600 Henry IV had accumulated, in arsenals in Paris and the French provinces (presumably not including those in frontier fortresses) 400 guns, with 200,000 shot for them and 4,000,000 lb of gunpowder.[35] The growth during the century in the sheer quantity of artillery in use had therefore been marked.

These sixteenth-century guns were still very far from being perfect weapons. Their rate of fire was slow: a careful investigation of this point has found no example of heavy siege guns achieving a rate of fire greater than one shot every six minutes. Usually, especially in the earlier part of the century, it was much less than this. When the Turks unsuccessfully besieged Rhodes in 1480 even their smaller and more manageable guns probably fired no more than fourteen rounds in a day; and when in 1495 the French besiegers of the Castel Nuovo in Naples managed to fire over 300 cannon-shots in three hours this was regarded as an impressively intense bombardment. In Henry VIII's invasion of France in 1513 the biggest guns he took with him (they fired an iron ball weighing 260 lb which needed 80 lb of powder to propel it) could get off only five shots in a day.[36] Most important of all, artillery was always more or less expensive. It was often extremely difficult and therefore costly to move, especially over hilly or mountainous country, given the primitive roads of the age. This again was most marked in the early part of this period, when guns were often much heavier and less mobile than they later became. The artillery train of the duchy of Milan in 1472 amounted to only sixteen guns, though these were all large; but they needed 227 carts and 522 pairs

35. *Histoire militaire de la France*, i, p. 226; Guilmartin, *Gunpowder and Galleys*, p. 211; C. Duffy, *Siege Warfare. The Fortress in the Early Modern World, 1494–1660* (London, 1979), p. 114.

36. E. Brockmann, *The Two Sieges of Rhodes, 1480-1522* (London, 1969), p.69; Pepper and Adams, *Firearms and Fortifications*, p. 15; F.L. Taylor, *The Art of War in Italy, 1494–1529* (Cambridge, 1921), p. 97; C.G. Cruickshank, *Army Royal: Henry VIII's Invasion of France, 1513* (Oxford, 1969), p. 74.

of oxen to transport them. The French guns in the invasion of Italy in 1499 needed 1,800 horses to pull them; but 2,500 had to be requisitioned to drag them and their ammunition across the Alps when Francis I invaded the peninsula in 1515.[37] Apart from the cost of the guns themselves, moreover, the shot and still more the powder they needed were not cheap. Saltpetre, one of the essential constituents of black gunpowder, was always in more or less short supply and therefore costly: in 1609 the Venetian government allocated 36,000 ducats a year, a considerable sum, for its purchase alone. Artillery and the men and materials needed to serve it therefore accounted as the century went on for a growing part of the cost of any army. In 1500 they may have made up only 6–8 per cent of military expenditure in France; but by 1600 it was commonly estimated that gunpowder weapons and their services added a third to the cost of a campaign, and one calculation put this extra cost as high as a half.[38]

That cannon fundamentally changed warfare is too obvious to need stressing. As early as 1498 the Venetian Senate declared that 'the wars of the present time are influenced more by the force of bombards and artillery than by men at arms'. This was an exaggeration; but contemporary events gave it some support. The French victory at Fornovo in 1495 was perhaps the first battle in which artillery played a major role; another French success at Ravenna in 1512 was the first in which it decided the issue. Sometimes, when artillery in any quantity was still a novelty and for that reason all the more frightening, its mere moral effect could be profound. In September 1494 during the invasion of Italy a French force was able to land at Genoa without resistance merely because of the impression made there by the guns mounted on the vessels that carried it.[39] Yet 'bombards and artillery' were not necessarily decisive on the battlefield. At Pavia, one of the most complete victories of the century, the defeated French mustered 53 guns against the mere sixteen of their opponents; but the miscalculations of Francis I more than nullified this advantage. It was in the attack and defence of fortresses that artillery came most fully into its own and had the most far-reaching results.

37. M. Mallett, *Mercenaries and their Masters: Warfare in Renaissance Italy* (London, 1974), p. 161; F. Lot, *Recherches sur les effectifs des armées Francaises des Guerres d'Italie aux Guerres de Religion, 1494–1562* (Paris, 1962), p. 27; G. Dickinson, ed., *The Instructions sur le Faict de la Guerre of Raymond de Beccarie de Pavie, Sieur de Fourquevaux*, (London, 1954), p. 43.

38. *Histoire militaire de la France*, i, p. 245; J.R. Hale, *War and Society in Renaissance Europe, 1450–1620* (London, 1985), p. 47.

39. M. Mallett, 'Diplomacy and war in fifteenth-century Italy', in G. Holmes, ed., *Art and Politics in Renaissance Italy* (Oxford, 1993), p. 140; *Histoire militaire de la France*, i, p. 259.

Very soon after the first French onslaught on Italy in 1494 it became clear that the new menace of artillery attack was forcing big and expensive changes in the techniques of fortification. Walls now had to be much thicker to withstand bombardment. At least equally important, the defenders had to be able to use artillery to defend themselves. This meant the development of the bastion, a solidly built structure projecting from the wall, at first usually curved in plan but soon becoming angular. On this could be mounted guns covering a stretch of the wall and exposing to their flanking fire any enemy attack. The first true bastion is usually said to have been the Boulevard d'Auvergne in the great fortress of Rhodes, built in the 1480s, but it soon began to appear in Italy. There the ease with which cities and castles succumbed to French attack in 1494–95 was startling proof that the defensive methods of the past were no longer adequate. The successful defence of Padua in 1509 by the Venetians against the forces of the Emperor Maximilian I, which included a considerable artillery train, showed clearly the potentialities of a determined and sustained resistance to attack by cannon; but the refortification of Verona in 1520 was the first application of the new methods on a large scale. In the 1530s Francesco Guicciardini, the greatest Italian historian of the century, could quite justifiably claim that in Italy at least 'the towns now being defended have been made very safe and cannot be taken by storm'.[40] From Italy the new type of fortification, the 'trace italienne', then spread to the rest of Europe. By the early seventeenth century the bastion had reached Russia: it appears there first in some fortifications built in Moscow in 1618.

More than ever in the past, the attack and defence of fortresses was now becoming a science, something that involved careful design and planning, exact calculation and formal rules. This process culminated in the long struggle of the Netherlands revolt from the 1570s onwards, a series of wars in which sieges, at least after the first few years, completely predominated over battles in the field. A chair of surveying and fortification, the first of its kind anywhere, was created in the University of Leyden in 1600; and twenty years later a French soldier wrote admiringly that 'Nowadays the Spanish and Dutch officers have made the capture of towns an art, and they can predict the duration of resistance of a fortress, however strong, in terms of days'.[41]

The new fortifications, with thick walls and increasingly elaborate

40. F. Guicciardini, *The History of Italy*, trans. S. Alexander (New York/London, 1969), p. 341.
41. Duffy, *Siege Warfare*, p. 100.

and numerous bastions, were extremely expensive. Their cost meant that even in Italy, where they had first emerged on a significant scale, it was often difficult to adopt them wholeheartedly. Though a few cities – Treviso, Ferrara, Civitavecchia – were provided in the early decades of the sixteenth century with extensive bastioned defences, this remained rare because of the cost. Even the fortification along largely traditional lines of a moderate-sized town such as Tournai, after its capture by the English in 1513, shows the drain on scarce resources that such a project could involve. By the beginning of 1516 there were available for the work 24,000 quarters of lime (new lime-kilns had to be built for the purpose), 60,000 ft of hewn stone, 8,000 tons of filling or rag stone, 700 tons of timber and 1,000 loads of sand, as well as a large quantity of tools and equipment. Not surprisingly, Henry VIII had to scale down the project, making the walls thinner and the towers lower. A scheme for new defences of Rome, which were to include eighteen bastions, had to be abandoned in 1542, when one alone was found to have cost at least 44,000 ducats and taken seven years to build. Two years later an architect estimated that up-to-date fortifications for Vicenza, even if they were built of turfed earth rather than stone, would need the labour of 2,000 men for four months. Certainly the amount of labour involved in even modest projects of this kind was substantial. A minor place such as Great Yarmouth, when it strengthened its fortifications to resist the Spanish armada in 1588, found that this meant building earthworks 40 ft thick. The French saying that 'When you fortify a place you have to shut your eyes and open your purse' was only too well justified. Even by the end of the century none of the greatest cities of Europe possessed a complete and fully bastioned system of the new-style fortifications.[42]

Defences of this kind were expensive to take as well as to build. From very early in the Italian wars it became clear that the besieging army must be protected against the artillery and firearms of the garrison. At first this was done by trenches and fascines (bundles of branches and brushwood bound together and acting as a sort of palisade); but soon the besiegers began to create a kind of improvised fortress of their own, of earthworks, trenches and fortified houses, which provided a defence not merely against fire or sudden sallies from the besieged fortress but also against possible attack by a relieving army. 'Lines of circumvallation' of this kind were first used

42. C.G. Cruickshank, *The English Occupation of Tournai, 1513-1519* (Oxford, 1971), p. 115; Boynton, *The Elizabethan Militia*, p. 129; Judith Hook, 'Fortifications and the end of the Sienese state', *History* 62 (October, 1977), 373; Pepper and Adams, *Firearms and Fortifications*, pp. 28–9.

in the siege of Milan in 1524; but it was once more in the Netherlands that they were carried to their highest pitch, one which impressed all Europe. The enormous siege-works built by the Dutch around Geertruidenberg before they finally took it in the summer of 1593 are a good example; while even in the siege of the relatively small fortress of Grace, a French envoy reported in 1602 that 'The works which Prince Maurice has made before this place are truly gigantic. Every redoubt, no matter how small, has its own wet ditch and drawbridge, and the continuous line is so huge and vast that it takes nearly five hours to make the circuit'.[43] Moreover, as fortresses became stronger it became more necessary for the besiegers to outnumber heavily the garrison they were attacking. A French expert at the end of the sixteenth century thought that to attack any well-fortified place successfully a ten-to-one superiority, in guns as well as men, was needed. Certainly in the Netherlands, as the struggle with Spain went on, the numbers of guns used in sieges increased. This was a good indication of the growing strength of fortresses and the difficulty of taking them except by starving out the defenders. The rapid and easy capture of any important one, as with the French taking of Calais in 1558 or the Spanish one of Maastricht in 1579, became increasingly hard to achieve as the century went on, and attracted correspondingly more attention when it happened.

There were other ways in which the methods and techniques of warfare were developing. An important one was the use for the first time of the most important of all the intellectual tools of the commander – reasonably accurate maps. Venice, leading the way in this respect, had already made some use of them in military planning from the 1460s onwards, while Charles VIII in the 1490s commissioned a map of the Alpine passes to help future invasions of Italy. During the French campaign on the Rhine in 1552 Henry II used another specially commissioned map showing roads, and also villages in which his soldiers might be lodged for the night. When in 1567 the Duke of Alba directed the movement of a large force along the 'Spanish Road', the military supply-line which ran from northern Italy to the Netherlands, he had the help of a very accurate map of Franche-Comté through which the road passed. He also set on foot much mapping work in the Netherlands to make Spanish rule there more effective. Even in Poland, maps were used for the first time for military purposes in 1579, in a campaign against the Russians.[44]

43. Duffy, *Siege Warfare*, p. 93.
44. D. Buisseret, ed., *Monarchs, Ministers and Maps* (Chicago/London, 1992), pp. 6, 101, 103, 138–43, 170.

War by the end of this period was thus becoming more profession-alized and 'modern' than ever before. In this respect, as in so many others, the Dutch, because of the protracted struggle against Spanish rule which had begun in the early 1570s, now led Europe. In 1597 the words of command used in their army were established in a stand-ardized form. A decade later Jacob de Gheyn published in his *Wappenhandlinghe* the first important textbook of military drill. This was merely one of the most significant of the growing flood of books on all aspects of military affairs being produced all over western Europe in the later sixteenth and early seventeenth centuries. A decade later again, in 1617, John II of Nassau (who had commissioned de Gheyn's book) set up in Siegen in west Germany the first recognizably mod-ern military academy. It is significant that he, and the other leading Dutch commanders of the period, Prince Maurice of Nassau and Prince William-Louis, had all studied at universities and that the greatest Dutch mathematician of the age, Simon Stevin, served as a high-ranking member of Maurice's staff. War had now taken on an intellectual aspect it had never had before.

The legacy of the past

All this paints a picture of progress, in the sense of growing if often increasingly destructive efficiency. Yet side by side with this there re-mained a substantial though diminishing legacy of attitudes rooted in the past and values derived from late-mediaeval chivalry. Origin-ally these had rested on the ideal of a code of conduct that tran-scended all national divisions and a knightly caste bound together, at least in theory, by Christian unity in struggle with the infidel. By the end of the Middle Ages this ideal had been radically changed. Now 'chivalry was exploited to focus purely secular allegiance upon the person of the prince' and 'in France, Burgundy, England and the German Empire by the second half of the fifteenth century chivalry found new vitality and a new direction'. The supranational ideal had been replaced by one of aristocratic state service.[45]

Even in this altered and perhaps debased form the chivalric legacy was a significant factor to the end of this period. Much importance was still attached to observance of the proper formalities in the declaration of war by one ruler on another; and it was still assumed that a siege

45. M. Vale, *War and Chivalry: Warfare and Aristocratic Culture in England, France and Burgundy at the End of the Middle Ages* (London, 1981), p. 168; S. Anglo, ed., *Chivalry in the Renaissance* (Woodbridge, 1990), p. 32.

would begin by the garrison being formally summoned by a herald to surrender. Even under Elizabeth an English treatise took it for granted that this remained the norm; and almost to the end of the century there were purists prepared to argue that an operation of this kind was hardly legitimate without such a summons. The ransoming of important prisoners continued to be governed by elaborate rules with roots deep in the mediaeval past.[46] It was still common in the earlier decades of the sixteenth century for a commander before giving battle to deliver a formal oration to encourage his troops (though this derived from Roman tradition as much as from any chivalric one). There were still occasional proposals in these decades for the outcome of a battle to be decided by single combat between the two opposing commanders. Gaston de Foix, the French commander, suggested before the battle of Ravenna in 1512 that the result depend upon such a duel between himself and the viceroy of Naples, though the Spaniards declined the offer. Later Charles V was more than once to propose quite seriously, in 1528 and again ten years later, that an entire war be decided by personal combat between himself and Francis I.

But all this was more and more artificial, increasingly out of touch with reality. War, so far as the ordinary rank-and- file soldier and the civilian exposed to its effects were concerned, had always been brutal and destructive. The struggles in Italy from 1494 onwards were carried on with a cruelty at least equal to anything seen before: this in itself did something to expose the hollowness of chivalric ideals. More important in this respect, however, from the 1530s onwards, was the change in the way wars were fought in western and much of central Europe. The ideal of chivalric warfare centred on battle in the open field, battle in which heavy cavalry, for centuries the quintessential knightly arm, was normally decisive. Until the peace of 1529 battles had been relatively numerous in Italy; and the mailed horseman had still played an important though diminishing role in them. Their frequency, it has been argued, offered 'an unusually fertile soil for some expressions of the cult of chivalry'. The process may also have worked in reverse: battles, seen as the greatest opportunity to display honourable behaviour and gain personal reputation, may have been frequent because the thinking of so many commanders was still strongly influenced by chivalric ideas and values.[47] Even though the 'Ladies' Peace' of 1529 was itself short-lived, the generations which followed saw full-scale battles become markedly less numerous and the part

46. Cruickshank, *Army Royal*, pp. 82, 110 and chap. IX.

47. Vale, *War and Chivalry*, p. 174; S. Gunn, 'The French wars of Henry VIII', in J. Black, ed., *The Origins of War in Early Modern Europe* (Edinburgh, 1987), p. 36.

played in them by heavy cavalry, when they did occur, less important. More and more it was now the siege which bulked large. This, with the patient effort, the digging, the entrenchments, the mining of walls, the use of artillery with its dirt and its artisan associations, was the antithesis of chivalric warfare.

The dream of chivalry kept a hold on the west European mind: Cervantes in *Don Quixote* was satirizing attitudes which were not yet dead. Chivalric romances continued to appear in large numbers. In the first half of the sixteenth century they were published in Spain at an average rate of almost one a year; and in France the output was much bigger.[48] But all this was an increasingly thin veneer covering a reality more and more shaped by the unyielding facts of professionalism, technology and finance.

War at sea

Naval warfare was very much a poor relation of war on land. Often it was merely an offshoot of military operations and subordinate to them. The most important function of a fleet was to cover the movement of land forces when it was necessary to transport them by sea. Great concentrations of ships were usually meant to carry invading armies across stretches of water, sometimes short ones, and land them on hostile territory. The successful attack on Tunis by Charles V in 1535 and his disastrous failure at Algiers six years later, the even worse defeat of the Spaniards by the Turks at Djerba in 1560, are merely the most obvious examples of this. All of these, and even much less well known enterprises of the kind, involved very large maritime forces. Charles V took to Algiers in 1541 65 galleys which protected more than 450 transports carrying 24,000 soldiers. For a projected invasion of England in 1545 it was hoped to use 300 French merchant ships and 37 galleys, while in 1574 a successful Turkish attack on Tunis involved 280 galleys and almost 50 other vessels. But forces of this kind were not meant to fight at sea. Laden with soldiers and supplies, a large-scale naval battle was usually the last thing they wanted. The crushing victory of a Christian fleet over a Turkish one at Lepanto in 1571 merely throws into sharper relief the extreme rarity of decisive conflicts at sea during this period. Even the disaster of the Spanish armada was the result of weather far more than of the fighting power of its English opponents.

---

48. Anglo, ed., *Chivalry in the Renaissance*, pp. 193–228, 254.

Apart from transporting troops and protecting them while they were at sea there were other ways in which navies could play some role in war. Ships and their guns could sometimes help directly land operations by an army. There were examples of this in France's invasion of Italy in 1494 and her struggles with Spain and England in the years that followed.[49] Strength at sea might allow a state to launch destructive raids against an enemy coastline. It could even make possible short-lived efforts to blockade enemy ports, though it was to be two centuries or more before effective cutting-off of an enemy's trade in this way became a real possibility.[50] But all this was subordinate to what mattered most in war – the success or failure of armies.

War at sea was seen clearly by contemporaries as secondary to that on land. Many of the substantial naval powers – Genoa, the Hanse cities, Portugal – had small territories and small armies; Spanish predominance under Philip II rested on the fact that Spain, uniquely, was a first-class force both on land and at sea. Compared to the large output of treatises on military affairs, naval warfare was very little written about: when it was it usually figured as a mere afterthought to discussions of armies and fighting on land. When economies were needed, few states hesitated to sacrifice strength at sea to military power; and it was possible, even normal, for commands of the highest importance at sea to be given to men whose previous experience was entirely military. The Duke of Medina-Sidonia, who commanded the armada of 1588, is the most obvious example; but his English opposite number, Lord Howard of Effingham, had relatively little seagoing experience and his command in 1588 was a military as well as a naval one.

Privateering and private initiative

Even to talk of 'navies' in the sixteenth century is often misleading. Everywhere privately owned and controlled vessels played a role, often a dominant one. This was less marked in the Mediterranean than in the Atlantic. Yet even here private energies and interests were often significant. Although the Spanish government made a great and largely successful effort to build up its Mediterranean galley-fleet in the 1550s and 1560s, there was much debate as to whether it might be more efficiently maintained by private individuals than by govern-

---

49. *Histoire militaire de la France*, i, pp. 294–5.
50. See below, pp. 34–6.

ment officials. It was argued on the one hand that privately provided galleys tended to be less reliable and often of poorer quality than those under complete state control. Against this it was generally though not universally agreed that private enterprise would do the job more cheaply; and in fact efforts to maintain effective direct government control became much weaker from the 1570s onwards.[51]

But it was in the Atlantic that the inability or unwillingness of states to build large navies of their own was most marked. There for most of the century war 'was a war not of states but of subjects, not of navies but of privateers, corsairs and armed merchantmen'.[52] Since as yet there was no clear distinction between a man-of-war and a merchant ship and the one could easily be transformed into the other, and since a navy, man-for-man, was much more expensive than an army and made considerable technological demands, such a policy usually made much sense. By the 1580s and 1590s there were some signs that this situation was beginning to change, with the development of a sustained and very demanding Anglo-Spanish struggle at sea. But throughout this period the naval strength on the ocean of all the west European powers consisted mainly not of royal ships but of privately owned ones chartered from their owners or pressed into service in the seaports for some special occasion. Even in the later years of the century this non-governmental element remained very important. Philip II and his ministers reacted to the disaster of 1588 by an ambitious programme of naval building, which meant the creation for the first time of a substantial fleet of royal ocean-going ships of war. Yet of the 84 which made up the new armada meant for use against England in 1597, 52 were still commandeered merchantmen, and under Philip III direct building by the crown virtually came to an end, so that in 1606 'no less than half the home fleet consisted of glorified merchantmen serving the king for hire'.[53]

On the English side the situation was similar. Both Henry VII and his son had significant numbers of royal ships: Henry VIII had about 60 at his death in 1547. But under Elizabeth this element in English naval strength became less important: in the great struggle of 1585–1604 with Spain half or less of the war effort at sea was the work of royal ships.[54] Of the vessels which fought the Spanish Armada, seven were the personal property of the English commander, Lord Howard of Effingham, and two belonged to Sir Francis Drake. Of the 150

51. Thompson, *War and Government in Habsburg Spain*, pp. 173–5.
52. Ibid., p. 185.
53. Ibid., pp. 192, 195.
54. D. Loades, *The Tudor Navy* (London, 1992), p. 275.

which took part in the attack on Cadiz in 1596 only about a tenth were owned by Queen Elizabeth. The rest, apart from a Dutch contingent, were supplied by English port towns or private owners. Even a generation later, of the 30 ships sent on the futile Cadiz expedition of 1625 only the three flagships seem to have been men-of-war and all the rest hired merchant ships. In France the first serious effort to create a navy under royal control came only under Henry IV in the first years of the seventeenth century; and his murder in 1610 meant that it was very short-lived.

The limited effectiveness of governments where war at sea was concerned was reflected in the prevalence of privateering. By the beginning of this period it was already well established that any ruler, if his subjects suffered loss or injury at sea for which they had failed to gain redress, might license them to take reprisals by attacking ships of the state whose subjects had inflicted the original loss. 'Letters of marque' of this kind, and the privateering that they legitimized, played an important role in every naval conflict in western Europe. Thus a great deal of fighting at sea, and in particular a great deal of destructive commerce-raiding, was left to private individuals; and widespread abuses were the inevitable result. Ships might go privateering with no letters of marque at all, which made them outright pirates. Such licences might be issued by incompetent or corrupt officials in an uncontrolled way. A captured ship might simply be looted rather than being brought into port to have its cargo properly appraised. Worst of all, innocent neutral ships might be indiscriminately attacked.[55] The dangerous fluidity of the situation can be seen in the ease with which, at least in the early part of the sixteenth century, men of very high social rank might alternate between service on the ships of their monarch and what was in effect no more than ordinary piracy.[56]

On several occasions from the 1450s onwards there were efforts by different states to control more effectively the issue of letters of marque. The Anglo-Castilian treaty of Medina del Campo of 1489 was one such, while in 1497 an Anglo-French agreement attempted to curb piracy by ordering that seamen on each side should give a bond restraining them from harming the shipping of the other. There were also attempts to settle the numerous grievances, the claims and counter-claims, which such a situation inevitably produced: the most

---

55. K.R. Andrews, *Elizabethan Privateering: English Privateering during the Spanish War, 1585-1603* (Cambridge, 1964), ch. 2, discusses such abuses in detail.

56. E.g. the case of the Spanish Marquis de Villamarina, in A. Tenenti, 'I corsari in Mediterraneo all'inizio del Cinquecento', *Rivista Storica Italiana* LXXII (1960), 252.

important was a meeting in 1537 at Bayonne between French, Portuguese and imperial representatives. Occasionally the right to take reprisals of this sort might be suppressed altogether, at least in theory and for a limited time: an earlier example is an Anglo-French agreement of 1474. Prize courts intended to subject captures of this kind to some legal restraint had begun to emerge in the mid-fourteenth century; and there was now some effort to regulate them and make them more effective. But all this had only very limited effect. By the last years of the sixteenth century privateering in the Atlantic was at a higher pitch than ever before. It was clearly an important element in the emergence of England as a naval force. The expedition led by Drake and Sir John Norris in 1589, which attempted unsuccessfully to capture Lisbon and the Azores, was essentially a private venture financed by investors who hoped to gain heavily from the enterprise. In this and the two following years at least 236 English privateers are known to have been at sea, and since they took at least 300 prizes it is likely that many of them made a modest profit.[57] The expedition to the West Indies led by the Earl of Cumberland in 1598 was made up entirely of privately owned ships (five of them and a smaller pinnace the property of Cumberland himself).[58]

This sort of private-enterprise, free-market warfare was in part forced on governments by their poverty; and in favourable circumstances and within limits it could be effective. But it meant that there were important aspects of any struggle at sea that were beyond government control. In 1589 Drake and Norris could probably have destroyed the remnants of the great armada of the previous year if they had attacked them in the ports of northern Spain, particularly Santander, as Elizabeth had ordered. This would have struck a crippling blow at Spanish seapower, with very important repercussions on the whole course of the war. Instead the hope of plunder for themselves and profit for those who had sunk money in the expedition led them, after the rather pointless capture of Corunna, to go on to Lisbon without attempting anything further. A few years later the English government proposed the formation of an auxiliary fleet to protect trade in the Channel and adjacent seas. But this, it was envisaged, would be made up of privately owned ships, mainly from London, and be organized by an independent committee, though with government help. To us this seems a striking abdication of a government's

57. R.B. Wernham, *After the Armada: Elizabethan England and the Struggle for Western Europe, 1588–1595* (Oxford, 1984), p. 249.

58. Idem, *The Return of the Armadas: The Last Years of the Elizabethan War against Spain, 1595-1603* (Oxford, 1994), pp. 252–3.

basic responsibilities. But contemporaries, in England or elsewhere, saw it differently. In that age, as a recent historian has said, 'In every possible way, from the supply of victuals to the planning of a campaign, the state eagerly shifted its burdens on to the shoulders of private individuals, and was not concerned that this meant sacrificing any uniform, consistent, overall control'.[59]

Here again can be seen the blurring or complete lack in this period of so many of the clear dividing-lines we now take for granted – between war and peace, between the territories of adjoining states, between belligerents and neutrals, between conflict as an expression of government policy and as an outlet for private greeds and ambitions. Devastating as it could be and often was, war in that age was still a concept with distinctly fuzzy edges. Yet it was also the force which, more than any other, drove the relations between the states of Europe. Preparing for a war that was foreseen or desired, guarding against one that was feared, were major preoccupations of the diplomatic network that now increasingly bound these states together. No strand in the history of this period is more important than that of inter-state conflict; and the course and results of these conflicts inevitably depended on the way in which they were fought and the means available to fight them.

59. J.R. Hale, 'Armies, navies and the art of war', *New Cambridge Modern History* iii (Cambridge, 1968), p. 201.

CHAPTER TWO

The Instruments of International Relations: Trade and Finance

The limits of economic warfare

It was difficult for states during the sixteenth and early seventeenth centuries to use economic pressure as an effective weapon in international relations. In the conflicts that make up so much of the history of the period it was hard for any government to mobilize efficiently even the resources of its own territory and subjects. To wage effective economic war was even more difficult. Administrative machines were still small, usually inefficient, all too often corrupt. Populations were deeply resistant to anything that interfered with normal economic life: the imposition of new taxation, or the cutting-off or restriction of a customary trade, would always face at best grumbling and at worst active evasion or outright resistance. Economic difficulties that struck at the living standards of the ordinary man (which meant essentially anything which raised food prices) were the surest of all triggers of widespread discontent and usually the only thing that could win the masses over to new doctrines in religion or politics. In the Netherlands, a good case in point, the marked growth in the early 1530s of Anabaptism, the most radical of all the new religious sects of that age, was stimulated by the very high food prices of 1531–32, while the outburst of image-breaking of 1566, with all its political repercussions, had in part similar roots. To create economic difficulties for a rival or potentially hostile ruler was therefore a sensible and obvious line of policy; and efforts of this kind were often made. The Spanish ambassador in London was ordered in 1562, for example, to do what he could to impoverish Elizabeth's government. This, it was hoped, would force her into concessions on trade with the Spanish-ruled Netherlands, increase her dependence on Spanish goodwill and perhaps force her to abandon the Anglican church establishment that had taken shape only three years earlier.

Indeed, the mutual dependence of England and the Netherlands on the trade between them, especially the export of English cloth for finishing in the cities of Flanders and Brabant, meant that on both sides there was deep resistance to anything that threatened to interrupt it. Thus in 1528 the Emperor Charles V, as ruler of the Netherlands provinces, was forced to allow them to withdraw from the war with England in which he was then involved; while almost 40 years later the English ambassador to France said that 'I may call the peace with France one of discretion, with Flanders and Brabant one of necessity'.[1]

However, purely economic pressures were normally only a secondary weapon in the struggles of that age. The bigger and more self-sufficient a state, inevitably, the less likely it was to be much affected by external forces of this kind. Some smaller ones – Venice, Florence, the Netherlands provinces, even England – were relatively vulnerable to such forces; but in the Habsburg–Valois struggles that dominated the first half of the sixteenth century neither France nor Spain was significantly affected in this way. France in particular remained throughout the century the most self-reliant, and inherently the strongest economically, of all the states of Europe. There were a number of basic commodities which could not be produced everywhere in adequate quantities. Control of their export to areas where they were in short supply could therefore sometimes be used as an effective weapon. Salt was one such: the fact that the whole Baltic area had no good domestic source of supply and therefore relied on imports from Portugal or the west coast of France could thus at times become an important factor in Baltic rivalries. The big, strong horses needed by armies for their heavy cavalry, another strategic commodity of which an exportable surplus was produced in only a few areas, could also on occasion be used as a political weapon. Most basic and obviously important in this way, however, was grain; and though most European states were usually more or less self-sufficient in this respect, there were some at least partial exceptions. Venice drew a considerable proportion of her grain supplies from parts of the Balkans which were now under Ottoman rule: this was a powerful inducement to her to remain on good terms with her great Muslim neighbour. Sometimes an importing state could simply solve the problem by conquering one which produced a surplus. Spain, so much of which was barren and infertile, benefited in this way from

1. R.B. Werrnham, *The Making of Elizabethan Foreign Policy, 1558–1603* (Berkeley/Los Angeles/London, 1980), p. 330.

her acquisition of Sicily, then the greatest exporter of grain in Europe, in the first years of the sixteenth century. The decline of Sicilian exports, for reasons which are not entirely clear, in its later decades, and the resulting need for Spain to draw more of her grain from the Baltic, considerably weakened her strategic position.

But the whole concept of sustained and effective economic warfare was still embryonic. Administrative systems were usually too weak to exert any rigorous control over the activities of individual traders. Navies were quite unable to mount any effective blockade of an enemy's coastline. Indeed, the idea of a systematic economic policy of any sort, and the machinery to implement one, were still only taking shape. Unified customs systems on a national scale were emerging. England had one from the reign of Henry VIII, and a new tariff was introduced there in 1558, though France had no similar machinery until 1581. Customs arrangements as the century went on slowly ceased to be mere fiscal expedients and increasingly became an aspect of commercial policy, while trade treaties grew in numbers.[2] Nevertheless, all-out economic struggle between states was not merely impracticable but hard to imagine. Some types of commercial and productive activity seemed so important that there was great reluctance to interrupt them completely in time of war. The outbreak of hostilities therefore by no means necessarily meant the end of trade between the combatants; and often when two maritime states were at war an at least semi-official *trêve pêcheresse* might allow the fishermen of both still to work with some degree of security. There was also no general agreement on what constituted contraband: this was to be a disputed issue for centuries to come. Apart from arms and munitions it was often argued that grain, the basic foodstuff, fell within the definition. In 1558, for example, Henry II of France, in the last stage of his struggle with Philip II of Spain, explicitly allowed the export to the enemy of grain of all kinds, as well as artillery and other munitions of war. But the situation in this respect was far from clear: in 1590 the Dutch firmly rejected an English effort, as part of the naval war against Spain, to have grain declared contraband. Nor was there any clarity about the rights and obligations of neutrals. Any agreement on this was still far in the future; and such issues did not usually seem very important to the writers who were now laying the foundations of a structure of international law. Contemporary historians also, still under the spell of classical values and precedents, were often unwilling to admit that rulers and governments could be in-

2. G. Zeller, *Les Temps Modernes: De Christoph Colomb à Cromwell* (Paris, 1953) (vol. ii of *Histoire des Relations Internationales*, ed. P. Renouvin), pp. 14–16.

fluenced in any significant way by something so crass as merely economic considerations.

However, as the sixteenth century drew to a close economic pressure was beginning to be used on an unprecedented scale as a weapon in international conflict. In England the struggle with Spain from 1585 onwards generated proposals to strike at the roots of the enemy's maritime strength and indeed at her whole economic life. This was to be done partly by cutting off the supplies of essential naval stores, masts, pitch, tar and hemp, which Spain drew from the Baltic. It would also be achieved, in an even more far-reaching way, by intercepting the treasure-fleets which brought her the American silver on which her ability to pay her armies, and thus her position as the greatest European power, in part depended. This, urged the Earl of Essex, the leading advocate of such a strategy, would fatally weaken Philip II, since it would 'stop and divert his golden Indian streames . . . and lett out the vitall spirites of his estate'.[3] Such schemes had little success. Spain was able to make great and largely successful efforts in the 1590s to rebuild her naval strength. The treasure-fleets, the most glittering prize of all, were not intercepted. English efforts to cut off supplies to her exposed Elizabeth to diplomatic pressure from Poland, Denmark and the Hanse towns of north Germany, which resented interference with their trade in naval stores and grain with the Iberian peninsula, and even to some effort at commercial retaliation from the Holy Roman Emperor, Rudolf II.[4] There were protests as well from Tuscany and Venice over English interference with their shipping, so that Leghorn, now one of the greatest Mediterranean ports, was briefly closed to English ships. None the less, this was a vision of economic warfare bolder in conception and more sustained in its application than anything seen hitherto.

Philip II and his ministers showed equal boldness and tenacity. In 1585 they imposed an embargo on all trade with the rebellious Dutch provinces which lasted until 1590; and though this was at first widely evaded it was much more effective than has usually been recognized. In 1587–89 there was a sharp and damaging decline in Dutch trade with the Iberian peninsula (Portugal had been under Spanish rule since 1580). After several years of relaxation the embargo was reimposed in 1598 and rigidly enforced for the next decade. The peace treaty which Spain signed with England in 1604, as well as the trade

3. L.W. Henry, 'The Earl of Essex as strategist and military organiser (1596–7)', *English Historical Review* LXVII (1953), 364.
4. R.B. Wernham, *The Return of the Armadas: The Last Years of the Elizabethan War against Spain, 1595–1603* (Oxford, 1994), pp. 199–201, 280–1.

agreements she made with France in the same year and the Hanse towns in 1607, all included clauses designed to make it more effective. In 1595 Philip II even hoped to obtain a base in Poland from which he could attack Dutch trade (the Polish king, Sigismund III, was under strong Jesuit and pro-Spanish influence). There was also in the 1590s growing pressure in Spain for a still more active assault, by large-scale commerce-raiding and attacks on the very lucrative Dutch North Sea fisheries. The impact on the economic life of the rebel provinces was deep and widespread; and from 1603 onwards there was a determined effort to extend the Spanish embargo to the Caribbean, where Dutch trade had begun to be active. Spain also banned English trade until the peace of 1604; and this, like the efforts to strike at the Dutch, had considerable diplomatic implications. In 1589, for example, the Duke of Parma, commanding the Spanish army in the Netherlands, tried to use anti-English feeling in the Hanse towns as a weapon against English commercial links with Germany. The Spanish–Dutch truce of 1609 meant the restoration of normal commercial relations; but when the struggle between Spain and the rebel provinces burst out once more in 1621 it at once produced a new Spanish embargo which lasted until 1647. All this was economic war of a seriousness and duration never seen before.[5]

Finance and international relations

Sustained and at least partly effective economic warfare, then, was only beginning to take shape by the end of the sixteenth century. But inevitably economic needs and pressures, and the relative economic strengths of different states, always played an important, sometimes decisive, role in international relations. Every ruler and government was in constant need of money. Without it armies could hardly be raised; and if it were in really short supply this could mean truly disastrous defeat. The destruction of a Hungarian army by the Turks at Mohacs in 1526, a catastrophe which decided the fate of Hungary for almost two centuries, might have been averted, claimed the agent of the great German financial house of Fugger, if the king, Louis II, had

5. J.I. Israel, 'Spain, the Spanish embargoes and the struggle for mastery of world trade, 1585–1660', in his *Empires and Entrepots: The Dutch, the Spanish Monarchy and the Jews, 1585–1713* (London/Ronceverte, 1990), pp. 191, 201, 204ff.; idem, *Dutch Primacy in World Trade, 1585–1740* (Oxford, 1989), pp. 57–60; R.B.Wernham, *After the Armada: Elizabethan England and the Struggle for Western Europe, 1588–1595* (Oxford, 1984), pp. 256–7; R.A. Stradling, *The Armada of Flanders: Spanish Maritime Policy and European War, 1568–1668* (Cambridge, 1992), pp. 21–32.

had only 150,000 ducats more in cash.[6] This was a gross exaggeration, but underlying it was a crucially important truth. Moreover, as has been seen,[7] when an army had been raised it might be critically and destructively unreliable unless it could be paid with some approach, however remote, to regularity. In an age so dominated by war, and by war which was rapidly becoming more expensive, an age moreover in which political structures were often composite and multi-national and patriotism was embryonic and unreliable, money was fundamental to the success, perhaps even the survival, of any state. Rulers also had to face the cost not merely of expensive armies and growing navies but (though this was much less crippling) of expanding bureaucracies as their administrative machinery became larger and more complex. Though very many officials were paid by the fees and dues they collected and not directly by the ruler they served, they made none the less some additional call on his limited resources.

Yet no ruler ever had all the money he needed. Few plumbed such humiliating depths of poverty as the Holy Roman Emperor Maximilian I. His marriage in 1494 to Bianca Maria Sforza, daughter of the ruler of Milan, brought him a handsome dowry of 300,000 ducats, which outweighed the fact that her grandfather had been little more than a peasant. Yet only two years later she and her ladies were on the point of going short of food for lack of money. In 1518, in the last months of his life, the emperor himself would literally have had nothing to eat but for loans from the financier Jacob Fugger. Maximilian was hardly typical; he was notorious for his extravagance and resulting poverty. One contemporary claimed that 'at times when he wished to set forth to war, his servants were so poor that they together with the Emperor could not pay their reckoning at the inn', while a Venetian ambassador contemptuously remarked that 'for a ducat he can be won for anything'.[8] But this was merely the most extreme illustration of a universal difficulty. Rulers everywhere struggled to meet financial demands with which it was more and more difficult to cope.

The essential weakness of all public finance in this age 'consisted in the fact that an antiquated engine was being used to draw a load for which it had not been designed'.[9] The engine was underpowered and unequal to the task for several reasons. Not only were new or in-

6. R. Ehrenberg, *Capital and Finance in the Age of the Renaissance: A Study of the Fuggers and their Connections* (London, 1928), p. 86.

7. See above, pp. 7–8.

8. Ehrenberg, *Capital and Finance*, pp. 60, 74; R.W. Seton-Watson, *Maximilian I, Holy Roman Emperor* (London, 1902), p. 118.

9. Ehrenberg, *Capital and Finance*, p.13.

creased taxes everywhere deeply unpopular and often hard to collect; tax systems in general suffered from severe weaknesses and inequities. Over most of Europe nobilities enjoyed privileges and exemptions which hamstrung efforts to increase government revenue. In 1538, for example, an effort to introduce in Castile a new tax on food from which there would be no exemptions faced at once in the Cortes (an assembly of representatives of the nobility and the towns) furious noble hostility, and had to be dropped. This decisive setback meant that any effort to spread the tax burden more equally was now abandoned, with serious long-term results. The jealousy with which towns guarded the tax exemptions that many of them enjoyed was at least as great. In Sicily, where inequity of this kind was exceptionally marked, the city of Syracuse, which had been granted such privileges in 1298, was still asserting them five centuries later.[10] Such attitudes inevitably threw an increasingly heavy burden on the great unprivileged majority of society which was much less able to defend itself against government demands. In Castile the *servicios* – taxes from which the nobility was exempt – made up a steadily growing proportion of the total tax yield during the reign of the Emperor Charles V. At its beginning, in 1519, they accounted for about 8 per cent of government revenue; when it ended, in 1556, this had grown to 19 per cent. 'The common people who have to pay the *servicios*', wrote Prince Philip, the future Philip II, to his father in 1545, 'are reduced to such distress and misery that many of them walk naked'.[11]

Moreover, as the weight of taxation increased the incentive to escape it inevitably grew in proportion. Thus when in 1591 a new tax was introduced in Castile, of the 3,319 male citizens of Burgos, one of the kingdom's most important cities, almost five-sixths claimed to be exempt (more than 1,700 on the grounds that they ranked as nobles and over a thousand others since they claimed religious status of some kind).[12] The position in Castile was made particularly difficult by the fact that by the middle of the century it was having to shoulder the deficits of other Spanish-ruled territories. At different times between the 1530s and the 1560s Naples, Sicily and even the Netherlands all became a drain on the kingdom's resources. When Charles V abdicated in 1556 it was already bearing alone 70–80 per cent of

10. D. Mack Smith, *A History of Sicily. Mediaeval Sicily, 800–1713* (London, 1968), p. 126.

11. H. Koenigsberger, 'The empire of Charles V in Europe', *New Cambridge Modern History* (Cambridge, 1958), ii, p. 321.

12. A. Castillo, 'Dette flottante et dette consolidée en Espagne de 1557 à 1600', *Annales*, 18e année, No. 4 (1963), pp. 750–1.

the financial burdens of the entire Spanish empire. In France, the other great contestant in the cycle of wars between 1494 and 1559, the demands these made on the common man also grew. One estimate (though precise calculation is impossible) is that they increased by 80 per cent between the 1490s and the 1550s.[13]

It would be wrong to paint an unrelievedly black picture of the impact of government demands on the population of Europe as a whole. It was growing in numbers, which helped it to bear heavier aggregate fiscal burdens; and the situation varied greatly at different times and in different parts of the continent. It seems likely that there was, in fact, a slow rise in general living standards from the later fifteenth century until the period of relatively sharp economic difficulty and contraction which began about 1620. But the deep unfairness of so much taxation was the greatest of all obstacles in the way of governments which sought to ease their financial difficulties.

It was not the only such obstacle. Inequity meant inefficiency. Not only did tax systems so often favour noble, clerical and urban wealth, and thus limit the power of governments to raise revenue: these systems were themselves inefficiently administered. The farming of taxes, which could deprive a government of much of their yield; lax or corrupt officials; the sheer physical difficulty of making any sort of central control of tax collection effective in large states with poor internal communications: all these were difficulties which faced many governments. Considerable efforts were made in several states to tighten the hold of the government on the raising of revenue and to collect it in a more regular and regulated way and thus make it easier for governments to borrow when they needed to. In France a central treasury was set up in 1523; and the new post, soon to become very important, of controller-general of finance was created in 1554. In Castile, under Ferdinand and Isabella after their marriage in 1469, the tax system was probably more efficient than anywhere else in Europe. Ferdinand did something to improve it before his death in 1516; and a council of finance was set up in 1523. Even in Russia a similar impulse can be seen. In the early 1550s, as part of the reforming effort under the young Tsar Ivan IV, there were efforts to increase the government's control over the raising of taxes and ensure that their yield was paid directly to Moscow. But it was always easier in this age to devise policies than to carry them out effectively. In England, for example, the reforming plans in this respect of Thomas

---

13. P. Chaunu, 'L'empire de Charles Quint', in M. Duverger, ed., *Le Concept d'empire* (Paris, 1980), p. 260.

Cromwell in the 1530s were only partly put into effect: taxation issues were the only ones on which during his reign Henry VIII was forced to give ground in the face of popular opposition, notably in 1525, when new taxes to finance a war with France had to be withdrawn in the face of furious resistance.

Faced with all these difficulties, there were a number of expedients on which rulers and their ministers could fall back in their search for money. They could raise forced loans, compelling institutions or wealthy individuals to lend them specified sums of money. Francis I of France from the beginning of his reign in 1515 used this expedient to finance his efforts at conquest in Italy. They could sell rights of various kinds – to farm a particular tax, paying a lump sum to the government, collecting the tax and making a profit in the process; or to monopolize the import or sale of some particular product or commodity. Government offices were also sold. In France, where this practice went further and has been more intensively studied than anywhere else, Louis XII began such sales in 1512–13 to finance, typically enough, his efforts to reconquer the duchy of Milan; and Francis I revived it in 1521 to raise money for the war he had just begun with Charles V. It took such firm root that it was estimated that by the end of the sixteenth century there were over 50,000 official posts in existence in France, many of them created merely to be sold. In 1568 Charles IX allowed officials to transfer their offices to other holders (very often members of their own family) provided they paid a tax when the transfer took place. In 1604 a very wide range of such offices was made hereditary in return for the payment of an annual tax which was calculated as a proportion of their value. This tax, the *paulette*, consolidated a huge structure of venal offices which was to remain a feature of French administration and society until the cataclysm of 1789. Nowhere else did such a system become quite so widespread and deep-rooted; but in several parts of Europe, notably perhaps in Spain, sales of offices played a significant role in public finance.

The government in every major state also tried to tap the great reservoir of wealth controlled by churches and clerics. In Spain Ferdinand of Aragon in the last decades of the fifteenth century considerably strengthened the finances of the monarchy by accumulating in his own hands the grand masterships of the very rich military orders of Santiago, Calatrava and Alcantara; and these passed to Charles V when he became effective ruler in 1516. More important were the taxes known as the 'Three Graces' – the *cruzada*, the sale of bulls of indulgence to the whole population; the *excusado*, a tax on the clergy first granted by the papacy in 1567 to help finance the suppression of heresy in the Netherlands; and the *subsidio*, another and heavier levy on the clergy introduced in 1560. These had much influence on Philip II's often strained relations with the papacy. Nor did France, Spain's inveterate rival, neglect such sources of income. The church there too was taxed, while in 1557, as his financial position became more critical, Henry II ordered the making of an inventory of the gold and silver objects it possessed so that in extremity they could be collected and melted down.[14] Adoption of the reformed religion greatly strengthened the position of a ruler *vis-à-vis* the church, so that in England Henry VIII was able in 1534 to assume the right to tax it freely, while the dissolution of the monasteries in 1536–40 gave him the opportunity (which was largely neglected) to gain for the crown a very large financial windfall.

Money might also be raised by selling crown land. This was as a rule the most damaging expedient to which any ruler could be driven, involving as it did the disposal of the most important of all his capital assets. None the less it might become unavoidable. Even Elizabeth I, whose careful financial management, not to say meanness, was her greatest strength, was forced in the immediate aftermath in 1589–90 of the great armada to finance in this way the expensive struggle with Spain, on land as well as at sea, on which she had now embarked. Feudal rights, some of them increasingly outdated and unpopular, were another source of income which might be more rigorously exploited: in the last three years of her reign Elizabeth managed to increase by almost half the amount she drew from the Court of Wards.

But all this was not enough. No major ruler of this period was able to meet merely out of income the financial demands made on him. This could mean only one thing – borrowing, and on a scale which in the second half of the sixteenth century sometimes meant bankruptcy. Even in its early years the more impoverished monarchs were sometimes forced to borrow in very primitive ways. The negotiation of the Treaty of Cambrai in 1529, which brought a temporary peace between Charles V and Francis I, involved long discussion of the emperor's debts to Henry VIII of England, and in particular of the return of a jewel, the Fleur de Lys, which had been pledged many years before by the Emperor Maximilian to Henry VII as security for a loan. But it was the wars of the 1540s that saw an unprecedented growth in the debts of all the major European rulers. Even before this war costs, overwhelmingly the greatest drain on their resources,

14. F.J. Baumgartner, *Henry II, King of France, 1547–1559* (Durham, NC/London, 1988), p. 193.

had often been very high. Francis I may have spent 7.5 million livres on his Italian campaign of 1515 alone; and the fighting of 1521–5 probably cost him about twenty million. But it was the middle years of the century that saw these burdens become truly crushing. In Antwerp, now establishing itself as the greatest of the continent's money markets, the bellicose and spendthrift Henry VIII in the four years before his death in 1547 borrowed about £1 million sterling – more than Charles V himself. It was only in the 1550s, however, that it became clear that the increasingly expensive Habsburg–Valois struggle was now creating a weight of debt that might well cripple both combatants.

Until then the debts of both Charles V and Francis I, though growing, had been manageable. In 1515, just before he set out for Spain, Charles had owed to the bankers of Antwerp little more than 10,000 livres; and even in 1551, when his last struggle with France began, the total was less than a million. But when he abdicated the Spanish throne only five years later this had grown explosively to the horrifying sum of seven million.[15] This huge debt had accumulated, moreover, in spite of the fact that the emperor was demanding sharply increased sums from his relatively wealthy Netherlands provinces and also receiving unprecedented ones from Spain: it was estimated that by September 1554 the country (in effect Castile) had provided him, in loans and subsidies, with about eleven million ducats since war broke out with France.[16] His rival, Henry II, was facing similar difficulties. The annual revenue of the kings of France from taxes, the royal demesne and other sources, had risen from five million livres in 1523 to more than nine million when Francis I died in 1547. Yet one contemporary estimate put the king's military expenses alone in 1553 at thirteen million. Whatever other expedients Henry resorted to (he increased markedly the number of venal offices as a means of raising money), here again borrowing on a large scale was the only way in which the war could be financed. In March 1555 he raised in Lyons, the greatest centre of financial dealings in France and one of the greatest in Europe, an unprecedentedly big loan, giving official recognition for this purpose to a syndicate of financiers known as 'Le Grand Parti'. This was the first government loan anywhere in Europe to which the general public, as distinct from a small group of wealthy financiers, was able to subscribe. It was a success: many humble

15. F. Braudel, 'Les emprunts de Charles-Quint sur la place d'Anvers', in *Charles-Quint et son temps* (Paris, 1959), graph facing p. 196.

16. M.J. Rodriguez-Salgado, *The Changing Face of Empire: Charles V, Philip II and Habsburg Authority, 1551-1559* (Cambridge, 1988), pp. 58–9, 62.

people rushed to lend. But it was also an indication of the king's increasingly difficult position.

As both Charles and Henry were driven to borrow more they were forced to pay higher, sometimes cripplingly higher, rates of interest. In 1520–42 the emperor had been able to borrow in Spain at an average annual rate of 18 per cent. In 1543–51, as his position became more difficult, this rose to 28 per cent. In his last years, 1552–56, this rose further to a crushing 33 per cent. Moreover, the fact that virtually all loans to monarchs in this period were for short periods (often as short as six or even three months, though they were then usually renewed repeatedly over many years), and that almost all such debt was floating debt, meant that the financial position of every heavily indebted government was more unstable and unpredictable than it otherwise would have been. It was also quite normal for a substantial addition to be made to the rate of interest to allow for the all too likely delays in repayment of the principal. In 1554 Charles's ministers in Spain had to face not merely a basic rate of 43 per cent but also a supplementary 14 per cent to cover such contingencies. One loan to him of 339,000 ducats appears to have involved a total repayment of 898,000. Figures of this kind illustrate the ruinous expedients to which any government was now likely to be driven if it wished to wage war on a large scale over any considerable period. So great were the emperor's difficulties that in August 1555 the Duke of Alba, the Spanish commander in Italy, had to leave his own son as a hostage in the hands of unpaid soldiers who had mutinied in an effort to secure what they were owed: their pay was then 800,000 ducats in arrears.[17]

By the later 1550s Philip II, who had now succeeded his father as king of Spain, was being driven to more arbitrary measures. In 1557 he raised a million ducats by seizing without warning in Spanish ports bullion and other valuable commodities just brought back from the Indies, overriding completely the rights of their owners. The crown bonds he offered in compensation, as Charles V had already done in rather similar circumstances, were hardly an adequate recompense. In June of the same year the rate of interest payable on his debts was reduced by government decree to a mere 5 per cent, the first of several measures of this kind over the next four decades which were, in effect, admissions that the king was bankrupt. The regents who ruled Spain (Philip was still in the Netherlands) strongly opposed the decree and it was never effectively applied in practice. The king's big-

---

17. These figures are taken from Rodriguez-Salgado, *The Changing Face of Empire*, pp. 66–7, 145. The financing of the wars of Charles V in the early 1550s is discussed in detail on pp. 50–72.

gest creditors, the Fuggers and the Genoese banking houses whose international importance was now rapidly growing, were therefore able to evade its worst effects. But smaller lenders had to face a suspension of payments on the king's debts until Philip returned to Spain for good in 1559 and arrangements for meeting their claims could be introduced in 1560–61.[18]

Difficult as the position of the Habsburgs had become, however, and strong as the resulting pressures to make peace now were, the situation of Henry II was just as bad. By the time of his sudden death, in 1559, the French government was about 40 million livres in debt and its credit in ruins. The calling of a states-general in 1558 (the first since 1484) in a last effort to raise more by taxation was a failure. Annual revenue had now reached twelve million livres; but much of this never reached the treasury and the pay of all royal officials was in arrears.

It was, in fact, the French who first proposed, in October 1558, the negotiations which led more than five months later to the peace settlement of Cateau-Cambrésis. Though this was a symbolic victory for Philip he was well aware of the underlying weakness of his own position. He even empowered his representatives at the negotiations to surrender the duchy of Milan, the key to Italy and the focus of so many ambitions on both sides, if this were essential as the price of peace. In March 1559 he told his ambassador in London frankly that 'I tremble whenever I think of something that might break this peace, if it is concluded, because I lack the strength to do anything more'. When he returned to Spain in 1559 it is estimated that his debts may have reached the frightening total of 29 million ducats.[19] But the equal exhaustion of France meant that no such ruinous territorial sacrifice was needed. The two greatest monarchs in Europe had been driven to make peace by sheer financial necessity. This was not a totally new situation. In 1537 Charles V and Francis I had been forced by mutual financial exhaustion to agree to a truce and begin unsuccessful peace talks; though Francis had begun the war in 1536 with a reserve of 1.5 million livres, its first year alone cost him more than three times as much. Again, the peace they signed in 1544 was forced on them since neither could face the cost of further fighting: the war of 1542–44 had cost France some seventeen million livres. But by 1559 the financial pressures were more irresistible than ever in the past. In this way the later 1550s were something of a turning-point. They showed, more clearly than anything that had gone before, the extent to which Europe's international relations were now influenced

18. Rodriguez-Salgado, *The Changing Face of Empire*, pp. 236, 251.
19. Ibid., pp. 306–7, 325.

by the relative economic strength of the contending states, and most of all by the efficiency of their fiscal and financial structures.

For almost a century after 1559 Spain was the supreme imperial power within Europe as well as outside it, and immensely impressive in terms of her strength and successes. Yet it became more and more impossible for her to bear the cost of this imposing structure of military and political greatness. The struggle to subdue the rebellious Netherlands provinces in particular, a war of sieges and correspondingly expensive, rapidly became the most sustained and debilitating drain of all on her resources. Government annuities (*juros*) already under Charles V made up the major part of the state debt: by the early 1540s about two-thirds of the ordinary revenues of Castile was going to their payment. But under Philip the weight of the burden grew rapidly. *Juros* were issued at the beginning of his reign at an annual rate of about 1.6 million ducats; but when he died in 1598 this had almost trebled, to 4.6 million each year. The cost of the Spanish army grew at a similar rate, from 700,000 ducats a year in 1560 to two million at the end of the reign. In 1556–75 sixteen million ducats worth of *juros* were issued, but in the next quarter-century something like 50 million. Taxation became increasingly heavy. The level of ordinary taxes in Castile, which under Philip II bore perhaps 70–80 per cent of the total cost of his empire, was in 1584–98 twice what it had been in 1556. The Spanish possessions in Europe also had to face growing financial demands. In the kingdom of Naples, for example, much government expenditure, used hitherto for more or less useful domestic purposes, was increasingly diverted from the 1560s onwards into 'shoring up imperial power, literally from one end of Europe to the other'.[20] But there was a level beyond which such demands could not be pushed. The result was further government bankruptcies (really forcible conversions of floating short-term debt at high rates of interest to longer-term indebtedness at lower ones) in 1575 and 1596. These had serious results both in economic and political terms. When in September 1575 Philip had to suspend payment on his debts, this produced in the following year a collapse, sudden and complete though temporary, of Spanish authority in the Netherlands as the unpaid army there mutinied. Decades of costly effort could not undo the long-term effects of this disaster. The bloody and destructive 'Spanish Fury' of 1576 in Antwerp was a turning-point in the commercial and financial history of sixteenth-century Europe, while

---

20. Castillo, 'Dette flottante et dette consolidée', 748–9, 757; A. Calabria, *The Cost of Empire. The Finances of the Kingdom of Naples in the Time of Spanish Rule* (Cambridge, 1991), p. 130.

the Genoese bankers who were now a major prop of Habsburg power were also severely affected. The bankruptcy of 1596 in its turn produced crisis or near-crisis conditions in all the main financial centres of Europe; and in Spain it dealt a final blow to the formerly very flourishing fairs of Medina del Campo, for long a major centre of the country's commercial life. Its political effects were more important and lasting. It paved the way to the Treaty of Vervins of May 1598, in which Philip abandoned the dreams of dominance in France that had lured him for the last decade and restored, in effect, the situation established in 1559. In rather the same way another Spanish government bankruptcy in 1607, the result in part of the notoriously expensive court of Philip III, was the prelude to the truce of 1609 with the rebel Netherlands provinces.

American silver and Spanish power

Spain provides the clearest and most striking example in this age of the growing role, though one not always clear to contemporaries, that money now played in international relations. The aggregation of political and military power that the Spanish Habsburgs controlled, impressive in so many ways, was simply too big and too demanding in the later sixteenth century to be carried for long by the predominantly Castilian economic foundation on which it rested. Yet even in purely financial terms Spanish power seemed to many observers threateningly great and potentially overwhelming. This was because of the stream, both dazzling and menacing to contemporaries, of American silver that was now flowing into Spain. Silver-mining began in Mexico in the 1540s. More important, the very rich silver deposits at Potosi in Peru were discovered in 1543. The introduction of the 'amalgamation' process of refining the ore by the use of mercury, first in Mexico and a little later in Peru, greatly increased production (and also stimulated an important export trade in mercury from Spain to her American possessions). By 1570, even before the new method had become fully effective, Potosi had a population of 120,000 and was the largest town in the Spanish overseas empire. A system of forced labour, imposed on the Indian population in Peru in 1572 and in Mexico three years later, helped production to grow still further: output at Potosi leapt by 600 per cent in 1572–79.[21] By the 1580s, and

21. D.C. Goodman, *Power and Penury: Government, Technology and Science in Philip II's Spain* (Cambridge, 1988), pp. 172–94, gives a good account of precious metal production in Spanish America.

still more the 1590s when it was at its peak, the flow of American silver to Spain was becoming a torrent. The contribution of precious metals imported from America to the structure of Spanish power had already grown by a factor of five (of course from a low original base) under Charles V. Under his son it quadrupled.

Philip II and his government benefited both by the levy of a tax, the *quinta* or royal fifth, on the imported bullion and by the ability, in case of pressing need, to seize cargoes of it and use them for their own purposes. A general correlation can, it has been suggested, be seen between on the one hand relatively plentiful imports of silver and on the other Spanish victories and successful expansionism in Europe. The difficulties, both financial and political, of the middle and later 1570s, for example, coincided with a period when trade with the American empire was failing to grow rapidly, whereas the remarkable successes of the 1580s – the conquest of Portugal, Parma's successful offensive in the Netherlands, large-scale intervention in France – fell in years when American bullion was flowing into Seville at an unprecedented rate. Such claims push monetary determinism to unjustifiable lengths: decisions made in Madrid, conscious choices between different courses of action, were at least equally important. The fateful decision in 1566–67 to crush the unrest in the Netherlands by force was taken at a moment when American silver was flowing in at an unprecedented rate; but it was not this that made up Philip II's mind. However, contemporaries were justified in seeing bullion imports from across the Atlantic as one of the foundations of Spain's whole international position.

Indeed not merely in Spain but all over western Europe the safe arrival of the treasure-fleets from America came to be awaited eagerly as some guarantee that money would be plentiful, credit relatively easy to obtain and the wheels of commerce therefore adequately lubricated. In 1595, notably, the lateness with which that year's consignment of silver reached Seville was seen in every financial centre as adding to the serious difficulties that already existed. It must be remembered that the Spanish government always drew the major part of its income from the increasingly hard-pressed resources of Castile. These American silver could never replace. Yet of the extent of its contribution to Spain's overstretched finances there is no doubt. By the middle 1590s, with the flow of silver at its height, Philip and his ministers could rely with some confidence on receiving three million ducats each year from America, four times as much as twenty years earlier. Without this it would have been impossible to carry the burden of war, in the Mediterranean, later in France, most demanding of all in the Netherlands (which alone had cost perhaps 110 million ducats in all by 1608).[22] Moreover, the Spanish government drew very substantial indirect as well as direct financial advantages from the empire across the Atlantic. It was American silver that provided the main inducement for bankers (predominantly Genoese) to lend on so massive a scale and over so long a period to Philip.

Yet he was never without serious money worries; and these became markedly more serious as his reign went on. American silver was a palliative, not a cure, for his difficulties. 'From 1570', the most penetrating study in English has concluded, 'the sense of permanent fiscal crisis is overwhelming. Every major campaign was as much a financial confidence trick as a military exercise.'[23] There were fundamental defects in Spanish (or more accurately Castilian) fiscal machinery – poor accounting, with a lack of uniformity in the way in which accounts were kept and a resulting difficulty in making accurate estimates of costs; confusing division of responsibility between a plethora of different administrative bodies; dishonest or corrupt tax-collectors or paymasters who exploited the system, or lack of it, for their own advantage. But there is no reason to think that these defects were worse in Spain than in any other major state. What nullified the effect of the American silver and fatally undermined the heroic striving of Castile to keep the whole imperial structure intact was the essential economic weakness that underlay all these efforts.

Much of Spain was infertile, arid and with a difficult and extreme climate. Her population was much smaller than that of her great rival – perhaps eight million in Spain and Portugal (united since 1580) as against twice as many in France. A good many types of skilled worker were scarce or non-existent in Spain and had to be sought in foreign countries. Her industries, though some of them were by no means negligible, were often unable to meet her need for their products, a deficiency that was particularly marked where many kinds of war material were concerned. Thus of the 32,000 arquebuses needed for the difficult suppression of the Morisco revolt in southern Spain in 1568–70 only 6,000 were produced in Spain and the rest had to be bought abroad. Philip also had to import artillery in large quantities from Germany, the Netherlands and on at least one occasion England. Though Spain had rich native resources of both iron and copper, the essential raw materials of gun-founding, lack of both money and technological ability meant that they were not effectively de-

22. I.A.A. Thompson, *War and Government in Habsburg Spain, 1560–1620* (London, 1976), pp. 68, 70.
23. Ibid., p. 73.

veloped.[24] Contemporaries therefore were struck by the speed with which the river of American silver that flowed into the country flowed out again, either to pay for needed imports or to maintain Spanish armies abroad, without Spain's own productive power benefiting from this enormous windfall. An English observer, writing at the end of the sixteenth century from a prison in Seville itself, noted that a consignment of silver from America 'within a few days that it is unladen vanisheth without show or appearance'.[25] None of this altered the fact that Spain was the greatest power in Christendom and remained so until the middle of the seventeenth century; but already fundamental and intractable weaknesses were clearly visible.

The rise of Dutch power

The Spain of Philip II is therefore a striking illustration of the fact that military power and political success now depended, to an extent never seen before, on an essential underpinning of economic strength. This lesson was driven home by the sharply contrasting experience of her most tenacious opponent, the rebellious provinces of the northern Netherlands. By the 1590s these provinces, above all Holland, by far the most important of them, were securely launched upon 'the most prodigious burst of colonial and maritime expansion ever seen in the world until that time'.[26] This spectacular achievement developed with a speed which took contemporaries by surprise. The Dutch had for long been important in the transport of heavy and bulky commodities with relatively low unit values – grain, timber and fish – from the Baltic and North Sea to southern Europe. But their trade now suddenly expanded to cover much of the world. The middle 1590s saw a considerable though eventually unsuccessful effort to break down the trading monopoly claimed by Spain in the Caribbean. In 1602 the United East India Company, an amalgamation of a number of previously existing competing groups, was formed and at once launched a successful attack on the trade of the Portuguese in Indonesia, and therefore on the revenues which Spain, after the union of 1580, drew from it. As early as 1605 the company had taken the islands of Amboina, Tidore and Ternate and seized and fortified bases in the Spice Islands. In the Mediterranean Dutch trade had been growing since the 1580s; and by 1612 an agreement

24. Ibid., p. 25; Goodman, *Power and Penury*, pp. 109–10, 115–17.
25. Wernham, *The Return of the Armadas*, p. 251.
26. Israel, *Dutch Primacy in World Trade*, p. 18.

with the Turkish government had placed that with the Ottoman Empire on an equal footing with those of France and England. The same year saw the appearance of the first Dutch ambassador in Constantinople. Moreover, this explosively growing Dutch trade was far from being one merely in low-value bulk commodities. The 'rich' trades in such things as textiles, metals, sugar and spices played an equally important role in it. The new United Netherlands had considerable textile industries of its own and fulled and dyed much cloth produced in England; this, and the refining of both salt and sugar, provided the basis for significant export trades. The distribution of Swedish copper was another facet of Dutch commercial activity, while its conquests in the east gave the new East India Company a virtual monopoly of the world's exports of nutmeg, mace and cloves. Pre-eminence in trade, moreover, led quickly to a corresponding leadership in international finance. The Wisselbank in Amsterdam, set up in 1609, and the Amsterdam Loan Bank, which began operations five years later, became at once the most important institutions of their kind. The former 'was the first major public bank in Europe outside Italy and, for over a century, much the greatest'.[27] The fact that capital in the Dutch provinces was relatively plentiful and interest rates therefore correspondingly low rapidly aroused the admiration and envy of competitors, notably in England.

Dutch commercial and financial primacy was very largely the primacy of Amsterdam; and this was the obverse of the loss by Antwerp of her former leadership in these respects. The sack of the city in 1576 by mutinous Spanish soldiers dealt it a terrible blow: nevertheless it regained much of its former economic activity and importance in the early 1580s. What put its past greatness beyond hope of recovery was the great siege of 1585 and the recapture of the city for Spain by the Duke of Parma. Its population had by then declined sharply. In 1586 it was probably no more than about 55,000, a fall of something like two-fifths in the last two disastrous decades.[28] Even more damaging was the fact that the mouth of the River Scheldt remained in rebel hands after 1585. This allowed the Dutch to prevent seagoing ships sailing up the river directly to Antwerp, and thus to inflict crippling difficulties and extra costs on its trade. Henceforth the closure of the Scheldt was to give Amsterdam and other Dutch ports a crucial advantage over their great potential rival; and the mainten-

27. Ibid., pp. 76–7. Chapters 2 and 3 of this book give much the best account in English of the growth of Dutch trade and financial supremacy.

28. R. Boumans, 'Le dépeuplement d'Anvers dans le dernier quart du XVIe siècle', *Revue du Nord* XXIX (1947), 181–94.

ance of this closure was to remain a primary objective of Dutch diplomacy. By the beginning of the seventeenth century, therefore, the position of Amsterdam as the greatest trading centre in Europe was beyond challenge. Of her possible competitors in northern Europe apart from Antwerp, Lübeck, the greatest of the Hanse cities, was now in rapid decline, while the great days of London and, on a smaller scale, Hamburg, were still to come.

For the Dutch, economic strength bred political and even military importance. By the time of the Twelve Years Truce with Spain in 1609 the United Netherlands, in spite of its deep provincial and urban rivalries and its complex and cumbersome constitution, was a very substantial military power (not least because its economic strength allowed it to pay its soldiers with relative regularity). By 1606 it had 60,000 men in pay, an enormous force for a state so small in territory and population. Already in the 1590s a series of important successes on the eastern and southern frontiers, particularly the capture of Groningen in 1594, had produced important economic benefits by opening trade routes into Germany. That the Dutch rebels, apparently condemned in the 1560s and 1570s to rapid and complete defeat, were now a real international force was shown clearly when the United Netherlands successfully resisted the efforts of the ambitious Christian IV of Denmark in 1611 to raise sharply the tolls paid by shipping passing through the Sound, the narrow channel between the Baltic and the North Sea. This resulted in the imposition of 'something like a *Pax Neerlandica* on the waters of the Baltic and the north'.[29] For several generations the new state was to be one of the decisive forces in the political life of northern Europe.

Spain and her rebel provinces, then, in different ways and with very different outcomes, were the outstanding illustrations of the fact that true and lasting international greatness was by the end of this period, more than ever before, impossible without at least an essential minimum of economic power. Yet it was still unusual for rulers and their ministers to think primarily, or sometimes even at all, in economic terms. Policies were seldom framed in the light of a realistic evaluation of the resources available (a very difficult exercise in any case when statistics of any kind were so fragmentary and inaccurate) and of the likely costs of any particular line of action. Dynastic ambitions and claims, continuing deep sensitivities where the personal prestige of rulers, and hence that of the states they personified, was concerned, a still active sense of religious obligation: all these still marked international relations in the early seventeenth century.

29. Israel, *Dutch Primacy in World Trade*, p. 95.

CHAPTER THREE

The Instruments of International Relations: Diplomats and Diplomacy[1]

The origins of modern diplomacy

The sixteenth century saw the emergence for the first time of a network of organized diplomatic contacts which linked together more or less continuously the states of western Europe. By the early seventeenth century areas hitherto on the margins of this system, Russia, Poland and the Ottoman Empire, were beginning to be, at least in some sense, parts of it. A true European state system was emerging; and foreshadowings, though faint ones, of the basic idea underlying such a system, that of the balance of power, were beginning to be visible.

Alliances between a number of different states, sometimes wide-ranging ones, were by no means unknown in mediaeval Europe. In the late twelfth century, to take only one of the more obvious examples, the Plantagenet rulers of England had been the allies of the kings of Aragon and the Guelf dukes of Bavaria against Philip Augustus of France, who himself had the support of the Holy Roman Emperor. Europe, and even its western parts, were still in the Middle Ages far from being a truly unified political system. But already there can be seen friendships and enmities which were acquiring the force of tradition and which were, in some cases, to influence the events of the sixteenth century. There was a marked readiness from the fourteenth century onwards of France and Scotland to combine against England; and that of England to look for allies against France to Flanders and Castile was at least visible. The legacy of Angevin rule in Naples meant that there was a distinct thread of French interest in

1. This chapter relies heavily on M.S. Anderson, *The Rise of Modern Diplomacy, 1450–1919* (London, 1993), ch.1 and pp. 150–4.

Italy long before Charles VIII crossed the Alps in 1494. But diplomatic representatives were still sent by one ruler to another only for specific and often ceremonial purposes, and remained in post only until that was accomplished. Diplomacy was as yet intermittent, fragmentary and limited in its scope.

It was in Italy that this situation first changed decisively and permanently. That she should have led Europe in this respect, as in many others, is not surprising. The peninsula was dominated by a small number of significant but not really large states – Florence, Venice, Milan, the kingdom of Naples and the papal territories – supplemented by a few smaller ones such as Mantua and Genoa. Most of these were well developed and highly organized. They were also intensely competitive, active or potential rivals for power, for territory, for security and even survival. Their geographical proximity, and the strength of local patriotisms and antagonisms, made these rivalries the most intense in Europe. Each felt compelled to watch closely the attitudes and actions of its neighbours and competitors: this, combined with the relative efficiency of their governments, meant that their foreign policies were more continuous and better organized than those of the greater powers north of the Alps.

The result was a system of permanent diplomatic contacts, one which involved the stationing by each government in the capitals of its rivals of a representative who remained there until he was replaced, and whose main function was usually not to negotiate but rather to watch carefully events in the state to which he had been sent. The military strength and intentions of a rival, potentially threatening alliances which it might hope to conclude, any internal weakness in it which might be exploited; none of these must escape the eye of a competent diplomat. Several explanations have been given of the origins of the permanent embassy: that it developed from the *bailo*, the essentially commercial agent who had already for long been maintained by Venice in Constantinople, or from the procurators kept by many rulers at the papal *Curia* who by the fifteenth century were sometimes given the title of ambassador. Most probably, however, it was the outcome of a slow and almost unconscious development, as the temporary and *ad hoc* embassies of the Middle Ages became more frequent and lasted longer. Whatever its roots, the middle years of the fifteenth century saw the rapid establishment of the new institution in Italy. By the 1450s all her major secular states – Milan (which seems to have led the way), Venice, Florence and Naples – had permanent embassies stationed in each other's capitals.

The advantages to the small Italian states of having such an agent also in the major European capitals meant that representatives of this new kind soon began to appear north of the Alps. Milan had an ambassador in Paris from 1463 onwards, Florence from 1474, Venice from 1479. The first permanent Milanese ambassador arrived in London in 1490, the first from Venice in 1496. The greater states of western Europe, however, followed the Italian example only after a delay of some decades. Since the new diplomacy was generated by a combination of ambition and insecurity, it was natural for states which were powerful, or relatively secure against attack, to feel less need for information about the strength and intentions of their neighbours than was the case in Italy. Thus although the prudent and wary Ferdinand of Aragon sent a permanent ambassador to London in 1488 and the Emperor Maximilian I one in 1493, it was only in 1509 that England, from the security of its island situation, sent one to any foreign court. France, the most powerful state of all, was also the slowest to make use of the new methods. Its first permanent embassy, to the emperor, was also despatched in 1509; and at the accession of Francis I in 1515 it had still only this one. It was only the creation by a series of dynastic accidents of the empire of Charles V, and the threat this seemed to offer to France's ambitions in Italy and even her own security, that changed this attitude. At the death of Francis I, in 1547, France had ten permanent embassies in foreign capitals; and she was now for generations to come to possess a larger and more elaborate diplomatic machine than any of her rivals. In spite of more than a generation of devastating though intermittent civil war she had in the later sixteenth century, it has been claimed, 'the most extensive ambassadorial system in Europe'.[2]

The linking of the states of Europe by the new form of diplomacy was not a smooth and uninterrupted process. Nor was it complete by the early seventeenth century. The developing diplomatic network was seriously disrupted for a generation or more after 1560, as the Counter-Reformation gathered strength and religious antagonism sharpened. It took some time to establish the principle that an ambassador had the right to practise a form of religion which differed from that established in the host country. In March 1551 the imperial ambassador in London even threatened war if he, and the Catholic Princess Mary, were not allowed to celebrate Mass freely, while in the spring of 1568 Philip II flatly refused to allow the English ambassador in Madrid to have Anglican services in his house. The same religious antagonisms, as they inevitably became associated with secular inter-

2. De Lamar Jensen, 'French diplomacy and the wars of religion', *Sixteenth Century Journal* V, No. 2 (Oct. 1974), 44.

state rivalries, also opened the way for a series of embarrassing incidents when ambassadors were shown to have taken part in plots designed to overthrow rulers of a different religion. Two Spanish ones were expelled from England, in 1571 and 1584, for their share in the Ridolfi and Throckmorton conspiracies against Queen Elizabeth, while in 1563 the English ambassador in Paris was arrested after a long series of intrigues by him meant to strengthen the growing Huguenot faction in France against the government.

England, now emerging somewhat reluctantly as the spearhead of Protestantism, had no resident ambassador in Madrid after 1568 until the Anglo-Spanish peace of 1604, while the last decades of the century saw a long break in diplomatic relations between the Italian states and Protestant Europe. Religious prejudice also helped to delay the growth of such relations between Scandinavia and the Catholic states. The first years of the seventeenth century, however, saw diplomatic contacts begin to span once more the religious divide of the previous decades. A series of important peace settlements – between France and Spain in 1598, between England and Spain in 1604, temporarily between the rebellious Dutch provinces and Spain in 1609 – ended the most acute and destructive phase of religious hostility in western Europe. Even in Spain the ministers of Philip III after 1609, though they still had no doubt that the Dutch must be subdued, now saw them in secular terms, as a threat to Spanish power and most of all to Spain's overseas empire, rather than as religious dissidents whom it was a sacred duty to crush. In these years of slowly relaxing religious prejudice (though it still remained very powerful with the ordinary man and with what embryonic public opinion existed) it was possible to reconstruct the ruptured network of diplomacy fairly quickly. In the early years of the seventeenth century English resident ambassadors reappeared in Madrid and Venice, Spanish and Venetian ones in London, Dutch ones in Venice and Paris and French and Spanish ones, though only intermittently, in Denmark and Sweden.

Eastern Europe lags behind

To the end of this period, however, eastern Europe remained largely outside the network of resident ambassadors and continuous diplomatic relations that was emerging in the west. In this respect Europe was still a duality. Between the western states, France, Spain, England, the Italian principalities, later the new Dutch republic, these relations were beginning to develop some aspects which foreshadow the diplomacy of today. But in the east, in Poland, Russia, the Ottoman Empire, even to some extent Scandinavia, the short-lived and temporary embassy, sent *ad hoc* for some specific and limited purpose, was still the norm. The Polish–Lithuanian crowned republic, within its pre-partition frontiers the largest state in Europe, still attracted little attention in the west. Though Henry VIII and Elizabeth sent one or two special embassies to the country, these were peripatetic and 'circular' ones which went also to other destinations (usually Denmark, Prussia and the Hanse towns), so that Poland was only a part, perhaps a minor one, of their sphere of activity. Not until 1610 did England have any resident representative there; and though he held the post for six years he was merely a humble agent, paid at the lowest rate.[3] In rather the same way Philip II, when in 1572 he thought briefly of putting forward an Austrian Habsburg, the Archduke Matthias, as a candidate for the Polish throne, could do so only through the Spanish ambassador to the Holy Roman Emperor, as he had no representative of his own in the country. Even France, in whose foreign policy Poland was so often to figure prominently from the later seventeenth century onwards, showed during this period little concern for her: the fact that a Frenchman, the future Henry III, reigned briefly, reluctantly and ineffectively in Poland in 1573–75 did nothing to alter this.

More important were the abnormality and one-sidedness of the relations between the western states and the Ottoman Empire, and the sketchy and intermittent nature of those with Russia. The position of the Ottoman Empire was peculiar. It was unquestionably a great power. To contemporaries it seemed the greatest of all, with the possible exception of Spain, because of its alarming military strength and what appeared, for much of the sixteenth century at least, to be the excellence of its government. Its Balkan conquests, its penetration into central Europe and the possibility that it might dominate the Mediterranean, meant that it was a great force in international affairs. It was bound, therefore, to attract the attention of the west European states. From the 1520s onwards there were largely unsuccessful French efforts to use Turkish power as a weapon in the struggle with Charles V. From the 1570s onwards Protestants in many parts of Europe – England, the Dutch provinces, the Huguenots in France – hoped with even less result for at least indirect Turkish help in the struggle with Catholic Spain. Western diplomatic repre-

3. G.M. Bell, ed., *A Handlist of British Diplomatic Representatives, 1509–1688* (London, 1990), pp. 217–18.

sentation in Constantinople therefore grew during the sixteenth century in scale and importance. From its early years the Holy Roman emperors and from the 1530s France paid growing attention to this eastern colossus; and the increasingly frequent and important embassies they sent to Constantinople were later supplemented by those of other powers. England, stimulated by a growing trade with the Levant as well as hopes of support against Spain, was represented in the Turkish capital from 1583 onwards, and the emerging Dutch republic a generation later.

Yet none of this could get round the fact that the Turks were, unalterably, the enemies of Christendom, a foe against whom, ideally, all Christians must unite. To the men of the sixteenth century, as to their ancestors a hundred years earlier, 'the Turk was a species different *in kind* from Christian states whether Catholic or Protestant, a political pariah excluded by his very nature from membership in the family of European states'.[4] This feeling of unbridgeable difference, moreover, was fully reciprocated by the Ottoman government. There was no effort to establish permanent Turkish diplomatic representatives in the main capitals of Europe until the 1790s, and no successful attempt of this kind until the 1830s.

To west Europeans Russia seemed much more remote than the Ottoman Empire, and much less important and interesting. England did indeed develop during the second half of the sixteenth century a relatively good working relationship with the strange, little-known and apparently semi-barbaric empire on Europe's eastern fringes. In 1553 a small group of Englishmen led by Richard Chancellor, who had reached Russia via the White Sea, appeared in Moscow; and four years later the first Russian ambassador ever seen in England arrived in London. In this way there began a series of contacts which, though never close and from the English side focused entirely on commercial objectives, were fairly frequent and relatively harmonious.[5] But no French representative reached Moscow until 1586; and he, significantly, was a mere merchant of Dieppe, while no Russian one was seen in Paris until 1615. With the states and rulers on or near her western frontiers – Sweden, Denmark, Poland–Lithuania and the Holy Roman Emperor – Russia could hardly avoid having some political and diplomatic contacts. Her first treaty with Sweden was signed

4. F.L. Baumer, 'England, the Turk and the common corps of Christendom', *American Historical Review* L (1944–5), 27. Many of the points made in these paragraphs are further developed at pp. 228–31 below.
5. On these see M.S. Anderson, *Britain's Discovery of Russia, 1553–1815* (London, 1958), ch. 1.

in 1482 and one with the Emperor Maximilian I in 1490; while it has been claimed that another with Denmark in 1562 was the first ever negotiated by her with any west European state on a basis of complete equality.[6] There were even intermittent contacts with the papacy, and the dream of the conversion of Russia to Catholicism was already attracting attention in Rome. But in Moscow as in Constantinople most of Europe, its problems and potentialities, seemed remote and irrelevant. Not until the early years of the eighteenth century, when the reforming energies of Peter the Great had transformed the situation, did diplomatic relations between Russia and the states of western Europe become systematic and continuous, something seen by both sides as of permanent importance. The network of diplomacy that was growing up in sixteenth-century Europe, therefore, for all its undoubted significance and potentialities, was still confined, at least in any well-developed form, within restricted geographical limits.

The diplomat and his problems

The new diplomacy meant the emergence in western Europe for the first time of what can fairly be called professional diplomats, men with substantial diplomatic experience who saw themselves as members of a distinct though as yet small group with traditions and standards of its own. The emergence of the permanent embassy meant that an ambassador might stay in the same post for long – sometimes for what would now seem dangerously long – periods. An extreme case is Honoré de Caix, who acted as France's resident representative in Lisbon during the years 1518–41 (though there were during that period six special French embassies sent to Portugal for specific purposes and limited periods). Also, more significantly, the same individual might well lead a whole series of different missions over many years, since competent men willing to serve abroad were never easy to come by. The minor Styrian nobleman Sigismund von Herberstein, who in 38 years in the service of the Austrian Habsburgs in the first half of the sixteenth century was employed on as many as 70 missions to various destinations, most of them of course very short, is an outstanding example. The special ambassador sent for some particular purpose – to congratulate a new ruler on his accession, to add lustre to a royal marriage or to attend a coronation – was still almost

---

6. W. Kirchner, 'A milestone in European history: the Danish–Russian treaty of 1562', *Slavonic and East European Review* XXII (1944), 44; see also pp. 269–70 below.

always a noble and often of very high rank. To appoint for such ceremonial purposes someone known to be personally close to the ruler
whom he represented was often desirable. To do so was to pay a com-
pliment to the ruler who received him; and in an age morbidly sensitive to the finest shades of ceremonial distinction this was an
important consideration. But the humbler resident ambassador, who
might spend a considerable time in the same post and who was
usually a source of information, of advice and warnings, rather than
an active negotiator, was much more likely to be a professional of a
recognizably modern stamp. Of considerably less exalted birth and
very often either a lawyer or a churchman, he might well spend much
of his working life in diplomacy, acquiring the experience and the
distinctive outlook on which a genuine professionalism could be
based.

It was precisely this information-gathering function, however, that
explained the suspicion with which many rulers in the fifteenth and
early sixteenth centuries regarded the new-style resident ambassador
and the reluctance with which they received foreign diplomats of this
kind. Such an agent, observing over a considerable period events in
the state where he was stationed, noting and reporting in particular
on its military strength and preparedness, could easily be seen as no
more than a licensed spy. Even more dangerous, he might help to
weaken and undermine the ruler who received him by intrigues with
domestic opponents or some discontented court faction. Henry VII
is said to have contemplated on his deathbed in 1509 expelling from
England all ambassadors sent by other rulers, while in 1500 a Venetian ambassador to the Emperor Maximilian I found his lodgings
guarded by soldiers so that no one should talk to him. After the first
decades of the sixteenth century, as the new diplomacy spread and
began to be taken for granted, this suspicious defensiveness became
somewhat less marked, at least in western Europe. Nevertheless it was
slow to die. As late as 1618 one commentator, after issuing strong
warnings about the danger of foreign diplomats collecting damaging
military information, urged that any representatives sent by a foreign
ruler in time of war should not only be deprived of any arms they
might be carrying but should also have their clothes searched to
make sure that nothing dangerous was concealed in them.[7] This
nervous distrust lasted longer in Russia than anywhere else and hardly weakened until far into the seventeenth century. In particular,
fears that foreign diplomats might foment sedition meant constant

---

7. O. Krauske, *Die Entwicklung der ständigen Diplomatie vom fünfzehnten Jahrhundert bis
zu den Beschlüssen von 1815 und 1818* (Leipzig, 1885), pp. 14–15.

efforts, notably by the close guarding of their houses, to prevent their having contact with anyone but government officials.[8]

But the advantages of closer and more continuous contacts between states and of a more ample flow of information were too great to be denied, at least in western Europe. In spite of suspicions and conservatism, diplomacy of a more continuous, more professional, in a word more modern kind was taking root there. This was reflected in the fact that something like a generally accepted hierarchy of diplomatic ranks and a recognized nomenclature for them were slowly beginning to emerge, though this was a slow process which was not complete until the eighteenth century.

A sixteenth-century diplomat had many difficulties to contend with. He had to face the physical problems and demands of travel, of poor roads, bad weather and uncomfortable living quarters, in reaching some perhaps distant foreign court. The strain of constantly accompanying a ruler who was himself in constant movement could be even greater. A Venetian ambassador to the Emperor Maximilian in 1507 complained that during the twenty months he had spent in Germany in attendance on the imperial court he had been almost continually on horseback.[9] This was exceptional; but in eastern Europe in particular the difficulty and discomfort of travel could be daunting. The Jesuit Antonio Possevino, drawing on his own experience, warned in the 1580s that any envoy sent to Russia must equip himself not only with a tent, for use when no better lodging was available, but also with a bed which would protect him against the flies 'which bite fiercely and, unlike elsewhere, are active at night, working their way through the linen to cause intense discomfort'. He also needed curtains which could be used if necessary to divide, in the interests of privacy and decency, the single room in which the entire embassy staff might well be forced to spend the night together.[10]

Nor could the diplomat confronting these rigours console himself with the thought that he was being well paid for what he had to endure. Since no ruler of this period was normally well provided with ready cash the temptation to neglect, when money was short, men who were far away and had little means of pressing their claims was strong. Even the wealth of the Indies could not always protect Spanish diplomats against difficulties of this kind. La Quadra, Philip II's

---

8. On this see B. Picard, *Das Gesandschaftswesen Ostmitteleuropas in der frühen Neuzeit* (Graz/Vienna/Cologne, 1967), pp. 14–15.

9. M.A.R. de Maulde-la-Clavière, *La Diplomatie au temps de Machiavel* (Paris, 1892–3), iii, p. 7.

10. *The Moscovia of Antonio Possevino, S.J.*, ed. and trans. H.F. Graham (Pittsburg, Pa. 1977), p. 40.

ambassador in London, died in August 1563 in such poverty that his creditors retained his corpse as security for what they were owed, and it could not be sent to his family in Naples until March 1565. Disorder at home and disruption of the normal routine of government, as in France during the wars of religion, might mean really serious difficulty and even hardship for a diplomat in some foreign capital. Few were reduced to such straits as the French ambassador in Copenhagen, who in 1580, after years of very irregular payment, was in fear of imprisonment for debt. In the following year he was unable for months on end to appear at court, and thus carry out his duties effectively, because of debts he could not pay; and when he died in 1589 all his papers were seized by his creditors.[11] Both of these were extreme cases. But irregular payment, long delays, and allowances inadequate to cover the often heavy expenses involved if a diplomat were to do his work effectively, were the rule rather than the exception. Even when money was available its transmission to a foreign capital might be difficult and slow. An English ambassador in Brussels in 1551 had to buy cloth in England and sell it in the Netherlands to obtain the local currency he needed, while the £300 paid by bill of exchange to another in Madrid in October 1561 did not reach him until six months or more later. It is not surprising, therefore, that complaints about lack of money and slow or incomplete payment of what was due figure prominently in much diplomatic correspondence of the period. Since organized and effective diplomatic machinery was still only evolving, what a diplomat in fact received depended not on any fixed scale of salaries and expense allowances but rather on his social rank and the effectiveness with which he, or someone on his behalf, could press his claims. The noble ambassador, sent with much display and ceremony to carry on some important negotiation or perform some prestigious ceremonial function, would often feel honoured by serving his prince in this very public way; but his humbler counterpart who was largely an observer and reporter had often to think in more material terms.

Diplomats could profit in a quite different way from the presents they were given, usually at the end of a mission, by the ruler to whom they had been accredited. Gold chains, their weight and value carefully proportioned to the rank and importance of the recipient, were the most common form that these gifts took; but on occasion silver plate, horses, furs, jewels, expensive garments and even cash might

11. G.D. Ramsay, *The City of London in International Politics at the Accession of Elizabeth Tudor* (Manchester, 1975), pp. 97–8; G. Baguenault de Puchesse, 'Un ambassadeur de France au Danemarck au seizième siècle', *Revue d'Histoire Diplomatique* (1911), 192–3.

be given. A successful or lucky ambassador might reap a significant windfall in this way. Thus the more important of two English ambassadors sent to the Emperor Charles V at Bologna in 1529 received a present worth 2,000 ducats and his less important colleague one of half that value, while a French ambassador to England at the end of the century was given by Elizabeth a 'cupboard of plate' worth 4,000 crowns.[12] But it was the special ambassador of high social rank who normally benefited most in this way. His humbler and more professional counterpart who remained in post over a longer period could expect less ostentatiously generous treatment. That such gifts should still bulk relatively large in the whole picture of remuneration (diplomats as a rule were not slow to complain when they received one of what they thought less than the appropriate value) shows that true professionalism was still some distance in the future. Diplomacy, then, was not an occupation in which any man could reasonably hope to make money. It is not surprising, therefore, that it was often far from easy to find suitably qualified men willing to undertake a foreign embassy which might well involve much difficulty and discomfort for little profit.

It was not even completely clear by the end of this period that an ambassador must be maintained exclusively by the ruler whom he represented. In the later fifteenth century it was not uncommon for diplomats to be given by the states to which they were sent not merely living accommodation but even allowances for the expenses of themselves and their retinues. In 1466 the Venetian senate explicitly forbade its representatives to accept any payment in money or kind from the monarchs at whose courts they were stationed; while at the same time it tried to end any obligation for the republic to maintain diplomats sent to it.[13] This was probably the first clear assertion of what now seems an obvious principle. But it was only slowly that it became generally accepted; and the process was by no means complete even in the early seventeenth century. In England the rule that resident representatives of foreign states must pay for their own lodging seems to have been asserted from 1556 onwards; but in the emerging Dutch republic they were housed at public expense until as late as

---

12. R.J. Knecht, ed., *The Voyage of Sir Nicholas Carewe to the Emperor Charles V in the year 1529* (Cambridge, 1959), p. 43; G.B. Harrison and R.A. Jones, eds, *A Journal of all that was accomplished by Monsieur de Maisse, ambassador in England from King Henri IV to Queen Elizabeth, Anno Domini 1597* (London, 1931), p. 89. A list of the presents given by foreign rulers to English ambassadors in 1569–86 can be found in G.M. Bell, 'Elizabethan diplomatic compensation: its nature and variety', *Journal of British Studies* XX, No. 2 (1981), 25.

13. D.E. Queller, *Early Venetian Legislation on Ambassadors* (Geneva, 1966), p. 22.

1649. Envoys from states outside or on the fringes of Europe, in particular, still looked for free maintenance after the practice had been abandoned by most western ones. The sporadic Russian embassies to western Europe continued until the end of the seventeenth century to expect to be paid for by the rulers to whom they had been sent; and as late as 1650 an important English writer on international law still had no doubt that 'the reception of ambassadors further requires that hospitality should be provided befitting their rank, and necessities supplied to them'.[14]

On another major aspect of modern diplomacy, the immunity of the accredited diplomat, the sanctity of his person and his freedom from any legal action, the position was somewhat similar. The assumptions we now take for granted were gaining ground, but only slowly and unevenly. There was a general acceptance that the person and goods of a diplomat were entitled to some degree of protection; but this did not prevent rulers and governments from sometimes behaving in a highly arbitrary way, especially in the earlier decades of this period. Thus in 1512 the papal envoy to England was arrested for allegedly revealing secret information to the French ambassador; and in 1516 his successor (at least according to the Venetian ambassador) was even threatened with the rack. In 1528 the imperial ambassador to France spent almost six weeks in prison after angering Francis I; while in 1540, in perhaps the most serious incident of this kind, the French ambassador in Venice had his house surrounded by soldiers and cannon trained on it to force him to surrender three Venetian subjects who had taken refuge there after allegedly betraying state secrets to him. The intensified religious antagonisms of the decades from about 1560 onwards, as has been seen,[15] made questions of this kind more pressing and acute.

Diplomatic immunities, none the less, were slowly becoming better established and generally recognized as the sixteenth century went on. To some extent practice outstripped theory. It was still possible for writers to argue that a diplomat who fomented treason or rebellion was a criminal and could be treated as such. But the Spanish ambassadors who plotted against Elizabeth suffered nothing worse than expulsion; and the principle that the house of an ambassador was inviolable was gaining increasingly wide acceptance. A Catholic ambassador and his household in a Protestant state, it was generally agreed, had the right to worship freely within the embassy,

14. R. Zouch, *Juris et judicii fecialis . . . explicatio* (Washington, 1911; first published 1650), ii, p. 21.

15. See above, pp. 54–5.

as had a Protestant one in a Catholic state. There were still many difficulties and uncertainties; and diplomats sometimes misused their immunities – most glaringly by allowing their houses to be used as a refuge by common criminals. In the seventeenth century this was to lead to considerable friction in both Madrid and Rome. As late as the 1760s a legal theorist could argue that an ambassador who, on his own initiative, fomented sedition in the state where he was stationed could be punished by death; whereas if he acted on the instructions of the ruler he represented he could be held as a hostage until the latter had given satisfaction for his offence.[16] But long before then diplomatic immunity, though its exact extent and application might still be debatable in various ways, had been placed on a secure footing.

Ceremonial and precedence

Nothing illustrates better what seem to twentieth-century eyes the archaisms, the unmodern aspects of sixteenth- and seventeenth-century international relations, than their intense preoccupation with every aspect of ceremonial. Titles, precedence, all the external symbols of the standing and prestige of the European monarchs, were a constant focus of both fear and ambition. Minute details of this sort, which now seem of no real significance, could and did arouse deep and strong feeling. Victory in such disputes often tasted sweeter than any purely material gain, while defeat might be more difficult to stomach than a severe military setback or a significant territorial loss. The importance of prestige and reputation seemed to every ruler almost impossible to exaggerate. These imponderables, if carried to a high enough pitch, seemed able by themselves to compensate for deep-seated material weaknesses. 'Reputation', said the Count–Duke of Olivares, the chief minister of Spain in 1622–43, 'can many times triumph without arms and resources.'[17] This was merely an extreme statement of an attitude which had for long been universal. Inevitably, then, ceremonial and prestige-laden issues bulked large in the responsibilities of diplomats. None of their duties was more important than ensuring that the standing of the monarchs they represented suffered no slight through some act or omission of protocol. 'An ambassador', wrote an anonymous author of the early

16. J.-J. Burlamaqui, *Suite des principes du droit politique* (Geneva/Copenhagen, 1764), ii, pp. 213–15.
17. J.H. Elliott, *El conde-duque de Olivares y la herencia de Felipe II* (Valladolid, 1977), p. 98.

seventeenth century, 'must not permit or allow anyone to challenge or in any other way offend the honour of his Prince on any subject at all.'[18] The ostentatious public entry made by special and high-ranking ambassadors into the capital of the ruler receiving them, the care taken to make such entries as impressive as possible in terms of the numbers taking part, the richness of their clothes, the number and quality of the horses, was one index of this sensitivity. The more lavish the show, the more emphatic the assertion of the importance of the ruler represented. The importance attached to the treatment of an ambassador at the first audience granted him by the monarch to whom he was sent was another obvious reflection of the same attitude. The way in which he was conducted into the ruler's presence; the details of the deportment of both; the ceremonial speech (often long and tediously verbose) made by the ambassador or one of his retinue: all these were the objects of anxious interest. The widespread use until well into the sixteenth century of the term 'orator' as a synonym for 'ambassador' or 'envoy' is significant; and ambassadors were sometimes chosen merely for their ability to deliver an impressive speech.

Underlying all the ceremonial duties of the ambassador was the question of precedence. He must safeguard and vindicate by every possible means any rights of this kind over other monarchs claimed by the one whose direct personal representative he was. The sensitivity of rulers in this respect, their intense desire to assert against rivals their importance and the greatness of the territories they ruled, underlay much of the international relations of this period and gave them an emotional edge which nothing else could. 'The dignity and reputation of princes', said Philip II in the 1550s, 'is of no less importance to them than their states.' Two generations later a diplomat of long experience could echo the same idea in very similar terms: 'Princes and sovereign states often hold more dear the conservation of their rank and dignity than that of their lands and possessions.'[19]

These were not empty words. In exchange for some concession of this kind a ruler might well be willing to make a substantial material one. When in 1582, at the end of a long and finally unsuccessful struggle, Tsar Ivan IV of Russia finally made peace with King Stephen Bathory of Poland, his dominant preoccupation was to make sure

18. E. Griseille, 'Un manuel du parfait diplomate au dix-septième siècle', *Revue d'Histoire Diplomatique* (1915), 775.

19. M.J. Rodriguez-Salgado, *The Changing Face of Empire: Charles V, Philip II and Habsburg Authority*, *1551–1559* (Cambridge, 1988), p. 25; J. Hotman, Sieur de Villiers, *De la charge et dignité de l'ambassadeur*, 2nd edn (Paris, 1604), pp. 58–58 v.

that in the negotiations his titles as Tsar of Kazan and Astrakhan were fully recognized. 'In his eyes', wrote the Jesuit who acted as mediator, 'none of the fortresses he was preparing to surrender to the King remotely compared in importance with this salutation.'[20] It is true that the tsars were, and long remained, even more touchy and difficult on issues of this kind than their west European counterparts. But in this they were merely extreme representatives of a universal attitude. Disputes over precedence between different rulers, and hence between the diplomats who represented them, had been frequent in the later fifteenth century. They were little appeased when in 1504 Pope Julius II tried to reduce such quarrels by arranging the more important monarchs in a formal hierarchy. What, after all, gave one a justified claim to superiority over another? A quasi-rational answer to this question in terms of extent and wealth of territories or strength of armies could be challenged on several different grounds. The fact that one state had been converted to Christianity earlier than another; pseudo-historical claims of a ruler to some feudal superiority over another; the fact of his having received the sacred unction at his coronation or claiming to have the power to cure the 'King's Evil' by his magically healing touch: all these could be used as arguments in controversies of this kind. Such disputes easily took on a deeply wounding tone and aroused particularly bitter personal feelings. In particular the refusal of some title or mark of respect which had been granted in the past could arouse more bad feeling than almost any other aspect of this intensely sensitive subject; and sometimes this refusal was brutally expressed. Ivan IV, for example, in the 1560s quarrelled violently with Erik XIV of Sweden when the latter ventured formally to address him as 'brother', asserting that 'the [Holy] Roman Emperor and other great sovereigns are our brothers, but it is impossible to call you a brother because the Swedish land is lower in honour than these states'.[21]

The diplomatic network which increasingly bound together the states of Europe was therefore in some respects recognizably the ancestor of that of today. Formal relations between these states were becoming more continuous than ever before. Governments now received a flow of information about the situation in other states and their possible intentions, supplied by diplomats who remained in the same post for significant periods of time, which was more copious than ever before. Diplomacy was slowly becoming something resem-

20. Graham, ed., *The Moscovia of Antonio Possevino*, p. 128.
21. A. Yanov, *The Origins of Autocracy: Ivan the Terrible in Russian History* (Berkeley, Ca, 1981), p. 209.

bling a profession; and the men who carried it on were beginning to feel some sense of common standards and rights. But some of the most important purposes which this diplomatic machinery served were still strikingly unmodern, to our eyes even irrational.

The balance of power

Insofar as any single unifying idea has underlain European diplomacy in the 500 years from the mid-fifteenth to the mid-twentieth century, it was that of the balance of power. The belief that the safety and independence of individual states depended most of all on their tendency to combine to resist the threatening power of any one or any group among them was very durable. Stability and security for the smaller ones, it was often argued during these centuries, depended upon an equipoise between opposing powers or combinations of powers. Since the permanent ambassador and the professional diplomat evolved first in Italy it is not surprising that the idea that was to govern much of their work also first appeared there. The situation which produced the diplomatic machinery – a group of highly developed states in close and continuous contact but with deep underlying rivalries – also generated theories as to how that machinery should be used. By the sixteenth century several Italian writers can be found talking, in a somewhat general way, in balance of power terms. Thus the Florentine historian Francesco Guicciardini claimed in the 1530s that Lorenzo de Medici, as *de facto* ruler of Florence more than two generations earlier, had done his best to create a balance between the competing states of Italy; while the Venetian republic liked to think of itself as holding a balance of power in the peninsula between the kings of France and their Habsburg rivals.[22]

Slowly, as time went on, monarchs and ministers north of the Alps also began to speak in these terms. A primitive balance of power was in operation, however, long before the use of the particular terminology to describe it. The alliance of England, the Spanish kingdoms and the Archduke Maximilian (soon to be the Emperor Maximilian I) in 1490, in a belated and unsuccessful effort to prevent the absorption by the French crown of the duchy of Brittany, was a case in point. So, more clearly, was the better-known League of Venice of March 1495, which brought together the pope, the emperor, Spain, Venice and Milan in resistance to the French irruption of the previous year

22. Anderson, *The Rise of Modern Diplomacy*, p. 151.

into Italy.[23] The efforts of several states to combine against Charles V, again, after his apparently overwhelming victory at Pavia in 1525 seemed to threaten his domination of much of Europe,[24] was seen by many later writers as an early effort to create an effective European balance. Some more or less explicit statements of the balance of power as a guiding principle of international relations can be found. Mary of Hungary, the sister of Charles V to whom he had entrusted the government of his Netherlands provinces, said in 1535 of the minor Italian princes that 'their fear of the greatness of the two rivals [i.e. Charles V and Francis I] leads them to balance their power'. Almost two decades later she spoke once more of the threat to the small Italian states and their resulting efforts 'to balance their power' when dealing with France and the Habsburgs. In 1584 a French pamphlet spoke of 'la balance' between the great rivals, France and Spain. This seems to be the first use of such terms in writing of this kind, a forerunner of the great outpouring of pamphlet literature on the balance of power, its nature and justification, which began about 1680.[25]

By the first decades of the seventeenth century the idea of such a balance as something inherent in any state system, and as one of its essential and desirable characteristics, was clearly becoming more widespread. The Venetian Giovanni Botero wrote in 1605 of the balance of power as rooted in 'the order of nature and the light of reason'. Even though each ruler might think in terms only of his own advantage, he went on, none the less this selfishness worked to the benefit of the whole state system.[26] By the 1640s there can be found the first references in treaties to the balance as something that had a stabilizing and pacifying effect on Europe as a whole, and therefore ought to be supported and fostered. The end of the period covered by this book saw Europe more unified in international relations terms, more of a coherent state system, than ever before. Almost inevitably, therefore, statesmen as time went on thought increasingly in terms of states and combinations of states which might confront each other on more or less equal terms within this system. These attitudes as they developed acquired a new vocabulary, one which is still with us today; and though this process was still incomplete in the early years of the seventeenth century, it was well under way.

23. See below, p. 77.
24. See below, p. 96.
25. Anderson, *The Rise of Modern Diplomacy*, pp. 151–2.
26. Ibid., pp. 153–4.

CHAPTER FOUR

The birth of Valois–Habsburg Rivalry, 1494–1529

The preliminaries to the invasion of 1494

The invasion of the Italian peninsula in 1494 by a powerful French army commanded in person by the king, Charles VIII, was quickly seen by contemporaries as opening a new epoch in relations between the states of western Europe. This judgement has been generally accepted by historians, and with reason. In the decades that followed, the ruling houses of France and the Spanish kingdoms (essentially Castile) emerged clearly as rivals for primacy in the west, powers with which no other could compete. Italy, from which for so long cultural leadership and example had radiated to the rest of Europe, now had her political division and military weakness, and her resulting helplessness in the face of determined foreign attack, brutally exposed. The complete inability of the increasingly divided Holy Roman Empire to act as any kind of effective unit was once more harshly underlined. The conventional view which sees the events of 1494 as marking a new era in international relations has therefore more substance than most generalizations of this kind.

That France should in 1494–95 win successes that startled many observers is not surprising. Her military achievements in these years, though destined to be very short-lived, rested on solid foundations. Racked little more than two generations earlier by a struggle with England which was also a civil war, and apparently on the brink of conquest or partition, she was now by every quantitative criterion the greatest power in Europe. Her population of perhaps fifteen million was twice that of the Spanish kingdoms (Aragon, Castile and Navarre), four times that of England and probably ten times that of the Austrian territories of the Habsburgs, soon to become almost by

accident her greatest and most tenacious opponents. This population, so great for that period, was also increasingly prosperous: in the
last two decades of the fifteenth century well over 300 new fairs and
markets were established in different French towns, a good index of
growing economic activity and wealth. The country's cultural life was
also flourishing. By 1500 at least 30 French towns had printing
presses: Lyons, a great centre of the new industry, alone had over
100.

Moreover, France was expanding not merely in an economic or
cultural sense but in a territorial one. Her kings clearly had an appetite for such acquisitions at least equal to that of any contemporary
ruler. Good luck and opportune deaths, factors always of supreme
importance in an age so completely dominated by dynasticism and at
the mercy of dynastic accidents, in the two decades before the invasion of Italy worked very markedly in favour of the French monarchy.
In 1481 Provence had fallen under the direct control of the French
crown. In 1477 the death in battle, leaving only a daughter to succeed him, of Charles the Bold, Duke of Burgundy and ruler under
different titles of a great assembly of territories stretching from the
Swiss frontier to the North Sea, had already opened the way for Louis
XI of France to make other important gains. Five years later the
Treaty of Arras gave him control of Artois, Franche-Comté and the
county of Auxerre. By 1494 Brittany, after the death of its last semi-independent duke, Francis II, three years earlier, was also under more
effective royal control than ever before.

France then was becoming more of a unity, and not merely in a
political and administrative sense. True national feeling of anything
like a modern kind was still in the future. For the ordinary man, as
over most of Europe, loyalty was still owed to the town, the locality, at
most the province, rather than to anything so nebulous and hard to
envisage as the nation. To French rulers, as to others, it still seemed
entirely natural and reasonable to surrender entire provinces if
necessary in pursuit of some purely dynastic ambition. Yet some of
the foundations of French national consciousness were being laid.
There was in particular a significant growth of linguistic unity in the
later decades of the fifteenth century, as the *langue d'oil*, the
speech of northern and central France, gained ground at the expense of the *langue d'oc* still spoken over much of the south. A kind
of national pride can be seen, at least in the surrogate form of
glorification of the status and rights of French kings. Already can
be heard the argument that they ranked above the Holy Roman
Emperor himself, since kings, it was contended, for example those

of the Old Testament, had existed long before emperors had been known.[1]

The strength of France was underlined by the relative weakness of its neighbours. The quality of the Castilian infantry, the finest in Europe, was soon to underpin an imposing structure of Spanish power. But as yet this was some years in the future; and the kingdoms of Castile and Aragon, in spite of the marriage of Ferdinand of Aragon and Isabella of Castile in 1469, had quite different histories and interests. Their linking in any effective unity was out of the question. England was at best a second-rate power, and in military terms now perhaps hardly even that; while the innate caution of Henry VII and the fact that his own domestic position was still not entirely secure set severe limits to any international ambitions he might have. The Holy Roman Emperor Maximilian I (elected in 1493 on the death of his father, Frederick III) was already showing all too clearly the often humiliating chasm between ambitions and resources which was to dog the whole of his reign. His short-lived marriage to Mary, the daughter of Charles of Burgundy, was the most important dynastic union of the period. It brought the Habsburgs the Netherlands territories which Charles had ruled; and these included some of the greatest and wealthiest cities in Europe – Ghent, Bruges, above all Antwerp. But these provinces were already showing the dislike of anything that smacked of intrusive alien control which, two generations or more later, was to make them so durable and costly a thorn in the side of the Spanish Habsburgs. Pro-French feeling in some of them, notably Flanders, and their ability to play off their new Habsburg rulers against their rivals in Paris, added to the difficulty of the situation. Moreover in 1492 Charles, Duke of Guelders, returned to his duchy, which welcomed him enthusiastically (it had been confiscated, on very dubious grounds, by Charles of Burgundy and had later passed into the hands of the Habsburgs). This began an intermittent and destructive struggle that went on for decades, during which the duke became the most inveterate of all enemies of the emperor and his successor, Charles V.

On his accession to the imperial throne Maximilian struggled to establish some effective control of these rich but turbulent provinces; but with little success. After the early death in 1482 of Mary of Burgundy Flanders, the richest and most important of them, ratified the Treaty of Arras without even the pretence of consulting its titular

---

1. M. François, 'L'idée d'empire en France à l'époque de Charles-Quint', in *Charles-Quint et son Temps* (Paris, 1958), p. 28.

ruler; while the estates of the province took control of Maximilian's young son, Philip. Maximilian could not assert himself as the guardian of his own son until 1485; and even then he was forbidden to remove the boy from the Netherlands. Three years later, on a visit to Bruges, he was surprised by a sudden rebellion there, taken prisoner and held captive for three months. He was able to free himself only by promising to withdraw all foreign troops from the Netherlands within eight days and to end an inconclusive frontier struggle he was then waging with France. When he returned to Germany at the end of 1488, after more than a decade in the Low Countries, he left behind him a record of ineffectiveness and failure.

In Germany his situation was at least equally difficult. The Holy Roman Empire was now more than ever ineffective and disunited, a prey to the rivalries and ambitions of the rulers of its individual states and of its free cities: the efforts made under Maximilian from the 1490s onwards to overhaul its organization, provide it with some central judicial organs and, most important of all, levy taxes which would give the emperor a substantial and regular income, were largely fruitless. Already there were clear signs of its territorial disintegration. After their victory over Charles the Bold in 1476–77 the Swiss cantons, hitherto at least in theory imperial territories, sent no more representatives to the Reichstag. In the 1490s efforts to summon some of their cities before imperial tribunals led to a short but important war in which, by 1499, Maximilian was forced to admit defeat. Henceforth *de facto* Swiss independence was securely established; and the loose confederation of cantons was if anything an expanding force. In 1501 it was joined by the German cities of Basel and Schaffhausen, while the Swiss mercenary infantry, its reputation already established by its victories in the 1470s, was for the next generation to remain the most feared military force in Europe. When Charles VIII led his army across the Alps, therefore, effective resistance to his ambitions was scarcely more to be feared from the Habsburgs than from England and very much less, as events were soon to show, than from the Spanish kingdoms.

To present-day eyes the French invasion of Italy seems an expensive and destructive irrationality. Even at the time there were well-informed Frenchmen who advised against it. But this was, and throughout more than six decades of struggle in Italy was to remain, very much a minority view impotent to influence events. This was an age of dynasties rather than of nations, of dynastic claims and ambitions, not of national, still less popular, rights. Rulers might on occasion use various primitive propaganda devices to mobilize popular support for their policies; and this could involve some appeal to embryonic national feeling (often in the shape of hostility to some particular foreign group rather than in any positive form). Royal proclamations and manifestos read from the pulpit on Sundays; pamphlets supporting, often with much pseudo-historical detail, some royal claim; medals and woodcuts; even printed leaflets: all could be pressed into service.[2] But the effect of such efforts is very difficult to measure and was almost certainly slight. In an age when hardly any large state was linguistically homogeneous, when the concept of a clearly defined frontier was still largely embryonic[3] and the idea that such boundaries should if possible be 'natural' was unknown, when only a small minority would ever see a map of their country, national feeling in any developed form was always likely to be weak.

The relations between the European states, then, were driven by the characters, the ambitions and the claims of their rulers; and in 1494 Charles VIII lacked neither ambitions nor claims to support them. The dynastic and legalistic complexities of these claims are not in themselves important: ambition and power, not rights, were what mattered. Charles, however, could assert a right to the kingdom of Naples inherited from the last Angevin count of Provence, who had died in 1481 and bequeathed his lands and titles to Louis XI, Charles's father.[4] When in 1493 the claim was submitted to a committee of the Parlement of Paris, the highest French court of law, it duly reported that Charles had as much right to Naples as to France itself. Besides this, there was a French claim to the duchy of Milan. In 1387 Valentina Visconti, the daughter of its reigning duke, had married into the French royal family; and the dying-out of the Visconti line of rulers in 1477, it could be asserted, had now left Louis, Duc d'Orléans, Charles's cousin, as legitimate ruler of the duchy.

There was scarcely a ruler in Europe who could not, if he chose, find some alleged right of this kind to put forward. Generations of dynasticism, of royal marriages, opportune or inopportune deaths, disputed successions and family compacts, had left much of the continent liable at any moment to have its life disrupted by conflicting ambitions and assertions of this kind. The French claims in Italy were made important, however, by two things. The first was the character of Charles VIII. A young man of at best mediocre intelligence,

2. On this see J.H. Hale, *Renaissance Europe, 1480–1520* (London, 1971), pp. 84–6.
3. See above, pp. 4–5.
4. The details of this Angevin claim to Naples are discussed in detail in J.S.C. Bridge, *A History of France from the Death of Louis XI* (Oxford, 1921–36), ii, pp. 11–17.

physically very unprepossessing, he was governed by ambitions unrealistic even by the undemanding standards of that age. Military victory and territorial conquest in Italy would bring him glory and reputation, the personal prestige which to the mind of that age seemed the most natural and laudable objective of any ruler. They might, moreover, lead on to even greater things. Once established in Italy, Charles might be able to reach the pinnacle of glory and make himself incomparably the greatest of European monarchs by defeating the Turks, recovering Constantinople and recreating in some form the Byzantine empire with himself as its ruler. By 1494, after his first apparently brilliant Italian successes, a French agent had persuaded Andrew Paleologus, the nephew and heir of the last Byzantine emperor, to renounce, in return for a pension, all his claims to rule in Constantinople in favour of Charles.

Equally important, there were significant forces in Italy which, for reasons of their own, actively encouraged French intervention. Deep divisions between the Italian states, and within some of them, did more than anything else to make possible the invasion of 1494. Well before the French army crossed the Alps it was clear that the Angevin claim to the kingdom of Naples might be a useful weapon in the perennial rivalries of these states: both Venice and the papacy had already tried to use it for their own purposes. Within the kingdom, moreover, there was a considerable Angevin faction among the nobility. In 1485 this rose in rebellion against the ruler, King Ferrante; and though the rising was crushed the situation in Naples, and indeed in much of Italy, remained very unstable. Antonello di San Severino, Prince of Salerno, one of the leaders of the rebellion, as a refugee in France pressed Charles to intervene and assert forcibly his claims. Other voices urged the same course. Cardinal della Rovere, a leading member of the papal *Curia*, who was on very bad terms with the new pope, Alexander VI (he had been an unsuccessful candidate when Alexander was elected) and afraid for his own safety, fled from Rome at the end of April 1494, also took refuge in France, and became another vocal advocate of French intervention.

Most important of all those calling on Charles to cross the Alps, however, was Ludovico Sforza (Ludovico il Moro), who ruled the duchy of Milan as regent for his young nephew, Gian Galeazzo. He was widely suspected of wishing to supplant his nephew and become duke himself; and when Gian Galeazzo died in October 1494 (probably not poisoned by his uncle, in spite of the inevitable suspicions his death aroused) he did in fact achieve this. But Ludovico had already been driven by his own fears and ambitions into actively encouraging a French invasion. Gian Galeazzo's wife, much more able and energetic than he, was a member of the ruling family in Naples and complained bitterly to her father and grandfather there of the control of Milan by Ludovico and the slights to which it exposed her. Faced by the threat of Neapolitan intervention and his resulting loss of power, Ludovico had been driven by the spring of 1493 into actively encouraging French action which he hoped would safeguard his own position. None of the Italians who helped to make possible the invasion of 1494 understood the cataclysm they were about to unleash. To them French intervention was no more than a weapon to use against their enemies; and their short-term interests bulked much larger than any thought of what action by Charles might lead to. Ludovico may well have believed that the mere threat of French intervention would by itself be enough to serve his purposes. But the deep disunity of Italy, combined with selfish personal and group ambitions, helped to make the peninsula for a generation or more the main battleground of Europe.

Charles's political preparations for the Italian adventure were far-reaching and expensive. By a series of treaties he did his best to protect France against attack by any neighbouring power while he and his main military force were south of the Alps. Henry VII promised at the end of 1493 permanent Anglo-French peace in return for a substantial money payment. More important, Ferdinand of Aragon had already in January of the same year recovered the counties of Roussillon and Cerdagne in the Pyrenees, long disputed between France and Aragon (Treaty of Barcelona), while the Emperor Maximilian was in his turn bought off by the cession of Artois and Franche-Comté (Treaty of Senlis). These agreements were one of the most glaring examples in European history of the sacrifice of the substance for the shadow. The money promised to the thrifty Henry VII mattered relatively little. But the territorial cessions, though not crippling, were important and lasting. Roussillon and Cerdagne were not to be finally reincorporated in France until 1659. It was only at the same date that Artois became once more French territory, while Franche-Comté was recovered only in 1674. The surrender of these provinces, which meant giving up most of what Louis XI had gained after the collapse of Burgundian power in 1477, therefore had results that were to endure for generations.

The invasion and its results

At the beginning of September 1494 Charles VIII crossed the Alps at the head of a fine army of perhaps 17,000 men (he was then joined by almost as many more in Italy) and with probably the most powerful artillery train hitherto seen anywhere in western Europe.[5] His virtually unopposed progress southwards through the peninsula was a military promenade rather than an active campaign. The Italian states, paralysed by their divisions, in some cases by serious internal weaknesses and in others by fear of French power, offered no significant resistance. Milan under Ludovico il Moro was the ally of France. Venice, the strongest of the Italian states, remained resolutely neutral. In Florence, under the ineffective Piero di Medici, there was widespread pro-French feeling. Even before he was overthrown early in November Piero had been forced to abandon his support for Naples and surrender to the French, agreeing to hand over to them a number of strong points, notably Leghorn and Pisa, and to lend Charles 200,000 ducats. For many years to come French influence was to dominate in Florence. Already in September the Colonna, one of the greatest and most turbulent families of the papal state, who sided with the French, had seized the port of Ostia and thus cut off Rome from seaborne supplies – yet another example of the weakness and disunity that made Italy so fatally vulnerable. Charles entered Rome in December, impressing onlookers most of all by the 36 cannon he brought with him. Alexander VI was forced not merely to give the French free passage through his territories but to agree that all the towns of the papal state should have governors appointed or approved by them and that some of the most important, such as Viterbo and Civitavecchia, should remain in French hands.

Nor did Naples put up any more effective opposition. King Ferrante, before his death in January 1495, had already offered to recognize French suzerainty and pay a tribute to Charles: his son and heir Alfonso tried to carry on these negotiations but Charles refused to listen. Both the will and the ability to resist had collapsed. Alfonso abdicated in favour of his son, Ferrantino, and on 22 February Charles entered the city of Naples, with a lavish use of imperial symbolism

---

5. F. Lot, *Recherches sur les effectifs des armées françaises des Guerres d'Italie aux Guerres de Réligion, 1494–1562* (Paris, 1962), p. 21. Contemporaries, as Lot emphasizes, regularly and often grossly exaggerated the size of fifteenth- and sixteenth-century armies; but the force under Charles's command was undoubtedly a great one by the standards of that age.

that emphasized his Byzantine ambitions. He was received, as the greatest Italian narrator of these events later recorded, 'with such general applause and rejoicing that it would be difficult to attempt to express it, since both sexes, people of every condition, every quality, every faction, flocked to greet him with incredible exaltation, as if he were the father and founder of the city'.[6]

Charles was understandably delighted with what he had achieved. 'No one in Italy', he wrote, 'talks of anything but my exploit and of my artillery, with which they have made an acquaintance somewhat differing from their expectation. Our nation has acquired the greatest honour and renown, and there is no more talk of Italy being the graveyard of the French.'[7] Yet this whole glittering structure of success collapsed almost at once like a house of cards. Victory apparently so complete inevitably aroused the fears and jealousies of other powers. The Emperor Maximilian resented French success and was particularly angered by Charles's dreams of a reconstituted Byzantine empire with himself as its ruler: in his eyes there was room in Europe for only one imperial title. (The fact that he had not been crowned by the pope and therefore was strictly speaking only emperor-elect probably sharpened his feelings.) Ferdinand of Aragon, already ruler of Sicily, was casting covetous eyes on the kingdom of Naples. There Catalan influences had for long been strong. Trade with Catalonia was important in the life of the south Italian seaports; there had been a good deal of Catalan immigration; and until about 1480 the treasury accounts of the kingdom had been kept in Catalan. Moreover, King Ferrante had married Ferdinand's sister. Nor could any Italian ruler, and certainly not Ludovico il Moro in Milan, feel comfortable in the presence of so threatening a foreign presence as that of France. The result was the League of Venice, signed on 31 March 1495, the product in the main of Ferdinand's diplomacy. Ostensibly meant to last for 25 years, it united, at least on paper, the emperor, the Spanish kingdoms, the pope, Venice and Milan for the mutual defence of their territories.

The alliance, for all its pretensions, proved predictably shaky and short-lived. Nevertheless it had real significance. The involvement of the emperor and Spain meant that the affairs of Italy were now an integral element in an emerging balance of power that embraced much of western Europe. One nineteenth-century Italian historian claimed that the League of Venice 'substituted the equilibrium of Eu-

---

6. F. Guicciardini, *The History of Italy*, trans. S. Alexander (New York/London, 1969), p. 75.

7. Bridge, *A History of France*, ii, p. 174.

rope for that of Italy, thus attesting the political end of the Middle Ages and the beginning of modern times'.[8] This is too sweeping a judgement. Wide-ranging combinations of different states had, after all, been by no means unknown much earlier.[9] Nevertheless, from the end of the fifteenth century the concept of a balance of power that was European and not merely regional, even though incompletely articulated, became increasingly rooted in the thinking of rulers and governments.[10] In this balance Italy was a victim rather than an autonomous participant, a field for the expression of the ambitions of greater powers. She had now lost, for generations to come, control of her own destiny.

Faced by growing hostility, far from France and in an exposed position, Charles VIII with most of the French army left Naples on 20 May 1495, though substantial garrisons were left in the main Neapolitan fortresses. As he marched north the opposition to him grew. When the important fortress-city of Novara, about 40 miles west of Milan, was seized by the French in June this intensified the fears and hostility of Ludovico; it also antagonized Venice, which until then had shown little desire to hinder actively Charles's retreat. When on 6 July a composite Italian army of the League, commanded by an experienced soldier, Francesco Gonzaga, met the French at Fornovo, south-east of Parma, the battle was indecisive and the whole French baggage-train was lost. Yet the League forces, though they had a considerable superiority in numbers, suffered much the heavier losses and failed to halt the French withdrawal. Many Italians claimed the battle as a victory; but others soon came to see it as evidence of a military inferiority that was to have devastating results. At Fornovo, wrote the historian Paulo Giovio in the early 1530s, 'Italy lost her ancient military renown. Foreign nations, which had been in awe of us until a short time before, began to regard us with a shameful contempt, and to the deplorable results of this unfortunate battle are to be attributed the miseries which have since come upon us in the enslavement of Italy.'[11] Charles was able to continue his march and reach France in safety, helped by the fact that Ludovico hurriedly changed sides once more and made peace with him in October.

8. Quoted in ibid., p. 222.
9. See above, p. 52.
10. See above, pp. 67–8.
11. Quoted in Bridge, *A History of France*, ii, p. 265.

The second French invasion: Spain becomes a major player

Charles's invasion of Italy had been a failure. It was clothed with a certain false glamour; but this did nothing to offset its very real costs. This fact was driven home by the collapse in 1495–97 of his position in the kingdom of Naples. The French there, in spite of their enthusiastic welcome, almost at once made themselves very unpopular by their plundering, their failure to favour the Angevin faction of the nobility as the latter had hoped, their generally oppressive behaviour and their unconcealed contempt for the local population. Moreover the Duc de Montpensier, the French commander, was now faced by the greatest soldier of the age, the Spaniard Gonsalvo de Cordoba, the 'Great Captain', who systematically reconquered the kingdom. By February 1496 the Castel del'Uovo, the last French foothold in the city of Naples, had fallen. When Taranto was lost in January 1497 the last remnant of French power in southern Italy vanished.

Yet these failures did not end the appetite for further adventures of this kind. The peace settlement with Ludovico, which returned Novara to Milan, also involved a promise by the duke to support any further French invasion. Also the anti-French league showed all the fragility that was to mark every future combination of this kind. By the beginning of 1498 it had in effect collapsed. Ferdinand was now ready to come to terms with Charles VIII. Alexander VI had quarrelled with Venice. The Venetians had not forgiven Ludovico for making a separate peace. Maximilian was angered by his failure to play any effective role in Italy. The way seemed clear for a new French initiative; and when Charles suddenly and unexpectedly died in April 1498 it was widely believed that another French invasion of Italy was imminent.

Louis XII, the cousin and successor of Charles VIII, is in some ways a more sympathetic figure. He felt some real interest in the well-being of his subjects and knew his own military limitations: he did not command in person in the field. But he had no doubt of the justice of his claim to Milan, inherited from his Visconti grandmother.[12] He had hoped to acquire the duchy during the invasion of 1494–95 and had been deeply mortified by his failure to do so; and from the moment of his accession he described himself as 'King of France and Duke of Milan'. He was determined to enforce his rights against Ludovico, who had by now made himself unpopular with his subjects

12. This claim is discussed in detail in ibid., iii, pp. 38–43.

through his heavy taxation and arbitrary rule. Louis's claim to Naples as the heir of its former Angevin rulers, though he felt less strongly about it, was also an inducement to act; and his chief adviser, Georges d'Amboise, Archbishop of Rouen, who hoped that victory in Italy might win him a cardinal's hat and perhaps the papacy itself, strongly supported his plans. Almost from the moment of his accession, therefore, preparations for a new Italian adventure began. Negotiations were opened with Venice; and when Venetian ambassadors were sent to France it was noted that two royal residences were provided as their living quarters and – a thing without precedent – their maintenance was paid for by the French government.

In April 1499, after long negotiations, an alliance was made by which France and Venice agreed to cooperate against Milan, to divide the duchy between them and unite against the Emperor Maximilian if he attacked either of them. A month earlier Louis had made an agreement with the Swiss cantons which allowed him, in return for a subsidy, to recruit soldiers there, while no Swiss was to serve against France. In May 1499 the Duke of Savoy, whose territories astride the Alps made him a factor of some strategic importance, also took the French side against Milan. Elsewhere in Italy the ambitions of states and rulers once more worked to France's advantage. The Florentine republic hoped to use a new French invasion to help her recover Pisa, lost in 1494: the desperate struggle of the Pisans to preserve their independence intensified the very bitter rivalry between the two cities. Pope Alexander VI hoped the French might help in the creation of a principality in central Italy to be ruled by his son, Cesare Borgia, who had just acquired a French wife (Charlotte d'Albret, a member of a junior branch of the royal family) and a French title. Italy therefore was no more united or better equipped to resist foreign attack than she had been five years earlier.

To a considerable extent the events of 1494–95 repeated themselves. Easy and rapid French initial successes were very soon followed by mounting difficulties. Ludovico's lack of popular support was combined with a failure to take effective defensive measures; and in September the French army entered Milan. (It was commanded by a professional soldier, Trivulzio, a member of the Milanese nobility formerly in Ludovico's service, who had quarrelled with him and gone over to the French. Italians often played a leading role in the foreign armies that were to devastate Italy over the next generation or more.) Yet almost at once the excesses of the French soldiers, arbitrary rule and still heavier taxation, made the new regime in Milan deeply disliked. Moreover, the demands of the Swiss in French service for the pay owed them now became a serious source of trouble. The result was that in February 1500 Ludovico, who had been well received by the Emperor Maximilian in the Tyrol and was now helped by men supplied by the Swiss, was able to retake Milan. He was given an enthusiastic welcome: the people of Milan in 1499–1500 showed themselves as fickle as those of Naples in 1495–96. But this was no more than a short-lived episode in a complex struggle. In April he was again defeated, captured and taken off to end his life in comfortable captivity in France.

Louis XII had therefore won a considerable success in northern Italy. It had not been without cost. In the east of his newly acquired duchy of Milan he had to cede territory, notably the city of Cremona, to Venice in virtue of his agreement of 1499 with the republic. Later, in 1503, he gave up a smaller territory, Bellinzona, to some of the Swiss cantons. But a much more important threat to French power in Italy was the shape events were now taking in the kingdom of Naples. Louis had not abandoned his ambitions there. If he had been wise he would have accepted the offer of its young ruler, King Federigo, to hold it as a French fief. Instead he agreed with Ferdinand of Aragon in November 1500, by the Treaty of Granada, to partition the kingdom. France was to take the cities of Naples and Gaeta, with the Abruzzi and the Terra di Lavoro, Ferdinand Apulia and Calabria in the extreme south of the peninsula.

Faced by two such enemies Federigo had no hope of successful resistance; though in June 1501, in desperation, he offered to allow 15,000–20,000 Turks to cross the Adriatic to his assistance – a good indication of the willingness of Christian rulers to make use of the infidel when it suited their own purposes.[13] The extremely brutal sack of Capua by the French in July 1501 showed once more how destructive foreign invasion could be for any Italian state. It was hardly conceivable, however, that French and Spaniards would agree for long in the division of the territorial spoils. Quarrels very soon broke out about the parts of the kingdom (Basilicata and Capitanata) that had not been mentioned in the agreement of 1500; and by the spring of 1502 when the French commander, the Duc de Nemours, attacked the Spaniards, war had broken out. The short struggle that followed was important both militarily and politically. It showed clearly for the first time the quality of the Spanish infantry, now becoming the most formidable in Europe since, unlike the Swiss, its only competitors for this distinction, it depended largely on firearms and not on massive

---

13. J.N. Hillgarth, *The Spanish Kingdoms, 1250–1516:* ii, *1410–1516, Castilian Hegemony* (Oxford, 1978), p. 556.

and increasingly outdated formations of pikemen. Gonsalvo de Cordoba, at the height of his powers as a commander, was forced to remain on the defensive during the winter of 1502–03; but this was followed by brilliant success. In April 1503 he defeated the French at Cerignola; and in the last days of the year he won a victory on the river Garigliano which forced the French army into a disastrous retreat in which it suffered terribly. On 1 January 1504 Gaeta, the last Neapolitan stronghold still in French hands, surrendered.

Military triumph was followed by political success. In March 1504 Louis XII had to accept a truce which gave Ferdinand of Aragon possession of the kingdom of Naples for three years. This meant, though few people in France were yet ready to recognize it, that any hope of lasting French conquest in Naples was now becoming quite unrealistic. Not for more than 50 years were French hopes of victory there to be finally abandoned; and the Angevin claim to the kingdom had by no means been surrendered. Certainly Louis himself was very far from accepting the terms of the truce as permanent. In September 1504 he tried to make sure of at least the neutrality of the Emperor Maximilian in any new Italian adventure by agreeing that his son, the Archduke Philip, should marry Louis's daughter Claude (who was not yet five years old) and that if Louis died without male heirs she should inherit Brittany, Burgundy and Milan, together with the French claim to Naples. This willingness to make such concessions for purely dynastic objectives showed clearly that the French king's hopes of conquest in southern Italy were still very much alive. Clearly also the convolutions of this exceptionally complex period in the relations of the European states could still spring many surprises. In October 1505 Ferdinand of Aragon, who was now on bad terms with Maximilian and felt himself dangerously isolated, married as his second wife Louis's niece, Germaine de Foix, and in return for a promise of a million crowns secured French recognition as ruler of Naples. But behind this bewildering kaleidoscope of shifting alliances and dynastic ambitions an important decision had been taken. For two centuries to come southern Italy was to be under Spanish control. A long step had been taken in building the structure of Spanish power which for generations was to alarm statesmen all over Europe.

The attack on Venice

The precarious equilibrium established in Italy in 1504 could not last for long. The power of France still seemed threateningly great, especially when Genoa, now virtually a French protectorate, was racked in 1506–07 by serious internal unrest, the result of widespread resentment of the dominance of a few noble families, which was suppressed by a French army. The Emperor Maximilian, moreover, was deeply suspicious of any possible attempt by Louis to obtain the imperial title for himself. He had already tried in 1501 to make the French king swear not to make any such effort; and in February 1508 he tried to strengthen his own exclusive claim to the imperial dignity by having himself formally proclaimed as Holy Roman Emperor in the cathedral in Trent (though he still recognized the right of the pope to crown him in Rome). However, it was the papacy that most obviously threatened the *status quo*. The efforts of Cesare Borgia to build up for himself a principality in the Romagna, after a promising start, had been frustrated by the death of his father, Alexander VI, in August 1503. But Julius II, who succeeded Alexander after a short interval, was one of the most ambitious and secular-minded of all popes. A Venetian ambassador reported that he wanted ' to be lord and master of the world's game'.[14] He made determined and largely successful efforts to gain effective control of the whole papal state, to sweep away the local despots who ruled in many of its cities and recover territory it had lost. He was determined to make the papacy at least the equal in secular terms of any other Italian state, and also to drive foreign 'barbarians' from the peninsula. The first of these ambitions involved him in serious friction with Venice; and it was against the republic, which had occupied a number of cities in the Romagna after the collapse of Cesare Borgia's ambitions there, that the next outburst of fighting in Italy was directed.

Venice, now at the peak of her power and wealth, was correspondingly feared and envied by the other Italian states: in 1497 the Florentine government had even tried to persuade the Turks to attack her. Julius, always a good hater, made no secret of his desire to humiliate her. He told a Venetian diplomat that he meant 'to reduce your Venice to the original condition of a fishing village'.[15] Nevertheless he was not one of the original members of the alliance which was now forming to defeat the republic and partition her territories. Maximilian in 1508 had tried to force a passage for his army through Venetian territory in a futile effort to assert the waning power of the Holy Roman Empire in Italy, make good his claims to suzerainty over Genoa and Milan, which were now a complete dead letter, and

---

14. Guicciardini, *The History of Italy*, p. 210fn.
15. Ibid., p. 201.

achieve his great ambition of having himself crowned in Rome by the pope. His perennial lack of money made the attempt a humiliating failure. The Venetians barred his path effectively; and he was forced in June 1508 to accept a three-year truce by which Venice kept almost all the territory it had occupied in its struggle with him – Istria, Trieste and Fiume, which had been Habsburg lands in the past and which Maximilian much wanted to recover. He had therefore genuine grievances against Venice. Indeed his feud with her had always to him been more important than the fate of Milan, much less that of Naples.

In December 1508 at Cambrai he reached an important agreement with Louis XII. There was to be peace between them for their joint lives and one year thereafter, while Louis was to be invested by the always impecunious emperor as Duke of Milan in return for a payment of 100,000 crowns. More important, by a secret treaty signed on the same day the two rulers agreed to attack Venice and deprive her of much of her territory. She was now to pay the price of her remarkable past success and to lose the gains she had made in Italy during the last century or more. It seems likely that the way had already been cleared for this alliance when Louis and Ferdinand of Aragon met face to face at Savona at the end of June 1507. In the east, it was now agreed, Maximilian was to annex Venetian territory up to the River Mincio, including the important city of Verona; while in the west a strip of territory between the Mincio and the Adda was to go to the duchy of Milan. The ports in Apulia, notably Brindisi, which had been in Venetian hands for over a decade, were to be recovered by Naples; and Mantua and Ferrara, small states which had lost territory to Venice in the past, joined the league and were promised the recovery of what they had lost. Julius II did not become formally a member of the alliance until the outbreak of fighting was imminent; but as soon as the war began he excommunicated Venice and increased still further the very heavy odds against her.

In May 1509 a French army crossed the River Adda and invaded Venetian territory. A few days later, at Agnadello, the republic suffered a crushing defeat. Never again until its final collapse in 1797 was its situation to be so desperate. The cities under Venetian rule offered no resistance to the invaders: Venice itself seemed in grave danger. But from this apparently hopeless situation the republic was able to emerge surprisingly unscathed. The French army was a formidable opponent; but Maximilian, as always, was hamstrung by lack of money, and though he tried to forbid all trade between the Holy Roman Empire and the republic it was impossible to enforce the prohibition. The Venetian- ruled cities soon saw that their new masters were likely to be more oppressive than the old ones and showed no enthusiasm for rule by France or the emperor: the rapid recovery of Padua by Venice was an important sign of her resurgence, even though from March 1510 onwards her government was forced to sell offices on a growing scale to finance the war. Most important of all, the alliance against her was from the beginning undermined by the conflicting ambitions and outlooks of its members and the complete and only too well justified lack of trust between them.[16] It proved quite as fragile and short-lived as all the others formed during these years of continual change and instability.

Julius II soon began to direct his hostility against a new and greater target – the French and their influence. He had now recovered the cities in the Romagna whose occupation by Venice had so much angered him. This allowed him to think of the republic as a possible ally against France: in July 1509 he opened negotiations with her and in February 1510 made peace with her. The duchy of Ferrara, over which Julius was determined to assert his suzerainty (the duke was technically a papal vassal), was now the main focus of his ambitions. But Ferrara was a French protégé: allies were therefore essential. In March the pope was able to make an agreement with the Swiss cantons by which, in return for a subsidy and diplomatic support, they agreed to provide him with 6,000 men if they were not themselves at war with some other power, and not to make any other alliance of which Julius disapproved. In July he made sure of at least the benevolent neutrality of Ferdinand of Aragon by investing him formally as king of Naples. But the effort to conquer Ferrara and make it part of the papal state was a failure, though during it, at the siege of Mirandola in January 1511, the fire-eating old man scandalized much contemporary opinion by directing operations in person, wearing armour, reviewing his troops in the snow and 'retaining of his pontificate nothing but the garb and the name'.[17] Later in the year Bologna, of which Julius was also very anxious to gain control, was lost. By October 1511, however, he had created the Holy League, an alliance of Ferdinand of Aragon, the Venetians and himself. It was meant to drive France from Italy; but it was joined in the following month by England, which had no Italian interests. She made a separate agreement with Ferdinand for an invasion of Guyenne: the chimera of territorial conquest in France was to haunt Henry VIII

16. Ibid., pp. 197–9, 203.
17. Ibid., p. 213.

throughout his reign. Louis XII for his part tried to strike at Julius by backing the meeting in Pisa of a church council which, it was envisaged, might even lead to the election of a new pope. This also was a complete failure. No other ruler supported it; and after three ineffective meetings the council moved to French-held Milan and finally took refuge in France.

The result of these manoeuvres was another spasm of fighting, relatively brief but at least as brutal as any that had gone before: the sack by French soldiers in February 1512 of Brescia, which the Venetians had just retaken, was particularly notable for its savagery. Two months later, at Ravenna, the French defeated a Spanish and papal army in the most evenly contested battle of the Italian wars hitherto. Both sides lost heavily, and the battle was followed by a bloody and destructive sack of Ravenna itself. But in spite of this success the position of the French in northern Italy collapsed in the summer of 1512. Their able young comander, Gaston de Foix, had been killed in the battle and was succeeded by a much less effective one. More important, the Swiss now entered the picture as an independent force in their own right and in a decisively anti-French sense. They were a truly formidable enemy; and their military prestige was now at its height. 'The unity and glory of their armies', wrote Guicciardini two decades later, 'have made this savage uncultured people famous, for as a result of their innate ferocity and their disciplined organization, not only have they always valiantly defended their own country but they have been consummately praised for their military services in foreign wars.'[18] For some years their relations with France had been under growing strain. Disputes over trade, since the impoverished 'forest cantons' depended heavily on the duchy of Milan for food, and inevitably over the payment of Swiss mercenaries in French service, were well-established sources of friction. Matthias Schinner, Archbishop of Sion, a cleric almost as belligerent and politically minded as Julius II, was now able to make the Swiss, as members of the Holy League, the most effective of all the anti-French forces. Invading Italy through the Brenner Pass, they brought with them Massimiliano, the elder son of the deposed Ludovico il Moro, whom they set up as a puppet Duke of Milan.

Julius and Maximilian now for a moment dreamed of a victory that extended far beyond Italy. In November 1512, when the emperor joined the Holy League, they made an agreement which envisaged nothing less than a partition of France. She was to lose Dauphiné and

18. Ibid., p. 240.

Provence, to be conquered by the forces of Massimiliano and the pope, while Maximilian overran Burgundy and Picardy. Simultaneously Henry VIII and Ferdinand of Aragon would seize Normandy, Guyenne and Languedoc. This scheme, another illustration of the unreality of so many of the hopes and ambitions involved in these struggles, had never the slightest chance of being carried out. Maximilian was far too weak to play the role assigned to him; and though an English force meant to reconquer Guyenne had already landed in northern Spain in the summer of 1512 it achieved nothing. (Ferdinand wanted to use it to conquer Navarre, where Pamplona was taken by his own forces in July.) The Swiss, if they could be held together for any length of time, were clearly the most dangerous of France's enemies: the Italian states were no more united than in the past. In March 1513 the Venetians, who deeply distrusted Maximilian and resented the dictatorial attitudes of Julius II, made an alliance with Louis XII directed against the always fragile Holy League; while already Ferdinand had secretly agreed to a year's truce with him.

Nevertheless, 1513 was a bad year for France. A renewed alliance with Scotland, which it was hoped would hold England in check, led only to the catastrophic defeat at Flodden in September of a Scottish army and the death of the Scottish king, James IV. In northern France an English army under the young Henry VIII captured Tournai and Thérouanne, costly victories but none the less gratifying to him and wounding to French pride. In August 1514 an Anglo-French peace treaty allowed Henry to keep his conquests with all the expense they involved; while in October Louis married Mary, the English king's sister. Much more important militarily, yet another French invasion of the duchy of Milan was decisively defeated, mainly by the Swiss pikemen, at Novara in June. Three months later this was followed by a Swiss invasion of Burgundy and the appearance of their forces before its capital, Dijon. The commander of the French garrison, La Trémouille, who knew that the city could not be defended against serious attack, made an agreement with the Swiss by which Louis XII abandoned his claim to Milan; and the siege was then raised. Louis at once refused to be bound by the agreement, which had been made without his consent; but for the time being at least Milan, the focus of so much effort and expense, had once more escaped from French control. Death deprived the king of any further opportunity to conquer it (he died on the first day of 1515); but territorial ambition and war in Italy had now become a deeply rooted tradition of French foreign policy.

Francis I and Charles V: the first trials of strength

The Duc d'Orléans, who as Francis I succeeded his cousin Louis XII, was not the man to abandon the dream of victory and lasting conquest beyond the Alps. Louis had been driven by a determination, very understandable in the light of the assumptions of that age, to enforce dynastic claims in which he sincerely believed. Francis was not indifferent to such considerations. But more than either of his predecessors, he was impelled by the desire for personal glory, the wish to stand forth as the greatest of European monarchs. Like Charles VIII, he dreamed vaguely of an eventual conquest of Constantinople, though now, with the Ottoman Empire approaching the zenith of its power, such an idea was even more visionary than it had been in the 1490s. In August 1515, after buying the neutrality of Henry VIII with the promise of a French pension of 100,000 crowns a year for the next ten years, he crossed the Alps at the head of a fine army in a new effort to secure Milan. This breathed some new life into the largely moribund Holy Alliance of 1511; but the situation was now in many ways favourable to France. In Milan the rule of Massimiliano Sforza was unpopular. Pope Leo X, who had succeeded Julius II in 1513, after some hesitation took the anti-French side; but he was a much weaker man than his formidable predecessor. Maximilian was as unable as ever to act effectively. Spanish troops sent north from Naples were not enough to turn the military balance; and a small force of papal cavalry had even less effect. The defence of Milan therefore fell largely upon the Swiss; and they were divided. For some years they had acted as an independent force in international affairs. But neither their organization, or lack of it, nor their history equipped them well for this role. Until 1509 France had been the main employer of Swiss mercenaries and a welcome source of pensions and bribes. There was still, therefore, a strong pro-French party in some of the cantons, which wished to revert to the old situation. The short-lived episode of independent Swiss action was coming to an end.

This important change was driven home and made permanent by the French victory in September at Marignano, a few miles from Milan (with important indirect help from their Venetian allies, who tied down the Spanish troops around Verona). Milan immediately surrendered to Francis, while Massimiliano in his turn retired to France as a pensioner of the king. After the battle the Swiss remained an important military factor in the struggles in Italy; but their defeat in this hard-fought battle meant that they had lost the aura of quasi-invincibility that had hitherto surrounded them. They now reverted to being merely a weapon which greater powers manipulated for their own purposes, a source of mercenaries for the use of others. In November ten of the cantons made peace with Francis; and a year later Schinner negotiated with the French the 'perpetual peace' of Fribourg. In this Francis agreed to pay the cantons a substantial lump sum as well as an annual subsidy to each of them. In return it was agreed that the Swiss henceforth should not serve any employer against him, either in Milan or in France itself.

Three months earlier Francis had consolidated his position in Italy by signing the Treaty of Noyon with the young Charles, the grandson of the Emperor Maximilian and ruler of the Netherlands. For three decades the rivalry of these two men was to be the pivot around which the relations of the west European states turned. It was already clear that Charles was destined to be one of the greatest monarchs of Europe. He was the product (born in 1500) of the marriage in 1495 of Maximilian's son, the Archduke Philip, and the Infanta Juana, daughter of Ferdinand and Isabella and heiress to both Castile and Aragon. This dynastic linking of the Austrian Habsburgs with Spain, largely a reaction to the French invasion of Italy in 1494, was to influence the history of the continent for generations. The early death of his father in 1506 made Charles the ruler of Franche-Comté and the rich Habsburg Netherlands territories. The death in January 1516 of his maternal grandfather, Ferdinand of Aragon (who never met him), made him ruler of Aragon and Castile. (His mother, Juana of Castile, though she lived until 1555, was permanently insane and quite incapable of ruling.)

But his position was by no means easy. He had been brought up entirely in the Netherlands and as yet spoke no Spanish. His central interest was the preservation of what remained to the Habsburgs of the Burgundian inheritance and the recovery if possible of the parts of it lost after the death of Charles the Bold in 1477. More than three decades later, in his political testament of 1548, he was still urging his son never to abandon his claim to the lost duchy of Burgundy, 'which belongs to me and will belong to you by the same right'. Such issues were far closer to the heart of the adolescent Charles than anything that happened in Spain or Italy. His chief minister, Guillaume de Croy, Lord of Chièvres, had great influence over him. In Charles's early years he even had his bed placed in the young prince's room 'so that, should he wake up, he will have someone to talk to'.[19] But

19. M. Fernandez Alvarez, *Charles V* (London, 1975), p. 17.

Chièvres was a leading member of the Walloon nobility, French-speaking and traditionally in favour of good relations with France.

In 1516 such relations were essential. A breathing-space was urgently needed in which the rule of Charles in the Spanish kingdoms could be established. His position there was potentially very difficult. There were great differences of history, outlook, interests and even language between Castile and Aragon; and it was far from certain that the very tenuous union between them would continue. Ferdinand himself in his last years had hoped that Charles might become ruler merely of Castile, where Ferdinand had acted as regent for the mad Juana since the death of Isabella in 1504, while Aragon could be inherited by his younger brother, the Archduke Ferdinand. In Castile in particular a turbulent nobility, profiting from the long interregnum, threatened serious disorder. The xenophobia latent in every European people ran strongly in Spain and meant that Charles was seen as an unknown and unwelcome foreigner. Not until September 1517, after elaborate and time-consuming preparations, did he set foot in the country that was soon to become of central importance to him.

All this meant that the Noyon agreement was at least as welcome to Charles as to Francis. It envisaged the establishment of lasting good relations between the two rulers by the expedient, the inevitable and almost the only conceivable one in that age, of a dynastic alliance. Charles was to marry Francis's daughter Louise (who was not yet a year old). If she died before the marriage could take place he was to marry her younger sister (who was not yet born); and Charles even wrote to Francis (who was only six years older than himself) as 'Monsieur mon bon père'. Nothing came of these provisions. They were merely one of the dozens of abortive schemes for dynastic marriages with which the history of the sixteenth century is littered. In addition Charles promised, as ruler of Aragon, to pay a tribute of 100,000 crowns a year for the kingdom of Naples, an implicit recognition of Francis's alleged right to the kingdom, and to make concessions in Navarre. If the agreement opened the way for the consolidation, at least for the time being, of French power in northern Italy, it also gave Charles a valuable breathing-space in which to begin to establish his authority in Spain.

It can be argued, indeed, that there was now some chance that conflict in Italy might become less acute and even be brought to an end. The personalities who had for long bulked large in it were disappearing. Within less than three years Julius II, Louis XII and Ferdinand of Aragon had left the stage. The Emperor Maximilian was to follow them in 1519. There were still powerful forces making for war: intensely prestige-conscious monarchs, nobilities whose main or only function was to fight, saw to that. But there was perhaps some possibility in these few years, even if only a remote one, of a new start in international affairs and the beginning of a more peaceful age. Any prospect of this kind, however, was ended by the imperial election of 1519 and the victory in it of Charles, who now became the Emperor Charles V.

It was inevitable that he should be a candidate for the imperial title. A traditionalist little touched by Renaissance humanism (he had no knowledge of Greek and only a mediocre one of Latin), he would inevitably strive for the highest secular authority and the most prestigious title in Europe, especially as there was by now an unbroken line of Habsburg emperors stretching back over eight decades. Maximilian had wished Charles to succeed him: shortly before his death he made efforts to have him accepted by the imperial electors, the seven German princes, clerical and secular, who chose each emperor, as King of the Romans, in other words as recognized heir to the imperial dignity.

But it was clear well before the election took place that Francis I would do his utmost to prevent Charles becoming emperor and to obtain the title for himself. Personal prestige played an important role in this. The glory of becoming, at least in formal terms, the greatest secular ruler in Europe, and of leading it in resistance to the growing Ottoman threat, was a potent lure. There were also obvious French strategic interests, even considerations of French security, involved. How much his election as emperor would add to the real power of Charles was open to question, given the whittling away of effective imperial authority that had been in progress for generations. But it seemed to tighten around France a formidable Habsburg ring, in which possession of Spain, the Netherlands, Franche-Comté and the Austrian lands would now be supplemented by leadership of the German world. 'You understand the reason which moves me to gain the empire', wrote Francis to one of his agents, 'which is to prevent the said Catholic king [i.e. Charles] from doing so. If he were to succeed, seeing the extent of his kingdoms and lordships, this could do me immeasurable harm; he would always be mistrustful and suspicious and would doubtless throw me out of Italy.'[20]

It was also clear that the election would be decided very largely by

20. L. Schick, *Un grand homme d'affaires au début du XVIe siècle, Jacob Fugger* (Paris, 1957), p. 163.

money, for which the imperial electors were unashamedly greedy. None of those concerned had any illusions on this point. As early as 1517 Maximilian had urged Charles to send large sums to Germany to be used in buying support; and in May 1518 he confessed frankly that 'People will believe more in the ready money of the French than in our words and promises'. In February 1519, as the decisive moment drew nearer, the electoral agent of Francis I told the French chancellor that 'The business comes down to this, which of the two, that is our king and the Catholic one, will give and will be able to promise most'. Almost simultaneously one of Charles's representatives thought that he had 'never yet seen men so greedy for money', while another was afraid that 'all our undertaking is likely to disappear in smoke, for where we offer a thousand the French give ten thousand'.[21] These fears were exaggerated, for Charles was always more likely than his rival to win. None the less he had to spend a great deal of money. In this struggle the backing given him by the great German banking house of Fugger was crucial. Of the more than 850,000 florins he had to spend over 543,000 came from it, as loans secured on the silver and copper deposits of the Tyrol. (The rest was provided by a second German banking firm, that of Welser, and by Italian bankers in Florence and Genoa.) These resources turned the scale. Lavish payments to most of the seven electors (the Elector Palatine, a west German prince with territories in the Rhineland, did best of all with 139,000 florins) and also to their advisers and courtiers carried the day. On 28 June 1519 Charles was elected. Four years later Jacob Fugger was able to claim with full justification, in a letter to the young emperor, that 'It is well known and clear as day that Your Imperial Majesty, without me, could not have obtained the Roman Crown'.[22]

But the election was not entirely a matter of money. Francis I also spent freely and had no illusions about the need to do so. 'In times like the present', he said, 'whatever a man sets his heart upon, be it the papacy, be it the empire or anything else, he has no means of obtaining his object except by force or corruption'. He seems (there is some uncertainty here) to have raised a large loan of 360,000 crowns from Italian bankers in London. He sold royal lands and government offices. He scraped together money by every possible means, even confiscating the personal property left by the Seigneur de Boisy, Grand Master of France, the holder of one of the greatest court of-

21. Ibid., pp. 160–1, 168, 172.
22. Ibid., pp. 161, 175–9.

fices, who had just died. Such expenditure drew hints or promises of support from several of the electors.[23] He also negotiated with King Sigismund of Poland, the guardian of the young Louis II of Hungary and Bohemia, since it seemed likely that Sigismund might cast the Bohemian vote in the election, though this did not in fact happen. He claimed, moreover, that he would be better able than Charles to protect Christian Europe against the Turkish threat, pointed to his rival's youth and limited experience and argued, with some justification, that Charles if he were elected would be unable to give adequate attention to any of the multitude of territories and responsibilities that would then weigh upon him.

But Francis was faced by a groundswell of anti-French feeling in Germany which became a significant factor in the situation. German humanists had already done a good deal to stimulate such attitudes among the educated minority there; and Charles's agents were able to exploit them to considerable effect. The papal legate in Germany, who had eventually come round to supporting Francis, even feared for his life, so marked was the hostility to France; while in April 1519 the Swiss cantons, won over in part by Charles's money, wrote to the French king to demand that he withdraw his candidature. An English diplomat reported that in Germany it was dangerous even to speak a good word of a Frenchman, while a number of German and Netherlands cities forbade their merchants to help in the transfer of money from France for use in electoral bribery. All this made 1519 something of a turning-point in European history. Public opinion, in however embryonic a form, was now for the first time influencing a great international event.

New struggles: Pavia and its results

Charles's electoral victory in Germany made a new trial of strength between France and the growing Habsburg power inevitable. In June 1520 Francis and Henry VIII had near Calais the series of interviews, accompanied by conspicuous display lavish even by the standards of that age, that has gone down in history as the Field of Cloth of Gold. This did not lead to the English support against Charles for which Francis may have hoped. But on both sides preparations for a new struggle were well under way. In Castile a serious revolt, set off by resentment of increased taxation, began in May 1520 and for a time

23. R.J. Knecht, *Francis I* (Cambridge, 1982), p. 75.

threatened the complete collapse of Charles's authority. By the spring of 1521 it had been defeated; but Francis gave some encouragement to the rebels and used his rival's difficulties in an unsuccessful attempt to recover the territory lost in Navarre eight years earlier. In February 1521 he took into his service a useful auxiliary, Robert de la Marck, Duke of Bouillon and Lord of Sedan, giving him a lump sum and an annuity and encouraging him to invade Luxemburg, one of Charles's territories. On his side Charles launched an attack on north-eastern France in August 1521. This was made ineffective by the resistance of a single small fortress, Mézières, and was followed by the French devastation of Hainault in the early winter; but the emperor had already reached a secret agreement with the pope in May and in November their combined forces captured Milan. Charles also seemed to have gained English support. In August 1521 a treaty signed at Bruges provided for his marriage to Mary, the daughter of Henry VIII, and for a combined English–imperial attack on France in March 1523. All this was accompanied by protracted and futile talks at Calais between French and imperial representatives with England acting as an ostensible arbitrator. These collapsed in November 1521.

In 1522–23 the tide of success continued to run strongly for Charles. In April 1522 a new French offensive in northern Italy was badly defeated at Bicocca; and this was followed by imperial forces capturing Genoa, a French satellite whose navy made it an important prize. In May England entered the war as the ally of Charles. The death of Leo X in December 1521 had already been followed by the election to the papacy of the Dutchman Adrian of Utrecht, Charles's former tutor and regent in Spain. (Francis I described him as 'the emperor's schoolmaster'.) Charles seemed clearly to have the upper hand in Italy; and his interest in the peninsula and its affairs was growing. The fact that Chièvres had just died helped forward this important change of attitude: the emperor's rivalry with Francis was now becoming focused on Italy as well as on the eastern and north-eastern frontiers of France.

Finally in September 1523 the constable of France, Charles, Duke of Bourbon, the greatest of French nobles, of the blood royal and a semi-independent ruler in his own right, rebelled and went over to the emperor. Bourbon had had a distinguished military career. He had commanded the van of the French army at Marignano and then been appointed as Francis's lieutenant-general in Milan. But he had legitimate grievances against the king: both Francis and the Duchess of Angoulême, another member of the royal family, had laid claim to the lands of Bourbon's wife, who had died two years earlier. Whatever its motives, his action was a serious threat. Already in the spring and summer of 1523 he had been negotiating secretly with Charles V and Henry VIII. In July it was agreed that he should marry one of Charles's sisters and have a force of 10,000 German mercenaries put at his disposal, while southern France would be invaded from Spain. These schemes proved as ineffective as so many similar ones of that age; but in the summer of 1524 Bourbon led an invasion of Provence, took Aix and laid siege to Marseilles. Nevertheless there was no active support of this potentially dangerous move from either Spain or England, while Bourbon, like so many commanders of that age, was crippled by lack of money (he was forced to borrow from his captains in order to pay his men) and had to retreat.

Almost inevitably, moreover, as the pendulum swung in favour of Charles counterbalancing forces tried to assert themselves. In December 1524, as his power in Italy seemed to become menacingly great, Venice, Florence and the papacy formed an alliance with France. Yet another French invasion of Italy captured Milan and besieged Pavia while a smaller force was detached to march south towards Naples. The scene was now set for the most spectacular conflict of the Italian wars.

From Pavia to Cambrai

On 24 February 1525 the French army was decisively defeated by the imperial forces outside Pavia. The slaughter of French nobles was the greatest since Agincourt; and Francis I himself was taken prisoner. The defeat was the most striking example during these wars of the way in which military common sense could be overridden by considerations of prestige and what seemed appropriately chivalric behaviour. Francis had been urged by some of his commanders to abandon the siege of Pavia (a prolonged siege, it will be remembered, was likely to be the most costly of all military operations in terms of manpower)[24] and withdraw to the relative comfort of Milan for the winter. He refused because of the loss of prestige he felt such a move would involve, saying that no king of France had ever laid siege to a town without taking it. Now fate seemed to have placed Charles V in a position of unprecedented strength. His greatest rival was his prisoner. The fighting qualities of the Spanish infantry and

24. See above, pp. 9–10.

German *Landsknechte* who made up his army had been displayed once more, while the Swiss who fought on the French side had made a very poor showing. He seemed master of Italy and able to deal appropriately with the smaller states there, notably the papacy, which had supported his enemy.

In fact the victory was less overwhelming than appeared at first sight. Lack of money, that perennial bugbear, meant that it could not be pressed home in a military sense; while fear of Charles's threatening power increased the readiness of some of the Italian states to combine against him. His demand that he be given possession of the citadel of Milan, while at the same time refusing formally to invest as duke Francesco Sforza, the ruler of the duchy, seemed to many observers a particularly ominous portent. Henry VIII at first hoped to exploit the new situation to his own advantage. After the battle he proposed to the emperor a partition of France which would have destroyed her as a power, giving England Normandy or Picardy and involving the permanent exclusion from the throne of the Valois dynasty. By August of the same year, however, he had swung clearly in the French direction. In a peace agreement signed in that month he promised to do his best to obtain the release of Francis on reasonable terms: in return he was promised a huge subsidy of two million *écus* to be paid in annual instalments of 100,000. In France Louise of Savoy, the captive king's mother, who was acting as regent, showed ability and resolve in coping with the new situation. She did her best to stimulate opposition to Charles V in Italy; and in December an envoy sent by her appeared in Constantinople to urge the sultan to support Francis and prevent Charles becoming 'master of the world'. Though this had no result it foreshadowed significant later developments.

Most important of all, the emperor failed to obtain from his victory what he wanted above everything else – the recovery of the Burgundian territories lost to France after 1477. Francis was taken, after some delay, to Spain; and this was followed by nine months of negotiations over the terms for his release. Mercurino di Gattinara, Charles's grand chancellor, who until his death in 1530 was to be the emperor's most influential adviser, pressed for severe terms – the abandonment of all French claims in Italy, the handing over to the Constable of Bourbon of Provence, to be held as a fief of the Holy Roman Empire, the surrender of the whole Burgundian inheritance. The first of these did not present too much difficulty; but on the others agreement was much harder. Burgundy was the essential sticking-point. In August Francis formally declared, before the French ambassadors sent to Madrid to negotiate his release, that any surrender of the duchy he was obliged to make contrary to his duty as king would have been extracted by force and therefore could not bind him. In January 1526, at the moment of his release, he repeated the declaration before a number of French dignitaries, including the new constable, Anne de Montmorency, and the president of the highest French law-court, the Parlement of Paris. By the Treaty of Madrid signed in that month he made huge concessions. All the French claims in Italy and Navarre were surrendered. The parts of the Burgundian inheritance seized by Louis XI after 1477 were to be given up. The Constable of Bourbon was to be pardoned and have his huge fiefdom restored. But Francis never had any intention of fulfilling these terms. Charles had made a great mistake in releasing his prisoner in return for mere promises; and events were soon to strengthen the French king's hand.

With Francis at liberty it soon became clear that the Burgundian inheritance was not to be reunited under Charles as he so much wished. The French people, an envoy of the emperor was told, would never tolerate such a surrender of the royal patrimony; and early in June 1526 the estates of Burgundy, probably under government influence, declared their wish to remain under French rule and denounced the Treaty of Madrid as 'contrary to all reason and equity'. In the following month Francis attempted to assert the principle that territories could not be transferred from one ruler to another without the consent of their inhabitants, a claim completely contrary to the whole tenor of international relations in that age of dynasticism and monarchical absolutism.[25] Moreover, the fears aroused by Charles's apparently overweening power were as much alive as ever. In May 1526 the Holy League of Cognac united Venice and the papacy with France against the emperor. In the following weeks Florence and Francesco Sforza, who had now been driven from Milan by the Spaniards, also joined it. The league was as ineffective as might be expected in an age so lacking in international good faith. Francis did nothing to help his Italian allies; and the vacillating Pope Clement VII, 'a sheep rather than a shepherd' as a contemporary dismissively described him, made and broke a series of truces with the emperor. Almost a year later, however, at the end of April 1527, Henry VIII, who had already urged Francis not to keep the promises he had made by the Treaty of Madrid and who had been sympathetic to the Holy League though not a member, went over to the anti-imperial side when he made the Treaty of Westminster with Francis. A few

25. Knecht, *Francis I*, pp. 207–8.

weeks later he agreed to subsidize a new French campaign in Italy.

Simultaneously Charles had to cope with a powerful distraction in central Europe. The Turkish conquest of much of Hungary in 1526, after the great victory at Mohacs, suddenly intensified the threat from the east to the Habsburg lands there. It also opened the way to a bitter struggle between the rival claimants to what remained of Christian-controlled Hungary, Charles's younger brother, the Archduke Ferdinand, who since February 1522 had administered the Habsburg territories in central Europe, and John Zapolya, Prince of Transylvania.[26] This meant that Francis had now a potential ally who, though distant, might have considerable nuisance value. He had already opened contacts with Zapolya in 1523; and early in 1527 a new French envoy reached the Transylvanian prince, to whom the possibility of marrying into the French royal family was now held out as a bait. In the autumn of the following year a Hungarian bishop arrived in Paris and signed an alliance with Francis I. This was the first appearance of a line of French policy which was to be intermittently significant for more than two centuries to come, that of supporting and manipulating for France's purposes opposition to the Habsburgs in east–central Europe. The battle of Mohacs thus had more important and lasting consequences than that at Pavia, in spite of the much greater attention paid to the latter in western Europe.

Charles's position, then, was by no means free from difficulty. None the less he won some important successes. In the Netherlands the depredations in 1527–28 of the Duke of Guelders, his most determined opponent, forced the estates of Holland and Brabant, in need of the emperor's protection, to support an extension of his powers. He was therefore able to obtain recognition of the rights he claimed as Count of Holland over Utrecht, and as Duke of Brabant over Gelderland and Overijssel. Much more spectacular was the capture of Rome by an imperial army under the Constable of Bourbon in May 1527. The emperor's feeling that he had been betrayed by the deeply untrustworthy Clement VII was strong. He had already encouraged in the previous year a raid on Rome and an effort to kidnap the pope by the Colonna, whose soldiers sacked the Vatican palace; and the uncontrolled killing and looting that marked the taking of the Holy City, together with the fact that Clement was for some months in effect a prisoner in the castle of San Angelo, deeply impressed contemporaries. In the event the capture of Rome was something of a two-edged victory, for Charles attracted widespread criticism for what

26. See below, pp. 236–7.

had happened and showed his regret by going into mourning and cancelling the festivities arranged to mark the birth of his son Philip. It seemed, none the less, a striking illustration of his power and the mastery he might now hope to exert in Italy. But a much more important practical success of the imperialists came in 1528, when Genoa went over to their side.

The city, in spite of many vicissitudes, had been a French satellite most of the time since 1499; and a new and apparently successful French invasion of Italy in August 1527, when an army under the Vicomte de Lautrec once more marched through the peninsula and at the end of April 1528 besieged Naples, owed much to Genoese support. Yet in July the Genoese fleet then blockading Naples, which was on the point of surrender, was withdrawn. This was followed a few weeks later by the retreat of the French army, now in any case greatly weakened by disease. In September Andrea Doria, the Genoese admiral and a member of one of the city's greatest noble families, seized Genoa and established a new and highly oligarchic constitution. Doria had mixed motives. He strongly supported the Genoese claim to the small port of Savona, which the French insisted on keeping. He also had personal grievances, particularly the appointment of a Frenchman to command the fleet blockading Naples; and Charles V had for some time been trying to win him over. But whatever his reasons, the movement of Genoa into the imperial camp (or rather the Spanish one, for the commercial and financial links between Spain and Genoa were already close and were soon to become closer) was a critical event in the international power struggle and had more lasting significance than any battle. It opened a very important door into Italy through which henceforth Spanish men and money were to flow. It was the greatest single step in consolidating in the peninsula a dominant Spanish position which was to last for two centuries; and it is not surprising that Charles rewarded Doria by admitting him in 1531 to the great chivalric order of the Golden Fleece and that his family acquired a Spanish title. The French were not blind to the setback they had suffered; but an effort by them to recover the city was defeated in June 1529 at Landriano. Simultaneously Clement VII, by the Treaty of Barcelona, moved decisively into the imperial camp.

When two months later peace was made neither side could claim complete victory: in sixteenth-century conditions such a victory was hardly possible when large and powerful states fought each other.[27]

27. See above, p. 6.

The Treaty of Cambrai, the 'Ladies Peace' negotiated by Louise of Savoy and the Archduchess Margaret, the aunt of Charles V and his regent in the Netherlands, involved sacrifices on both sides. Francis I abandoned once more his claims in Italy as well as the suzerain rights he claimed in Flanders and Artois. The emperor, for his part, had to recognize that it was impossible, at least for the moment, to make good his claim to the whole Burgundian inheritance, though he was careful to retain the title of Duke of Burgundy. The death of the Constable of Bourbon in the capture of Rome, shot while climbing a scaling-ladder at the beginning of the attack on the city, meant that his enormous possessions passed to the French crown, though the treaty guaranteed the rights of his heirs. Francesco Sforza became once more Duke of Milan. The two sons of Francis I, who had been left behind in Spain as hostages for their father's observance of the terms of the Treaty of Madrid, were to be released on payment of a huge ransom of two million gold *écus*, of which 1,200,000 were to be paid as a lump sum.[28] (The collection and payment of the money was difficult and took time: the two princes were not freed until July 1530.)

By 1529 Italy had suffered more than a generation of invasion and conflict which had left a bitter legacy. In Florence, formerly so wealthy, disruption of trade and agriculture combined with heavy taxation meant that by the later 1520s even the richest citizens were in difficulties: one was imprisoned for failure to pay his taxes while another had to sell even his clothes.[29] Great artistic and intellectual activity had been accompanied by widespread destruction and loss. Pride in Italian achievement had been tempered by a realization that the states of the peninsula were almost helpless when confronted by France or her Habsburg rival. France, in spite of years of costly struggle, had been defeated. The coronation of Charles V as Holy Roman Emperor by Clement VII at Bologna in February 1530, the last holder of the title to be so crowned, put a symbolic coping-stone on his success. Ruler of Naples and Sicily, dominant throughout most of Italy, he might now even succeed in the most difficult task of all, that of bringing the papacy to heel. The restoration in Florence in 1530 of the rule of the Medici family, after a short-lived republican interlude since 1527, consolidated Spanish influence there. The duchy of Milan was soon to lose what was left of its independence and become part of Charles's increasingly Spanish-dominated empire.

---

28. The peace negotiations and their immediate background can be followed in Joycelyne G. Russell, 'Women diplomats: the Ladies Peace of 1529', in her *Diplomats at Work: Three Renaissance Studies* (Stroud, 1992).

29. Melissa M. Bullard, *Filippo Strozzi and the Medici* (Cambridge, 1980), pp. 17–19.

Genoa, so strategically important, had become one of the pillars of Spain's whole international position. The success and reputation of the Spanish infantry were at their height.

There were clearly new difficulties, great and growing ones, which Charles V would now have to face. The advance of the Ottoman Turks seemed to menace all Christendom and to impose on him as emperor the obligation, which he felt deeply, to lead its resistance. In the western Mediterranean the Barbary corsairs were becoming a scourge of the coasts of Spain and southern Italy.[30] In Germany the Lutheran movement had now gained the support of significant territorial princes and was seriously complicating Charles's position and limiting still further his freedom of action. Moreover, both Turks and Lutherans might well become, in spite of any Catholic religious scruples, dangerous weapons in French hands for use against the emperor. The rivalry of Charles and Francis, of Habsburg and Valois, was now the central theme of international relations in the western half of Europe. In the conflicts to come Italy was still to play an important part. Control of the peninsula, with its long history as the centre of the Roman empire, still seemed to many observers the key to pre-eminence among the rulers of Europe. The recovery of Milan remained the main objective of Francis I. But these new struggles would not, like those of the past, centre on Italy. From the 1530s onwards the boundaries of the Italian states were to be much more stable than in the last three or four disastrous decades. With surprisingly few exceptions they now remained unchanged until the early eighteenth century. The conflicts to come would be focused at least as much on the Netherlands and the eastern and north-eastern frontiers of France.

30. See below, pp. 232–3.

CHAPTER FIVE

The Empire of Charles V and Its Enemies, 1529–59

Charles faces new tasks: infidels and heretics

Charles V took seriously his obligation as the leading Christian monarch, the natural protector of Christendom, to face and repel the Ottoman Turkish advance which in the 1520s had suddenly become more menacing than ever before. God, it seemed, by endowing him with an unprecedented accumulation of kingdoms and lordships, had also placed on him duties of this kind which he could not shirk. The Habsburg possessions in the Netherlands; the Austrian provinces and Franche-Comté; the imperial title; the Spanish kingdoms and the rather tenuous Spanish foothold in North Africa; Naples, Sicily and Sardinia, and from 1535 onwards Milan, not to speak of the Spanish empire in America with its immense potentialities: all this gave him a position for which there was no precedent. Gattinara and the intellectuals with whom, until his death in 1530, he surrounded the emperor, argued that Charles was destined to carry on and consummate the work of Charlemagne. 'God', the chancellor told him in 1519, 'has set you on the path to a world monarchy'[1]; and there were many contemporaries who hoped, and many others who feared, that these words might be a statement of fact. It was all too easy for Charles to see both Francis I, the ally of the infidel, and Henry VIII, an apostate from the true faith, as unworthy and less than truly Christian princes and his moral inferiors.

The emperor's position, inevitably in that age, was reflected not merely in territorial possessions but in dynastic alliances which meant that he had during his reign links of this kind with almost every European ruling family of significance. His empire had been

1. *New Cambridge Modern History* (Cambridge, 1958), ii, p. 301.

created by fortunate dynastic marriages. Such marriages, more than war or conquest, were his chosen means of spreading his influence throughout the continent and thus perhaps inaugurating a unity, the product of personal and family ties between monarchs, of which he would be the leader and guardian. He himself married a Portuguese princess, while one of his sisters became the wife of his great rival Francis I, another married Christian II of Denmark, another Louis II of Hungary and yet another John III of Portugal. His son Philip was to marry in turn a Portuguese princess, the queen of England, a French princess and an Austrian archduchess, while one of his nieces married a king of Poland and another the last Sforza duke of Milan. God had been very good to Charles. To repay the debt by acting as the shield of Christendom against Islam in central Europe and the Mediterranean seemed an inescapable obligation. It was also one whose fulfilment would bring him great honour and reputation.

In meeting this obligation he claimed the support of his fellow-monarchs, though often in the full realization that this was unlikely to be provided. The Treaty of Madrid, to take only the most obvious example, had claimed in one of its clauses to pave the way for peace between all the rulers of Europe and joint action by them against both infidels and heretics. Yet the Turkish advance was not a direct and immediate threat to the emperor's international position in the way that a successful French offensive in Italy, the Netherlands or the Rhineland was. Nor did Charles see war against the infidel, whatever the moral obligation to wage it, as carrying the same prestige as the struggle with France, the greatest state of Christian Europe. The tradition of rivalry with her was an active and now ever-present one. The wars in Italy had been marked by many famous deeds of gallantry and striking feats of arms; by contrast, the struggle in the semi-barbaric Danubian plain seemed remote and unglamorous. The Turkish threat was unquestionably real. Yet the defence against it of what remained after 1526 of Christian-ruled Hungary, or even of the Habsburg central European provinces, never absorbed more than a small fraction of the resources Charles spent on the safeguarding of his possessions in the western half of Europe. Though for a short time after his victory at Pavia he thought of giving more attention to the situation in the east, nothing came of this. Nor did he pay any attention to an earlier proposal of Pope Adrian VI that a truce for two years be concluded in western Europe to allow more effective resistance to the Turks. His younger brother, the Archduke Ferdinand, regent for him in his central European territories, pleaded with him in vain from 1522 onwards for more effective support and greater resources. Only once, during the unsuccessful Ottoman advance of 1532,[2] did Charles himself set foot in Vienna; and then he spent only a few days in the city.

The Barbary corsairs in north Africa were a different matter. They now meant the extension of Turkish power to the western Mediterranean. Their greatest leader, Kair ed-Din Barbarossa, was now a vassal of the sultan; and the corsair statelet of Algiers was the centre of a continual piratical onslaught which meant the seizure of Christian shipping, the disruption of Christian trade and the carrying-off as slaves of many Christians from Sicily, the kingdom of Naples, the Balearic islands and the Mediterranean coasts of Spain. By the 1530s there were signs that seemed to foreshadow Muslim dominance of much of the Mediterranean; and the great Sultan Suleiman was now more aware than in the past of the usefulness of the Barbary corsairs as a weapon against Christian Europe and willing to back them with the resources of his empire in manpower and shipbuilding.

But these corsairs, even with Turkish backing, were a destructive, costly and sometimes humiliating nuisance rather than a real threat to Charles's power. Their activities stung him to action as the Ottoman offensive by land never did. He inherited with the Spanish crowns a tradition of effort to conquer and control the north African coastline; and it was incumbent on him to protect the coasts of his Spanish and Italian possessions against Muslim raids. Until the 1570s, long after his death, Spanish and often Italian resources were to be expended on a large scale in this struggle. The emperor himself was to lead in 1535 and 1541 great and costly efforts to consolidate and make permanent Spanish power in the Maghreb.[3] But for him such efforts were a matter of obligation and prestige, of a desire to act, and be seen to act, as the head and protector of Christian Europe, as much as of necessity.

Yet the Turks, and even the much weaker Barbary corsairs, were a significant factor in the international relations of the great west European powers. The demands they made on Charles's resources meant that they were a potentially very useful ally for his great rival, Francis I. They seemed a potent weapon, if they could be brought effectively into play, for use against Habsburg power in the Mediterranean and central Europe. Any overt alliance with the Ottoman empire and its north African satellites was certain to expose Francis to much outraged condemnation. Charles had already tried to make the French

2. See below, p. 238.
3. See pp. 26, 239.

king responsible before European opinion for the loss to the infidel of much of Hungary in 1526.[4] Yet the possible advantages of joint Franco-Ottoman action were great. It would face the emperor with a difficult struggle on two fronts and stretch Habsburg resources as nothing else could.

Francis was well aware that by sharing in a successful crusade he would gain widespread approval and personal prestige. In October 1529, in the aftermath of the peace made at Cambrai, he sketched to the imperial ambassadors who had just arrived in Paris a plan for war against the Turks with a great army of 60,000 men, of which Charles V would be the commander while Francis would lead the vanguard: he even proposed to meet the emperor somewhere in Italy to plan the campaign.[5] Realism and personal ambition dictated a very different attitude, however. 'I cannot deny', Francis very frankly told a Venetian ambassador two years later, 'that I keenly desire the Turk powerful and ready for war, not for myself, because he is an infidel and we are Christians, but to undermine the emperor's power, to force heavy expenses upon him and to reassure all other governments against so powerful an enemy.' Nor was Turkish support for the French king merely a defensive expedient or a means of rectifying a threatened balance of power. It also promised effective help in realizing that perennial dream – decisive victory in Italy, and particularly the final and lasting conquest of the duchy of Milan. In 1533 Francis allegedly spoke still more frankly, saying that 'Not only will I not oppose the invasion of Christendom by the Turk but I will favour him as much as I can, in order the more easily to recover that which plainly belongs to me and my children, and has been usurped by the emperor'. A year later Thomas Cromwell, newly established as chief minister of Henry VIII, commented according to the imperial ambassador in London that 'The king of France, to reconquer the Milanese, will not be held back by any scruple from drawing the Turks, and even the devil himself, into the heart of Christendom'.[6]

Moreover, in Constantinople the possible usefulness of Francis as an ally against Habsburg power and an aid to further Ottoman successes in central Europe or the Mediterranean did not go unrecognized. The early 1530s, therefore, saw a rapid growth of Franco-Ottoman contacts. An emissary of Barbarossa met Francis I in July 1533 at Le Puy; and this was followed by the arrival in France of an ambassador from the sultan, who urged the king to continue his hos-

4. J. Ursu, *La politique orientale de François Ier (1515–1547)* (Paris, 1908), p. 39.
5. K. Brandi, *The Emperor Charles V*, trans. C.V. Wedgwood (London, 1939), p. 281.
6. R.J. Knecht, *Francis I* (Cambridge, 1982), p. 225; Ursu, *La politique orientale*, p. 79.

tility to the emperor and promised him Turkish military help. In November 1534 another envoy from Barbarossa arrived, ostensibly to announce the corsair leader's capture of Tunis but probably also to discuss future joint military action, and was given an official reception. Already in February of that year, when a French ambassador, La Forêt, was sent to both Barbarossa and the sultan, his instructions showed how far Francis was now prepared to go in his search for an effective alliance. La Forêt was to urge Barbarossa to an attack on Genoa, in which France would cooperate and provide munitions and supplies. Suleiman was to be asked for joint action against Charles V. This he could provide partly by giving France large financial support, and also by ordering Barbarossa to attack Sicily and Sardinia, where a puppet ruler, nominated by the French but tributary to the sultan, was to be installed. A new Turkish offensive in central Europe, it was stressed, would be unwelcome. Action of this kind with its implied threat to Germany (Turkish raiding parties had penetrated as far as Regensburg during the 1529 offensive against Vienna) was likely to rally the German princes to the side of the emperor. Attacks on Italy or Spain, on the other hand, were welcome since 'the Germans will not act because of the danger to Italy and the joint fleets of France and Turkey will be able to cut the sea passage from Spain to Italy'.[7]

There is no doubt, then, that the French king had real hopes of what a Turkish alliance might achieve. But these instructions also show how difficult effective joint action would be. Distance, slow and difficult communications, the distrust that was bound to persist between states each of which regarded the other as infidel and therefore inherently suspect; all these made up a large part of the difficulty. But underlying them was the fact that the interests of the two powers coincided only to a limited extent. Both, more particularly France, might benefit from effective cooperation in Italy if this could be achieved. Elsewhere, even in principle, it would be much more difficult. A new Turkish onslaught in Hungary would probably be counter-productive from the French point of view. But a French offensive in Flanders or on France's eastern frontier would equally be seen in Constantinople as a diversion of resources to theatres of war too remote to give the Ottomans any worthwhile help. When a new war between France and the Habsburgs broke out in 1536 Suleiman therefore complained bitterly of French action of this kind as a betrayal.[8]

7. Ursu, *La politique orientale*, pp. 88–91.
8. Ibid., p. 103.

Nevertheless there was on both sides a willingness at least to explore the possibilities of joint action; and this was strengthened when, in July 1535, a large force led by Charles V in person (100 warships convoying three times as many transports) took Tunis from Barbarossa. This was one of the high points of the emperor's reign. More emphatically and justifiably than ever before he could now claim to be the champion of Christendom, a claim underlined by the 10,000 Christian prisoners who gained their freedom when he captured the town. His success could be presented as a model for his fellow-monarchs to imitate and brought with it precisely the sort of prestige so dear to the hearts of all rulers of that age. (Before the attack on Tunis was launched Charles had asked Francis I for help in the enterprise, counting on his refusing and thus providing propaganda ammunition for use against him.) The following year saw further moves in the Franco-Turkish rapprochement. In 1536 La Forêt may have signed in Constantinople a commercial agreement, the Capitulations, which gave French trade in the Ottoman empire the rights long enjoyed there by Venetian merchants. This, however, in spite of the attention historians have often given it, survives only in a draft, and it seems likely that no formal treaty of the kind was ever drawn up. There may well, nevertheless, have been more discussion of military cooperation and some agreement, though only a verbal one, for future joint action.[9] Effective alliance against Charles V was still an aspiration both in Paris and Constantinople, therefore, rather than a reality. But the aspiration, if it were ever realized, would be pregnant with unpleasant possibilities for the emperor.

The same was true of the Lutheran movement which had now clearly put down roots in Germany. Charles V was himself conventionally and devoutly Catholic: persecution of the new heresy had begun in the Austrian territories of the Habsburgs as early as 1523. Throughout the 1520s, however, he was much too preoccupied elsewhere to act effectively to enforce Catholic orthodoxy in the Holy Roman Empire; and by the early 1530s the Lutheran movement there was becoming menacingly strong. The Archduke Ferdinand, in his efforts to hold his own against the Turkish menace, was forced in the absence of effective help from his brother to demand, or rather plead for, men and money from the German princes. The Lutheran leaders thus quickly realized that the Turkish danger and the need for their support against it provided them with an ideal opportunity

---

9. R.J. Knecht, *Renaissance Warrior and Patron: The Reign of Francis I* (Cambridge, 1994), pp. 329–30.

to extort concessions in Germany from the archduke and even from the emperor. In 1526 the imperial diet, meeting in Speyer on the eve of the Mohacs disaster, demanded that the religious problem be solved before any help could be given to the Hungarians; and though it eventually agreed to provide 24,000 men for this purpose the concession came far too late to have any practical effect: the decisive battle was fought only four days after the diet adjourned. Though the Lutheran princes gave some help in the defence of Vienna during the Turkish siege of 1529, this was the last time they did such a thing without first obtaining religious concessions of some kind. In 1532, another year in which the Turkish threat was particularly acute, the emperor was forced to agree to the teaching of the new religious doctrines in hitherto Catholic territories as well as in those already conquered by Lutheranism. To say, as one student of the subject has done, that the success of Lutheranism in Germany 'should be attributed to Ottoman imperialism more than to any other factor' is something of an exaggeration;[10] but it is an exaggeration which embodies an important truth. Moreover the Catholic princes of Germany, whatever their religious feelings, often showed themselves as ready as the Lutheran ones to exploit the situation as a means of whittling away what remained of effective imperial authority.

Lutheranism therefore had now become a serious complication, a source of German weakness and division, so far as Charles and his brother were concerned. What made it a real danger was the possibility that it might be used, like the Turks, by France as a weapon against Habsburg power. Given that Habsburg–Valois rivalry was now well established as the central conflict around which the international relations of western Europe revolved, it is not surprising that some of the Lutheran leaders should have quickly begun to look to France for backing against the Catholic Habsburgs. Philip, Landgrave of Hesse, the most dynamic and aggressive of the princes who had gone over to the new faith, began even as early as 1528 to think in terms of a possible French alliance. A little later the Swiss reformer Ulrich Zwingli, though not doctrinally a Lutheran, shortly before his death in battle in October 1531 envisaged a great anti-Habsburg alliance in which France would be the most important element and even sent Francis a statement of his religious ideas, though he can scarcely have hoped for the king's conversion. On his side Francis was now actively exploring possibilities of this kind. From his stand-

10. S.A. Fischer-Galati, *Ottoman Imperialism and German Protestantism, 1521–1555* (Cambridge, Mass., 1959), p. 117.

point the ideal was the creation of a powerful league of both Lutheran and Catholic princes that would defend 'German liberties', in other words continued political weakness and fragmentation, against any effort by Charles or Ferdinand to reassert their authority.

In 1531 a first step in this direction was taken. A French agent succeeded in persuading the two Catholic dukes of Bavaria to make an alliance with the Lutheran princes who had just formed the League of Schmalkalden (named from the small town on the border between Saxony and Hesse where early meetings of the league often took place). In March 1532 Francis promised the allies financial support; and in May an agreement linking France with Hesse, Saxony and Bavaria was signed. Equally important, French backing was now being offered for a Lutheran attack on the south-west German state of Württemberg. Its ruler, Duke Ulrich, had been expelled in 1519; and in 1530 Charles V had given the duchy to his brother, the Archduke Ferdinand. This inevitably aroused the fears and jealousies of every enemy of the Habsburgs in the German world; and there is no doubt that the emperor acted here in an arbitrary and illegal way. The exiled duke, a violent and unpleasant man, had now become a Lutheran and was related to Philip of Hesse. The situation therefore provided an excellent opportunity for the use of French influence to inflict a serious defeat on Charles. Moreover, the usefulness and importance of the Lutherans as an anti-Habsburg weapon was being increased in these years by the apparent likelihood that England, which in the past had sometimes at least seemed a possible French ally in the restraint of threatening Habsburg power, would now be seriously weakened as a factor in international relations by her own peculiar internal religious problems. Henry VIII's break with Rome, made final by the Act of Supremacy of 1534, appeared to put a large question-mark against the country's unity and the value of any alliance with her even if one could be obtained.

In January 1534, therefore, Francis and Philip of Hesse met at Bar-le-Duc in north-eastern France. Francis promised subsidies to support the attack on Württemberg, while Philip promised to declare war on the Archduke Ferdinand within three months. In the early summer the duchy was overrun with little resistance and Duke Ulrich restored. Ferdinand was faced by too many other difficulties to be able to act effectively. Charles V, far away and deeply involved in preparations for his attack on Tunis in the following year, could offer his brother only some financial help; and even this came too late to achieve anything. This was a significant success for the German Lutherans and their French backer. Württemberg occupied an important strategic position, between Alsace and the Habsburg possessions of Franche-Comté and the Tyrol. Moreover in hostile hands it cut off the main body of Habsburg territories from the small and isolated ones in south-west Germany from which the dynasty had originated. The ease with which the duchy was abandoned in 1534 contrasts markedly and surprisingly with the readiness of Charles V to carry on a long series of expensive struggles in order to hold Milan.

The events of the early 1530s, therefore, showed very clearly that the rivalry of Valois and Habsburg was undiminished, and that the determination of Francis I to challenge Charles V and undermine his position was as strong as ever. A new war could hardly be long delayed.

New struggles but no decision, 1536–44

In February 1536 a French army invaded Savoy and Piedmont: Turin fell in the following month. Francis I justified his action by claiming that the Duke of Savoy, Charles II, was still occupying territories which rightfully belonged to the French king's mother, Louise of Savoy. (He had already made a series of sweeping territorial demands in January which he used to provide moral backing for his action.) But his real objective was the one that had been central to every French initiative in Italy for well over three decades: the duchy of Milan. More than anything else it was the death in October 1535 of the childless duke, Francesco Sforza, the last of his line, that made a new struggle over the repeatedly contested duchy inevitable. From Francis's point of view Savoy and Piedmont, though of genuine strategic value in themselves, were desirable chiefly as a bargaining counter which he could use in new efforts to secure Milan, or as a base from which he could launch a new attack in Italy if negotiations over the fate of the duchy broke down.

Clearly hostility and distrust between the combatants was as great as ever. When in August 1536 the eldest son of Francis, the Dauphin Francis, suddenly died, the French government without a shadow of proof accused Charles V and his viceroy in Milan, Ferrante Gonzaga, of having connived at his murder by poison. Yet the war that followed was shorter than the struggles of the 1520s and offers less in the way of military drama. Charles V reacted forcibly to the French action in Savoy. By June his forces had recovered the occupied territory. In the following month another imperial invasion of Provence was decided on. It was no more successful, however, than Bourbon's attempt twelve years earlier: once more the lesson was repeated that new and stronger fortifications, distance, disease, supply problems and shortage of money made extremely difficult any successful large-scale invasion of a major European state.[11] At least as much as ever in the past, this was still one of the essential limitations within which international relations had to be carried on. The following year saw the French recover control of Savoy and Piedmont; while in the Netherlands Charles of Egmont, that inveterate enemy of the emperor, put his territories under French protection, though this was followed by his death a year later. In fact neither side could inflict really serious damage on the other. Francis had begun the war in 1536 partly because he believed that Charles's forces and attention would be largely tied down in resistance to the Muslim threat in the Mediterranean; but any reliance he and his ministers had placed on Turkish help proved unfounded. The appearance of a French naval squadron off Constantinople in September 1537 did not lead to the cooperation in attacks on the coasts of southern Italy, Sicily or even Spain that had been hoped for. Some Turkish military success in Hungary was not coordinated at all with the simultaneous French successes in northwestern Italy: effective joint action by these very disparate states was as far away as ever. The war was shortened most of all, however, by that most irresistible of all forces, shortage of money, and by the fact that to go on fighting soon became almost impossible for both sides. Francis I began the struggle with a cash reserve of 1.5 million *livres*; but its first year alone cost him three times as much. The fighting of 1537 was even more expensive, at a cost of 5.5 million; and very quickly both he and Charles were in desperate need of money.[12]

The result was a truce signed at Monzon in Spain in November 1537, which was followed by peace talks at Leucate, near Narbonne. These broke down after a few weeks, essentially over the perennial question of Milan; but in June 1538 a series of personal meetings in Nice between the rival rulers and the pope, Paul III, produced a truce meant to last for ten years. For the most part this reaffirmed the Cambrai settlement of 1529. But the provision that each side should retain any conquests made during the war meant that France remained in control of Savoy and most of Piedmont. Compared to the acquisition of Milan, so much hoped for and so often attempted, this was very much a second-best. Nevertheless it did something to pro-

11. A detailed account of the failure of this attack on Provence can be found in Knecht, *Francis I*, pp. 281–5.
12. Ibid., pp. 285, 287.

tect Provence against any new attacks like those of 1524 and 1536; and it began a long period of control by France of this strategic area astride the Alps, a gateway through which she might launch still further incursions into Italy. The truce was followed by an important meeting between Charles and Francis at Aigues-Mortes, on the Mediterranean coast of Provence. The two rulers agreed to join in repressing heresy, a sign of the increasing seriousness of the religious division of Europe and the way in which its role in international relations was growing. Of more practical importance, Francis's hopes of Milan were kept alive by a provision that his second surviving son, the Duc d'Orléans, should marry Mary, the daughter of Charles V, and that she should bring with her the duchy as her dowry. This dynastic alliance was to be reinforced by the eventual marriage of the eight-year-old Philip, the emperor's son, with Marguerite, Francis's daughter. The Orléans–Habsburg marriage never took place: it joined the very long list of abortive projects of this kind with which the history of this period is filled. Milan was the key to the whole Habsburg position in Italy. It was essential to the communications between the Austrian lands and the peninsula, and the jumping-off point for its more tenuous ones with the Netherlands. That Charles should have been willing to contemplate sacrificing it for purely dynastic reasons shows how conservative and tradition-bound his thinking was. To the end of his life considerations of purely military advantage, of making his great assembly of territories more strategically united and defensible, were to be for him quite secondary to dynastic ones.

But the truce of 1538 was merely that. No lasting peace between the adversaries was as yet in sight. In 1539, when a serious revolt broke out in Ghent, Charles V travelled from Spain across France to supervise its repression. This gesture, his reception by Francis and the festivities that accompanied it, indeed the entire journey, attracted much attention. But in fact nothing had changed. Real friendship or trust was non-existent. Before he crossed the Pyrenees the emperor was careful to obtain invitations not only from Francis but also from his chief ministers and his heir, the Dauphin Henry. One from the king alone, it was felt, might be invalidated if he should die suddenly. In that case, stranded in potentially hostile territory, Charles might find himself in an awkward and even dangerous situation. Milan was as big a stumbling-block as ever in the way of any lasting peace. In 1540 Charles suggested what amounted virtually to the recreation of the agglomeration of territories ruled by Charles the Bold before 1477. If his eldest daughter married Francis's younger

son the emperor would endow them with his Netherlands possessions and Franche-Comté, provided that on his side Francis handed
over to them the duchy of Burgundy. In addition, however, he must
evacuate Savoy and Piedmont and give up all claim to Milan. These
terms the king rejected. Once more Milan was the insuperable difficulty. 'Francis wanted nothing else, while Charles was as determined
as ever to prevent it passing into French hands.'[13] The result was that
in October 1540 Charles formally invested his son Philip as ruler of
the duchy and thus underlined his determination to resist the claims
Francis had pressed for so long.

On the French side it was equally clear that rivalry with the Habsburgs, now deeply engrained, was as active as ever. It seemed that a
formidable new rival to Charles V in the Netherlands might be found
in the young Duke William of Cleves. The death of Charles of Egmont in 1538 had made him the claimant to Gelderland and Zutphen. He already ruled, as well as Cleves, the small but strategically
placed west German principalities of Jülich, Mark and Ravensberg,
and had the backing of a number of other German princes. Moreover, in January 1540 Henry VIII of England married Anne, the
duke's elder sister. The marriage was very short-lived and almost far-
cically unsuccessful; but it meant that for the time being Henry had
aligned himself with Charles's enemies. All this made Duke William a
potentially very useful weapon in any new French challenge to the
emperor. He was therefore encouraged from Paris to take up a suitably hostile attitude to Charles; and in June 1540 Francis I arranged
his betrothal, in spite of the lady's deep unwillingness, to Jeanne
d'Albret, the heiress of Navarre. Another possible ally against Charles, though a remote and relatively weak one, was Denmark. In 1523
Christian II, the emperor's brother-in-law, had been driven from the
Danish throne. For the next two decades Charles supported first his
claims and then those of his daughter Dorothea to rule in Copenhagen – another good illustration of the importance of dynasticism
in his thinking. (Denmark's control of the entrance to the Baltic and
her ability therefore to interfere with the very large Baltic trade of
Charles's Netherlands subjects was another, though secondary, reason for wanting a friendly regime there.) In 1534–35 the Duke of
North Schleswig, who had become a Lutheran, succeeded after a
considerable struggle in becoming king of Denmark as Christian III.
This inevitably aligned him with the emperor's opponents; and in
November 1541 he made with France an alliance in which William of

13. Ibid., p. 299.

Cleves was included. There were therefore in northern Europe conflicts which Francis might well exploit to embarrass his great opponent.

Moreover, the hopes placed in the Turks and their north African allies were still very much alive. When in 1541 Sultan Suleiman won considerable successes in Hungary Francis tried to claim credit in Constantinople for having contributed to this by diverting so much of the resources of the Habsburgs away from the Danube valley. When in October of the same year Charles V launched a disastrously unsuccessful attack on Algiers, Barbarossa was helped to defend it by French agents who kept him informed of the emperor's preparations.[14] In such an atmosphere the renewal of the Valois–Habsburg struggle could be only a matter of time.

In July 1541 two French agents, Antonio Rincon, en route to Constantinople, and Cesare Fregoso, on his way to Venice, were assassinated near Pavia on their way down the river Po. The action had not been ordered by Charles V, but was probably carried out on the initiative of the Spanish viceroy in Milan (Rincon, a renegade Spaniard, had for many years been active in building up close Franco-Ottoman contacts). Francis I did not at once react forcibly. However, the humiliating failure of the emperor in his attack on Algiers encouraged the king to a new trial of strength; and in March 1542 the French ambassador, the Baron de la Garde, returned from Constantinople with promises of large-scale Turkish support, both military and naval, in such a conflict. Early in July, therefore, came a French declaration of war. The two monarchs whose rivalry had dominated so much of international relations for so long now faced each other for the last time.

The war that followed was again short and indecisive, in spite of considerable efforts by both sides. Charles V had already achieved one important success in the Netherlands. In August–September 1540 he decisively defeated the Duke of Cleves, forcing him to submit to the emperor and abandon his claims to Gelderland and Zutphen. This was a significant step in strengthening Charles's hold on his Netherlands territories and consolidating his regime there, a process which was carried further when in the same year he was able to build a citadel and station a garrison in the city of Cambrai. Moreover, the defeat of the duke deprived France of a potentially important weapon for possible use against the emperor. It also struck a severe blow at Protestantism in north-west Germany: Duke William reverted to Catholicism in 1546. Charles was also successful in win-

14. Ursu, *La politique orientale*, pp. 136–7.

ning England to his side and inducing her to play an active, though financially very costly, role in the war. In February 1543 Henry VIII made a secret alliance with the emperor. By this they agreed that neither would make a separate peace with Francis, who was to be called on to end his scandalous relations with the Turks and even to compensate the Holy Roman Empire for the expenses it had incurred in resisting their last offensive in the Danube valley. The French king must also pay the debts he owed to Henry and hand over to him Boulogne, Montreuil, Ardres and Thérouanne as security for regular future payment of the pension he had promised the English king some years earlier. If he refused these terms Charles and Henry would each, within the next two years, invade France with an army of 25,000 men and force the cession of Burgundy to the emperor and Normandy and Guyenne to the king. In December a second agreement envisaged a still greater effort: each of the signatories was now to provide an army of 40,000 men; and these were to converge, in an ambitious plan of campaign, on Paris itself. It was in this year, significantly, that the English government made for the first time a serious effort to raise a substantial force of mercenaries in Germany, the great military reservoir of western Europe. These schemes of conquest and partition proved as impossible to realize as earlier ones of the same kind. Nevertheless they were not totally without result. The English, commanded by Henry VIII in person, captured Boulogne in September 1544. Simultaneously an imperial offensive in Champagne, though its momentum was lost through the determined resistance of the little fortress of St Dizier, seemed to threaten Paris.

The French on their side were not without successes. The later stages of the war saw them win in April 1544 a considerable victory at Ceresole in Piedmont. But for France the most striking aspect of the war was that it displayed to Europe Franco-Ottoman cooperation of a closeness and openness never seen before. Barbarossa was now an old man (he died in 1546) but he had lost little of his energy and his appetite for attacks on Christian Europe. In 1543 he launched another destructive raid on southern Italy which culminated in the taking and burning of Reggio in Calabria. He was then joined by a French squadron commanded by no less a person than the Duc d'Enghien, a Bourbon and hence member of a junior line of the royal family. Together they attacked and took Nice in August, though the citadel held out against them. Joint action of this kind was striking enough; but it was followed by what seemed to many contemporaries far worse. Barbarossa's ships spent the winter, with the active support of the French government, in Toulon.

The use of the port as a base for Turkish or Barbary corsair attacks in Italy was not altogether a new idea. Francis I had already offered Toulon for this purpose in 1537.[15] It was now put into effect, however, with what seemed to many observers shocking thoroughness. All the French inhabitants of the town except heads of households were ordered on pain of death to leave with their belongings. Each of Barbarossa's captains was given a house for himself and his servants and slaves. Islam became for a moment the dominant religion. For eight months Toulon ceased in effect to be part of France and was transformed into a Turkish colony planted in the dominions of the Most Christian King. Cooperation between the French and their guests was by no means complete. Barbarossa complained that he was given no support either for raids on the Italian coast or for the recapture of Tunis; and when he finally sailed in May 1544 he found provisions for his fleet partly by looting five French ships in the harbour. But the whole episode startled much contemporary opinion. The help openly given by a great Christian state to an infidel force (one contemporary commentator complained that Barbarossa and his men had been paid 800,000 crowns before they left Toulon) seemed deeply shocking and gave rise to much condemnation. In Germany the imperial diet denounced Francis I as 'as much an enemy of Christendom as the Turk himself'.[16]

Nevertheless, so far as the outcome of the war was concerned the Toulon episode was no more than a picturesque sideshow. The struggle was ended as its predecessor had been, by the financial exhaustion of both sides and their resulting sheer inability to go on fighting. The war cost France almost five million *livres* in 1542 and over six million in each of the two following years. The result was 'a frantic search for money in which every known expedient was pushed to the limits'.[17] Offices were sold, clerical tenths were levied, money was borrowed from the Lyons bankers, efforts were made to improve the yield of the salt tax; but still the demands of the war could hardly be met. On his side Charles V was hardly in a better position. In June 1544 he admitted that his money would not hold out beyond the end of September; and in spite of some success in the imperial offensive towards Paris, with the capture of Château-Thierry and Soissons as well as St Dizier, a peace was signed at Crépy-en-Laonnais on 18 September. In essence this was again a restatement of the terms reached at Cambrai fifteen years before. Francis further agreed to give the

15. Ibid., p. 145fn.
16. Ibid., p. 150.
17. Knecht, *Francis I*, p. 377.

emperor substantial help against the Turks and, by a secret agreement, if necessary also against the Lutherans in Germany. The peace was, yet once more, to be cemented by a dynastic marriage. The Duc d'Orléans might marry either Anne, the second daughter of the Archduke Ferdinand, in which case he would receive the duchy of Milan, or Mary, the daughter of Charles V, who would bring with her as her dowry The Netherlands and Franche-Comté. The emperor was to decide within four months which of these alternatives he preferred; and this led to much discussion among his ministers of the relative value of the wealthy but hard-to-govern Netherlands as against the poorer but strategically important Milan. But this elaborate arrangement proved as barren of results as previous ones of the kind; and it is doubtful whether Charles ever seriously meant to surrender territory on this scale, especially in The Netherlands. In any case Orléans died a year later, in September 1545.

The struggle takes on new dimensions, 1544–47

The peace of Crépy had ended the long-drawn-out struggle for the time being; but it had done nothing to bring closer a durable peace. France and England were still at war: they did not come to terms until June 1546, when the Treaty of Ardres was signed. This provided for the payment to Henry VIII of a French pension during his lifetime. More important, England was to retain Boulogne, her one conquest of the war, for eight years, after which France might buy it back for 800,000 crowns. This provision illustrates once more what to modern eyes must seem the marked lack of realism and common sense that underlay much of international relations in that age. Boulogne was of no real use to England: it merely did something to keep alive the dream, now completely unrealizable, of conquests in France comparable to those of Edward III or Henry V. Moreover, it was expensive to garrison, the culmination of a long course of lavish military spending. During the last nine years of the reign of Henry VIII (1538–47), it has been calculated, total extraordinary spending of this kind, on a substantial programme of coastal defences in the early 1540s, on the war of 1543–46 and now on Boulogne, amounted to the crushingly large sum of at least £2,135,000.[18] But to condemn the retention of the town is to think in terms of twentieth-century values, not in those of the sixteenth century. To abandon for crude material reasons a

18. R. B. Wernham, *Before the Armada: The Growth of English Foreign Policy, 1485–1588* (London, 1962), p. 162.

gain of this kind from the traditional enemy, and the prestige such a success brought, demanded a cast of mind foreign to that age. On the French side the loss of Boulogne was seen as humiliating and something to be reversed as soon as possible. For Francis I in his last years its recovery became his central objective and took precedence even over possession of Milan.

Hostility to England now acquired in Paris a sharper edge than hitherto; and this expressed itself in growing efforts to support pro-French influences in Scotland. There the 1540s saw a bitter struggle between the forces which adhered to the traditional policy of friendship with France and competing ones which stood for better relations with England. So long as the former had the upper hand England might find any policy she attempted to pursue in continental Europe impeded by the hostility of her weaker northern neighbour. One pope later in the century commented that the frontier with Scotland made England 'only half an island';[19] and though Scottish alignment with France could hardly in itself be a serious danger, it might well on occasion become a considerable nuisance. Henry VIII and his ministers tried to protect their position in the north with an energy which often became brutality, defeating the Scots in battles at Solway Moss (1542) and Pinkie (1547) and devastating much of the country in a particularly destructive invasion in the spring of 1544. Underlying all this was a constructive idea, that of permanent peace and union of the two countries, to be produced by a marriage of the young Prince Edward, Henry's heir, with the baby Queen Mary of Scotland, who had been born only in 1542. But the violent methods used were self-defeating. A decisive victory for cooperation with England rather than France was not to be won until 1560: until then the situation remained fluid and offered opportunities for interference of which France could take advantage. In June 1543 French military help arrived in Scotland, and again in May 1545. In June 1547 several thousand more French soldiers landed to strengthen the anti-English party; and this was followed by the arrival of an even larger force a year later. In August 1548 it was agreed that Mary, not yet six years old, should be sent to France, there in due course to marry the Dauphin: a permanent union of the French and Scottish crowns was envisaged, so that Henry II, Francis I's son who had succeeded him in March 1547, could claim that 'France and Scotland are now one country'. The political defeat for England, though not in the event irreparable, was serious. The short-lived war that Henry declared

19. Ibid., p. 19.

against England in August 1549 was inspired by his intense desire to recover Boulogne; but when it ended in March 1550 the English government agreed not merely to abandon the town in return for a mere 400,000 crowns but also to withdraw all its forces from Scotland.

The essential struggle after 1544, nevertheless, was what it had been for a generation – that between Valois France and the power of the Habsburgs. The central focus of this had now moved decisively north of the Alps, to the Netherlands and west Germany. Italy remained important. French ambitions there and Habsburg, essentially Spanish, determination to frustrate them were still very much alive. In each Valois–Habsburg struggle, even in each campaign, the main centre of activity might shift quite suddenly between the Netherlands, west Germany and the Italian peninsula. But Italy was at last ceasing to be the great cockpit of Europe. With most of the peninsula controlled by Spain or at least under strong Spanish influence, she was beginning to move towards the sidelines of international relations, a position she would increasingly occupy from the 1560s onwards.

It was the German world which after 1544 gave most scope for anti-Habsburg intervention by France. The Lutheran reformation had now assumed proportions which seemed to threaten the overrunning by heresy within a few years of the whole Holy Roman Empire. For two decades Charles V had clung, like the great majority of his contemporaries, to the hope that the religious schism could and would be healed by the calling of a general council of the church. This, it was assumed, would carry out the reforms needed to restore unity. For twenty years one pope after another had equivocated and delayed, inspired by the fear that such a council must seek to limit papal power. Inevitably also, considerations of their own political advantage influenced the attitudes of secular rulers to the idea, as demands and proposals followed one another in an ineffective succession. Francis I, for example, had objected for his own purposes to the holding of a council in 1533 and again in 1536. At last Pope Paul III summoned one to meet in March 1545 at Trent in northern Italy. It was eventually to prove of immense importance and to transform the Catholic Church. But its calling had been delayed too long; and even after it met it was to be many years before it achieved much of significance. Long before then, however, Charles V had been growing more and more worried by the situation in Germany. The Schmalkaldic League was split by internal divisions and the differing and often conflicting ambitions of the Lutheran princes who dominated it, many of whom were quite willing to subordinate religious belief to personal or family advantage. In June 1541 Philip of Hesse showed its fragility when he made an agreement with Charles and recognized the Archduke Ferdinand as his successor. Only a year later, however, the Schmalkaldic princes were able to force Henry, Duke of Brunswick-Wolfenbüttel, the one significant Catholic prince left in north Germany, to flee from his territories, which were then converted to Lutheranism. Most seriously of all, the league by its mere existence was a perpetual temptation to intervention in Germany by the emperor's enemies. Apart from its relations with Francis I (who in 1546 guaranteed a loan it raised from a group of Italian bankers in Lyons) there had been negotiations as early as 1535, as Henry VIII's breach with Rome became complete, for some form of alliance between it and England.

Charles was now increasingly anxious to take effective action to counter the tide of heresy and enforce religious unity in Germany. In 1543 Paul III, who still hoped to avoid the calling of a general council, offered him substantial help in men and money if he took an initiative of this kind. While the war with France lasted it was hardly possible for the emperor to do much: indeed, his desire to free his hands for action in Germany was a secondary but significant reason for Charles's readiness for peace in 1544. He was also helped by the fact that for a number of years from 1545 onwards, when Ferdinand made a truce with them, the Turks were relatively inactive in Hungary. The need to compromise and temporize in search of Lutheran support against them had for the time being at least ceased. Moreover Francis I, so ready to make trouble everywhere for the emperor, was for the moment less well placed than in the past to support the German Protestants. His intense wish to recover Boulogne did something to divert his attention from events east of the Rhine. Also the rivalry of different groups and individuals at the French court, something almost inescapable everywhere in this age of absolutism, was now unusually strong. Francis's two sons, the Dauphin Henry and the Duc d'Orléans, headed competing factions, while the king's declining health helped to make the situation still more uncertain.[20] There was also an obvious inconsistency, with which Habsburg propaganda made much play, between his support for heretics in Germany, and their increasingly severe repression in France itself. Active persecution of the new religious doctrines and their adherents was now growing there: the Sorbonne, which led the Catholic reaction, published a new index of forbidden books in 1544, while in the fol-

20. For details see Knecht, *Francis I*, ch. 26.

lowing year came a very brutal massacre of members of the old Vau-
dois sect in south-eastern France. Inevitably also, the better French
relations with heretics in Germany, the worse they were likely to be
with the papacy, which had sometimes in the past been a useful anti-
Habsburg force and might well be again in the future. It seems also
that Francis and his ministers overestimated the ability of the Schmalkaldic League to offer effective resistance to Charles once he was at
liberty to act freely. French envoys were negotiating with the Lutheran leaders by April 1545. But it was not until the first weeks of 1547
that it was realized in Paris that the emperor was on the verge of winning a very important victory.

By the summer of 1546 a great struggle in Germany was clearly imminent. Charles had strengthened his position by winning over to his
side Maurice, Duke of Saxony, an able and ambitious man who
wished to obtain for his own branch of the Wettin family the electoral
dignity held by the senior one headed by the Elector John Frederick,
the most important member of the Schmalkaldic League. In October
1546 he obtained from the emperor a promise that this transfer
would take place, while in May Charles had already begun to mobilize his army for the coming trial of strength. Lack of unity and decision meant that though the Schmalkaldic League began the war with
considerably larger forces it soon lost the initiative, so that during the
winter of 1546–47 the imperial ones steadily consolidated their control of south and much of west Germany.[21] They then, in the spring
of 1547, moved into Saxony itself. There, at Mühlberg on the Elbe,
Charles on 24 April won a crushing victory. The Elector John Frederick was captured in the battle and Philip of Hesse, who had rejoined
the Schmalkaldic League in 1544 after his temporary desertion to the
emperor, surrendered a few weeks later.

The power of Charles seemed for a moment almost beyond challenge; and the fact that both Francis I and Henry VIII had already
died in this same year (Henry in January and Francis in March)
strengthened this impression by leaving him as the only survivor of
the struggles of the last three decades and apparently without a rival.
Events soon showed how hollow these pretensions were. In Germany
any real religious settlement seemed as far off as ever. In June 1548
the imperial diet accepted a new such effort, the Interim, which reflected to some extent the Catholic successes of 1546–47. This, however, was a compromise and suffered the normal fate of compromises: it pleased neither of the contending parties. In the autumn

---

21. There is a detailed account of this campaign in Brandi, *The Emperor Charles V*,
pp. 549–56.

of 1547, in the aftermath of his victory, Charles vainly proposed what would have been, if successful, a considerable step towards greater German unity. He suggested a league of princes headed by himself, of which each member should pay a contribution towards the cost of a joint army (an idea he had already put forward more than once). This had no success. Particularism and the interests of individual rulers and ruling families were too powerful for it to have any chance of acceptance; and in spite of his victory and prestige Charles was simply not strong enough to force it into effect. His relations with the papacy were also deeply disappointing and angered him intensely. The pope clearly had no interest in using the newly assembled council as Charles had hoped. In the spring of 1547 its meeting-place was transferred, in spite of imperial protests, from Trent (very near the frontier of Habsburg territory) to Bologna (where it would be more vulnerable to papal influence) and later its meetings were suspended altogether. It was not to begin functioning again until 1551. 'You yourself know', the emperor told his son Philip in his testament of 1548, 'how unreliable Pope Paul III is in all his treaties, how sadly he lacks all zeal for Christendom, and how badly he has acted in this affair of the council above all.' Underlying all other difficulties, however, was the continuing hostility of France, something that her new ruler, Henry II, felt at least as keenly as his father. This must be faced as in the past. 'The French', Charles told his son in the same document, 'will always be casting about for excuses to resume their royal claims on Naples, Flanders, Artois, Tournai and Milan. Never yield to them, not so much as an inch; they will take an ell'.[22] Henry II had already shown his readiness to make difficulties for Charles, for soon after his accession he demanded that the emperor come in person to the French court and there do homage for Flanders, over which Henry still claimed suzerainty. This was a clear breach of the peace of 1529, which had ceded the province to Charles in full sovereignty. Obviously the long struggle had still many years to run.

More conflict in Italy: the imperial position in Germany collapses, 1547–52

It was not long before it once more burst out actively. In France repeated disappointments had not dulled the appetite for adventures across the Alps. Italian influences were strong in Paris: the court of

22. Ibid., pp. 583–4.

Henry II, it has been said, 'often included more Italians than French-men'.[23] In particular political exiles from Florence, refugees from the establishment of Medici autocracy there in 1530, pressed for French intervention to restore them to power; and there were smal-ler groups of such *fuorusciti* from some other Italian states. Moreover the direction that French policy should take was now being hotly con-tested by the Constable Montmorency and his great rivals, the Guise family from Lorraine, who were supported by Henry's mistress, Diane de Poitiers, and who pressed for yet another attempt at Italian conquests. When in 1548 François, Duc d'Aumale and soon to be Duc de Guise, the leading member of the family, married Anne d'Este, a member of the ruling dynasty of the duchy of Ferrara, this strengthened further the Guise interest in Italy and their insistence on a forward policy there. Though the king was much influenced by Montmorency, who was interested primarily in France's eastern and north-eastern frontiers, he was also anxious to maintain the position in Savoy and Piedmont which France had gained by her invasion in 1536. In 1549 he issued letters of naturalization to the inhabitants of Piedmont, a step towards the full and permanent incorporation of the province in France.

Moreover the complexities of Italian politics meant that in the later 1540s opportunities for French intervention were not lacking. The pope, Paul III, had as a major objective the creation in north–central Italy of principalities for his two sons. From 1545 the Farnese family, to which he belonged, held the duchies of Parma and Piacen-za, though not without opposition. In 1547 their ruler, Pier Luigi Far-nese, was murdered as the result of a Spanish-inspired plot; and Pope Paul himself died in November 1549. A year later Charles V ordered Ottavio Farnese to give up Parma and was supported in this by the new and anti-French pope, Julius III. The result was a struggle in which France fought as the ally of Farnese and the emperor as that of the pope. In May 1551 Henry II agreed to supply soldiers and an an-nual subsidy to support Farnese, who invaded the papal state in the next month; but this was followed by his retreat and a siege of Parma by the imperial forces. These Italian complications were not in them-selves of great importance. But they emphasized once more the fatal division and political weakness of Italy and made inevitable a new ap-pearance of foreign armies there. By August 1551 Henry II had de-cided in favour of open intervention and was again urging the sultan to use his fleet against the Italian coasts. When in the same month,

---

23. L. Romier, *Les origines politiques des Guerres de Réligion* (Paris, 1913–14), i, p. 30.

with little resistance, a Turkish force captured Tripoli on the north African coast, hitherto held by the knights of St John, it was accompanied by the French ambassador to Constantinople, the Baron d'Amaron, who played an important part in persuading the commander of the garrison to surrender. This produced a new wave of ineffective international condemnation of France as the ally of the infidel.

More serious was the revolt against Spanish rule that broke out in Siena at the end of July 1552. This last effort to resurrect the type of city-republic that had bulked so large in Italy's mediaeval history inevitably looked from the beginning to France for support. The Spanish garrison was driven out to the accompaniment of cries of 'Francia, Francia'; and in November Sienese ambassadors sent to Paris had an audience with Henry II and were given promises of support by him. His involvement in Italy was now growing both geographically and in scale. In August 1553 French troops landed at Bastia, in the north of Corsica, and soon almost all the island was under French control. The same summer saw a joint French and Turkish raid on the island of Elba in which many of the inhabitants were massacred. None of this, however, meant any real strengthening of the French position. The conquest of Corsica might claim some strategic justification as a threat to Spain's sea communications with northern Italy; but since the island was formally a Genoese possession (though one very difficult to control) its occupation tended to push the republic still more completely into the Spanish camp. The Florentine exile Piero Strozzi, an experienced soldier who had been sent from France to lead the defence of Siena, was badly defeated in August 1554; and a siege of the city, one of the most bitter of the century, then began. It ended, after a heroic resistance led by a French commander, with its surrender in April 1555. Soon afterwards Charles V granted Siena to his son Philip. Two years later, in July 1557, it was acquired by Cosimo di Medici, Duke of Florence, and became part of what was soon to be the grand duchy of Tuscany. The mediaeval republic had now disappeared from Italian life (the little one of Montalcino, south of Siena, lived on until the final departure of the French from Italy in 1559; but this was never of any importance). 'In the history of Italy', wrote the author of the most detailed study of these years, 'the date 1555 really ends the middle ages and begins modern times'.[24]

These Italian struggles had dramatic aspects, notably in the heroic

24.   Ibid., pp. 455–6; a more recent account of the struggles over Siena and Corsica can be found in M.J. Rodriguez-Salgado, *The Changing Face of Empire: Charles V, Philip II and Habsburg Authority, 1551–1559* (Cambridge, 1988), pp. 111–18.

and doomed defence of Siena. But they did not alter the essential fact of the Italian situation – Spanish dominance of the peninsula. Of the Italian states not already part of Charles V's empire only Venice by the mid-1550s retained real independence and was able to play a significant role in international affairs. In Germany, however, the position was different. There France won a success that had important long-term results and was to be her one real gain from so many years of demanding anti-Habsburg struggle. In the summer of 1551 French envoys opened negotiations with Maurice of Saxony, who was now moving into opposition to the emperor; and in October the ambassador of Henry II, the bishop of Bayonne, signed an agreement at Lochau with Charles's Lutheran opponents. The king was to provide subsidies to allow them to challenge Charles once more. In return he was to have possession of 'those towns, which although they have belonged to the Empire for all time, are yet not of German speech', the three bishoprics of Metz, Toul and Verdun, 'and any others of the same kind'. Henry was to rule these, in a face-saving form of words, only as imperial vicar. It could be claimed, therefore, that no outright surrender of the territory of the Holy Roman Empire was involved. Nevertheless this was in effect such a surrender, and a territorial gain by France pregnant with consequences for the future. The Lutheran princes also promised to support the king in any attempt he might make to become Holy Roman Emperor in a future election: the hopes that Francis I had cherished in 1519 were not yet altogether dead. In January 1552 these terms were repeated in a treaty signed at Chambord, one of the French royal residences. The full importance of these agreements was not understood when they were made: it was hardly realized that the approaching French occupation of Metz, Toul and Verdun was to be permanent. Some German Protestant theologians were misguided enough to hope that Henry II might now become a supporter of the Reformation, or even himself a Protestant. However, the position of Charles was now under serious threat, a more serious one than he was at first willing to recognize. Spain and Spanish influence were intensely unpopular in Germany. 'Kein Welsch soll uns regieren', ran a popular saying, 'dazu auch kein Spaniol' (No Italian shall rule us, a Spaniard even less so). Henry II's propagandists were therefore able to argue that French and Germans should now combine against an alien Spanish emperor; and in February 1552 the rulers of Hesse and Mecklenburg joined the alliance against Charles V.

A month later, in mid-March, a large French army entered Lorraine and occupied the three bishoprics. There was little resistance:

the campaign was a military demonstration rather than a matter of serious fighting. The newly appointed bishop of Metz was a French partisan; and only one small fortress put up any real resistance to the invaders. Moreover Charles V, in poor health and with his attention focused on the situation in Italy, remained very inactive during the winter of 1551–52 in face of the approaching threat. The result was that a French army had approached the Rhine for the first time since the Carolingian era (though any idea of the river as a natural French frontier still lay far in the future). Lorraine, an area where French influences merged gradually into German ones, had been given an important push in the French direction. The reigning duke was a child and hitherto his mother, Christina of Denmark, Duchess of Lorraine, the niece of Charles V, had acted as regent for him. She was now replaced by her brother-in-law, the Comte de Vaudémont, who although a Lorrainer was favourable to France, while the young duke was carried off to the French court to be bound to the Valois family by marriage to Henry II's daughter.

Simultaneously Charles was facing the most spectacular and humiliating personal setback of his entire reign. As the French moved into Lorraine Maurice of Saxony and Albert Alcibiades, the Margrave of Brandenburg-Kulmbach, moved against the emperor, taking him by surprise and forcing him to flee to Innsbruck in the Tyrol, an area traditionally loyal to the Habsburgs. From there, after a period of hesitation and uncertainty, he was forced to make a still more hasty retreat, in very arduous conditions with a small following, across the Alps to Villach in Carinthia. His entire position in Germany had for the time being collapsed. 'I find myself actually without power or authority', he wrote bitterly to his brother Ferdinand on 4 April. 'I find myself charged to abandon Germany, not having anyone to support me there, and so many opponents, and already the power in their hands. What a fine end I shall have for my old age!'[25]. Moreover Henry II did his best to add to Charles's difficulties. He spurred on the Turks to take once more the offensive in Hungary and the Mediterranean; while in Italy French influence encouraged an unsuccessful revolt by one of the greatest Neapolitan nobles, the Prince of Salerno (after its failure he fled to join the French forces), and the more serious rising in Siena in July.

Yet the recovery was almost as striking as the collapse. Charles's enemies completely lacked unity. They were fighting not for any ideal or principle but merely to increase their own power and privi-

---

25. *The Autobiography of the Emperor Charles V*, trans. L.F. Simpson (London, 1862), Introduction, p. xxiv.

leges. Both Maurice and Albert Alcibiades had interests and ambitions of their own to serve. The elector hesitated and equivocated. As early as April he had opened negotiations with the Archduke Ferdinand; and early in August, after difficult negotiations, Charles was able to come to at least a temporary arrangement with him by a treaty signed at Passau. In mid-September Maurice even became commander of the imperial forces fighting the Turks in Hungary. Albert Alcibiades was merely a military leader, a German *condottiere* out to profit personally from the situation. By November he had come over to Charles's side, bringing with him a formidable force of 15,000 men after the emperor, very reluctantly, had confirmed agreements which the margrave had forced on the bishoprics of Würzburg and Bamberg compelling them to provide him with large sums of money. Moreover Charles, in spite of the defeats of the early spring, still had great resources on which to draw. Anton Fugger made him a large loan: the fate of the whole Fugger enterprise had now for long been so completely bound up with that of the Habsburgs, above all in Germany, that they stood or fell together. Spanish troops under the Duke of Alba, already one of the best of Spain's commanders, arrived in the Rhineland. The Catholic princes rallied to the emperor's support.

None of this could alter the fact that the year ended with the most catastrophic military failure of Charles's reign, the disastrous siege of Metz which began in October. The city's fortifications had been considerably strengthened by Francis de Guise; and under his command it put up a determined defence. The main responsibility for the disaster, however, must fall on the emperor himself and his insistence, against the advice of his generals, on undertaking the siege in the worst possible conditions in midwinter. The result was a failure far more costly in human terms than that at Algiers in 1541. Yet in Germany Charles's position as 1552 drew to a close was far less disastrous than had seemed likely in the early spring.

The Habsburg inheritance, the abdication of Charles V and the Treaty of Cateau-Cambrésis, 1552–59

The struggle with France was not to end until 1559, when Charles himself was in his grave. His last years, however, were dominated less by the military fluctuations of the war than by two other considerations: the disposal of his heterogeneous territorial inheritance and an effort to draw England permanently into the Habsburg camp. That he should have been deeply preoccupied by the succession problem was inevitable. Thoughts of abdication and retirement from the demands of the world were now more and more in his mind. The burdens of his position, both physical and psychological, had always been heavy and became heavier as he grew older. He could not escape a sense of failure. Heresy was now more deeply rooted in Germany than ever and spreading to other parts of his dominions, notably the Netherlands, while the reform of the church for which he so much wished seemed as far off as ever. The Holy Roman Empire was more disunited and ineffective than when his reign began, while the physical demands on him were increasingly hard to bear. It has been calculated that between 1517, when he first arrived in Spain, and his abdication in 1556 he spent 3,600 days, a quarter of his reign, in travelling. For 500 of these days he was on campaign and 200 others were spent at sea, while he slept during these four decades in 3,200 different beds. He himself complained that 'My life has been one long journey'.[26] Even for an emperor travelling with every possible advantage this meant in sixteenth-century conditions a heavy drain on his energies. His health was also a growing preoccupation. He had for long suffered from painful attacks of gout (the first in 1528, when he was still a young man) which he meticulously recorded in the skeleton narrative of the main events of his reign, his so-called autobiography, which he dictated in Germany in 1550.

Serious negotiations within the Habsburg family over what should happen when Charles left the scene had begun in the 1540s; and they proved delicate and difficult.[27] His outlook and values were uncompromisingly dynastic. To him his enormous and disparate possessions were essentially a kind of gigantic family enterprise in control of which it had pleased God to place him. He governed his territories, it has been said, 'like the head of one of the great sixteenth-century merchant houses where the junior members of the family served as heads of the foreign branches of the firm'.[28] The facts of geography forced him to rely on viceroys in many parts of his dominions. But these were in most cases close relations – his brother Ferdinand in the Austrian territories and Germany, his aunt the

26. P. Chaunu, 'L'empire de Charles Quint', in M. Duverger, ed., *Le Concept d'Empire* (Paris, 1980), p. 258; H. Kamen, *Spain 1469–1714: A Society of Conflict* (London, 1983), p. 62.
27. M. Fernandez-Alvarez, *Charles V, Elected Emperor and Hereditary Ruler* (London, 1976), pp. 145ff.
28. H. Koenigsberger, 'The empire of Charles V in Europe', in *New Cambridge Modern History* (Cambridge, 1958), ii, p. 309.

Archduchess Margaret and his sister, Mary of Hungary, in the Netherlands. Only in Italy was this not so; and even there his son Philip was Duke of Milan. Yet he was forced to recognize that his empire could not be disposed of merely as an accumulation of personal property and in terms of his own wishes.

His ideal solution was for Philip to succeed him not merely in Spain, the Netherlands, Franche-Comté and the Italian possessions, but in the Holy Roman Empire as well. It seems likely that in the winter of 1546–47 he hoped to persuade Ferdinand to give up in favour of Philip his title of King of the Romans, which he had possessed since 1531, and therefore his expectation of being the next emperor. In 1549, as part of his father's efforts to secure the imperial succession for him, Philip made an official progress, accompanied by the erection of triumphal monuments and the performance of courtly pageants, through a number of German cities, culminating in a lavish ceremonial entry into Augsburg. Yet his succeeding his father as emperor was hardly a practical possibility. Apart from the natural resentment of Ferdinand and his son, the Archduke Maximilian, Philip as a Spaniard speaking only Spanish and an uncompromising Catholic, with no experience of or interest in Germany, was quite unacceptable to German opinion.

In 1551, in an atmosphere of growing acrimony, a compromise was achieved. It was agreed in a settlement reached at Augsburg that Ferdinand should succeed his brother as Holy Roman Emperor; but he was then to induce the imperial electors to choose Philip as King of the Romans and also appoint him as imperial vicar in Italy. When Philip in his turn became emperor Maximilian was to be chosen as King of the Romans. In other words henceforth there should be a separation between the two branches of the Habsburg family, the German and the Spanish–Burgundian, with the imperial title alternating between them. It is unlikely that this arrangement could have worked for long even if there had been a genuine effort to apply it. No such attempt was made, however. Ferdinand never tried to put the agreement into effect; and even to Charles it was very much a second-best. In April 1550 he had already obtained recognition of Philip as his successor in the Netherlands; but during the following winter his efforts to have him accepted also as imperial vicar in Italy had been stultified by the very strong anti-Spanish feeling in Germany. The Habsburg family was now deeply divided; and in the German crisis of 1552 Charles seriously suspected his brother and nephew, both of whom were on good terms with Maurice of Saxony, of encouraging his enemies.

Nevertheless, in 1554 the emperor and his son seemed to have won a different and very important political and strategic victory. Early in that year Philip married Mary Tudor, who in June 1553 had succeeded her half-brother Edward VI as ruler of England. Even this *coup* (as a reigning monarch she was the most prestigious match in Europe) was accompanied by clear signs of the spirit of rivalry that now separated the two branches of the Habsburg family. As soon as they received news of the death of the young Edward VI, Charles on behalf of Philip, and Ferdinand on behalf of his younger son, the Archduke Ferdinand, sent competing envoys to England to ask for the hand of the new queen, though the Austrian candidate was never a serious contender. Charles may well have seen the English match not merely as a weapon against France but even more as a way of strengthening Philip's position against his Austrian relations and rivals.

The marriage was always unpopular in England. Philip was always suspect there, partly as a devout and uncompromising Catholic in a country where Protestantism was now striking root. But he was disliked most of all simply as a foreigner, and one who, it was feared, would if allowed any real power sacrifice the country's interests and resources for purely Spanish ends. Before he set foot in England the imperial ambassador, Simon Renard, even asked Mary's council whether it could guarantee the prince's physical safety. He was so impressed by the strength of anti-foreign feeling that he also suggested, as a safety precaution, that Philip should make the Spanish grandees who accompanied him replace their servants by soldiers, disguising them in servants' liveries and taking care that their luggage should contain arquebuses. Within a month of the marriage one of Philip's companions was talking of possible ways of helping him to escape from the country, where he felt 'oppressed'.[29] The French ambassador, de Noailles, reported that 'Of the twenty-five or thirty who compose the Queen's Council, there are not three who approve the said marriage . . . and in general gentlemen as well as others in the land are utterly opposed to it'.[30] This highly unwelcoming attitude was reflected in the terms of the marriage agreement. Philip must have 'a convenient number' of Englishmen in his court and household. He must not take Mary out of England and was to lose all rights there if

29. E. Harris Harbison, *Rival Ambassadors at the Court of Queen Mary* (Princeton, NJ/ London, 1940), pp. 141, 185, 203; the best recent account of this marriage is D.M. Loades, *The Reign of Mary Tudor: Politics, Government and Religion in England, 1553–1558* (London, 1979), pp. 120ff.

30. Harbison, *Rival Ambassadors*, pp. 158–9.

she died childless, while the marriage was not to involve England in the Franco-Spanish war. It was also unpopular in Spain, where England was seen as a semi-barbarous and largely heretical country; and Philip bitterly resented the limitations placed on him and the fact that he was not crowned as king.

Yet the marriage seemed to portend a significant change in the international balance. If England were permanently in the Spanish camp this would make more formidable than ever the ring of Habsburg power that threatened to surround France. The marriage treaty provided that if Philip and Mary had a son he should inherit England, the Netherlands and Franche-Comté. But if Don Carlos, Philip's son by his first wife, Mary of Portugal, were to die childless then Spain and its dependencies, the Italian possessions and the American empire, were also to fall to Philip's son by Mary Tudor. This would have meant the recreation of the empire of Charles V in, for France, an even more threatening form, freed from the difficulties and distractions of Germany and the Turkish onslaught in the Danube valley. Even if such long-term dangers were avoided, the marriage might very well expose France to more of the attacks on her northern coastline and in Guyenne of the sort Henry VIII had launched in the past. It would also do much to safeguard the sea communications between Spain and the Netherlands and might well weaken French influence in Scotland. Almost two decades later, in 1571, a French ambassador in London claimed that 'the first of the two great kings now reigning in France and Spain who gains England to his side will not merely trim his fellow's locks but shear him to the skin'.[31] This overstated the importance of what was still a second-rate power; but the same idea, expressed in more moderate terms, commanded wide acceptance in the 1550s.

The French reaction to this situation was to support conspiracies and rebellions against the increasingly unpopular Mary, since her overthrow would mean the end of any actively pro-Spanish orientation of English policy. The most serious of these attempts, that led by Sir Thomas Wyatt in February 1554, was encouraged by both Noailles and d'Oyssel, the French ambassador to Scotland, while Henry II sent some money to the conspirators. A similar plot two years later led by Sir Henry Dudley received similar encouragement: Dudley met Henry himself at Blois in March 1556, while a year later Thomas Stafford also had an audience of the king before launching his very ineffective rebellion. None of these risings and intrigues changed the

31. Ibid., p. 57.

international situation. But clearly during the decade which followed the death of Henry VIII there was some danger that England, apparently divided and unstable and ruled in turn by a sickly boy and an unpopular woman, might become the arena of contending French and Habsburg ambitions, rather as Milan had so long been.

On 25 October 1555, in the great hall of the palace in Brussels before the Netherlands states-general, Charles V took the first and decisive step in the process of stripping himself of his territories. In a ceremony which deeply impressed the onlookers he abdicated as ruler of the Netherlands. He renounced his Spanish dominions in a semi-private ceremony, also in Brussels, in January 1556. This meant that the Netherlands, the Spanish kingdoms and their Italian dependencies were now ruled by Philip; and by the last weeks of 1556, with his father beginning his short-lived retirement in Spain, the new ruler was in control of these territories. Franche-Comté Charles retained until his death in September 1558, since an agreement with Henry II providing for its neutrality in the war between them specifically excluded their successors from its scope. A new era in international relations was beginning. The Spanish and Austrian branches of the Habsburg family were now formally separate, though the imperial electors did not accept until February 1558 Charles's abdication as Holy Roman Emperor, while Ferdinand refused to confirm the position of Philip as imperial vicar in Italy as had been agreed in the family compact of 1551. The 1530s and still more the 1540s had seen the Spanish element in the empire of Charles V become steadily more important and the emperor himself more and more Spanish in feeling and outlook. The empire of Philip II was to be even more completely a Spanish one, centred on and controlled by Spain (in effect by Castile). For three generations to come Spanish power and the threat of Spanish hegemony were to be the central issue around which the international relations of western Europe turned.

The disappearance of Charles from the stage did not mean the end of the Franco-Habsburg, or rather now Franco-Spanish, struggle. The inability of either combatant to strike a decisive blow, the general superiority of defensive over offensive warfare, was as marked as ever. The French campaign of 1554 in Artois, for example, was made ineffective merely by the resistance of the small fortress of Renti. The following year, however, saw French hopes of victory in Italy revive once more. In May 1555 a fiery old Neapolitan of the Caraffa family became Pope Paul IV. He was obsessively hostile to Spain and her influence in Italy: Philip had before his election denounced him as 'entirely unsuitable', which ensured him the votes of the

French cardinals. In October he made an alliance with France, which promised him support in men and money in case of war, while it was agreed that both Naples and Milan were to go to the younger son of Henry II. By September 1556 Paul's anti-Spanish attitude had become so marked and provocative that the Duke of Alba led an army from Naples in an invasion of the papal state. This provided ostensible justification for a last French invasion of Italy. Its real object was the conquest of Naples; and it was closely tied up with the family ambitions of the Guises and led by the Duc de Guise, who now had great personal prestige in France because of his successful defence of Metz in 1552. The expedition failed like its predecessors. In May 1557, when Guise was already in a difficult military position and having trouble with his Italian allies, Henry II ordered him to abandon the effort to conquer Naples and retreat to Tuscany or Lombardy. Three months later, on 10 August, the main French army was crushingly defeated at St Quentin, little more than 70 miles from the French capital, by a Spanish one commanded by Emmanuel Philibert, the young Duke of Savoy. The losses were very heavy: the Constable Montmorency, who commanded on the French side, and other French leaders were taken prisoner. The king at once ordered Guise to abandon Italy altogether. This was the end of more than 60 years of efforts at French conquest there. In the following month Paul IV, who had begun to prepare for the excommunication of Charles and Philip and had even threatened to call for Ottoman help against them, was forced to end hostilities with Spain. Alba had already brought his army to the walls of Rome, and the sack of 1527 might well have been repeated but for fears of the likely reaction of Catholic opinion throughout Europe: Spanish influence over the papacy was now greater than ever before.

For a moment the position of France seemed very serious, for early in June 1557, two months before the disastrous battle, England had also declared war on her. Soon, however, the pendulum swung once more in her favour. The great victory at St Quentin could not be exploited because of a crippling lack of money.[32] War with France in support of Spain was unpopular in England, where the council gave way only with great reluctance to Mary's wish to give such aid to her husband. Though a substantial English contingent fought at St Quentin the country's role in the war was limited and far from glorious. On the first day of 1558 a sudden surprise attack, led once more by the Duc de Guise, took Calais, which was very incompetently

32. See above, p. 7.

defended. The town had been an English foothold in France for well over two centuries, and its loss was therefore seen in England as a deeply humiliating defeat and put the coping-stone on Mary's unpopularity. Its capture was greeted with corresponding rejoicing in France. Henry II, who had always had the recovery of the town as one of his main objectives (plans for its recapture had begun to appear in 1547–49), visited it in person as soon as it was in French hands. France therefore, after a short-lived but acute moment of crisis, seemed to have made a remarkable recovery.

Both sides were now ready to make peace. Henry and Philip agreed in their fear and loathing of heresy and desire to stamp it out. The French king was frightened and angered by its spread in his dominions and anxious for peace on any honourable terms so that he could act effectively against the 'Lutheran scum'. Philip had been urged by his father, in Charles V's last days, to take very severe measures against the Lutherans and to 'root the movement out, as rigorously as possible'.[33] But the most irresistible of all pressures making for peace was once more the financial exhaustion of both combatants. By 1559 the total indebtedness of the French government was about 2½ times its whole annual income, so that in August 1559 the young Francis II, who had just succeeded his father Henry II, was forced by lack of money to revoke all alienations of the royal domain made by his predecessors. Philip II for his part told his ambassador in England as the final negotiations were drawing to a close that 'I tremble whenever I think of something that might break this peace, if it is concluded, because I lack the strength to do anything more'.[34]

Intermittent efforts to reach a settlement had already been going on for several years. There was a series of negotiations in different places on or near the border between France and Flanders, beginning with meetings early in 1555 at the village of Marcq, between Calais and Gravelines, in which English representatives attempted to mediate between the French and imperial ones. In February 1556 a truce agreed at Vaucelles, a short distance south of Cambrai, proved temporary and ineffective; and in late October 1558, after the French had been seriously defeated at Gravelines in July, there were fresh negotiations at Cercamp. These soon broke down. Henry II, however, now took the crucial decision to make peace by surrendering if necessary all France's other conquests provided he retained Calais

---

33. Romier, *Les origines politiques*, ii, p. 287; Fernandez-Alvarez, *Charles V*, p. 184.
34. Rodriguez-Salgado, *The Changing Face of Empire*, p. 325.

and some strong points in Piedmont. This was a clear victory for the relatively moderate and pacific tendencies represented by Montmorency (who had been released from captivity so that he could influence the king in this direction) and a defeat for the Guise party. The royal council was amazed and horrified by Henry's decision: the Duc de Guise, when asked by the king for his opinion of it, replied: 'I would have my head cut off rather than say it is honourable and advantageous for Your Majesty.'[35]

When peace negotiations were resumed at Cateau-Cambrésis in February 1559 they centred around two issues – Piedmont- Savoy and Calais. On the first the French made substantial concessions. More than two decades of French occupation after 1536 had reduced Duke Charles II of Savoy to humiliating penury and helplessness: when he died in 1553 he had with him only his faithful barber and was able to leave his son, Emmanuel Philibert, a mere 35 crowns, all the money he then had.[36] The young victor of St Quentin now emerged, none the less, as a major gainer by the peace. He recovered his father's lands apart from five fortresses and the marquisate of Saluzzo, which France still retained. Even this limit to his success was not to last for very long: by 1574 all the French-held fortresses had been regained, as Saluzzo was in 1588. This aspect of the settlement was a considerable success for Spain both in prestige and practical terms. Charles V had always refused, as a matter of honour, to abandon the claims of the dispossessed Charles II and his son. In his political testament of 1548 for Philip II he had stressed at length the need to help them recover what they had lost; and it was also important that the ducal territories, in friendly hands, provided the easiest line of communication linking the Spanish possessions of Milan and Franche-Comté. Moreover, it was agreed that the young duke should marry Marguerite de Berry, the sister of Henry II (at first somewhat against his will, since she was four years older than he and, he feared, unlikely to produce the male heir he needed). Emmanuel Philibert was now well placed to become, over the next two decades, one of the most successful absolute rulers of the sixteenth century.

Calais was a more difficult issue. The French were determined not to surrender it, yet Philip II was anxious to recover it for England. The death of Mary in November 1558 meant that he had lost what influence he had possessed there. But if England failed to regain the town he feared that disappointment and wounded pride might lead her to change sides, abandon the Spanish alignment that had proved

35. Romier, *Les origines politiques*, ii, p. 314.
36. Ibid., i, 477–8.

so disappointing and come to some understanding with France. This might well tilt the Franco-Spanish balance decisively against him. Until late in the process of peacemaking, therefore, he was even willing to contemplate a renewal of the fighting if a settlement satisfactory to England could not be obtained. Calais, however, was the territorial gain above all others that the French could never abandon, though they were willing to offer a money compensation if they kept it. At the beginning of March 1559, as the negotiations entered their last stages, there was even a Spanish proposal that the town should be demolished to end the stalemate;[37] but the treaty signed on 3 April provided for its remaining French for eight years. After that it might become permanently part of France on payment of a money compensation – a mere face-saving device. Injured pride was still strong in England and the dream of recovering Calais remained alive. But any realistic prospect of this had now vanished.

The other clauses of the treaty were much easier to settle. Corsica was evacuated by the French and fell once more under ineffective Genoese suzerainty. Spanish Navarre, conquered by Ferdinand of Aragon in 1512, was to remain in Spanish hands, in spite of efforts by Antoine de Bourbon, ruler of the French part of this Pyrenean kingdom, to recover it. (There were suggestions in the negotiations of 1558–59 that he might be compensated with either Sardinia or Tunis; but Philip II never meant these seriously.) Apart from the fortresses she still held in Piedmont–Savoy all that remained of France's conquests in Italy was abandoned, in spite of the resistance of many French military commanders and the queen, herself a member of the Medici family, who begged the king on her knees not to make so shameful a surrender. The treaty was to be reinforced by the customary expedient of a dynastic marriage. Philip II was to take as his third wife Elizabeth de Valois, the elder daughter of Henry II, who was to bring with her a substantial dowry of 400,000 crowns.

The disappointment of so many French soldiers is easy to understand. The settlement of 1559 was in effect a recognition that almost three generations of French effort in Italy had ended in failure. Spanish power there was now too deeply entrenched to be shaken, especially by a France about to become the prey of personal and factional rivalries and religious hatreds. Yet there was now a growing recognition, among French statesmen and diplomats if not soldiers, that the whole protracted Italian adventure had been a mistake, its glamour

37. J. Lestocquoy, 'De la prise de Calais au traité de Cateau-Cambrésis', *Revue du Nord* XI (1958), 43–4.

false and destructive. 'Italy was never any use to us French', wrote the historian Etienne Pasquier, 'except as a tomb when we invaded it'; and the ambassador in Constantinople, La Vigne, urged that 'A second Salic Law should be passed to have the first man who advises the renewal of the Italian wars . . . burnt as a heretic'.[38]

After 1559 relations between the Spanish and Austrian branches of the Habsburg family remained close and intermarriage between them frequent. But the separation that had been taking shape for a number of years, notably in the family compact of 1551, was now formally complete. The Austrian branch, in spite of the imperial title that had become *de facto* its hereditary possession, and the prestige it still conveyed, was now clearly the less important of the two. With no source of wealth comparable to the Netherlands or the Indies, ruling territories that were highly disunited, difficult to govern and for the most part poor, it could not compete with the enormous resources, if they could be effectively mobilized, at the disposal of Philip II. The Holy Roman Empire and its problems were now considerably less central to international relations than they had been even a decade earlier. It played no part in the peace negotiations of 1555–59; and though France kept her gains in Metz, Toul and Verdun, these were not mentioned in the Cateau-Cambrésis treaty. Her position there remained merely that of a military occupier: not until 1648 was it to be given a more secure legal footing. France's possession of the 'three bishoprics' was not in fact a serious threat to the empire; and though the Emperor Ferdinand in January 1560 demanded their surrender, this was never seriously pressed. It was Spain, whose increasingly important line of land communication between northern Italy and the Netherlands they helped to threaten, that was really concerned to see French garrisons there; but she had no legal standing that would allow her to raise the issue at Cateau-Cambrésis.

'The course of events in the world', said a Venetian ambassador to Spain in 1559, 'has reduced many powers, formerly distinct and separate, to three princes alone. One of these is this king [i.e. Philip II], the second that of France and the third the Turkish Signior.'[39] This reflected an important general change which had developed inexorably since the first French invasions of Italy. States or pseudo-states that had had some independent importance, even if only in the form of nuisance value, such as the Swiss cantons or the duchy of Guelders,

38. F.J. Baumgartner, *Henry II, King of France, 1547–1559* (Durham, NC/ London, 1988), p. 228.

39. R. Romano, 'La Pace di Cateau-Cambrésis e l'equilibrio europeo a metà del secolo XVI', *Rivista Storica Italiana* LXI (1949), 536.

now saw their significance much reduced or completely destroyed. In Italy there were some, such as Savoy or above all Venice, that could still conduct meaningful policies of their own. The ambassador of Cosimo di Medici, on reading the Cateau-Cambrésis terms, even claimed, though with ludicrous exaggeration, that 'My master has become the greatest prince Italy has known since the Romans'.[40] But the future now belonged, more than ever before, to the big batallions. They alone, for all their administrative and other inefficiencies, could meet the demands that war now made. Of these big batallions the biggest, for 80 years to come, was Spain. Her strength, the way it was used and the reactions it aroused were to be the central theme in west European international relations for the rest of the sixteenth century and far beyond.

40. Romier, *Les origines politiques*, ii, p. 349.

CHAPTER SIX

Spanish Power and Resistance To It, 1559–85

Religion and politics in a changing world

By 1559 Europe was entering a new era. Philip II faced both opportunities and challenges which differed from anything his father had confronted. Religious divisions were now a permanent and increasingly important force on the international scene. It was still possible for optimists to hope that discussion and some readiness to compromise might be enough to close the fissures of this kind that had been widening since the 1520s. The Emperor Ferdinand, for example, hoped for a time that Protestant representatives, including English ones, might take part in the last sessions of the Council of Trent in the early 1560s. But the legacy of four decades of increasingly bitter dissension could not be willed out of existence in this way. For both Catholics and Protestants the nature of the religious cleavage was changing. It was becoming sharper and more difficult to bridge, as on both sides attitudes hardened. In Germany, hitherto the main theatre of religious conflict, some kind of equilibrium had now been established. The religious Peace of Augsburg in 1555 marked the final defeat of the hopes and efforts of Charles V: its recognition of the Augsburg Confession of 1530 meant that henceforth Lutheranism in the German world had an official standing and permanence that could not be denied. But it was already losing much of its original impetus and ceasing to be the conquering and expanding force of the last four decades. Religious rivalry and ill-feeling were still very much alive in the Holy Roman Empire. From this as from most other points of view, however, Germany in the second half of the sixteenth century was a backwater. It was now the more violent and far-reaching religious conflicts in much of western Europe that took the centre of the stage.

On the Protestant side Calvinism now played the dynamic role; and it had new potentialities and posed new problems. Its intellectual and doctrinal foundations were already well laid: Calvin had published his *Christianae Religionis Institutio* in 1536 and his French translation of the Bible in 1551. More than Lutheranism it was a creed of the educated, or at least of the literate; and largely for this reason it was more uncompromising and doctrinally more radical. Undoubtedly its violent rejection of 'superstition', of a great many of the customary outward trappings of religion, such as statues, altars, clerical vestments and stained-glass windows, did much to limit its appeal in many parts of Europe. The killing of priests and monks by Calvinists (though it was never on a large scale) probably had less influence on public opinion than attacks of this kind. But Calvinism's political implications, both for individual states and for international relations, were more far-reaching than those of Lutheranism. Until the 1560s the Reformation, for all the popular support it could sometimes arouse, had relied for its success on the backing of the powers that be. In Germany its fate had depended on the leadership of a small number of territorial princes: Philip of Hesse and Frederick III of Saxony are the most obvious examples. In Sweden and Denmark its success was deeply indebted to royal support. Without backing of this kind Lutheranism could not have developed as it did. Calvinism, however, drew support from a wide range of social classes and often showed an ability to generate active, sometimes fanatical, popular enthusiasm. Moreover it was not included in the Peace of Augsburg and did not enjoy in Germany the official recognition, however reluctant, conceded to Lutheranism by that agreement.

Everywhere in 1559 Calvinists were still a small minority often only beginning to be fully conscious of themselves as a distinct group. But in France, Scotland, the Netherlands, Transylvania, parts of west Germany and even Poland they were now becoming the cutting edge of the Reformation. To them the support of the powerful, of nobles and even members of ruling dynasties, was inevitably very important. Calvin's own correspondence shows the significance he attached to this. But Calvinism none the less had a dynamism and potential radicalism that its Lutheran forerunner had neither achieved nor desired. It was never a democratic movement in anything like the modern sense of the term; but it could in some circumstances become a quasi-revolutionary force. In some parts of western Europe, therefore, committed Calvinists could turn into a kind of fifth column within their own societies. Moreover, Calvinism rapidly became an international force. The repressive policies of several Catholic rulers – Charles V, Philip II and Mary Tudor – by forcing large numbers of religious dissidents into emigration, helped it to develop in this way; and Geneva (whose population more than doubled between the early 1540s and Calvin's death in 1564), later London and in Germany Frankfurt and Emden, became centres from which religious radicalism of this kind radiated to much of western Europe. There was never an organized and coherent Calvinist international, any more than there was a Catholic one; but there did develop a scholarly and theological network that gave a growing intellectual unity to the movement, and from its beginnings Calvinism had a supra-national character that Lutheranism never achieved. Geneva, where Calvin was established from 1536 onwards, had no Lutheran parallel.

Against Calvinism was ranged a Catholicism that was now increasingly uncompromising and determined in its resistance; and this found practical expression most of all in the power of Spain and the determination of her king. Spain's unique history, one of the slow reconquest of the country over centuries from Muslim invaders, meant that there Catholicism had always a distinctive character. More than anywhere else in Europe it was a national faith, one with strong overtones of racial pride and exclusiveness. By the middle years of the century it was clearly becoming more rigid, exclusive and intolerant. The first Spanish index of prohibited books was issued in 1545 and was followed by others in 1551 and 1559. The reading of the Scriptures in the vernacular (a major attraction of all the reformed sects) was condemned in very severe terms in 1551, while in 1558 the import of foreign books was prohibited and in the following year Spaniards were forbidden to study abroad. Simultaneously there developed a heavy emphasis on purity of blood (*limpieza de sangre*). Henceforth purity of Catholic belief must be combined, at least in holders of any significant office, with purity of descent and freedom from the taint of any Muslim or Jewish ancestry.[1]

Philip II shared to the full the hatred of heresy, the rigid orthodoxy, that now ruled in Spain. He had no doubt that it was his duty to preserve and defend the Catholic religion; and in this belief he was encouraged in the years after the Cateau-Cambrésis treaty by the pope, Paul IV. Paul, to whom 'the slightest divergence from orthodoxy was a crime for which there was no remedy but death',[2] illustrates well the profound change in the leadership of the Catholic

1. These developments are well discussed in J.H. Elliott, *Imperial Spain, 1469–1716* (London, 1963), ch. vi.
2. C.G. Bayne, *Anglo-Roman Relations, 1558–1565* (Oxford, 1913), p. 20.

Church that was now taking place. It was becoming more uncompromising and self-confident, and thus more determined in its resistance to any form of heresy. The Council of Trent, in its last and most
productive sessions in 1562–63, reasserted and defined more auth-
oritatively many aspects of Catholic doctrine as well as introducing a
series of far-reaching reforms. Moreover, this new spirit was given
effect with impressive speed. Within a few years there was a rapid rise
in the number of Catholic clergy, and a marked improvement in
their quality and behaviour thanks to regular episcopal visitations.
But this flowering of Catholic reform was yet another force sharpening religious differences and increasing their importance in the
general picture of international relations.

Of this Catholic reaction Philip II was the obvious, indeed the only
possible, secular head. It was a role for which he was well fitted.
'Rather than suffer the least damage to religion and the service of
God', he asserted in 1566, 'I would lose all my states and a hundred
lives if I had them; for I do not propose nor desire to be the ruler of
heretics.' During his reign he 'solidified the concept of piety as a
Habsburg virtue, and the Cross and Eucharist as dynastic preserves'.[3]
Yet Philip could never allow policy to be decided merely by religious
emotion. However strong his faith he was always sensitive to any
threatened clerical infringement of his authority within his own
dominions. He allowed the decrees of the Council of Trent, of whose
work he was not an admirer, to be published in Spain only after delay
and with a declaration that they were valid only without prejudice to
the rights of the Spanish crown. His unflinching Catholicism was
founded in part at least on the belief, virtually universal in that age,
that religious and secular authority were inseparable. 'If the faith is
lost', he wrote later in his reign, 'I will lose my states and the nobles
will lose theirs; since these [heretics] do not wish to acknowledge the
authority of God, they will similarly reject that of their lords.'[4] Any
effort at a Catholic crusade must at once face the intractable realities
of the international situation and the need to preserve Spain's position
among the powers of Europe. Discretion, compromise, playing for
time, were often unavoidable; and to a man as cautious as Philip, and
usually as slow to take any big decision, they were congenial in them-

3. H.G. Koenigsberger, 'The statecraft of Philip II', *European Studies Review* i, No. 1
(1971), 11; Marie Tanner, *The Last Descendant of Aeneas: The Habsburgs and the Mythic
Image of the Emperor* (New Haven, Conn. /London, 1993), p. 143. The second half of
this book discusses the growth of a distinctively Habsburg form of Catholic piety
centred on the adoration of the Cross and the Eucharist.
4. M.J. Rodriguez-Salgado *et al.*, *Armada 1588–1988* (London, 1988), p. 10.

selves. Sometimes this caution could seem, at least to unfriendly observers, like mere hypocrisy. 'The king of Spain as a temporal sovereign', complained the instructions given to a papal legate much later
in his reign, 'is anxious above all to safeguard and increase his dominions. The preservation of the Catholic religion which is the principal aim of the pope is only a pretext for His Majesty, whose principal
aim is the security and aggrandisement of his dominions.'[5] This was an
unfair or at least an incomplete judgement. The king's religious faith
and hatred of heresy were very real; but they were inevitably tempered
by large doses of realism and modified by international realities.

England and Scotland

In the early years of Philip's reign it was above all in his relations with
England that this caution and realism showed themselves. To keep
England on the Spanish side, or at least to counter French influence
there, was one of his most important objectives. He therefore wished
Elizabeth to succeed Mary with as little trouble as possible, marry
soon and have children who would ensure the succession. He con-
gratulated her on her succession in November 1558 and in January of
the following year himself offered to marry her, provided that she
would live as a Catholic. The proposal soon petered out without result; but he still took pains to assure the young queen of his friendship. It is true that the victory in England of a somewhat diluted form
of Protestantism was not then complete. It was not until May 1559
that the queen gave her assent to the Acts of Supremacy and Uniformity which formally renounced obedience to Rome and restored the
prayer-book of Edward VI; and even after that both she and her chief
minister, William Cecil, later Lord Burghley, held out hopes to the
Spanish ambassador, De Quadra, of some restoration of the lost unity
of western Christendom. But it is clear that Philip was here governed
by purely political considerations. The necessities of the king took
precedence over the feelings of the Catholic.[6]

It was essential to keep Elizabeth, whatever her religious allegiance or lack of it, on the English throne. The alternative, the rightful
ruler in Catholic eyes, was Mary Stuart, Queen of Scots, through her
descent from Margaret, the eldest daughter of Henry VII, who in
1503 had married James IV of Scotland. But Mary had been brought

    5. J. Lynch, 'Philip II and the papacy', *Transactions of the Royal Historical Society* 5th
series, xi (1961), 23.
    6. Bayne, *Anglo-Roman Relations*, pp. 55–6, 90.

up partly in France and in April 1558 had married the Dauphin Francis. In July 1559 she therefore became queen of France. Her reign was brief: Francis died in December 1560. But Mary's return to Scotland, which followed, might well make her a more active threat to Elizabeth, particularly if she now married some powerful Catholic prince as Pius IV wished. French influence in Scotland in the later 1550s was, from the standpoint of both Elizabeth and Philip, dangerously strong. The regent who governed in Queen Mary's name, her mother Mary of Guise, was French. The French ambassador, d'Oyssel, had become from 1554 onwards virtually her chief minister. The great seal was in the hands of another Frenchman, de Roubay. French troops now held the main Scottish fortresses. England seemed in danger of losing permanently the struggle for influence north of the border that she had been waging intermittently for close on two decades; and in 1558 an English state paper gloomily described Henry II of France as 'bestriding the realm, having one foot in Calais and the other in Scotland'.[7] Philip therefore responded very coolly when just before his death the French king proposed that they unite to strengthen Catholicism and royal power in Scotland. He could not welcome anything that might increase further French influence there and make easier a future French invasion of England to put Mary in Elizabeth's place.

In the same way he opposed the desire of Pius IV to excommunicate the English queen: this would make more likely a Catholic revolt aimed at overthrowing Elizabeth, give more weight to the claims of Mary and legitimize a French invasion if one were attempted. This reaction, very paradoxically, made Philip 'the best friend of the English Reformation'.[8] In 1561 and again two years later he was able to prevent the excommunication of Elizabeth; and when in 1570 she finally suffered this fate at the hands of Pius V he forbade publication in his own territories of the bull excommunicating her and even tried to prevent it reaching England. His attitude was supported by his uncle, the Emperor Ferdinand, who disliked the papal threat to Elizabeth equally strongly. The dominions of the Austrian Habsburgs, an assembly of kingdoms, provinces and lordships lacking any sort of organizational or historical unity, were the extreme example of a 'composite monarchy' of the type so common in that age. As such they were particularly vulnerable to the divisive effects of religious conflict. Ferdinand until his death in 1564, and his son Maximilian II until his twelve years later,

---

7. R.B. Wernham, *The Making of Elizabethan Foreign Policy, 1558–1603* (Berkeley/Los Angeles/London, 1980), p. 2.
8. Bayne, *Anglo-Roman Relations*, pp. 224–5.

therefore clung to the hope that such divisions might even now be healed by a compromise which restored some sort of unity to Christendom: the Augsburg settlement of 1555, after all, had explicitly anticipated some development of this kind.

All this meant that Elizabeth was given valuable breathing-space in which the new regime could take root in England. The most important step in this process came in 1559–60 with the winning of a decisive success in Scotland. In May 1559 the repressive attitude of Mary of Guise and her ministers towards the Calvinism that was beginning to make headway in the country set off a revolt that was backed by English money. At the end of March 1560 an English army crossed the border, while in France religious divisions, and still more bitter factional rivalries, were now making effective counter-intervention almost impossible. By July 1560 the rebels, now encouraged by the regent's death and the capture of Leith after a long siege, were able to win a complete victory. The Treaty of Edinburgh and a separate and supplementary 'concession' provided that all French troops should leave Scotland at once and that no others should be sent in future. No Frenchman henceforth was to be appointed to public office. Mary was to abandon the arms and title of queen of England which she had assumed. The fortifications of Leith, Dunbar and Eyemouth were to be destroyed.

This treaty was one of the greatest achievements of Elizabeth's entire reign. Catholicism in Scotland was far from dead: the religious changes there, as everywhere in Europe, were the work of an active and determined minority. The country was still to suffer much disunity and factional struggle. But England was now freed from the fear of a northern neighbour controlled by a menacing continental enemy. The events of the next decade consolidated this success. By 1568 Mary, after seven years of folly and two brief spasms of civil war, was a fugitive and in effect a prisoner in England, while a group of Protestant nobles was in control in Scotland. More than ever Elizabeth was liberated from the threat in the north that had so exercised Henry VIII in his later years.

As France in the 1560s became more and more paralysed by internal divisions her ability to offer any effective threat to England, either directly or through a Scottish satellite, evaporated. This meant that the incentive for Philip II to protect Elizabeth and her regime was correspondingly reduced, especially as it became increasingly clear that that regime was now set on an essentially Protestant path. By the middle of that decade, however, the situation in France and the Low Countries was facing him with new and even more serious issues.

The wars of religion in France

When Henry II died suddenly in July 1559, mortally wounded in a tournament, the situation in France was already very difficult. The war that had just ended at Cateau-Cambrésis had been cripplingly expensive and imposed very heavy burdens on the country. Peace meant unemployment for many minor nobles and gentry. These, very often poor and with no aptitude or taste for any occupation but fighting, were to be for decades to come a force making for conflict and instability. There were now large numbers of such men ready to fight at home if they could not fight abroad. A contemporary described the French, with uncomfortable accuracy, as a warlike nation 'which has great difficulty in staying long at peace without this leading to a foreign or civil war'.[9] Moreover Calvinism was making great advances: one estimate at the end of 1561 was that there were 2,150 Protestant churches or communities in France. Ministers sent and directed from Geneva had been arriving in considerable numbers for several years; and the new doctrines often made a particular appeal to nobles, a target of Calvin himself. Calvinist communities, as the movement developed, often placed themselves under the protection of a local seigneur, and the growing Calvinist movement began to take on a quasi-military character.

All these disruptive forces might have been kept under control by a strong central government. But its strength everywhere still depended crucially on the character of the monarch; and after 1559 France suffered from a generation or more of weak rulers. Henry II himself had been determined to stamp out heresy. His desire to do so was an important motive for making peace at Cateau-Cambrésis; and in the peace negotiations a vague general agreement was reached with Philip II for joint action to crush religious dissidence in the dominions of both rulers. But Henry's death dealt a disastrous blow to any hopes of strong rule and stability in France. His eldest son, Francis II, was then only fifteen years old and lived for little more than a year. Charles IX, his younger brother, was only twelve years old when he became king in December 1560. Ineffective rulers and crumbling central authority were now to be the background against which French history unfolded.

Competing personalities and factions among the greatest French

9. G. Zeller, 'Saluces, Pignerol et Strasbourg: la politique des frontières au temps de la prépondérance espagnole', *Revue Historique* CXCIII (Jan.–March 1943), 100.

nobles had already been very important under Francis I and Henry II; but this new weakness at the centre gave such rivalries disastrous new scope. On the Huguenot side (that of the French Calvinists) the titular leader was Antoine of Bourbon, King of Navarre and married to a niece of Francis I. He was, however, too indecisive and unreliable, in effect much of the time a reluctant royalist, to be an effective party leader, though his younger brother, Louis, Prince de Condé, had more energy and power of decision. But the support of the Bourbon dynasty, closely related to the royal family and with many adherents and great influence, was a very important accession of strength to the reform movement in France. Even more significant in some ways was the leadership now being provided by Gaspard de Coligny. A nephew of the old Constable de Montmorency, he had been converted to Calvinism while a prisoner in The Netherlands after the battle of St Quentin. Until his murder in 1572 he was the most single-minded and effective of all the Huguenot leaders; and he brought with him many of the lesser nobles who formed part of the great Montmorency clientage system. Catholic resistance to the new religious currents was led by the Guise family. François, Duc de Guise, the defender of Metz and captor of Calais, had emerged from the wars of the 1550s with immense personal prestige; and his brother Charles, Cardinal of Lorraine, proved a skilful supporter. For a generation or more the power and ambition of the Guises was to be an important factor in the history of France. Related to the ruling house of Lorraine, sprung, they claimed, from Charlemagne himself, they saw themselves as more than ordinary nobles and as having a quasi-royal status.

Religious differences thus combined with factional rivalries and personal ambitions to form a highly explosive mixture. Catherine de Medici, the widow of Henry II, now began a long series of manoeuvres that was to last almost to her death in January 1589, in an effort to safeguard the position and authority of her sons by playing off the different factions against each other and thus compensating for the growing weakness of the monarchy. A meeting of Calvinist and Catholic divines at Poissy in the summer of 1561 was the first of these expedients; but like everything of the sort attempted since the Lutheran movement first took shape in the 1520s it was a failure. Moreover efforts to preserve some kind of peace by granting a limited toleration to the Huguenots merely irritated the Catholics still further. At the beginning of March 1562 some of Guise's retainers surprised a Huguenot congregation worshipping in a barn at Vassy in eastern France and killed about 30 people. By then civil war had begun.

The fighting was ended for the time being by an agreement of March 1563 which gave the Huguenots a very limited liberty of conscience. This set the pattern for the French 'wars of religion' – relatively short spasms of active hostilities separated by intervals of uneasy and insecure peace, while general disorder grew and the country suffered increasing economic damage. Already, moreover, could be seen the most important result of these wars for international relations – the way in which they weakened France and the scope they gave for foreign influence and intervention there. In 1560 a Spanish ambassador extraordinary, Manriqe de Lara, sent to offer official condolences on the death of Francis II, had strongly urged Catherine de Medici to tolerate no innovations in religious affairs; and this pressure was kept up by the resident Spanish representative, Chantonnay. In 1562–63 a number of west German Protestant rulers, with English and Huguenot encouragement, provided a force of mercenaries which invaded eastern France in an effort to help their co-religionists. More important, Condé made approaches for English help soon after fighting began; and in August 1562 Elizabeth agreed to lend him 10,000 crowns. In return she was to hold Le Havre until she had recovered Calais; and in October English troops occupied the port. This intervention was quite futile. It gave no effective support to the Huguenots, but helped to shock the opposing French factions into a temporary papering-over of their differences. Le Havre was retaken in July 1563: by the Treaty of Troyes of April 1564 Elizabeth abandoned, at least for the time being, the dream of recovering Calais.

But the example of foreign intervention had been set; and action by Philip II in support of the Catholic cause was likely to be far more effective than anything Elizabeth or the German princes could do. Indecisive conflict such as that of 1562–63, however, in many ways suited Philip well. He sincerely wanted France to be Catholic and the French Calvinists to be crushed: he was disappointed by their survival. But he also wanted France to be weak. Divided and in disorder she could hardly carry on an effective foreign policy. She could neither seriously threaten England nor regain her lost position in Scotland. The survival of the Huguenots, therefore, however much he might deplore it from a religious point of view, had great political advantages for Philip; and his attitude to France, as to England, inevitably contained a large element of ambiguity. Certainly some contemporaries were surprised by his failure to take more active advantage of the growing chaos in France in the early 1560s. The Emperor Ferdinand in 1563 gave him only lukewarm praise when he told a Venetian ambassador that 'Philip is a good prince and has lost great opportunities, which Charles V would not have done'.[10]

It was by now clear that disunity in France was deep-rooted and not to be easily ended. On both sides there was growing extremism. Already in 1560 Condé had been arrested for alleged complicity in a plot to seize the king and himself take power: perhaps only the death of Francis II allowed him, though a prince of the blood royal, to escape with his life. In May 1562 fighting in Toulouse between Catholics and Huguenots lasted for several days and cost over 3,000 lives. In February 1563 the Duc de Guise was murdered; and though Coligny may not have been responsible for the act he certainly rejoiced in his enemy's death and thus became the target of even more intense Guise hatred. Moreover in June 1565 Catherine de Medici had at Bayonne an interview with the Duke of Alba, the most important and one of the most intolerantly Catholic of Philip II's military commanders. This aroused intense interest and widespread alarm. It was widely (though quite wrongly) seen as proof that a Catholic crusade for the destruction of Protestantism everywhere was about to be launched. The movement in the summer of 1567 of a powerful Spanish army under Alba himself from Milan to the Netherlands along France's eastern borders [11] seemed to justify these fears; and in September a second bout of civil war erupted. Again the fighting did not last long: a temporary peace was patched up in March 1568. But the involvement of foreign armies, the extent to which civil war in France was tending to be part of a wider struggle between conflicting religious and political forces in Europe, became still more marked. Alba gave some help to the French government, while the Huguenots were supported by German mercenaries sent by the Elector Palatine (who had been converted to Calvinism in 1561). These *reiters* were to reappear frequently in France as the wars went on; and though their military achievements were mediocre they did much to make the fighting more destructive. Strong religious feeling might motivate many Frenchmen, but more and more it was political considerations that governed the course of events. 'What could once have been represented as a religious struggle pursued in the political sphere, became more and more a political struggle pursued partly in the name of religion'.[12]

10. R. Romano, 'La Pace de Cateau-Cambrésis e l'equilibrio europeo a metà del secolo XVI', *Rivista Storica Italiana* LXI (1949), 549.

11. See below, p. 154.

12. N.M. Sutherland, *The Massacre of St Bartholomew and the European Conflict, 1559–1572* (London, 1973), p. 21.

The peace of 1568, like its predecessor, was short-lived. A plot to capture the Huguenot leaders in August of that year showed once more the growing bitterness of the struggle; and the fighting which then erupted was the most savage seen hitherto. The Huguenots were defeated at Jarnac and Moncontour; but the leadership of Coligny helped to ensure that they were far from crushed. When another insecure temporary peace was reached in August 1570 at St Germain they made an extremely important gain. They were now to hold and garrison four towns – La Rochelle, Montauban, Cognac and La Charité – to give them greater security. They were still to face great setbacks. But any idea that they could be totally defeated, as the more extreme Catholics had hitherto hoped, was becoming quite unrealistic. They now had a stronger position than ever before. Far from being a defeated minority they had now become an autonomous force within the state that could not be overridden or disregarded. France was now more than ever divided and exposed to outside pressure and intervention. She was therefore more than ever weakened as an effective factor in international relations.

The Netherlands revolt begins

Well before the abdication of Charles V the obstacles in the way of effective rule in the Netherlands had become all too clear. Each province jealously guarded its own customs and privileges. Nowhere in an intensely conservative and tradition-bound Europe, therefore, was any far-reaching administrative change more difficult to carry through. What by the middle of the century was coming to seem foreign Spanish rule could easily arouse suspicion and resentment; and by the 1550s the spread of various forms of Protestantism was complicating the picture and sharpening feelings. Any sort of effective cooperation between the provinces was particularly hard to achieve. In 1534 Mary of Hungary, as regent for her brother Charles V, had proposed a defensive union in which each province should contribute to the upkeep of a standing army. Although it was promised that provincial privileges should not suffer as a result and the smaller provinces were generally in favour (since they hoped to benefit from the larger contributions to be paid by the bigger ones), the proposal was a failure. In July 1535 the states-general, in which thirteen provinces were normally represented, rejected it out of hand. To them a more efficient central government meant inevitably a more oppressive and authoritarian one. 'If we accept this project', they said, 'we would undoubtedly be more united – and we would be treated *à la mode de France.*'

Two decades later, when she resigned as regent, Mary addressed a last complaint to her brother on the difficulties of this kind she had had to face. 'Apart from the consultations all governors have to engage in', she wrote, 'here in the Netherlands one has to gain everyone's good will, nobles as well as commons; for this country does not render the obedience which is due to a monarchy, nor to an oligarchic regime, nor even to a republic'.[13] In 1548 Charles V gave his Netherlands territories a certain legal unity by separating them from the Holy Roman Empire, of which they had for centuries been only nominally a part: henceforth they were no longer subject to the imperial courts and took no part in the meetings of the imperial diet. In the next year he persuaded the states of each province to agree that after his death they would all continue to obey the same ruler. But each province retained to the full its feeling of separateness. In 1558 Philip II suffered a serious blow to his authority when, desperate for money, he was forced to agree that the subsidy he was demanding should be collected and administered by the individual provinces. Soon after, before he left for Spain, he had to consent to the withdrawal of Spanish troops from the Netherlands. He inherited, therefore, possessions in what are now Holland and Belgium which were rich but also recalcitrant; and the spread of heresy there greatly increased his difficulties.

Lutherans and a variety of more extreme dissident sects, notably Anabaptists, had already been active in the Netherlands for a generation or more and had suffered sporadic but sometimes very violent persecution. Now in the early 1560s the situation was being changed by the appearance of Calvinism, with its superior organization and power to appeal to the nobility and also to many magistrates and members of ruling urban oligarchies, an almost equally important group. The new creed became a political challenge more slowly than in France. But its growth was clear; and the cruelty with which Anabaptists, Mennonites and Lutherans had been treated for many years had already aroused much popular hostility.

Philip II and his ministers were not well placed to respond immediately to this new growth of heresy. The peace of 1559 was followed by a marked transfer of Spanish attention and resources to the Mediterranean and the struggle there with the Turks and their north African

13. H.G. Koenigsberger, 'Prince and states general: Charles V and the Netherlands', *Transactions of the Royal Historical Society* 6th series, 4 (1994), 144–5, 128.

satellites. Such a war was widely popular in Spain. It aroused religious passions in a way the conflict with France did not. When in 1555 the Spanish government announced its intention to recover Algiers, and also the minor port of Bougie, 100 miles to the east, which had just been lost, there was an outburst of popular enthusiasm. A considerable sum of money was raised by voluntary contributions and 8,000–10,000 men volunteered for the new campaign. This was in marked contrast to the resentment that had been aroused by the need to provide huge sums for the war with France in Italy and the Netherlands.[14] It proved far from easy to defeat the infidel. A Spanish army was badly beaten near Mostaganem, about 120 miles west of Algiers, in 1558. Two years later another suffered an even worse defeat on the island of Djerba, off the coast of Tunisia. Yet these setbacks did not halt the expenditure of resources on the war in the Mediterranean. Spain was now becoming, as never before and at very substantial cost, a serious naval power there. The Turkish siege of Malta in 1565, one of the decisive events of the sixteenth century,[15] saw the struggle reach a climax. After that Spain's position eased somewhat. Malta did not fall. In September 1566 Suleiman the Magnificent, after so many victories against Christian Europe, died. But in the early 1560s Philip II's Mediterranean preoccupations did a good deal to give Calvinism in The Netherlands, and resistance to what was seen as oppressive Spanish rule there, an elbow-room they would not otherwise have enjoyed. Those who, for whatever reason, wished to limit Spanish influence were well aware that the more difficult her position in the Mediterranean the less able she was to suppress dissent of any kind in the Netherlands provinces. The Count of Brederode, one of the leaders of resistance to Spanish control, did not hide his desire that the Turks 'were in Valladolid already': the connection between events on the northern and southern wings of Spain's empire in Europe was not lost on many contemporaries.[16]

Philip sincerely wished to reform and strengthen the Catholic Church in The Netherlands, where it had a well-deserved reputation for slackness and corruption: Charles V had in 1551–52 proposed far-reaching changes in the ecclesiastical establishment there, though with little practical result. Philip in his turn pressed from 1561 onwards a plan for the creation of fourteen new bishoprics which would

---

14. M.J. Rodriguez-Salgado, *The Changing Face of Empire: Charles V, Philip II and Habsburg Authority* (Cambridge, 1988), p. 271.

15. See below, p. 242.

16. G. Parker, 'The Dutch revolt and the polarization of international politics', in G. Parker and L.M. Smith, eds, *The General Crisis of the Sixteenth Century* (London, 1978), p. 59.

have done much to improve its very defective organization. But this threatened so many vested interests that it aroused widespread opposition. Many nobles, who saw in church reform the end of opportunities to provide suitable and lucrative posts for their younger sons, opposed the proposal hotly, while it also seemed to foreshadow still more foreign interference in the life of the Netherlands provinces. The controversy therefore helped to create a climate favourable to the growth of Calvinism. At least equally important, Philip's regent in the Netherlands, his half-sister Margaret, the widowed Duchess of Parma, was crippled by the almost hopeless financial situation. The state debt, which as recently as 1550 had been only 500,000 florins, had reached a crushing ten million by 1565. The interest on this, together with administrative costs, amounted to a good deal more than the ordinary revenue, so that the government was now running a deficit of about 500,000 florins a year,[17] while Philip's Mediterranean commitments set strict limits to any help that could be sent from Spain.

No government in this position could be anything but weak. Soldiers and officials could not be paid; and the regent was forced into appeals for help from the provincial estates which undermined her position still further. As everywhere in Europe, effective opposition could be led only by great nobles; and a group of these, notably William, Prince of Orange, and the Counts of Egmont and Hoorn, though still completely loyal to Philip, was now at the head of resistance to what they saw as oppressive Spanish rule. In 1564 they won an important victory when they forced the retirement of Cardinal Granvelle, Margaret of Parma's able but very unpopular chief minister (he had also powerful enemies at the Spanish court who at the end of 1563 were in the ascendant there). That Philip was willing to accept this reflected his urgent need to keep the peace while he was still so heavily committed in the Mediterranean. In May 1566 he even agreed to moderate the very severe laws against heresy in the Netherlands because of his continuing concern with the struggle against the Turks.

The Mediterranean was to remain a major Spanish preoccupation for a decade to come. But by 1566–67 it was possible for a greater share of Spain's resources to be devoted to the increasingly threatening situation in the Netherlands. The death of Sultan Suleiman was followed by the provincial unrest and military mutinies which the disappearance of any Ottoman ruler normally provoked. The flow of silver

17. G. Parker, 'Spain, her enemies and the revolt of the Netherlands', *Past and Present* 49 (Nov. 1970), 75.

from America to Spain was growing. Simultaneously the need for action in the north seemed to become more urgent. In August 1566 violent rioting broke out in many Netherlands towns. In Antwerp, Ghent and other cities mobs invaded churches and smashed images, altars and all the trappings of 'superstition' that good Calvinists so detested. This spectacular orgy of destruction was set off largely by economic stress. High food prices, unemployment, falling wages, interruptions to the normal course of trade (the staple for English trade had been moved in 1564 from Antwerp to Emden) meant that large numbers of unskilled workers were responsive to Calvinist preachers attacking what they saw as idolatry. Open-air services in Antwerp are said to have attracted audiences of 20,000–25,000 just before the riots began. This outbreak of image-breaking was the work of a minority; but there was little effective resistance to it and it could well be seen as not merely a display of heretical religious beliefs but also a warning of the political dangers such heresy inevitably brought with it.

The result was Philip's decision, in spite of the doubts of some of his ministers and even the pope, and against the advice of Margaret of Parma, to send a large army under the Duke of Alba to the Netherlands to crush heresy and reduce the fractious provinces to obedience. The repercussions of his decision were great. Spain (again in effect Castile) had now embarked on a struggle that was to last, at immense cost, for 80 years. For decades to come the finest army in Europe was to be tied down in a great and finally unsuccessful effort to assert Spanish authority in the Netherlands. The central focus of Spain's military effort had now moved decisively to northern Europe. The long struggle in Italy had ended in 1559. That in the Mediterranean was by the end of the 1570s to lose most of its importance. But that in the Netherlands was to grow more demanding and difficult as the years went on. It was also to become more and more intertwined with events in France and the policies of England, and thus to play a central part in the whole structure of international relations. Such possibilities were clearly to be seen from the beginning. The march of Alba's army from Milan to the Netherlands at once aroused widespread alarm. There were fears that it might attack Geneva, while the Duchess of Lorraine, regent for her young son, took steps to defend the duchy against possible Spanish invasion. In France Charles IX and his ministers were so uneasy that Condé and Guise were both asked to advise on defensive measures.

Alba reached Brussels in August 1567. He had been reluctant to accept the governorship of the Netherlands, for he was in poor health and well aware that his absence from Spain would give a freer hand to his enemies and rivals there. Moreover, even before his arrival the unrest of the previous year was under control and open Calvinist worship at an end. None the less he at once began a policy of terror, in effect superseding the comparatively moderate Margaret of Parma. Egmont and Hoorn were arrested: Orange had already fled abroad. The newly formed Council of Troubles, soon to be known as the Council of Blood, began a savage repression of heresy. A sustained attempt was made to subject the provinces to a central control far more effective than any seen before. Side by side with this went an effort sharply to increase taxation and thus give the central administration the money without which it could not function effectively. This repressive and authoritarian policy brought results. Twelve thousand of those alleged to have taken part in the riots of 1566 were tried by the Council of Troubles; and it became clear that, as in France, of those who felt some sympathy with religious dissent only a small minority would stick to their beliefs in the face of genuine persecution. The yield of taxation was substantially increased: it rose from 750,000 ducats in the two years 1566–67 to 4.4 million in 1570–71.[18] But Alba's efforts to impose a 10 per cent tax on the import, export and sale of all goods aroused furious and successful opposition. This meant that the Netherlands, in spite of their relative wealth, would not pay the cost of maintaining there a large Spanish army. Henceforth, for decade after decade, the struggle to subdue them was to be a huge and eventually crushing drain on Spanish resources.

More even than its cruelty it was the readiness of the new regime to disregard traditional rights of all kinds that aroused resentment. When the president of the Council of Troubles, a Spaniard, told the Netherlanders that 'Non curamus privilegios vostros' (We are not concerned with your privileges) he epitomized the attitude which more than anything else aroused opposition. Sir Walter Raleigh, observing the situation from England later in the century, had no doubt that the resistance of his subjects to Philip was justified, since the king meant to 'Turklike . . . tread under his feet all their national and fundamental laws, privileges and ancient rights'.[19] One thing might have saved the situation – the presence of Philip himself and his personal mediation of some acceptable settlement. Society everywhere was still

18. G. Parker, *Philip II* (London, 1979), p. 97. There is a good account of the establishment of Alba's regime in the Netherlands and the growth of resistance to it in W.S. Maltby, *A Biography of Fernando Alvarez de Toledo, Third Duke of Alba, 1507–1582* (Berkeley/Los Angeles/London, 1983), pp. 143–58.

19. C. Wilson, *Queen Elizabeth and the Revolt of The Netherlands* (London, 1970), p. 16.

very much a face-to-face one. No subordinate, however sympathetic and tactful (and Alba was very far from being either) could be an adequate substitute for the monarch in person. Philip seems to have thought seriously about going to the Netherlands in the autumn of 1567; and considerable preparations for such a visit were made. He did not do so, partly because Alba advised against it. Moreover the death in July 1568 of his only son, Don Carlos, left him without a male heir and meant that a journey to the Netherlands by sea was now an unacceptable risk. Finally a serious revolt of the Moriscos, the formerly Muslim population of Granada forcibly and superficially converted to Christianity, which broke out at the end of 1568 and lasted until the summer of 1571, made it certain that the king would not leave Spain. But his failure to take the initiative in this way had serious implications. More than any other decision he took it symbolized the fact that his empire was now increasingly a Castilian-dominated one ruled by a monarch who left Castile rarely and with reluctance.

In 1568 came the first organized attempt at resistance to Spanish rule, when in October William of Orange invaded Brabant from his brother's little German principality of Nassau with a force of German mercenaries. The military failure was complete: Alba's army was superior in numbers and still more in quality to anything that could be brought against it. Louis of Nassau, Orange's brother, was overwhelmingly defeated at Jemmingen, which ended any prospect of support from England or the German Protestant princes. The invasion of Brabant was a total failure. But events in the Netherlands had now taken on an international importance that they were never to lose. Orange was neither a religious nor a political radical. He had Lutheran connections, since in 1561 he had married into the ruling family of electoral Saxony; but he disliked Calvinist intolerance and did not become a Calvinist until 1573. He was the wealthiest of all the Netherlands nobles, with a palace in Brussels and a fine country seat at Breda, as well as ruler in his own right of the independent principality of Orange in France, on the river Rhône. He could therefore see his struggle with Philip II as one between two sovereign princes. He had been a loyal supporter of the Habsburgs and a favourite of Charles V: the gouty old emperor had leant on him for support when he entered the hall in which he announced his abdication in Brussels in 1555. He had been one of the Spanish plenipotentiaries in the Cateau-Cambrésis peace negotiations, while Philip II had made him a member of the great chivalric order of the Golden Fleece and stadtholder of Holland, Zeeland and Utrecht. He saw himself as driven to

rebellion by an attack on the rights and liberties not merely of the nobility but of the whole of Netherlands society, as well as by the religious intolerance which he so much disliked. But once embarked on
the struggle he was well aware that Spain must be opposed on an international rather than a purely local scale. Already there had been
some contacts between the Netherlands rebels and the Huguenots in
France: from now on events in the two countries were to be closely
linked. Also he already had an agent in Constantinople attempting to
stir up the Ottoman government to attack Spain, though this was a
vain hope: for a generation to come Spain's enemies intermittently
dreamed of using the Turks as a weapon against her, but these
schemes never bore fruit.

But the interest aroused in England by events in the Netherlands,
on the other hand, had, like that in France, both immediate and lasting importance. The essential objective of Elizabeth and her ministers was simple. They wanted above all to prevent these provinces, so
close to England and so threatening in unfriendly hands, from falling
under the control of France, the great enemy. They wished, therefore, to maintain Spanish rule there, and with it Spain's obligation to
defend the Netherlands against French attack. This rule, however,
was not to be so complete that Spain became overwhelmingly powerful and perhaps herself a threat to England. Elizabeth disliked the
presence of a large Spanish army in the Netherlands; but she feared
the presence of a French one. A return to the situation that had
existed under Charles V, in other words, suited England well; and towards this English policy was directed until the end of the century.

Elizabeth showed, however, that she was now ready on occasion to
give serious offence to Spain. In December 1568 five ships carrying
£85,000 in cash meant to pay Alba's men took refuge in harbours on
the English south coast to escape from bad weather and the Huguenot privateers who were already very active in the Bay of Biscay and
the Channel. The queen, after some delay, seized the money, arguing that most of it was still the property of the Genoese bankers
who had lent it to Philip, not of the king himself. Alba retaliated by
seizing English property in the Netherlands, to which Elizabeth replied by doing the same to Spanish goods in England. Though it had
been agreed by the end of 1569 that she should retain the Genoese
money as a loan, normal trading relations were not restored until
May 1573. The crisis was not of great importance in itself. It may well
have been that the seizure of the treasure-ships was a mistake, 'an episode as costly as it was senseless', since the customs revenue lost
through the interruption of trade with the Netherlands, and the cost

of the military precautions that had to be taken in England, amounted to more than the money that was impounded.[20] But the loss added significantly to Alba's difficulties: indeed, the seizure may have been meant in part to have this effect. Moreover, the incident showed that problems of communication between Spain and her recalcitrant provinces were to pose considerable problems for her in the future. As the sea route became more threatened and vulnerable she was forced to rely increasingly on the 'Spanish Road' which ran from Milan across the Alps and through Franche-Comté and the Rhineland to the southern Netherlands. Its protection was now one of her major preoccupations and an important complication of her whole international position.

By the end of the 1560s, therefore, the situation over much of western Europe was tense and complex, with religious, political and strategic factors intermingled and reacting on each other. France was more and more paralysed by bitter internal dissension. The Netherlands were full of discontent. The position of Spain, clearly the greatest power in Christendom, was very impressive; but the calls on her resources were great and likely to grow. The stage was set for the explosive conflicts of the next three decades.

The Netherlands revolt takes root

A continuous armed struggle against Spanish rule in the Netherlands began in April 1572. In that month the minor port of Brill in Holland was captured by determined opponents of Alba's regime operating from ports in south-east England. These 'Sea Beggars' (*Gueux de Mer*) had been active for some time as privateers, often indistinguishable from pirates; and they were passionately Calvinist. It at once became clear that in some parts of the Netherlands at least they had touched off deep anti-Spanish feeling. Within ten days of the taking of Brill several towns in Holland were in revolt against Spanish rule. Nevertheless it seemed likely that the rebellion would be swiftly crushed. Elizabeth, true to her view of English interests, wished to remain on at least reasonably good terms with Philip II. Even though the Spanish ambassador in London, de Spes, had been expelled in the previous year because of his involvement in a serious Catholic plot against her, she hoped that he might be replaced by a more discreet and tactful successor and that relations would not be broken off. She

20. Ibid., pp. 24–6.

had been trying to get rid of the Sea Beggars since at least June 1571 and was glad to see them leave England. William of Orange, for his part, was taken by surprise by the capture of Brill. He was also annoyed, since he was planning a new invasion from Germany, that he had been given no opportunity to work in concert with its captors, whose intolerant Calvinism he in any case disliked.

Alba's reaction was swift and ruthless. He had first to deal with a potentially serious crisis when in May 1572 Louis of Nassau captured Mons, only a few miles from the French frontier. For a moment this seemed to open the possibility that the Huguenots, with Coligny now apparently a dominant figure in Paris, might launch a full-scale invasion of the southern Netherlands. But the massacre of St Bartholomew put paid to any such possibility,[21] a small Huguenot force sent to raise the siege of Mons which Alba had begun was easily routed, and Orange's effort at invasion from Germany also collapsed. The way was now open to regain what had been lost in Holland. But there the active and determined Calvinist minority, in spite of its small numbers, was gaining ground. In July 1572 the states of Holland recognized Orange as governor of the province: ostensibly he was still acting in the name of Philip II, but in fact a considerable rebellion was now under way. In 1572–3 Alba won some significant successes, yet the revolt was not crushed. Holland was difficult to conquer because of the rivers that intersected it and the low-lying and often waterlogged country, some of which could be easily flooded as a defensive measure by breaching the dykes that held back the sea. Zeeland, the other province to which the rebellion had spread, was made up largely of islands and was even more difficult to subdue. Some of the rebel towns also held out with heroic stubbornness: the seven-month siege of Haarlem in 1572–73, or later the nine months it took to capture even the small town of Zierikzee in 1575–76, were crushingly expensive. The struggle was becoming increasingly bitter; and this bitterness had more than ever a specifically though by no means entirely religious tone. Clergy on both sides became particular targets: the Spaniards hanged Calvinist ministers and elders, while the Sea Beggars killed monks, priests and nuns.

At the end of 1573 Alba at last obtained the recall he had been seeking for some time: six years of extreme harshness had ended in failure and even Philip II was pressing for the abandonment of the Tenth Penny sales tax and the issue of some form of general pardon. Alba's successor, Luis de Requesens, at once took a milder and more

21. See below, p. 166.

conciliatory attitude: a former governor of Milan, in poor health and without clear instructions from Madrid, he had done his best to avoid taking up what would clearly be a very difficult post. Conciliation was demanded not merely by the strength of the rebel resistance but even more by Philip's growing financial difficulties. He was still fighting on a large scale in the Mediterranean. The alliance with Venice and the papacy made in May 1571 had won the great victory of Lepanto only five months later; but it could prevent neither the final Turkish conquest of Cyprus in the same year nor the loss of Tunis in 1574. During these years, therefore, Spain was spending heavily in two major theatres of war; and the burden was becoming too heavy to bear. In April 1574 Philip's chief financial adviser calculated that his total liabilities amounted to almost fourteen times his annual revenue. Government bankruptcy was imminent. Inevitably this lack of money made it much more difficult to sustain a large-scale offensive in the Netherlands, where unsuccessful sieges of Alkmaar and Leyden added to the drain on Philip's resources. Another force raised in Germany to support the rebels was crushingly defeated at Mook in April 1574; but any effect this might have had was lost when almost at once the Spanish troops mutinied for lack of pay.

The international significance of the revolt grew in 1572–73. Foreign help for the rebels was urgently needed, for apart from their military inferiority their financial difficulties were at least as great as those of Philip II and they had no German or Genoese bankers from whom they could borrow. In June 1573 Orange offered to hand over Holland and Zeeland to Elizabeth if she would head an anti-Spanish alliance embracing England, the rebel provinces and the Protestant states of Germany. This had no effect. The queen was still far from being fundamentally hostile to Spain, while she was temperamentally very unsympathetic to both Calvinists and rebels, especially when the latter were merchants and even artisans, as most of the Dutch ones were. Her predominant emotion was still fear of French influence, so that when in 1572 the Sea Beggars captured Flushing, which commanded the main sea approach to Antwerp, an English force was sent to occupy it and guard against the danger of its falling under French control. Insofar as Elizabeth was willing, reluctantly, to help Orange, it was merely because he seemed a lesser evil than either France or Spain. Charles IX in Paris, however, was a more promising source of help; for however many Huguenots might die in the massacres of 1572,[22] France's policy was still at bottom strongly anti-Spanish. In

22. See below, p. 165.

1573 Orange began to receive French money to encourage continued resistance while help from the Turks was sought once more. In
1574 he sent an envoy to Constantinople, while the French ambassador there tried to revive Franco-Ottoman cooperation against Spain.

None of this was of much practical importance. Charles IX died in
May 1574; and the Turks had only limited interest in half-understood
events in the distant Netherlands. The Spanish government bankruptcy of September 1575, however, when Philip had to suspend payment on his debts, had far greater significance. It completely
undermined Spain's position in the Netherlands (as Requesens had
warned that it would). This was, in terms of its political results, the
most serious financial crisis of Philip's reign because it was unexpectedly prolonged. The king could not reach an agreement with the
mainly Genoese bankers to whom he was in debt until December
1577. This meant that for more than two years he was almost completely hamstrung, outside his Spanish kingdoms, by lack of money.
Once more the sequence of financial difficulty, unpaid soldiers and
resulting mutiny, with uncontrollable political consequences, came
into play. The death of Requesens in March 1576 made an already
bad situation even worse. By the autumn of that year it seemed that
Spanish authority over all the provinces, loyal as well as rebel, might
well collapse. From a paper strength of 60,000 the army there had
now shrunk to an effective one of only 8,000.

Worse was soon to come. Early in November mutinous Spanish
troops seized Antwerp, the wealthiest city in Europe, looting and
plundering and killing more than 7,000 of its inhabitants. This 'Spanish Fury' was the most destructive incident of its kind of the whole sixteenth century. Like the devastation of Rome by Charles V's soldiers
half a century earlier it made a deep impression all over Europe. It
also helped to produce a union of the Netherlands provinces which,
though fragile from the beginning, seemed for a time to have destroyed Spanish authority. Even before the mutinous soldiers entered Antwerp Orange and the moderates, led by the Duke of
Aerschot, who were now in the ascendant in the southern provinces,
had come to a compromise agreement. This Pacification of Ghent
provided that all foreign troops should leave The Netherlands and
that any future changes in their government should be made only
with the consent of the states-general. The edicts against heresy were
to be withdrawn and a future states- general was to settle the religious
question.

This settlement with its promise of a united front of all the provinces against Spain was short-lived. Don John of Austria, Philip's half-

brother and the new governor-general, came to the Netherlands with the prestige of the victor of Lepanto. But he lacked money, soldiers and even support from Madrid; and he was no politician or diplomat. However, among the rebels growing differences between Calvinists and Catholics soon showed themselves. In the great cities of Flanders and Brabant also there was acute tension between radical popular movements strongly influenced by Calvinist preaching and Catholic conservatives. All this, coupled with personal rivalries between Orange and the Catholic magnates of the southern provinces, meant that united opposition to Spanish rule was impossible to maintain. When in July 1577 Don John seized Namur this showed that a Spanish campaign of reconquest was in prospect: in January 1578 he won a decisive victory at Gembloux over the forces of the states- general. Many of the moderate Catholic nobles then began to return to their Spanish allegiance. In January 1579 they formed the Union of Arras, which a few months later made an agreement with Philip II restoring Spanish rule in the southern provinces. Simultaneously the seven northern ones, headed by Holland, much the richest and most important, formed their own Union of Utrecht.

The events of 1576–79 were a turning-point in the history of the Netherlands. They opened a rift between north and south which was to harden as time went on and rapidly become unbridgeable. The Union of Utrecht, indeed, was a very loosely worded document, an alliance and not a constitution. It did not specify the membership of the union and created no common institutions, while many of its clauses never took effect. None the less the division of 1579 was final. More and more Calvinism came to dominate in the rebel provinces, even though a high proportion of their inhabitants still clung to the old faith: Amsterdam itself was officially Calvinist only from 1578 onwards, while even two generations later perhaps two-fifths of the whole population of the northern provinces was still Catholic. Orange, who still hoped for some general union of all the Netherlands, for this reason disliked the incomplete and divisive one of 1579.

But it was now clear beyond doubt that Spain had embarked on a difficult and costly struggle with very far-reaching repercussions on her international position. France, divided and weakened as she was, might still be able to use it to strike at her traditional enemy. England, in spite of the hesitations and indecision of Elizabeth, might well be induced or driven to play an active part in it. Spain's international position at the end of the 1570s was still very strong. Philip II's finances improved in the years after 1577. His final agreement with his bankers, and the feeling that they would in the end always back him, may have had an important influence in persuading him to carry on the struggle in the Netherlands.[23] There were still great banking houses, whether old like the Fuggers or new like the Spinolas in Genoa and the Ruiz in Castile, with relatively plentiful capital to lend at relatively low rates. The trend of silver imports from America was upward. The struggle with the Turks in the Mediterranean, which from Philip's point of view in the 1560s and early 1570s had been at least as important as events in the Netherlands, was now losing most of its former significance: the fact that there was no great Turkish offensive in the very difficult years 1575–77 was an important stroke of luck. In northern and western Europe, therefore, Philip's hands were now freer than in the past. The acquisition of Portugal and its overseas empire, the greatest achievement of his reign, was now imminent. The 1570s had seen severe setbacks for Spain in the Netherlands; but her power was still growing.

France nullified by civil war

The flimsy peace embodied in the St Germain settlement of August 1570 had little hope of lasting long. The Huguenots had suffered serious military defeats, yet now, provided with their 'places of surety', they seemed to threaten the creation of a state within the state. Popular religious hatreds were stronger than ever, and at least as much tied up with the factional rivalries given play by the weakness of the young Charles IX. Even more important, the struggles within France were more than ever becoming part of a wider European conflict. Contacts between the Huguenots and the Dutch rebels had been developing for several years. Coligny in particular was in contact with some of the rebel leaders, notably Louis of Nassau. Already in 1568 he, with Condé and other leading Huguenots, had made with William of Orange an agreement for mutual defence and assistance, while the Huguenot stronghold of La Rochelle, on France's western coast, was used extensively by the Sea Beggars before their successes in Holland and Zeeland in 1572. Joint action against Spain had attractions for the more radical religious reformers in both France and the Netherlands; and in England and some parts of Germany there were increasingly those who sympathized, though ineffectively, with the idea of a wide-ranging anti-Catholic alliance which might bring

23. A. Lovett, 'The General Settlement of 1577: an aspect of Spanish finance in the early modern period', *Historical Journal* XXV (1982), 21–2.

England, the Protestant German states and perhaps Denmark into active support of the Protestant cause.

The French government, however, was inevitably guided by political rather than religious considerations. Catherine de Medici struggled as she had done for the last decade to defuse religious intolerance and factional ambitions. Her whole life was to be dominated by an unavailing effort to ward off the civil war and anarchy that threatened to engulf France. In August 1572, after long negotiations, she succeeded in marrying her daughter, Marguerite, to the young Henry of Navarre, son of the Antoine de Bourbon who had played an inglorious role in the conflicts of the 1560s. Now head of the Bourbon branch of the royal family, he stood high in the line of succession to the throne: if none of Catherine's sons produced a male heir he would have a strong claim to become king of France. Moreover, he was a Huguenot, though not an ardent or devout one. The marriage, which Catherine hoped would be a step towards internal peace, could thus be seen as a confirmation of continuing Huguenot strength. More important, and a greater source of resentment and bad feeling, was the reappearance of Coligny as a leading force in the making of policy. His return to court and to membership of the royal council in September 1571 intensified the hatred with which the Guise faction now regarded him.

He soon gained an ascendancy over the young and impressionable Charles IX. This he used to urge on the king an escape from France's deep internal problems by a new war with Spain, which would centre on an attack by France in the Netherlands. The idea was not new. Louis of Nassau had already urged it in two interviews with the king and his mother in July 1571. But it now assumed a new importance, as by the spring of 1572 the situation appeared to be moving in favour of such an attack. The successes of the Sea Beggars were likely to tie down much of Alba's army in difficult and expensive sieges; while in Brabant the capture of Mons by Louis of Nassau, though the success was very transitory, also seemed to show that Spain's position was vulnerable to French attack.

But there were other considerations which told heavily against so risky a step. Elizabeth, though she signed a defensive alliance with France in April 1572, a sharp though short-lived reversal of traditional English policy, was as hostile as ever to any growth of French power or influence in the Netherlands. The German Protestant princes were unwilling to give any support. The French ambassador in Constantinople warned that no help could be expected from the Turks. Charles IX was impressed by the strength of Coligny's personality. He was also attracted by the general idea of a war which would give France relief from the disruptive forces that threatened her and himself the personal prestige so avidly sought by every ruler of that age. He had already contemplated intervening in Italy in support of the Grand Duke of Tuscany, Cosimo di Medici, whose acquisition of this new title had angered Philip II. How far he was ever completely won over to the policy urged by Coligny is less certain. War with Spain was opposed by several other members of the royal council as well as by his mother. It was also certain to be opposed by a good deal of Catholic feeling in France, while Spanish military power was as formidable as ever. Moreover, the Guise hatred of Coligny was now backed by the queen mother's growing alarm at his influence over her son.

The result was the most spectacular episode of the 'wars of religion'. In August 1572 there was an unprecedented assembly of Huguenot nobles and gentlemen in Paris for the forthcoming marriage of Henry of Navarre and Marguerite de Valois. The city was already intensely Catholic in feeling: from now on it was to be the greatest stronghold of the old religion in France. In December 1571 there had been serious mob attacks on Huguenots and apparently a plan to besiege Coligny in his house. These had forced Montmorency, the governor of Paris, to enter the city with a considerable force of cavalry to restore order; and the situation remained dangerously explosive. By the eve of the Bourbon–Valois marriage Catherine had decided that Coligny was too dangerous to be allowed to live. His personal influence was threatening and the policy he was urging potentially disastrous. Quick action was essential. Coligny was clearly on the point of marching for the Netherlands; and if he did it might be very difficult for Charles IX to disavow him. The Guises and their supporters were more than ready to see that he did not escape. On 22 August an attempt to assassinate him failed and thus heightened still further the atmosphere of tension. On the night of the 23rd–24th the great massacre took place. In a few hours, and on a smaller scale in the days following, perhaps 3,000 people were slaughtered in Paris: Coligny himself was killed with particular ferocity. This was followed by still greater bloodshed in many provincial towns which went on until early October and in which the death-toll may have reached 8,000.

Neither Catherine, who had persuaded the king to assent to the massacre, nor the members of the council who had agreed to it, had meant the killing to be on such a scale. Selective assassination rather than wholesale slaughter was what they had envisaged; and in his instructions to provincial governors Charles tried to prevent the spread of the massacres. But they had significant effects. The Huguenots were deprived of their most important leader. Henry of Navarre, who was for a time in real personal danger, abjured the reformed faith, wrote a letter asking the forgiveness of the pope and re-established Catholicism in his hereditary territory of Béarn. A month after the killings he was formally readmitted into the Catholic Church. To the body of moderate French Catholic opinion that was now emerging, the *politiques*, anxious for a compromise which might reassert some degree of national unity, the massacres were deeply unwelcome. Catherine de Medici now found herself unable to hold the balance between the Huguenots, inevitably alienated, and the Guise faction, and was forced into *de facto* alliance with the latter.

More fundamental, however, were the long-term results. The Huguenots had by no means been destroyed as a military force. But the events of 1572 struck a mortal blow at their position in much of France. The massacres were followed in the northern half of the country by large-scale abjurations of the reformed faith as well as by a considerable Calvinist emigration. In Troyes, about 100 miles southeast of Paris, for example, frightened Huguenot parents hastened to have their children rebaptized as Catholics; and this was a widespread reaction. The effect of these crucial weeks was never to be undone. 'By the close of 1572', a recent study concludes, 'the Calvinist struggle to establish its churches on a sure footing in northern France was all but over.'[24] In parts of the south and west the reformed religion was still strong; and in the years that followed, as the grip of the central government became more feeble, the areas of Huguenot strength became more autonomous. But the triumphal years of the early 1560s, when briefly Calvinism seemed on the point of carrying all before it, were irrevocably in the past. The Huguenots would now never be more than a minority in France: by the end of the century they amounted to less than a tenth of the population.

In Europe generally events as spectacular as those of 1572 could only sharpen religious tensions. In Spain Philip II welcomed the blow struck for Catholicism in France. In Rome a special commemorative medal was struck for the pope, Gregory XIII: it seems likely that he was strengthened in a conviction that violence against heresy was not merely justified but also the most effective way of combating it. Among Protestants, inevitably, the result was to intensify anti-Catholic

---

24. Penny Roberts, 'Calvinists in Troyes, 1562–1572: the legacy of Vassy and the background to St Bartholomew', in A. Pettegree, A. Duke and Gillian Lewis, eds, *Calvinism in Europe, 1540–1620* (Cambridge, 1994), p. 118.

feeling and feed fears of a reconquest of the areas earlier lost to the reformed churches.[25] Yet it was as true as ever that no ruler could shape policy merely in terms of religious allegiances or preferences. A France pacified and united, and thus dangerously strengthened, however Catholic, could never be really welcome to Philip II. In London Elizabeth disliked as much as ever the un-monarchical and even un-aristocratic new state which was beginning to be born in the northern Netherlands; and she had a well-founded distrust of crusading ideological impulses in international relations. By October 1572 she had agreed to be godmother to a newly born Valois princess, and by Christmas the French ambassador was once more in good standing at her court.

In France another burst of indecisive fighting was now unavoidable. It centred on a long siege of La Rochelle, which ended in an agreement of June 1573. This conceded liberty of conscience to the Huguenots but restricted their right to the public practice of their religion to La Rochelle, Nîmes, Montauban and the households of the greater nobles. But more and more in these struggles religious feeling, in some ways more powerful than ever, was being complicated by local rivalries and factional and individual ambitions. As the situation became more chaotic the grip of the central government relaxed still further. Henry III, who succeeded his brother Charles IX in June 1574, found himself in an impossible situation which raised more and more dangerous possibilities of foreign intervention. In 1575 the Elector Palatine and his son, John Casimir, forced Condé to promise them a lifetime grant of Metz, Toul and Verdun in return for their help in a new bout of fighting. This showed once more, as Elizabeth's effort to recover Calais in 1562–63 had already done, how civil war could threaten France with serious losses of territory. John Casimir led a large army into eastern France in the spring of the next year; and though he did not gain possession of the three bishoprics he was able to extort from Henry III a large lump sum to pay his army as well as a pension for himself.

The agreement that ended this latest burst of fighting, the so-called 'Peace of Monsieur' (so named because the Duc d'Alençon, the youngest son of Catherine de Medici, played a leading role in its negotiation), gave the Huguenots greater concessions than any earlier settlement of the kind. They were to be free to worship everywhere except in Paris and at court. They were to have eight 'places of

25. On the reaction in England and the Protestant parts of Germany see A. Soman, ed., *The Massacre of St Bartholomew: Reappraisals and Documents* (The Hague, 1974), pp. 52–70, 78–83.

surety', twice as many as conceded in 1570. In each *parlement* cases involving them were to be decided by a commission including members from both faiths. This peace was therefore the most serious effort hitherto to end the 'wars of religion' in France by compromise. It saw *politique* influence at its height and embodied the central *politique* idea – the preservation of essential political unity by some sacrifice, however reluctant, of religious uniformity. The fact that it coincided with the Pacification of Ghent meant that the year 1576 saw a unique though fruitless effort to pacify both the great areas of conflict in western Europe.

There were important differences between the two. In the Netherlands the driving force was resistance to effective Spanish rule or the threat of it. In France there was no comparable foreign dominance to resent, with the unifying results that such a feeling might bring. In the Netherlands the settlement broke down above all because of the refusal of Philip II to contemplate any concession on the religious issue, whereas in France neither Catherine de Medici nor Henry III showed the same intransigeance. But there were also some considerable similarities. William of Orange, with his determination that the Dutch revolt must not become an intolerant Calvinist crusade, can be seen as the supreme *politique*. In both France and the Netherlands the cause of compromise was undermined by deep-seated noble rivalries – in France those centring on the Guise family and its ambitions, in the Netherlands the resentment of Orange's influence felt by great Walloon nobles such as the Duke of Aerschot.

The collapse in 1578–79 of the effort to construct a loosely united but essentially autonomous Netherlands, and thus end the fighting there, was paralleled by the rapid breakdown of the peace of 1576 in France. Catholic distrust of a monarchy apparently dangerously ready to compromise with heresy meant the emergence from the later 1570s onwards of a powerful Catholic League, formed from a number of already existing Catholic unions and looking to the Guise family for leadership and to Spain for material backing. For two decades to come this was to be the major force making for tenacious and finally desperate Catholic resistance to any strengthening of the Huguenot position. Its deep distrust of Henry III, whom it saw as an unmilitary and even treacherous dilettante, meant that extreme Catholicism now offered a more serious threat to the monarchy than the Huguenots did. As the Guises and their allies made the provinces where they were strong, such as Champagne and Burgundy, into something like autonomous republics, and a similar process was seen in the Huguenot-controlled southern areas, the effective authority of

Henry III, unpopular and always short of money, became more and more circumscribed. In Paris he was even refused entrance to the cathedral of Notre Dame. France, under Francis I and Henry II the only effective counterbalance to Spanish power, was now more than ever unable to hold in check her great traditional rival.

By 1580, therefore, it was clear that Spain was committed to a renewed effort to regain the lost parts of the Netherlands and stamp out the revolt there. At the same time the intensifying disorder in France and the growing readiness of the more extreme Catholics there to look to Spain for support opened possibilities of Spanish influence and perhaps armed intervention. The power of Philip II was reaching its zenith, though the calls upon it were soon to become greater than ever.

Spanish greatness at its height: the conquest of Portugal

The union of Castile and Aragon in 1469 led naturally to the idea that the entire Iberian peninsula might be made at least a dynastic whole by a similar union with Portugal. The connections between the Spanish Habsburgs and the Portuguese royal family were close: Philip II's mother and first wife were both Portuguese princesses. In other ways, too, there were important Spanish–Portuguese links. Ruy Gomez de Silva, Prince of Eboli, one of the most influential of Philip's advisers during the first two decades of his reign, was Portuguese, while the trade of Lisbon came increasingly to depend on supplies of silver from Spanish America which paid for Portuguese imports of spices from Asia and Indonesia. In 1578 a union, with the increase in the already great power of Spain that it implied, suddenly became an imminent probability. The young King Sebastian of Portugal, Philip's nephew, was strikingly lacking in any sense of reality. Throughout his reign he was dominated by the dream of a crusade in Morocco which would wrest it from Islam and place it under Christian rule. In June 1578 he began an effort to realize the dream, an enterprise in which the whole of Portugal participated and which dangerously strained its limited resources. It was clear from the beginning to observers more level-headed than the king that this was a reckless gamble. Philip himself tried in vain to dissuade his nephew from embarking on it; and these forebodings were very soon shown to be all too well justified. In August the Portuguese army was destroyed at the battle of Alcazar-el-Kebir, one of the most crushing military victories of the sixteenth century. Eight thousand men, including the king, were killed on the Portuguese side and 15,000 taken prisoner.

The blow to Portugal was devastating, not merely in material terms (many Portuguese nobles were among the dead, while many others had been taken prisoner and were in severe financial difficulties because of the ransoms needed to buy their freedom) but also in terms of national morale. The disaster also raised in an acute form the question of the succession to the Portuguese throne. Sebastian was succeeded by his great-uncle Henry. But he was a cardinal and almost 70 years old. He was unlikely to live long and certain to leave no heir (though he considered obtaining a papal dispensation to leave the church and marry). Philip II had, through his mother, a good claim to succeed when Henry died. But he would face opposition both within Portugal and from England and France, which were certain to be alarmed by any addition to his already great resources.

Nevertheless Philip's international position was now stronger than at any time since his accession. The flow of silver from America was now greater than ever before: in the 1580s and 1590s he was able to spend on armies, fleets and support to potential or actual allies on a scale never hitherto approached. In the Netherlands his forces, under a new and very able commander, were making headway, if slowly and at high cost. Most important of all, the long struggle with the Ottoman Empire, which had for the last two decades absorbed so much of his resources, was receding to the fringes of international affairs. Negotiations for a treaty between the two old enemies had begun in 1577; and in the summer of the next year the Turks began a long and difficult struggle with the Safavid rulers of Persia. The result was a Spanish–Turkish truce agreed in March 1580. No formal peace was possible: on both sides tradition and ingrained religious hostility were too strong for that. But the conflict between the two great powers that had reached a climax only a few years earlier now died away with remarkable suddenness. Philip could therefore act in Portugal with a freedom otherwise impossible.

There was significant resistance to the union with Spain. Most of the Portuguese nobility and the higher ranks of the clergy supported Philip's claim to the throne, sometimes encouraged in this attitude by bribery. There was, however, marked popular hostility to Castile, which was shared by the bulk of the Portuguese church. Of the other pretenders to the succession the most important was the Prior of Crato, Antonio, the illegitimate cousin of the dead Sebastian. The death of King Henry in January 1580 made him the leader of resistance to Castilian influence; and it was clear that a considerable military effort would be needed to overcome this and make good Philip's claim. At the end of June a large Spanish army commanded by the Duke of Alba, who had now been partly restored to favour after his failure in the Netherlands, crossed the frontier. Resistance was fierce; but the Spanish forces were far superior and Alba conducted this, his last campaign, with great ability. By the end of October the conquest was complete: the Prior of Crato left Portugal for France in May 1581.

Philip showed much moderation in the administration of his new kingdom. In 1581, when the Portuguese cortes met at Tomar, he promised to leave Portugal as a virtually autonomous state: its union with Castile was to be essentially similar to that between Castile and Aragon more than a century before. Official posts in the country were to be filled only by Portuguese. It was to retain its own currency. A new Council of Portugal was to be set up to advise the king; but it would do its business only in Portuguese. Trade with the Portuguese colonies was to remain in Portuguese hands; and since Spain now had to shoulder significant new expenditure on defending the Portuguese overseas empire she may well have lost financially by her new conquest. Customs barriers between Portugal and Castile were swept away at once (they were re-established in 1593); but a real effort was made to leave Portuguese institutions and interests untouched. The king remained in Portugal for more than two years (December 1580–February 1583) – his only prolonged absence from Castile after his return to Spain in 1559.

His coronation in April 1581 as king of Portugal saw Philip's power and prestige at their height. To Spain's territories in Europe and America and her remaining footholds in north Africa were now added the Portuguese bases and trading-stations in India, south-east Asia and China.[26] Not surprisingly, such success fed a growth of imperial pride and ambition. Philip himself never lost his innate hesitancy and caution. But some of his subjects even hoped that the establishment of Spain in the Philippine islands, begun in 1571, might lead on to the conquest of China or Japan, or that there might be a Spanish reconquest of the Holy Land.[27] Such flights of fancy were not in themselves important. But Cardinal Granvelle, who after his return from the Netherlands in 1564 had been excluded from

---

26. G. Parker, 'David or Goliath? Philip II and his world in the 1580s', in R.L. Kagan and G. Parker, eds, *Spain, Europe and the Atlantic World: Essays in Honour of John H. Elliott* (Cambridge, 1995), p. 245.

27. Parker, 'David or Goliath?', pp. 247–8.

decision-making at the highest level and who typified the imperialist and expansionist aspects of Spanish policy, returned to power in the late 1570s. For several years he had great influence (he organized the invasion of Portugal in 1580), and he argued with much force that Spain's future as a great power now lay on the Atlantic rather than in the Mediterranean world. Events were to bear him out. Willy-nilly, as the Netherlands revolt dragged on and relations with England changed decisively for the worse, a change of attitude of this kind was to be forced on Philip and his ministers.

Spanish progress in the Netherlands, growing disunity in France

Don John of Austria, deeply chagrined by the difficulties he had had to face and his lack of success in dealing with them, died in October 1578. He was succeeded as governor-general in the Netherlands by Alexander Farnese, Duke of Parma, a nephew of Philip II, who soon showed himself a much abler agent of the king than any of his predecessors. At least as competent a commander in the field as Alba and an incomparably better diplomat, he was to remain until his death in 1592 one of the leading figures on the European stage. His situation after the vicissitudes of 1576–79 was inevitably far from easy. In negotiations with the Union of Arras he was forced to agree to withdraw Spanish troops from the southern provinces and leave their defence to locally raised forces, a concession Philip II accepted in May 1579; but this agreement was before long to be completely overtaken by events. Soon afterwards Parma won his first real military success by capturing Maastricht in a sudden attack; and it rapidly became apparent that the rebel provinces of the Union of Utrecht now faced a very formidable opponent. On both sides the stakes were rising. In May 1581 nine provinces (Flanders and Brabant as well as the seven northern ones) adopted an Act of Abjuration by which they formally renounced their allegiance to Philip II.

The foreign aid so much needed if the rebellion were to survive seemed most likely to be achieved by the acceptance of a foreign ruler. In the autumn of 1577, with Spanish control apparently collapsing, the Archduke Matthias, brother of the Emperor Rudolf, had been briefly installed in Brussels as governor-general with William of Orange as his leading subordinate. This achieved nothing. The archduke had neither the character nor the resources to make any impact in so difficult and complex a situation. In 1578 Elizabeth subsidized the self-appointed Calvinist knight-errant, John Casimir of the Palatinate, who led another mercenary force into the Netherlands as far as Zutphen in Gelderland; but he then retreated for lack of money to pay his troops, having in his turn achieved nothing. The queen had in any case acted only because of her continuing determination to block any French advance in this strategically vital area, not through any desire for the success of a rebellion she instinctively disliked. France, personified by the Duc d'Anjou (the title now assumed by the former Duc d'Alençon), the younger brother of Henry III, seemed the best hope of effective foreign help. An ugly little man of limited ability, Anjou was none the less ambitious to be a ruler in his own right. Already in July 1578 he too had intervened ineffectively in the complications of the Netherlands, when he led an army across the frontier from France, though he had beaten a retreat six months later without winning any success.

Nevertheless the rebel provinces, as the threat from Parma became more pressing, continued to put their faith in Anjou and the French support it was hoped he would bring with him. In September 1578 their representatives signed with him at Plessis-les-Tours an agreement that he should become 'Defender of the Netherlands', while Henry III secretly promised support to his brother, though this was to be given only after he had established himself in his new dignity. Later the states-general agreed, though with some dissentients, that Anjou should become their 'prince and lord'; and in February 1582 he entered Antwerp, where Calvinism and anti-Spanish feeling were still very strong. But he had virtually no resources of his own and was from the start a liability rather than an asset to his prospective subjects. His growing frustration with what he saw as a humiliating situation culminated in January 1583 in an attempt to seize Antwerp by force, while there were simultaneous efforts of the kind in the other Netherlands towns with French garrisons. They failed completely: more than half of the 3,500 French soldiers in Antwerp were killed. Anjou was forced to take refuge first in Dunkirk and then in Cambrai; and it was clear that his intervention had ended in tragifarce. Even now hopes of French aid were not dead. In April 1584 it was agreed that if Anjou died without any legitimate heir the rebel provinces should be united with France under Henry III. The duke did in fact die only two months later; but Henry, more and more beset by domestic problems, was in no position to contemplate foreign adventures, least of all against a Spain which now threatened what remained of his authority in France itself.

Anjou's death and the king's childlessness meant the end of the direct Valois line. There were various possible claimants to the succession; and the most obvious was Henry of Navarre. But he was a heretic. Worse, he was a relapsed heretic, since he had quickly revoked his forced conversion to Catholicism and returned to the Calvinism in which he had been brought up. That such a man should become king seemed to many Catholics an unthinkable disaster and a breach of the unwritten constitution of France. To Philip II it was equally repugnant for both political and religious reasons. A Protestant king of France could only be an enemy; and Philip's desire to see Catholicism triumph there was completely sincere. His contacts with the Guise faction had never ceased; and on the last day of 1584 his representatives signed with Henry, Duc de Guise, and his brother, the Duc de Mayenne, the Treaty of Joinville.

This revived the Catholic League of the later 1570s in the more active and dangerous form of a Holy League dedicated to the extirpation of heresy in both France and the Netherlands. Henry of Navarre was to be excluded from any right of succession: the throne on the death of Henry III would be inherited by Charles, Cardinal of Bourbon, an old man and a political nullity though he had at least an arguable claim to succeed. Philip was to subsidize the League at the rate of 50,000 crowns a month and also give it military help if necessary. These promises were the beginning of an increasingly lavish and eventually almost ruinous outpouring of Spanish resources in France. Spain for her part might recover the French part of Navarre as well as Cambrai, the one gain of Anjou's Netherlands adventures. In a declaration issued at Péronne in March 1585 the League leaders bitterly criticized Henry III for his failure to crush heresy, the overweening influence of his favourites and the heavy taxation of the last few years.

Both Henry and Catherine de Medici had been willing to strike at Spanish power if this could be done without too much risk. Apart from their contacts with the Dutch rebels and their covert backing for Anjou, in 1582 a French fleet had tried, very unsuccessfully, to establish the Prior of Crato in the Azores, the only Portuguese territory where he still had active support. But Henry was now so alarmed and under such pressure that in July 1585 he revoked all the rights previously conceded to the Huguenots, forbade the practice of their religion, declared them incapable of holding any public office and tried to deprive them of their places of surety. This, the most violently Catholic edict since the beginning of the civil wars, made it clear that Spanish influence in France was now stronger than ever before and that for the time being at least the Dutch rebels had no hope of

French help. Parma was making steady progress and bringing the southern Netherlands provinces under final Spanish control. Ypres and Bruges fell to him in the spring of 1584, Ghent in September of the same year, Brussels in March 1585 and Mechlin in July. Already in 1580 the north-eastern province of Groningen had resumed its allegiance to Spain when its governor abandoned his support for the revolt. In July 1584 William of Orange was murdered by a Catholic fanatic: Philip's greatest and most tenacious opponent was no more.

The English challenge to Spanish power

The position of Philip II was now very strong. Though he was widely suspected of aiming at 'universal monarchy' and dominance of all western Europe these fears were unfounded: he thought always in largely defensive terms. But the fears are understandable. Portugal and its empire were the greatest territorial gain made by any ruler of the age. Philip's financial position was now better than ever before, as the stream of American silver flowed in unprecedented quantity. At the end of the 1570s an agent of the great Fugger banking house summed up the situation in the Netherlands in terms which showed the crucial importance of this: 'there will be plenty of men on both sides and the only question is which paymaster will hold out longest';[28] and Philip's purse was deeper by far than that of any possible competitor. A squadron of galleys which arrived in Genoa in June 1584 may alone have carried a record 3–4 million crowns in hard cash.[29]

With France so weakened England, clearly a second-rate power and one traditionally pro- rather than anti-Spanish, now stood out increasingly as Philip's most obvious opponent. Indeed it was the temporary nullification of France, the great traditional foe, that made it possible for England now to oppose Spanish power more and more openly. For the time being at least good relations with Spain as a shield against the enemy across the Channel were no longer needed. There were many complaints that the king could bring against Elizabeth and her subjects. The queen, in spite of her deep dislike of rebellion and preference for at least nominal Spanish suzerainty in the Netherlands, had more than once, however reluctantly, given support to the Dutch revolt. She had subsidized John Casimir in 1578 to

---

28. L. Stone, *An Elizabethan: Sir Horatio Palavicino* (Oxford, 1956), p. 58.

29. F. Braudel, *The Mediterranean and the Mediterranean World in the Age of Philip II* (London, 1972), i, p. 496.

help make possible his futile military adventure of that year, as well as giving money to the rebellious provinces. She had provided funds in 1581–2 to keep Anjou's forces in existence.[30] Considerable numbers of English volunteers had fought against the Spanish army in the Netherlands. English pirates, as they were justifiably seen in Madrid, were increasingly raiding in the Spanish colonies and taking Spanish ships. Elizabeth herself had made money from the £150,000 worth of plunder taken by Francis Drake during his voyage round the world in 1577–80 and even knighted him on his return. The material loss to Spain was not in itself important, but Philip felt keenly the threat to his prestige if he showed himself unable to protect his subjects and their property: when in 1585–86 Drake successfully raided Spanish possessions in the Caribbean this angered the king as two decades of ordinary piracy had failed to do. By the mid-1580s again, English negotiations were in progress with the most important native ruler in Morocco, the Sharif of Fez, which might lead to the establishment there of an English naval base from which the Straits of Gibraltar could be blocked, while Elizabeth and her ministers were also trying to obtain an alliance with the Turks. William Harborne, who had arrived in Constantinople in 1583 as the first English ambassador to the Ottoman government, was ordered in the spring of 1585 to work for an Anglo-Turkish offensive alliance against Spain. Finally, and in some ways most important of all, the English government oppressed its Catholic subjects, who looked eagerly to Spain, as Philip believed, for the help they needed and deserved.

Moreover Mary, Queen of Scots, overthrown and deposed in 1567, had been in effect a prisoner in Elizabeth's hands since her flight to England in 1568. Yet her claim to the English throne was arguably far better than that of Elizabeth, who in Catholic eyes was not even of legitimate birth and whose deposition had been proclaimed by Pope Pius V in 1570. Hitherto Philip had been unwilling to support Mary's claims openly or energetically. Given her French background and partly French descent, her becoming ruler of England would be a very dangerous setback for Spain. Now the situation had changed. France, for some time to come at least, was drastically weakened. Support for Mary's cause, in the justice of which Philip certainly believed, could now serve Spain's interests as well as the Catholic cause. When in May 1586 she wrote to Mendoza, the Spanish ambassador in Paris, promising to make over to Philip by will her right of succession to the English throne and asking him to take her under his protection, this

---

30. Stone, *An Elizabethan*, ch. 3, gives a detailed account of the English financial help given to the Dutch from the later 1570s onwards.

emphasized still more the coincidence of political advantage and moral obligation which she now represented. (It is unlikely that such a will was ever made, but both Philip and Mendoza believed it had been.) On a wide range of different grounds, therefore, political, military, legal and religious, Philip saw England under its existing regime more and more as an enemy.

In July 1585 the states-general of the rebel Netherlands provinces, their hope of French help at an end, offered to accept Elizabeth as their ruler. She refused the offer; but she did agree, by the Treaty of Nonsuch signed in August after long negotiations and with her usual hesitation, to send to the Netherlands a force of 6,000 men under the command of her favourite, the Earl of Leicester. Moreover, as part of the treaty she was to receive from the Dutch, as security for the repayment of the money she was spending, three 'cautionary towns' (Brill, Flushing and Remmekens); and her possession of these could be seen as a kind of seizure of territory which Philip II still claimed as his own. After years of caution, parsimony and uncertainty which had sometimes deeply irritated her ministers, she had now embarked on military intervention on the continent on a scale not seen since the 1540s. Its demands were to weigh on her for many years to come. Yet it is arguable that action of some sort could hardly have been avoided in the new situation. There now seemed a real danger that the whole coastline of western Europe from Gibraltar to Jutland might soon be under Philip's control. 'If he [Philip II] once reduce the Low Countries to absolute subjection', wrote Burghley, the queen's oldest and most trusted minister, 'I know not what limits any man of judgement can set unto his greatness.'[31]

Leicester's intervention was a disastrous failure, largely because of his own arrogance and tactlessness. When he landed at Flushing in December 1585 he was given powers which reflected the apparent desperation of the Dutch position. A new council of state was set up which was to include two English members; and he himself was given the title of 'Excellency' (though not until July 1586 did Elizabeth allow him to use it). But he soon faced bitter opposition. He tried to end all trade with the Spanish enemy, and thus aroused resistance in Holland whose merchants profited in this way, though Zeeland which was more exposed to Spanish attack, and the inland provinces which had no seaborne trade, were more receptive to the idea. He supported the more extreme Calvinists against the more moderate 'libertine' ones and responded to one of their demands by calling a

---

31. Parker, 'The Dutch revolt and the polarization of international politics', p. 63.

general synod. He was hampered by the deep divisions between the rebel provinces and often within individual ones. He was constantly short of money. Much of the English money sent to support the rebels (Elizabeth in 1585 had taken on obligations equivalent to about half her government's normal annual income) was wasted through fraud and corruption for which Leicester himself was largely to blame. When he temporarily came back to England in November 1586 the trade restrictions he had introduced were virtually repealed and the council of state remodelled. His return to the Netherlands in July 1587 provoked further quarrels, particularly when he failed to raise Parma's siege of the strategically significant port of Sluys. His final departure in December marked the end of an adventure in which he had achieved little more than Anjou in 1582–83. But by then Spain and England had been at undeclared war for well over two years.

CHAPTER SEVEN

Spanish Power Checked but Unbroken, 1585–1609

The turning-point?: the armada of 1588

The idea of a Spanish invasion of England was far from new in the mid-1580s. As early as 1571 Philip II had suggested to Alba a possible direct attack of this kind on Elizabeth. This, however, was no more than a gesture; for the king gave his general none of the money or other resources that an enterprise of this scope demanded. In 1577–78, again, Don John of Austria had dreamed of leading such an invasion, placing Mary Stuart on the throne and then marrying her himself. But it was one of the virtues of Philip II, cautious and sometimes even timid, that he was untouched by such dreams. None the less Don John was fully justified in insisting that the subjection of England to Spanish influence would be the longest step of all towards the crushing of the Netherlands revolt. 'Everyone believes', he told Philip, 'that the only remedy for the disorders of the Netherlands is that England should be ruled by someone devoted to Your Majesty. If the contrary case prevails it will mean the ruin of these countries and their loss to your crown.'[1]

By the mid-1580s, with Elizabeth for the first time formally allied to the Dutch rebels and giving them military support, this argument had more force than ever. Moreover Philip now felt increasingly that his reputation, that most precious of all assets to any ruler of the age, was at stake. If he continued to tolerate without response the insolent attacks of English pirates on his ships and American settlements, doubt might even be cast on his standing as the greatest ruler in Christendom. Yet it was impossible by merely defensive measures to safeguard what was now a world-wide empire and the sea communi-

1. G. Mattingly, *The Defeat of the Spanish Armada* (London, 1959), pp. 54–5.

cations that linked its different parts. 'It is no longer possible to protect everything', urged his influential secretary, Idiàquez. 'We must set fire to their [the English] home and ensure it is so dangerous that they will be forced to drop everything and concentrate on putting it out.'[2]

In August 1583 the Marquis of Santa Cruz, Spain's best admiral and fresh from his crushing victory the previous year over a French fleet off the Azores, suggested that he should lead an invasion of England. But his proposal made it clear that this would be not merely risky but also enormously costly if it were to have any real chance of success: he envisaged the use of a huge fleet and a military force twice the size of that devoted to the actual attempt in 1588. However, from this time onwards the possibility of an attack on England was never lost sight of in Madrid; and in January 1586 Philip ordered Santa Cruz to begin planning for one. Exactly how such an attack might be made was the subject of considerable discussion. As plans began to take a more definite shape, consideration was given to a landing either in Scotland, where a number of powerful nobles were still Catholic, or Ireland, to which in 1579 and 1580 Pope Gregory XIII had sent small forces (some of the second one Spanish) to support a rebellion in Munster against English rule. Such ideas gained little backing. But in the Netherlands Spain already had the finest army in Europe under a first-rate commander. To invade England it had to cross only a relatively narrow stretch of sea. To use it in this way, then, seemed an obvious strategy; and though Parma at first urged that the reconquest of the rebel provinces should come before any attack on England, he finally agreed, in April 1586, that such an attack, if successful, would be a very great help in that reconquest. When early in August 1587 he captured the port of Sluys it seemed that this might provide an embarkation point for his army. Its movement would be covered by a powerful Spanish seagoing fleet, though just how this was to be done was never properly worked out; and in September 1587 Philip issued the first definite instruction for an invasion of England in which both a fleet from Spain and an army from the Netherlands would take part. Parma, knowing well the situation on the ground, soon became pessimistic about the chances of success. He

---

2. M.J. Rodriguez-Salgado *et al., Armada 1588–1988* (London, 1988), p. 20. I.A.A. Thompson, 'The appointment of the Duke of Medina Sidonia to the command of the Spanish armada', *Historical Journal* XII (1969), 200–1, argues interestingly that the armada was never intended to conquer England but rather merely to threaten Elizabeth, force her to drop her anti-Spanish policies and make her incur heavy defence expenditure, but produces no convincing evidence to support this view.

still had no good deep-water port suitable for large ships under his control. He also realized that the barges that were being collected to ferry his men over to Kent or the Thames estuary were very vulnerable to attack and would have to face not merely English ships but also Dutch ones, intent on preventing a crossing. The possibility of a French attack while the bulk of his army was tied up in England was yet another restraining factor. In Madrid, however, none of these considerations seemed decisive.

In England there were hopes almost to the last moment that the threatened blow might be averted. Elizabeth clung even now to the belief that it was possible to restore throughout the Netherlands some formal Spanish suzerainty, one not effective enough to arouse local resistance but still sufficient to guard against the French intervention and control that she feared above all. Philip should give up any idea of an effective centralized government and return to the position in this respect at the beginning of his reign. If at the same time he agreed to withdraw Spanish troops and tolerate heresy, at least *de facto*, in the provinces where it was strongest, such concessions could provide the basis for the kind of compromise the queen sought. In 1586–88 there were negotiations with Parma to this end, at first without the Dutch being informed and then accompanied by pressure on them to accept some agreement with Philip. It is not surprising that their leaders suspected Elizabeth of preparing to desert them; but both their fears and her hopes were unfounded.

On his side Philip's desire for a direct attack on England was strengthened when, in February 1587, Elizabeth overcame long hesitation and signed the warrant for the execution of Mary, Queen of Scots. This seemed to mark her more clearly than ever as a tyrannical heretic usurper whose overthrow was called for on religious and moral grounds. At the same time it ended any possibility that placing Mary on the throne might establish French influence in England. It was apparently the news of her death that convinced Parma that an attempted invasion was now inevitable. With France paralysed and the Dutch rebels apparently fighting for survival, complete Spanish dominance of all western Europe had never seemed closer.

The 'Enterprise of England' was dealt a considerable blow when in February 1588 Santa Cruz died. His successor, the Duke of Medina Sidonia, was one of the greatest of Spanish noblemen; and throughout an appallingly difficult command he showed both courage and dignity. Nevertheless even before the armada set sail it had become clear that it would face great problems. A raid on Cadiz led by Drake in 1587 considerably disrupted the preparations, as did disease and bad weather. Spain's economic and technological weaknesses meant serious and intractable shortages of materials of many kinds, of guns and gunpowder, worst of all of trained seamen. The efforts made to overcome these were remarkable, greater than any other state of that age was capable of; but the deficiencies of decades could not be made good in months. 'From the time of Medina Sidonia's appointment', it has been argued, 'the Armada was led in a fatalistic spirit, fore-doomed by self-fulfilling prophecies of disaster.'[3] Certainly the duke himself and many observers in Rome, Paris and Genoa had grave doubts of its prospects. Philip, however, did not share such feelings. He now saw himself more than ever as the champion of the true faith. With Catholicism apparently under serious challenge in a deeply divided France, he alone could act as its standard-bearer in western Europe. As such he was entitled to the support of good Catholics everywhere and could reasonably hope for divine favour in the attack on England. 'I consider this campaign so important', he wrote to Medina Sidonia two months before the armada sailed, 'that if my presence was not so necessary here to provide for what is needed there and in other parts, I would be happy to take part. And I would do so with great confidence that it would succeed.'[4]

The fate of the armada in August–September 1588, the most spectacular episode in all sixteenth-century warfare, is well known – the long and ineffective running battle in the English Channel, the damaging attack on it by fireships in Calais roads, the disastrous return voyage around the north of Scotland and west of Ireland. No landing was achieved. Parma's army never came into play. The losses were heavy: perhaps 11,000 men in all died and almost half the 130 ships that set out from Lisbon were lost. Whether this can be claimed as a victory for the English navy is much more open to question: the English ships, though their guns and gunnery were superior, did in general little serious damage to the Spanish ones and it was bad weather that really sealed the fate of the great expedition. The better-informed contemporaries were well aware of this: one very experienced English professional soldier thought that 'miracles alone had saved England from perdition.'[5] But the moral and psychological effect was profound and lasting. This was the greatest and most sus-

3. F. Fernandez-Armesto, *The Spanish Armada: The Experience of War in 1588* (Oxford, 1988), p. 106. The practical difficulties in fitting out the armada are well discussed in I.A.A. Thompson, 'The Spanish armada: naval warfare between the Mediterranean and the Atlantic', in M.J. Rodriguez-Salgado and S. Adams, eds, *England, Spain and the Gran Armada, 1585–1604* (Edinburgh, 1991).

4. Rodriguez-Salgado *et al.*, *Armada 1588–1988*, p. 33, fn. 10.

5. C. Wilson, *Queen Elizabeth and the Revolt of The Netherlands* (London, 1970), p. 106.

tained conflict at sea hitherto known in Europe. 'The size of the forces involved and the nature of their armament were unprecedented. No naval campaign in previous history, and none afterwards until the advent of the aircraft carrier, involved so many fresh and incalculable factors.'[6] Spain had made an effort surpassing anything of the kind she had attempted before; and the attack on England won more popular support than either the long struggle in the Netherlands or military intervention in France.

The first reactions to the disaster were remarkably swift and energetic. The Council of War told the king that 'What matters is that we should show great courage and continue what we have started': the king's reputation must be safeguarded by launching another such attack.[7] Philip's own first instinct was to react in precisely this way, until he realized how great the difficulties were. Many cities and individuals made offers of help, while the cortes of Castile, when it met early in 1589, accepted that increased taxation was needed to carry on the war. In England Burghley regretted that more effort had not been made to destroy the Spanish ships as they returned home; and there were fears that Parma might still attempt an invasion even without a naval force to cover it. Yet Spain had passed a watershed. 'If any one year', a leading authority has said, 'marks the distinction between the triumphant Spain of the first two Habsburgs and the defeatist, disillusioned Spain of their successors, that year is 1588.'[8] Moreover discouragement in Spain was soon paralleled by new confidence in England and to some extent throughout Protestant Europe. God, it seemed, had shown that he favoured the Protestant cause and had turned his back on the Catholic one. The stage was now set for a struggle between, on the one hand, England, the Dutch rebels and the Huguenots and moderate Catholics in France, and on the other Spain and the more uncompromising French adherents of the old church. Europe was about to see a great international conflict which was, more than anything hitherto seen, a 'war of religion'.

The crisis in France and the accession of Henry IV

The crumbling authority of Henry III was being threatened in the later 1580s not merely by the Guises and the Catholic League but by the more and more menacing situation in Paris. The strength of

---

6. Mattingly, *The Defeat of the Spanish Armada*, pp. 226, 237–8.
7. Rodriguez-Salgado *et al., Armada 1588–1988*, p. 35.
8. J.H. Elliott, *Imperial Spain, 1469–1716* (London, 1963), p. 283.

Catholic feeling in the capital had already been shown in 1572; and from the end of 1584 there began to emerge there a committee of ultra-Catholic middle-class leaders which came to be known as the Sixteen (from the sixteen quarters into which the city was divided, though its actual membership was considerably larger). Religious emotion and intense distrust of the king, who even came to be accused of sorcery, combined with more concrete grievances – heavy taxation and alleged interference by Henry III with municipal liberties. The atmosphere in Paris was now taking on overtones of popular revolution far removed from the aristocratic factionalism of the Guises; and the Sixteen began to appear, at least to Parisians, as something like an alternative government. For almost a decade the intense Catholicism of the capital was to be a factor not merely of French but of international significance.

In October 1587 Henry of Navarre won at Coutras a decisive victory over an army of the Catholic League. It was not followed up; but it was the first important success on the battlefield that the Huguenots had achieved since the beginning of the civil wars in France. It is typical of the complexity of the situation in an increasingly chaotic country that Henry III, though himself a devout Catholic, welcomed the outcome of the battle: he well realized that a victory for the League would have made it even more able to bully and threaten him. Almost simultaneously the Duc de Guise defeated at Auneau another army of German mercenaries, commanded by the Baron von Dohna, which had been slowly and painfully organized, with money in part supplied by Elizabeth, in yet another ineffective effort to support the Huguenot cause. The victory had little real meaning. Dohna's army had merely pillaged the areas through which it moved; and even before the battle was fought it was retreating and disintegrating from lack of pay. But his success raised the popularity of Guise in Paris, where he was seen as the saviour of the old faith, to new heights. The atmosphere of potential revolution there was now stronger than ever.

It seems likely that the extreme Catholics in Paris had begun to prepare for a forcible seizure of power there as early as the beginning of 1585, and that there was almost a rising in April 1587: it was prevented only by the opposition of Guise and Mendoza, the Spanish ambassador, who regarded it as premature. A year later, however, with the armada about to sail, such an outbreak made good sense from the Spanish standpoint. It would weaken Henry III and his government still further and free Parma from any remaining fear of French action in the Netherlands. This would allow him to concentrate his attention and resources on the vitally important invasion of England. Spanish influence in Paris was now strong: Mendoza was in close touch with the Sixteen and had considerable influence on events, while in March Philip II sent Guise a substantial sum of money with instructions to take some action in May which would distract Henry III's attention. On 12 May, in a last effort to prop up his authority, Henry sent troops, largely Swiss, into the city. The result was a humiliating fiasco. Within a few hours barricades had been thrown up throughout Paris to make their movement impossible and their lives were threatened: many then surrendered to the League forces. The next day the king fled from his capital: any French interference with Parma or the operations of the armada was now impossible.

The months that followed this 'Day of Barricades' saw Henry forced to submit more and more completely to the demands of the League and its leaders. In July he signed at Rouen a decree in which he repeated the oath taken at his coronation to drive all heretics from France 'without making any peace or truce': he also ordered his subjects to accept no heretic as king and promised to allow the publication in France of the decrees of the Council of Trent. In August he appointed Guise commander-in-chief of the French armies. But the worst humiliation of all came in November when the Duke of Savoy, Charles Emmanuel I, suddenly invaded the marquisate of Saluzzo on the south-eastern frontier. This was one of the few gains, and a strategically important one, made by France at Cateau-Cambrésis. The League had not inspired the attack, though Charles Emmanuel was strongly Catholic; but Henry believed that it had, and his resentment of Guise tutelage became still more intense. He was soon to have his revenge. On 23 December the Duc de Guise was murdered, stabbed in the presence of the king in the royal château of Blois. This was followed by the arrest of his closest associates – his brother, the Cardinal of Lorraine (who was at once murdered by his guards), the Archbishop of Lyons, the Comte de Brissac, who had played a leading role in the 'Day of Barricades'. The king even had the bodies of the duke and his brother burned in quicklime so that there should be no physical remains of them for devout Catholics to venerate.

Henry seemed for a moment to have achieved his objective – to assert the rights of the crown and its independence of Guise coercion. But the assassinations in fact made his position worse. The Sorbonne denounced him as a murderer and declared that his subjects no longer owed him allegiance. In Paris the atmosphere became even more extreme and revolutionary: known or suspected royalists were imprisoned and forced to pay ransoms for their release, and a forced loan was raised. The council of the League began to claim the right to appoint to all state posts, to send and receive diplomatic representatives and to collect all royal revenues. In the provinces most important towns were also now under strong League influence, with similar results. The Duc de Mayenne, the brother of the murdered Guise, was declared lieutenant-general of the kingdom and greeted with great enthusiasm when he entered Paris. The result was that by the early months of 1589 only a sixth or less of France was under any real control by Henry III. In April, therefore, he was driven to make an agreement with Henry of Navarre, who had already paved his way to the succession by promising never to deny Catholics freedom of conscience or worship. After joining forces the two laid siege to Paris; but at a moment when the fall of the city and a great defeat for the League seemed possible Henry III was in his turn assassinated by a fanatical young Catholic.

There were several possible candidates for the succession. The Duke of Savoy, Mayenne, the young Duc de Guise, even the Count of Zweibrucken, the son of the Duke of Lorraine, could all put forward some kind of claim; and disagreements between them, particularly between Mayenne and Guise, were a considerable source of difficulty for the League. But the two who really mattered were Henry of Navarre and Charles, Cardinal of Bourbon, who in the eyes of the League and its foreign supporters was now King Charles X. The story of the next three years or more is that of the victory of Navarre by a combination of military success and judicious, and inevitable, concessions to Catholic feeling. A few weeks after his accession he won an important victory at Arques over a League army commanded by Mayenne. In March 1590 he won another at Ivry and followed this up by laying siege once more to Paris. The months that followed saw terrible suffering in the starving city. Soldiers of the garrison on at least one occasion caught and ate three children, while in all perhaps 13,000 people died of hunger and a further 30,000 later in epidemics. But Henry IV, as he must now be called, was forced to raise the siege in September, when a Spanish army under Parma marched from the Netherlands to relieve the city. He was also very seriously handicapped, as he was to be for years to come, by lack of money, that ultimate restraint on all military operations in this age.

Nevertheless the pendulum was clearly swinging in his favour, as the struggle became more and more an international one between Spain and a hostile coalition, though a loose and disunited one. He received Dutch subsidies in 1588, 1589 and 1591. Elizabeth also supplied money, though with her usual reluctance and grumbling; and in 1590 3,000 soldiers were sent from England to support the king, though they achieved little and only about half of them lived to return home. In the following year another army provided by a number of German Protestant states – Brandenburg, Saxony, Hesse, Württemberg and the Palatinate – had assembled at Frankfurt by August: joining his own forces with this and supported by another contingent supplied by Elizabeth under her new favourite, the Earl of Essex, Henry attempted to capture Rouen. This siege was also a failure. Parma, in the last and most brilliant of his campaigns, relieved the city in April 1592.

But more important than any military operation was the growing disunity of the Catholic forces opposing Henry IV. A great aristocrat like Mayenne, who in any case lacked political skill or tact, could never find it easy to work with a radical group such as the Sixteen, whose increasing violence and extremism made any cooperation with them more and more difficult. In December 1591 the duke arrested several of its members. Nor was there any effective joint action between the League forces and those of Spain. After Rouen had been relieved Parma wanted to press on and inflict a decisive defeat on Henry, who had been completely taken by surprise by the speed of the Spanish advance; but the opposition of Mayenne and the other League leaders meant that the opportunity was lost.[9] Nor could the growing presence of Spanish forces in different parts of France, which could easily be seen as an occupation by the traditional enemy, ever be welcome to most Frenchmen. In February 1591 1,200 Spanish and Neapolitan troops entered Paris to strengthen the garrison of the city, while Parma demanded that the fortress of La Fère be handed over to him to ease communication between his army in the Netherlands and the French capital. In the provinces the situation seemed even more alarming. Several thousand Spanish troops invaded Languedoc, while in September 1590 3,500 more arrived in Brittany. They were sent to support the Duc de Mercoeur, another of the Guise clan, who had established himself as a semi-independent ruler in the duchy. But by occupying and fortifying the coastal strongpoint of Blavet and thus gaining control of most of the south-west coast of Brittany, they seemed to threaten the creation of a new Spanish base on the Atlantic.

Nor were Philip II's efforts to make good the claims to the French throne of his favourite daughter, the Infanta Isabella Clara Eugenia, whose mother had been a French princess, likely to gain widespread

9. H.A. Lloyd, *The Rouen Campaign, 1590–1592: Politics, Warfare and the Early Modern State* (Oxford, 1973), pp. 183–4.

support. Mendoza had pressed these claims strenuously; and there were suggestions that the infanta might marry a French prince and bring with her as her dowry Flanders or Franche-Comté, while in January 1590 Philip's ambassadors made with the League leaders an agreement by which he was recognized as 'Protector of the Crown of France'. Moreover the King of Spain was not the only foreign ruler whose ambitions seemed to threaten France's integrity and international position. Late in 1590 Charles Emmanuel of Savoy, still greedy for territorial gain, invaded Dauphiné and Provence. He entered Aix-en- Provence in November and Marseilles in March 1591, and demanded that the *parlement* of Grenoble, the supreme legal authority in Dauphiné, recognize him as king. Charles III of Lorraine, for his part, occupied with Spanish approval the bishopric of Toul, claimed the frontier duchy of Bouillon and hoped to secure Champagne for himself and perhaps even the French crown for his son. Cooperation between Philip II and the League was always difficult: in Brittany Mercoeur had ambitions of his own which were hard to reconcile with those of his Spanish allies. But in Paris Catholic feeling was still strong enough to override any reluctance to accept the tutelage of the traditional enemy. In September 1591 the Sixteen told Philip that 'we can certainly assure Your Catholic Majesty that the wishes and desires of all Catholics are to see Your Catholic Majesty hold the sceptre of the crown and reign over us'.[10]

From the first days of his reign Henry IV was anxious to conciliate his Catholic subjects. But this was now inconceivable without his becoming a Catholic. At the beginning of August 1589 he promised to 'maintain and conserve within the realm the Catholic, Apostolic and Roman faith in its entirety without altering anything' and said that he was ready to receive instruction in it by 'a good, legitimate and free general national council'.[11] The possibility of his conversion inevitably alarmed many of his Huguenot supporters: but his position made it inevitable. A Calvinist minister who protested against any possible change of faith was answered simply with the question: 'On the one hand he is being offered the French crown, on the other a couple of psalms. Which do you think he should choose?'.[12] Whatever the claims of religious faith, political necessity made only one answer possible. In July 1593, in the basilica of St Denis, Henry publicly declared himself a Catholic.

10. J. Mariéjol, *La Réforme et la Ligue. L'Edit de Nantes* (Paris, 1904) (E. Lavisse, ed., *Histoire de France depuis les Origines jusqu'à la Révolution*, vi), p. 344.

11. D. Buisseret, *Henry IV* (London, 1984), p. 28.

12. Mariéjol, *La Réforme et la Ligue*, p. 239.

The declaration came at a crucial moment. The estates-general, though one much smaller in numbers and less representative than was usual, had met in January. It was hoped in Spain that it might support the claim of the infanta to the throne, and Parma, before his death in December 1592, had pressed for it to meet in Soissons, where it would be within easy reach of his army in the Netherlands. Instead it met in Paris; and very soon it became apparent that, with the unity of the League now more fragile than ever, it was only a matter of time before it recognized Henry IV as king. France need no longer fear rule by a heretic. Moderate Catholic opinion, anxious for an end to civil war, could now accept Henry with a clear conscience: only the most fanatical and the most factious still resisted.

To the end there were Spanish efforts to prevent his acceptance by the estates-general and the capital. At the beginning of April a Spanish ambassador extraordinary, the Duke of Feria, arrived in Paris to press once more the claims of the infanta; but he was told firmly that a foreign ruler would not be accepted. In June it was proposed that if she were recognized as ruler of France she should marry the Archduke Ernest, the younger brother of the childless Emperor Rudolf II. If Ernest became emperor on his brother's death this would mean a huge dynastic union under him of France, most of the Habsburg territories in central Europe, the imperial title and perhaps the Netherlands, with which Philip might endow his daughter. But this was merely another of the visionary schemes, especially where dynastic marriages were concerned, that were so common in this age. The proposal had no result.

Philip II reacted to these setbacks by ordering a new Spanish army to invade France from the Netherlands under Count von Mansfeld, Parma's successor; but it exhausted itself in a long siege of the relatively minor fortress of Noyon. Clearly the fate of France was to be decided by Frenchmen, not by any foreign ruler, however powerful. In March 1594 Henry IV was able to enter his capital almost without opposition. There were still difficulties to be faced. He was crowned at Chartres, not as tradition demanded at Rheims, since the latter was still in the hands of the League. But the resistance of his remaining opponents was slowly overcome, largely by a lavish expenditure of money. When Mayenne was at last reconciled to the king in November 1597 he was paid an enormous indemnity of 2,640,000 *livres*. His brother Mercoeur, the last of the great League nobles to hold out, was also given an indemnity and a large pension when he finally came to terms at the beginning of 1598. Charles III of Lorraine made peace in return for a payment of 500,000 crowns.

It was also necessary, and very important, to be reconciled with the papacy. Its attitude to Henry had varied sharply under different popes. Sixtus V (1585–90), the greatest of the century, had a considerable admiration for the new king (and for Elizabeth in England). Though he had excommunicated Henry in 1585 as a relapsed heretic he soon regretted this and began to take a more conciliatory line in the hope that he could be reconverted. Also he was on increasingly bad terms with Philip II. In July 1587 he had promised support for the invasion of England; but after the failure of the armada he refused to pay the million escudos he had undertaken to provide, arguing that he was obliged to do so only after a successful landing had been made. By the last days of his pontificate his relations with Philip were so bad that he even threatened to expel the Spanish ambassador from Rome. Most important of all, he feared that a Spanish victory in France would fatally weaken the only power able to hold its own against the might of the Spanish king. Such an end to any semblance of a balance of power might well threaten the independence of the smaller states of Europe, of which the papacy was one. The Venetian republic, another small and vulnerable state, was also notably alarmed by this possibility, and Sixtus sympathized with its alarm.

His death in August 1590 was therefore followed by a determined and at first successful Spanish effort to make sure that his successors were more reliable supporters of Philip II. Gregory XIV met this requirement well, for he supported the League in France with both money and a substantial force of 6,000 men which joined Mayenne in October 1591. But his death two months later opened the way to the election in 1592 of Clement VIII who, in spite of heavy Spanish pressure, was at least willing to listen to any advances Henry IV might make. It was not until September 1595 that he agreed, after long negotiations, to absolve the king; but this did much to consolidate Henry's position and weaken the crumbling resistance of what remained of the Catholic League.

Philip II had therefore suffered, after a long struggle, a serious defeat. He could console himself with the thought that Henry, to reign in France, had been forced to become a Catholic, however much the more extreme adherents of the old faith might distrust his sincerity. Yet the conflict in France had been damaging to Philip in terms of prestige as well as very costly in men and above all in money. Moreover he was now faced by a hostile coalition in which England and the rebel Dutch provinces were joined by a France more united than for a generation or more. Yet he was still beyond question the most

powerful ruler in Christendom; and the contest on which he had embarked had still many years to run and was to outlive him.

The Anglo-French-Dutch war with Spain to 1598

In January 1595 Henry IV declared war on Philip II. The undeclared
struggle they had been waging for years was now open and formal. A
triple alliance against Spain of England, France and the emerging
Dutch republic was in the making: in the spring of 1596 Elizabeth
and Henry became allies by a treaty signed in London, and to this the
Dutch then also became a party. The idea of some far-reaching anti-
Spanish coalition was not new. In 1589 Burleigh had proposed one
that would embrace not merely England and France but Scotland,
Denmark and perhaps some of the Italian states such as Venice and
Tuscany, as well as the German princes alarmed by the power of
Philip II. Early in the following year there were unsuccessful English
efforts to create such an alliance.[13] But schemes of this kind were un-
realistically ambitious. No wide-ranging alliance in that age, or indeed for long afterwards, could be expected to hold together for
long; and even that of 1596 was to prove fragile and of limited effect.
War-weariness and conflicts of interest weakened it from the beginning. Nevertheless the 1590s saw international conflict on a scale and
of a complexity unequalled for 40 years past.

For England the high point of the struggle had been passed well
before the formation of the triple alliance. In 1589 a powerful expedition to Portugal under Drake and Sir John Norris, the most experienced English military commander, achieved little. Greed for
plunder prevented the destruction at Santander of the remains of
the armada of the previous year, which might have been easily
achieved. An effort to rouse Portuguese support for the Prior of
Crato, who seemed a potentially useful weapon against Philip II, was
a failure. Yet England was now fighting more seriously and energetically than for many decades: the government began for the first time
since 1574 to consider borrowing abroad to finance the struggle.

In the early 1590s Elizabeth began, however reluctantly, to commit herself to military intervention on the continent more lasting
and more justifiable politically and strategically than anything seen
earlier in the century. The military adventures of Henry VIII, however large-scale and expensive, had been inspired essentially by noth-

13. R.B. Wernham, *After the Armada: Elizabethan England and the Struggle for Western
Europe, 1588–1595* (Oxford, 1984), pp. 143, 193–4.

ing more than the search for personal prestige. By contrast, when Elizabeth now sent soldiers overseas it was for genuine and serious defensive ends – to prevent any crushing of the Dutch rebellion, to support the Protestant cause in France and check Spanish influence there, to prevent the Brittany coast becoming a launching-pad for Spanish attacks on English shipping and perhaps on England herself. The autumn of 1591 saw these military commitments at their height. There were then 7,000 English soldiers in the Netherlands, where throughout the 1590s Englishmen made up at least a third of the army of Maurice of Nassau, the son of William of Orange and Dutch commander-in-chief; and at the same time the Earl of Essex was commanding 4,000 others in the fruitless siege of Rouen. Simultaneously there were about the same number in Brittany: an English force remained there until 1595 to prevent the Spanish grip on the south coast of the duchy being extended to the north, where the port of Brest, in enemy hands, might become a serious threat. It has been estimated that in the years 1588–95 Elizabeth sent in all 47,000–48,000 men to fight on the continent, a large military effort for what was still a small and far from rich country.[14] After 1595 the situation altered. From then on the war became for England essentially one at sea, a change which considerably eased its heavy financial strain.

For the Dutch the 1590s saw important successes. Parma's last great victory was the capture of Antwerp in August 1585 after a long and dramatic siege, one of the greatest of the century. After that, though he took Deventer and the defences of Zutphen in 1587, this was largely because they were betrayed to him (by English commanders – another reason for the bad feeling between Leicester and the states-general). In his last years the need to spend resources and energies in intervention in France, notably in 1590 and 1592, meant that he could achieve little. His death spared him the recall in disgrace with which Philip II had already decided to reward one of his ablest servants. The 1590s under his successors saw frequent army mutinies, something from which Parma had been largely free; and this contributed to a run of significant successes for the Dutch under Maurice of Nassau and Johan van Oldenbarnevelt, *Landesadvocaat* of Holland and in effect foreign minister of the rebel provinces. In the early years of the decade Maurice was able to undo much of Parma's work and greatly to strengthen the defences of the provinces that had thrown off Spanish rule.

At the same time they, above all Holland, began to see an explo-

---

14. Ibid., p. 565.

sive growth in their trade and maritime activity, one without parallel in the sixteenth century and perhaps in all modern history.[15] Military and commercial success went to some extent hand in hand. As the rebel provinces expanded to the east and south, trade with Germany and even Italy became easier (the capture of the town of Groningen in 1593, for example, did much to ease communications with Germany); while growing wealth nourished greater military strength. It was now becoming clear that even without English or French help the Dutch rebels might well be impossible to subdue and that, almost unconsciously and unintentionally, a new and important state with a unique political and social structure was coming into existence. What had begun in the 1560s as a mere crushing of opposition in which the odds were all in Spain's favour had now become a war of attrition which she could not hope to win.

Long before the signature of the triple alliance of 1596, therefore, Spain had suffered a series of important defeats. Yet she was still unquestionably the greatest power in Europe; and her opponents were far from united. The alliance of 1596 had been achieved only after long and difficult negotiations; and it was never easy, and often hardly possible, for the allies to work together effectively. Elizabeth was persuaded only with difficulty and through the exertions of Henry IV to admit the independent status of the rebel provinces; and she raised once more the demand that had contributed so much to Leicester's unpopularity, for the cutting-off of Dutch trade with Spain and her American possessions. Once more this prohibition was evaded from the beginning; and there was a good deal of hypocrisy in the queen's demanding it, for it is clear that a substantial amount of English trade with Spain also continued throughout the struggle which began in 1585.[16] The conversion of Henry IV, again, had disappointed and antagonized many of the more extreme Protestants in both England and the rebel provinces, while Elizabeth, apart from her dislike and distrust of the emerging Dutch state with its peculiar quasi-republican constitution, still feared possible French ambitions in the Netherlands.

The situation in the 1590s was therefore by no means completely unfavourable to Spain; and her military and naval effort during these years was remarkable, even heroic, and in part successful. With England the situation was now essentially one of stalemate. In 1596 an ex-

15. On this see J. Israel, *Dutch Primacy in World Trade, 1585–1747* (Oxford, 1989), ch. 2.

16. Pauline Croft, 'Trading with the enemy, 1585–1604', *Historical Journal* XXXII (1989), 281–302.

pedition under the Earl of Essex captured and sacked Cadiz. It did much damage and took much booty (though little of this found its way to Elizabeth and her ministers, to their disappointment); but the strategic importance of this spectacular success was small. In the same year Philip II once more sent an armada to invade England; but once more the weather was destructively hostile: a considerable number of ships and 2,000 men were lost in a storm. Yet another invasion fleet in the following year was on a still larger scale and almost as imposing as the great effort of 1588. This too was made ineffective by bad weather: yet it took the queen and her ministers by surprise and narrowly failed to win an important success. At the same time English attacks on the Spanish colonial empire failed completely to do any serious damage. Strategic points in Spain's West Indian possessions were now for the first time being effectively fortified; and the expedition to the Caribbean led by Drake and Hawkins in 1595, in which both leaders died, could achieve nothing. Attacks on Spanish shipping produced occasional lucrative English successes, as when in 1592 one captured galleon, the *Madre de Dios*, yielded plunder worth £500,000, about half the value of all England's annual imports. But by itself this form of warfare could never bring Spain to her knees.

In the Franco-Spanish struggle also neither side could strike a decisive blow. Spain's army in the Netherlands was still the best in Europe. It captured Calais in April 1596, Amiens in March 1597 and Doullens in July of the same year. Henry IV was able to retake Amiens in September, but only after a long and expensive siege; and by then both sides were ready to discuss peace terms. Henry IV and Philip II were driven to end the struggle by the force which had pushed so many of their predecessors in the same direction – acute financial pressures. Henry had lived from hand to mouth from the moment he became king and had often been reduced to humiliating straits by lack of money. This poverty was particularly dangerous because it inevitably threatened the coherence and reliability of his army. 'Nothing is so necessary to us', he said in November 1590 'as to raise money towards maintaining the armed forces we must assemble'; and he tried to do this by selling crown lands, though his right to do so was still open to question. In the following year he had to postpone an interview with a new English ambassador in order to deal with mutiny and mass desertion among his German and Walloon mercenaries.[17] Loans from his richer English and Dutch allies were therefore essential to him; and his relations with Elizabeth in the

17. Wernham, *After the Armada*, p. 362.

early 1590s were punctuated by a series of pleas for money and auxiliary troops.

Elizabeth's finances were never so strained. By the standards of that age they were well administered; and she did not have to cope with civil war and its aftermath. None the less the calls on England's resources were heavy; and by 1590 the queen was already feeling the pinch. The reserve of £300,000 with which she had begun the war had by then vanished, while an effort in 1589 to borrow £100,000 in Germany was a failure. She had to resort, therefore, to selling crown land – in effect living off capital – and in the years 1588–95 war expenditure absorbed about half of the total revenues of the English government. In 1585–1603 the queen spent at least fifteen million florins in support of the Netherlands revolt.[18] It is understandable that one of her main objectives in negotiations with France and the Dutch was to be repaid the money she had at various times lent them.

The financial demands made on Spain, however, dwarfed those on any of her opponents. Her resources were great and seen to be so. An experienced English soldier feared that in any sustained and therefore expensive military operations 'their great means will eat our small'.[19] By the 1590s the indispensable American silver was being carried to Spain in a new type of ship, the gallizabra or frigate, smaller and faster than the cumbersome galleon and therefore able to outsail any ship whose attack it could not repel. These could sail alone, not as part of large and slow-moving fleets, which made them correspondingly more difficult for an enemy to intercept. The English had little success in capturing Spanish treasure-ships, in spite of all the hopes and dreams that centred around them: the heavy losses which the fleet from America suffered in 1591 were caused by bad weather, not by any enemy. But Philip was now spending on an unprecedented scale. The armada of 1588 may have cost ten million ducats, while in the early 1590s intervention in France raised his expenditure to a higher level still. Of the four million florins received by the Spanish military treasury in the Netherlands between August 1590 and May 1591, three-quarters was spent on the war in France.[20] By the time he died, at the end of 1592, Parma had raised loans totalling almost a million ducats on the security of his own estates,[21] while by the mid-1590s Philip was spending more than twelve million du-

18. G. Parker, 'War and economic change: the economic costs of the Dutch revolt', in his *Spain and The Netherlands, 1559–1659* (London, 1979), p. 179.

19. Lloyd, *The Rouen Campaign*, p. 39.

20. G. Parker, 'Spain, her enemies and the revolt of The Netherlands', in his *Spain and The Netherlands*, p. 36.

21. C. Martin and G. Parker, *The Spanish Armada* (London, 1988), p. 71.

cats a year. Inevitably this outpouring of resources had serious implications for Castile, which shouldered so much of the burden and
where a new and unpopular excise duty, the *millones*, was agreed by
the cortes after long negotiations in 1590 and extended to cover food
in 1596 (something which Philip had at first promised would not be
done). Equally inevitably, there were rumblings of discontent and
the beginnings of questioning as to whether it made sense to carry on
the apparently endless Netherlands struggle. In 1596 Philip became
bankrupt once more, as in 1557 and 1575. As on the earlier occasions, the immediate repercussions on confidence and business dealings over much of Europe were considerable. Though the silver from
America continued to flow and the Spanish army could still win victories, the pressures for peace were growing stronger on both sides of
the Pyrenees.

The Franco-Spanish Treaty of Vervins, signed at the beginning of
May 1598, in effect restated the Cateau-Cambrésis settlement of almost 40 years earlier. This was a stalemate, not a defeat for Spain.
Nevertheless it meant that a great and expensive Spanish effort in
France had been fruitless: Philip III, the son and successor of Philip
II, did not ratify the treaty until May 1601. The peace meant the
handing-back of Calais to France; and this finally extinguished any
lingering hope in England of recovering the town. Elizabeth had
clung to this dream almost to the end. In negotiations with Henry IV
in 1595–96 she had tried to make Calais the price of the English help
he asked for; but the king told his ambassador in London that he
would lose the town or come to terms with Philip II rather than return it to England. To both the English and the Dutch governments
the most serious aspect of the treaty seemed the possibility that
Spain, now freed from French distractions, might launch a new offensive in the Netherlands with increased prospects of success.
Oldenbarnevelt himself headed a Dutch mission to Paris in an effort
to dissuade Henry from abandoning the struggle with Spain; and the
English government, which claimed that the treaty was a breach of
the alliance of 1596, tried to impress on the king the need to ensure
that the Dutch were not now exposed to Spanish reconquest.

None of this had much effect: Henry IV in discussions with Sir
Robert Cecil (Burghley's younger son and the leading English negotiator involved) said that the demand in France for peace was now
too strong to ignore. Shortly before he died, in September 1598,
Philip II ceded his Netherlands provinces to his nephew, the Archduke Albert, son of the Emperor Rudolf, who was to marry the Infanta Isabella Clara Eugenia whom Philip had earlier hoped to make

queen of France. But this was largely a cosmetic change. The new regime had indeed a good deal of independence. In 1598 and 1600 it made serious though unsuccessful efforts to persuade the rebel provinces to accept Spanish suzerainty in return for complete autonomy and religious freedom. But it had already been agreed that not merely were the 'obedient' provinces to revert to the Spanish crown should the archduke and his wife die childless but, by a secret understanding, that they should still recognize the suzerainty of the king of Spain and that their main fortresses should have Spanish garrisons. The Dutch and English fears shown in 1598 were soon to be justified by a new and partly successful Spanish offensive.

The last stages of the struggle, 1598–1609

Franco-Spanish antagonism was by now far too deep-rooted to be ended by the Treaty of Vervins. Each power remained very ready to make trouble for the other when it could. The marquisate of Saluzzo was still contested between France and Savoy; and when in August 1600 Henry IV declared war and invaded the disputed area the Spanish government provided more than two million ducats to support the duke. The struggle, militarily a minor one, had important strategic implications. When peace was made in January 1601 Henry IV gave up his claim to Saluzzo; but he received in exchange a number of small territories – Bresse, Bugey, Gex and Valromey. This meant that the 'Spanish Road' between northern Italy and the Netherlands, which had been fundamental to Spain's strategic position since the northward march of Alba's army in 1567, now depended on a single bridge over the Rhône almost within sight of French territory and was thus terribly vulnerable to French attack. Such a victory for Henry IV and acceptance of such a defeat by Spain was a clear indication of how the balance of power in western Europe was changing; and Savoy was now a much less reliable ally of Spain than in the past. The result was that the Spaniards now began efforts to control the Engadine and Valtelline, the valleys further east linking Milan with the Tyrol which offered an alternative and safer route across the Alps. The following years saw a complicated struggle between Spain on the one hand and France, supported by Venice, on the other, in which each side sought to dominate the Valtelline and deny its use to the other. In 1603 the Count of Fuentes, the very energetic governor of Milan (he was Alba's nephew), suddenly built a powerful new fort at the entrance to the valley, clear evidence that

Spain would not allow her position to be undermined without a fight. Efforts were also made to strengthen her position in the Swiss Confederation as a whole. Already in 1587 a treaty of friendship had been signed with the Catholic cantons; and in 1604 Fuentes obtained from them permission for Spanish forces to march through their territory to the Rhine.

All this meant a serious change for the worse in Spain's strategic position. Without the use of the 'Spanish Road' the struggle with the Dutch rebels could hardly be carried on. Throughout Philip II's reign there had been no real threat to this vital line of communication: France, the only enemy able seriously to menace it, had been too divided and distracted to do so. Now the situation had changed. France was once more a great power with an active foreign policy: her recovery after the wars of religion was remarkably swift. In 1602 she made a defensive alliance with eleven of the thirteen Swiss cantons, while in the following year Henry IV took Geneva, the 'Calvinist Rome', under his protection. Among the Protestant princes of Germany, and still more in Italy, where there was widespread resentment of Spain's dominant influence, she was once again an active and threatening rival. From 1598 onwards, moreover, the Dutch rebels received French money and were occasionally allowed to recruit soldiers in France, while the dream of using the Turks as a weapon against Spain and her Italian possessions now revived in Paris. In January 1601 Henry IV urged his ambassador in Constantinople to give secret encouragement to Turkish attacks on Calabria and Sicily. The Vervins settlement, therefore, brought no more than a breathing-space in a rivalry that was not to end for another century.

The Anglo-Spanish war was ended only by the Treaty of London, signed in August 1604. Like the Vervins agreement this was essentially a recognition of stalemate, an acknowledgement that neither side could strike a decisive blow against the other. Yet it had for a moment seemed that Spain might strike such a blow by taking advantage of the serious revolt against English rule that broke out in Ireland early in 1595. The idea of using Irish discontent as a weapon against England was far from new. In 1534 Anglo-Irish nobles claiming to be defenders of the Catholic Church had sought help from both pope and emperor against the changes Henry VIII was beginning to introduce. In 1569 de Spes, the Spanish ambassador in London, had suggested that English rule in Ireland might be overthrown by supporting James Fitzmaurice, who was then leading a serious native rising. In 1579 and 1580 the hostility to Elizabeth of Pope Gregory XIII led to the sending of small forces of papal troops to aid a revolt in Munster against the English regime. However the rebellion in the later 1590s of much of Ulster, led by Hugh O'Neill, Earl of Tyrone, and Hugh O'Donnell, was by far the greatest threat the English had to face in Ireland during the sixteenth century. Tyrone and O'Donnell looked to Spain for backing: they told Philip II when asking for his help that 'We hope to restore the faith of the Church and so secure you a kingdom'; and in 1596 they asked that the Archduke Albert should become ruler of Ireland. In August 1598 the English suffered a serious defeat at the battle of the Yellow Ford: by then the war in Ulster was becoming the biggest and most frustrating military enterprise of Elizabeth's reign, one which cost her in all something close to the crushing sum of two million pounds.

But the war was won. A small Spanish force landed in southern Ireland in 1601. When it surrendered at Kinsale, after fighting well, in the first days of 1602, the revolt was over. Tyrone, O'Donnell and some other members of the old Gaelic aristocracy of Ulster fled to France, and finally to Rome, in the summer of 1607. Whether Philip II and Philip III lost an important opportunity by their failure to give more active support to the Irish rebels, as has sometimes been claimed, is doubtful. Distance and English strength at sea would have made such a strategy difficult. Yet their failure to intervene effectively in Ireland contrasts forcibly with English efforts to support native resistance to Spain, whether real as in the Netherlands or largely imaginary as in Portugal. Certainly many Englishmen saw Ireland as their country's most dangerous weak spot. In June 1608, after the war with Spain had ended, an experienced diplomat complained that 'We are afraid of every shadow lest it should give a pretence unto Spain to foment the rebellion we expect in Ireland'.[22]

Tentative Anglo-Spanish peace negotiations at Boulogne dragged on for some time from May 1600 onwards; but these were completely fruitless. Arguments over precedence, that intense preoccupation of every diplomat in that age, meant that the representatives of the two sides never met formally, while exchanges of letters and private meetings led nowhere. However the accession of James VI of Scotland to the English throne in March 1603 changed the situation. He had little of the anti-Spanish feeling that two decades of war and the threat of invasion had rooted in England. His accession therefore meant an immediate cease-fire, while Philip III and his ministers were willing to end a struggle which now seemed increasingly pointless. The peace meant that the Dutch were left alone to struggle

22. M. Lee, Jr, *James I and Henri IV: An Essay in English Foreign Policy, 1603–1610* (Urbana, Ill./Chicago/London, 1970), p. 121.

against Spain: the English government refused to negotiate in 1604 unless the emerging Dutch Republic was allowed to be a party to the negotiations if it wished, but in fact it refused to take part.

That the new state would have a quasi-republican political structure was still not quite certain. Any acceptance of Spanish suzerainty, even a purely nominal one, was now out of the question. During the Franco-Spanish negotiations of 1598 Elizabeth had made a last effort to secure some settlement of this kind, but with no success. However a number of factors – the peace of 1604, coupled with the loss of Ostend, which fell in the same year to a Spanish army after a three-year siege, and the heavy taxation that the continuing struggle demanded – led Oldenbarnevelt to make tentative advances to Henry IV as a possible ruler of the new state. But this was no more than a last flicker of the idea that the Dutch rebels must, for their own security and to gain international respectability, find a foreigner able and willing to become their monarch. Growing wealth, military success and the experience of independence had given birth to a psychology very different from that of the 1570s and 1580s. There were now important forces within the new state which opposed an end to the war. Prince Maurice, with his supporters and the military and naval commanders, feared that the coming of peace might reduce the power of the Orange family and undermine the still very imperfect unity of the rebel provinces by removing the threat of Spanish reconquest. This attitude was supported by the English and French governments, which were happy to see the war drag on. Peace might provide a breathing-space in which Spanish power, shaken by the events of the last decades, could revive. It was also likely to accelerate the spectacular growth of Dutch trade, which was already attracting attention and envy. In November 1607 two English diplomats in the Netherlands pointed out to Robert Cecil, now Earl of Salisbury, 'how convenient this war would be for the good of His Majesty's realms if it might be maintained without his charge'.[23]

But there were also powerful forces on both sides pressing for at least some respite in the apparently endless struggle. In the rebel provinces the financial strain of continued fighting was considerable, in spite of growing prosperity. In 1591, the first year in which the Dutch took the offensive, their armed forces had cost 3.2 million florins: by 1607 the annual cost had soared to 8.8 million.[24] Oldenbarnevelt was in favour of peace; and he was supported by the merchant-

23. Ibid., p. 94.
24. Parker, 'War and economic change', p. 191.

oligarchy of Holland. In the provinces still under Spanish rule, where the economic damage done by the war had been greater, the impoverished government felt the need of an end to the fighting even more keenly. In 1604–07, helped by the fact that she was now at peace with both France and England, Spain had considerable military success in the continuing struggle. But this did nothing to lighten the economic burden on the 'obedient' provinces. Both the Archduke Albert and his very able military commander, the Genoese aristocrat Ambrogio Spinola, pressed strongly for an end to the war: Spinola claimed in 1607 that he needed 200,000 ducats each month merely to keep his men from mutinying from lack of pay and 300,000 to fight effectively. He had already financed the campaign of 1606 largely by raising a huge loan in Genoa on his personal security.

As early as May 1606, therefore, the archduke made advances to both Prince Maurice and Oldenbarnevelt in an effort to open peace negotiations. He renewed the attempt in the following year, so that an armistice to last eight months was agreed in April 1607, much to the annoyance of Henry IV. In April 1608 his representatives arrived in Holland. The negotiations were prolonged and difficult. Their success for long hung in the balance, while the Dutch strengthened their hand by making a defensive agreement with France in January 1608 and another with England five months later. A series of difficult questions had to be faced. Were the rebel provinces to be formally recognized as independent, something on which the Dutch now insisted? Were they to be allowed to prohibit the public exercise of the Catholic faith in the territory they controlled, something deeply offensive to Spanish pride? Were the Dutch to be free to trade in the East Indies, where their activities were already arousing complaints from Philip III's Portuguese subjects? The last of these questions particularly divided opinion in the rebel provinces. Abandonment of the Dutch East India Company, whose activities clearly held out such commercial promise, and of the creation of the proposed West India Company, aroused much opposition in Amsterdam. Yet an end to the fighting and the Spanish trade embargoes[25] would give a great fillip to commerce with southern Europe. To the moment peace was made the debate on this issue went on. It was only when a renewal of the war seemed a real possibility that a compromise was found, largely through French mediation, in the form not of a peace treaty but of an agreement signed in April 1609 for a truce which was to last for twelve years.

25. See above, pp. 35–6.

This was a great success for the Dutch, the culmination of four decades of struggle. For this reason the truce was bitterly resented in Madrid and accepted only with great reluctance. Philip III had deeply disliked the armistice of 1607 and more than once talked of deposing the archduke who was apparently so ready to sacrifice Spanish interests and pride. The settlement of 1609 was in effect forced on him, a much less effective ruler than his father, by Spinola and the archduke and by a new Spanish government bankruptcy in 1607 which emphasized how difficult it would be to carry on the war. The king's resentment is understandable. The freedom of the provinces which made up the new United Netherlands was now recognized. Both Spain and the archduke agreed that they were dealing with them 'in the capacity of, and taking them for free lands, provinces, and estates, over which they claim nothing'.[26] This was something less than a complete and formal recognition of sovereignty, but a very important concession none the less. Moreover the rebel provinces gave up no territory and made no concession on the religious question. Antwerp continued to be strangled commercially by Dutch control of the mouth of the Scheldt, to the benefit of Amsterdam. The thorny question of trade with the East Indies was left shrouded in discreet vagueness; but at least the Dutch had not agreed to their exclusion from it. The one thing they had not achieved was a permanent settlement: in due course the question of what was to replace the twelve-year truce would have to be faced. But by 1609 the one lasting constructive achievement of the intricate west European struggles of the later sixteenth century was an accomplished fact. A new state with potentialities which far transcended its limited physical size and resources was now established.

Yet the conflicts of the later sixteenth century and the peace settlements of 1598–1609 which ended them were by no means a conclusive defeat for Spain. Nor were they seen as such by contemporaries. In retrospect it is clear that she now suffered from internal difficulties which in the long run were to cripple her. Much of the sixteenth century had been for her an age of economic and demographic expansion. For half a century from about 1530 onwards both the area under cultivation and the population had grown substantially. This process had now been reversed. In Castile at least by the end of the century agriculture was in decline, and there was a marked drift of population from the countryside to the towns. Disease had made devastating inroads: the bad harvests of 1596–97 and the great plague

26. Lee, *James I and Henri IV*, p. 131.

epidemic of 1596–1602 probably nullified all the population growth achieved during the previous century. Such setbacks, coupled with the failure to achieve victory abroad, meant that a mood of fatalism, of resignation and almost of despair, was now widespread. None the less Spain was still in the early seventeenth century a very great power. Apart from the losses in the Netherlands her empire in Europe was still intact. From the Turks in the Mediterranean she had now little to fear, though the Barbary corsairs from their north African bases were still a serious nuisance. Her army was still the finest in Europe. The skill and pertinacity of her diplomats was widely respected and even feared. The flow of bullion from America was now passing its peak; but this was hardly as yet visible to most observers. Spain had not been victorious; but both her efforts and her achievements had been remarkable. Neither Philip II as he lay dying in 1598, nor his son when he reluctantly agreed to the truce of 1609, was the ruler of a defeated country.

Indeed, to inflict a decisive defeat on any major state, to impose on it truly crushing peace terms, was in this age almost impossible. The most striking aspect of the long and costly international struggles of the sixteenth century is their limited results. The states of western Europe had remarkably little success in their constant efforts to expand at the expense of one another. The establishment of Spain as a dominant force in the Italian peninsula, and in a different way the emergence of a new independent state in the northern Netherlands, are the only important exceptions to this judgement. Elsewhere, after decades of warfare, the political frontiers of western Europe in the early seventeenth century were strikingly similar to those of 100 years earlier. Rulers did not lack the ambition to make striking changes in the territorial and dynastic balance. They might dream of dismembering the lands of a rival, as Charles V had done after Pavia, or of a great accretion of power to their own family, as when Philip II hoped to make his daughter queen of France. But events continually and cruelly underlined the weakness of both economic structures and state machines, a weakness which made such ambitions impossible to achieve. Limited economic resources made it impossible for any state, even for Spain when the American silver flowed most freely, to bear the burdens of a prolonged and large-scale war without very serious difficulty; and the growing predominance of sieges[27] meant that wars were very difficult to win quickly, while administrative machines could not mobilize effectively what

27. See above, pp. 9–10.

economic resources there were. The ambitions of rulers, the force of tradition, pulled every state towards the expansion of its territory and influence. But to maintain effectively over long periods the instruments, the armies and navies, through which alone this expansion could be realized, was extremely, often impossibly, difficult. Much of the international relations of this period is therefore a story of inflated ambitions, disappointed hopes and grudgingly accepted compromises.

CHAPTER EIGHT

Approach to Conflict, 1609–18

German weakness and the Jülich–Cleves question

For half a century from the 1550s onwards Germany and German affairs had played only a secondary role in international relations. After the achievement in 1552 of French control of the three bishoprics of Metz, Toul and Verdun, and the Cateau-Cambrésis peace of 1559, the preoccupations of the west European powers lay elsewhere, in the Netherlands, France and Portugal. After the Peace of Augsburg in 1555 religious antagonisms in the German world, though far from appeased and indeed becoming more acute, did not threaten international stability like those in France, the Netherlands provinces or perhaps even Scotland. It was only in 1609, as Spain's struggle to subdue her rebel Dutch provinces was temporarily suspended, that Germany emerged as the arena in which the rivalries of the powers were now most likely to find expression. But from then on the progression to the disasters of the Thirty Years War, which began in 1618, was rapid.

The second half of the sixteenth century was far from being an age of religious peace in the German world. The Peace of Augsburg, decreed by the imperial diet in September 1555, recognized the existence and status of Lutheranism, doctrinally embodied in the Augsburg Confession of 1530, side by side with the Catholic faith and on a footing of equality. Yet this was essentially a political settlement, or attempt at one, a compromise forced on the German states and their rulers by the fact that neither the Lutheran nor the Catholic side could crush the other. Religious uniformity, not diversity or toleration, remained the ideal; and in the decree lip-service was paid to the need for efforts to re-establish such uniformity. Equally serious,

Calvinism, now rapidly becoming active and militant in a way that Lutheranism had never been, was not mentioned at all: its status remained unsettled and questionable. Religious division and its political implications therefore continued to provide in Germany plenty of materials to feed the flames of some future conflict. The generation which followed the peace of 1555, though it saw no great crisis, also saw tensions in Germany become if anything more acute as the Counter-Reformation gathered momentum, as on the Calvinist side the Elector Palatine and on the Catholic one the dukes of Bavaria emerged as the most obvious leaders of antagonistic religious parties, and as it became clear that neither the emperor nor the imperial diet could control the conflicting groups. The ecclesiastical states, small, often badly governed and a tempting prey to neighbouring secular rulers, and the free cities, also often small and weak, were particular elements of instability; and in the early 1580s a serious crisis with ominous implications for the future erupted in the ecclesiastical electorate of Cologne.

The fate of the electorate had international significance because of its strategic position, on the middle Rhine and with a common frontier with the Spanish Netherlands. In 1577 a young nobleman, Gebhard Truchsess von Waldburg, was elected archbishop (though he was not as yet even an ordained priest). In 1583 he granted toleration to Protestants in the electorate and married, in a Lutheran service, a nun with whom he had fallen in love. This was a challenge both to Catholic feeling and to Catholic strategic interests that could not be ignored. The result was a desultory and badly conducted war which became yet another call on Spain's more and more stretched resources in the Netherlands and did not end until 1589: by then Spanish forces had driven those of Truchsess from the electorate and made sure that he would have a reliably Catholic successor, a member of the Bavarian ruling house. This was an important Catholic success. It was followed by others in several of the German ecclesiastical states, notably in the bishopric of Strasbourg, where Lutheran influence was decisively checked in the 1590s (though the city itself remained solidly Lutheran). Moreover, all this went on against a background marked by the powerlessness of both emperor and diet, a situation in which German political life became more chaotic and uncontrollable as its central institutions, such as they now were, became steadily weaker. Rudolf II, Holy Roman Emperor since 1576, had never been a strong or stable personality. As in his later years he sank into insanity and seclusion in the Hradschin palace in Prague, he was more than ever unable to meet the almost impossible demands that his position now made on him. The diet, for its part, was more and more paralysed when it met by the disputes and grievances of the different religious factions. This process culminated in the collapse with nothing accomplished of its meeting in 1608, followed by an equally ineffective one in 1613. By then the situation was more strained and dangerous than ever.

In 1607 tension and ill-feeling were heightened when in Donauwörth, a minor imperial free city in south Germany, long-standing friction between the Lutheran town council and an increasingly strong Catholic minority came to a head. The Duke of Bavaria, the most powerful of the neighbouring princes, intervened with imperial approval and then took advantage of the situation to annex the city to his own territories. The episode was not in itself of great importance. But it drew widespread attention and heightened the alarm of German Protestants of every colour. It also threw once more into sharp relief the vulnerability of many of the free cities, the greed of many of the territorial princes and the decay of imperial authority. Of far greater significance, however, was the question of the Jülich–Cleves succession which erupted in 1609. This group of territories (as well as the duchies of Cleves and Jülich it included the duchy of Berg and the county of Mark) had a strategic significance similar to, and even greater than, that of the electorate of Cologne. Non-German powers, Spain, the Dutch and rapidly reviving France, were certain to be deeply interested in its fate. This had already been made clear when in 1598 Spanish forces from the Netherlands invaded the duchies, only to be driven out by Dutch ones in the spring of the following year. The death in 1609 without a direct heir of their ruler, the insane Duke John William, was therefore an event of international importance. Of the many claimants to the succession two were significant: the Elector of Brandenburg and the Count Palatine of Neuburg. Both were Lutherans; and success for either would mean that the largest and richest secular principality in north-west Germany had moved from Catholic to Protestant control. On both sides of the religious divide, therefore, there was intense interest in the fate of these territories; and on both there were already ominous signs of preparations for conflict. The summer of 1608 had seen the foundation of the Union for the Defence of Evangelical Religion, a grouping of Calvinist princes with some Lutheran support led by the Elector Palatine Frederick IV. In the following year this was answered by the creation of a Catholic League which united the clerical electors of the Rhineland, those of Cologne, Trier and Mainz, with the Duke of Bavaria and some minor princes. Both of these were military alliances financed by contributions from their members. Both had enterprising leaders: Christian of Anhalt, the representative of Frederick IV, on the evangelical side, and Maximilian of Bavaria on the Catholic one. Neither was completely effective, for both suffered from disunity and shortage of money; but their very existence showed how potentially explosive the situation in Germany had now become.

There was little doubt that in strict law the territories in dispute ought to be administered by the emperor until the conflicting claims to them had been resolved. But this was quite unacceptable to the Dutch. The possibility that they might still be in Habsburg hands when the twelve-year truce with Spain expired was too dangerous to contemplate. Prince Maurice, given a free hand, would probably have invaded the duchies as soon as John William died; but Olden-barnevelt and the peace party, who feared that this would mean renewed war with Spain, were able to prevent such drastic action. In France also attitudes were divided, with some of Henry IV's advisers, notably his finance minister Sully, favouring immediate and forcible intervention while others urged caution and the king himself was un-decided. But one important change was now clear. The main focus of conflict had moved, for the first time in more than two generations, to Germany. Late in May 1609 the Brandenburg and Neuburg claim-ants agreed to joint administration of the duchies for the time being, until a final settlement could be reached. (Henry IV had already tried unsuccessfully to obtain some agreement between them before John William died.) The months that followed, however, saw the situ-ation become steadily more tense. In July the Archduke Leopold, ac-ting in the name of the emperor, seized Jülich. In October Henry IV demanded that he withdraw; and it was clear that a formidable anti-Habsburg coalition was in process of being formed. The princes of the Evangelical Union met at Hall in Swabia at the end of the year; and in February 1610 they agreed to raise an army to back the two Protestant claimants to the duchies. The attitude of Henry IV had hitherto been somewhat ambiguous, for as late as October 1609, in spite of bellicose gestures, he was still playing with the idea of mar-rying one of his daughters to a Spanish prince. But he now promised his support to the union and began to form an army in Champagne which could be used to invade the lower Rhineland. Almost equally threatening, a treaty signed late in April with the eternally acquisitive Charles Emmanuel of Savoy, on terms that involved large French concessions, was meant to pave the way for an imminent invasion of Italy and the overthrow of the still-dominant Spanish position there.

Even the cautious James I agreed to provide 4,000 soldiers to support the Protestant cause in Germany, though he refused to contemplate a conflict with Spain. A new war, another round in the century-old Franco-Spanish struggle, seemed on the point of breaking out.

The death of Henry IV: a breathing-space for Spain

This did not happen. Henry IV was the driving force behind the anti-Spanish alliance: without him it had little substance. For several years he had been making considerable efforts to strengthen his relations with the German Protestant states, especially the Calvinist ones; but these were neither strong enough nor reliable enough to be very effective allies. The pacific and hesitant James I was no more to be relied on. Charles Emmanuel of Savoy, with his eyes firmly fixed on his own ambitions in the duchy of Milan, was an equally shaky support; and in the Dutch Republic there was deep resistance to any renewal of the costly and demanding war that had just ended. Henry, however, was almost certainly determined to fight, though his exact intentions are still something of a mystery. Quite apart from any political considerations, he was driven by frivolous personal motives. A notorious womanizer, he was now besotted by the beautiful and very young wife of the Prince de Condé. Her husband had fled with her to Brussels to escape the king's attentions, and the government there had refused to return them to France as Henry demanded. Personal pique therefore reinforced political ambition in urging a campaign in the Spanish Netherlands. But on 14 May, almost in the moment of leaving Paris to join his army, Henry was murdered, stabbed in his carriage by a Catholic fanatic convinced that he was thus helping to safeguard his faith.

The whole international situation was transformed at once. The position of Spain, apparently under serious threat, immediately became much stronger as the coalition against her collapsed. France, by contrast, was sharply weakened. The death of Henry IV had results in some ways similar to those that had followed that of Henry II half a century earlier. The new king, Louis XIII, was an eight-year-old child. His mother, Marie de Medici, who became regent, was a foreigner and neither strong nor intelligent. Personal and factional ambitions revived at once among the leading French nobles; and a half-hearted attempt at revolt by some of the greatest of them (the Prince de Condé, the Duc de Bouillon, the Duc de Nevers and others) in 1614 intensified a growing political weakness and instability.[1] Moreover the regent and her advisers, notably Père Coton, the confessor of Henry IV, and the papal nuncio in Paris, were markedly Catholic and even pro-Spanish in outlook. At the end of January 1611 Sully, the *surintendant* of finance, who had pressed for the carrying-on of the anti-Spanish policy of Henry IV, resigned; but he had already lost all influence. In April it was agreed that the young Louis XIII should marry Anne of Austria, daughter of Philip III of Spain, while the Infant Philip, heir to the Spanish throne, was to become the husband of a French princess: the marriages took place at the end of 1615. These dynastic links seemed to symbolize a new unity of the two greatest Catholic states, especially as they were accompanied by the signature of a Franco-Spanish defensive alliance to last for ten years. Any appearances of this kind were misleading: French fear and resentment of Spanish power were as strong as ever; but for the time being at least they could not express themselves openly.

However, the death of Henry IV, though it ended the threat of full-scale war in western Europe, did nothing to settle the Jülich–Cleves question. Dutch forces with some French help captured the city of Jülich at the beginning of September 1610; but friction in the duchies continued between supporters of the rival Neuburg and Brandenburg claimants, intensified by the fact that the former had now become a Catholic and the latter a Calvinist. In 1614 the situation came to a head when in August a large Spanish force from the Netherlands entered the duchies to support the Neuburg claimant. There was now no real chance of French intervention, still less of any effective action by England; but the capture by the Spaniards of the Rhine crossing of Wesel, a strategic point of great importance, forced a Dutch reaction. The result was a compromise. The Treaty of Xanten of November 1614 left Cleves and Mark in the hands of the Elector of Brandenburg and Jülich and Berg in those of the Count Palatine of Neuburg. War had been averted; but the dangers posed by Germany's weakness and possible foreign intervention there were now unmistakable. The divisions of the German states were as glaring as ever: neither the Catholic League nor the Evangelical Union was united and neither could play any effective role in the settlement. The danger of foreign involvement in German quarrels was growing. In the spring of 1611 James I had arranged the marriage of his daughter Elizabeth to the Elector Palatine Frederick V, the most ac-

---

1. The difficulty of the French position after 1610 is illustrated in N.M. Sutherland, 'The origins of the Thirty Years War and the structure of European politics', *English Historical Review* CVII (1992), 601–18.

tive and ambitious of the German Protestant princes; and a year later
an English alliance with the Evangelical Union was signed and joined
by the Dutch in 1613. A Spanish garrison remained in Wesel and a
Dutch one in Jülich.

In the decade after 1610 Spain seemed to many contemporaries to
stand forth as the greatest power in Europe as clearly as under Philip
II. Energetic and aggressive governors such as the Count of Fuentes
in Milan and the Duke of Osuña in Naples defended and consolidated her position in Italy. A series of skilled and masterful diplomats
strengthened her influence at the major European courts. Iñigo de
Cardenas in France, the count of Gondomar in England, Balthasar
de Zuñiga at the court of the Emperor Rudolf in Prague and his successor, the count of Oñate, made up a galaxy of diplomatic talent
that no other state could equal. Spanish military prestige remained
very high. When in 1612 Charles Emmanuel of Savoy, hungry as ever
for territorial gain, seized the duchy of Montferrat, a detached possession of the Duke of Mantua who had just died, he set off a war with
Spain which lasted until papal mediation engineered a peace in October 1617. In this struggle Charles Emmanuel was supported by
many of Spain's enemies. Venice, traditionally anti-Spanish, backed
him with secret subsidies. The French government, in a temporary
access of strength, promised him support in 1616 in an effort to pro-
long the war. His army included 4,000 Protestant mercenaries recruited in Germany. Yet the tide of military success ran in general in
Spain's favour; and in 1618 fear of Spanish power and aggression in
Italy was intensified by the revelation of a plan (the details are still
mysterious, but Osuña was certainly implicated) for the seizure of
Venice by a *coup d'état.*

Yet this view of Spain as still immensely powerful, a state whose influence over her neighbours, enmeshed in her intrigues, was dangerously great, was not shared by Spanish opinion in general or by the
Spaniards best qualified to assess her situation. They, on the contrary, were driven more and more into angry defensiveness, a prey increasingly to a sense of threat, even of impending disaster. For such
forebodings there was considerable material justification. Spain's
economic and demographic weakness, visible by the end of the sixteenth century, was growing. The expulsion of the Moriscos, the remaining population of Moorish descent, which began in 1609, meant
that over the next five years the country lost about 275,000 mostly
productive people: the population of the kingdom of Valencia, the
worst-hit area, fell by about a quarter. The flow of American silver, on
which the power of Spanish rulers to borrow so much depended, was

declining sharply. At the end of the sixteenth century Philip II had drawn about two million ducats a year from this source; but by 1615–16 this had fallen to only a million and by 1620 to a mere 800,000.[2] But material factors of this kind were less important than a pervasive sense of failure, a vague but strong feeling that things had gone badly wrong and that not merely sweeping internal reforms but also a reassertion of Spain's status abroad were urgently needed.

What rankled most of all with many Spaniards was the sense that the country's prestige, its *reputaciòn*, had been badly damaged. This seemed the greatest threat of all, given the supreme importance in that age of such prestige, of a state being respected, even feared, by its neighbours. 'In my view', Zuñiga is alleged to have said, 'a monarchy that has lost its *reputaciòn*, even if it has lost no territory, is a sky without light, a sun without rays, a body without a soul.'[3] A series of setbacks, most galling of all the enforced truce with the Dutch rebels in 1609, had undermined Spain's international standing; and memories of the great achievements of the previous century made the sense of loss all the sharper. An active foreign policy, it could be argued, was therefore essential. Caution and passivity would merely give Spain's enemies the time and opportunity to bring about her final downfall. In such a forward policy the German world was now to become central.

The approach to the Thirty Years War

During the decades that followed the abdication of Charles V, relations between the two branches, Spanish and Austrian, into which the Habsburg family was now divided were not particularly cordial. The Emperor Maximilian II (1564–76) was so ready to tolerate Lutheranism that he was even accused of apostasy and may on his deathbed have refused the Catholic sacraments: while his son and successor, Rudolf II (1576–1612), though a very different type of man, played an equally secondary role in the calculations of his great Spanish cousin. France, the Netherlands, England and Portugal bulked far larger in thinking in Madrid than the affairs of central Europe; while for the Austrian Habsburgs the supreme problem was still that of relations with the Ottoman Empire. Yet repeated intermar-

---

2. J.H. Elliott, 'Spain and its empire in the sixteenth and seventeenth centuries', in his *Spain and its World, 1500–1700* (New Haven, Conn./London, 1989), p. 24.

3. Idem, 'Foreign policy and domestic crisis: Spain, 1598–1659', in *Spain and its World*, p. 122.

riage meant that family links remained very close. Maximilian married the sister of Philip II and Philip the daughter of Maximilian, while one of Philip's daughters was the wife of one of Maximilian's sons. Spanish influences remained strong in Vienna and Prague (though there were no corresponding German ones in Madrid), and by the end of the sixteenth century they were beginning to grow. Nor had the idea of a renewed personal union of the Spanish monarchy and the Holy Roman Empire, a recreation of the empire of Charles V, disappeared. In the 1590s Pope Clement VII urged Philip II to secure the imperial dignity for his son; and at the end of 1609 Zuñiga, then Spanish ambassador at the court of Rudolf II in Prague, was ordered to prepare the way for the election of Philip III as the next Holy Roman emperor. This initiative, however, was essentially a response to the danger of war with France as the Jülich–Cleves question approached its crisis; and with the death of Henry IV it was abandoned.[4] Zuñiga was opposed to the scheme; and neither the Duke of Lerma, Philip III's favourite and chief minister, nor the king himself liked the idea.

None the less the position of the Austrian Habsburgs in Spanish policy was now becoming steadily more important. If the dignity of Holy Roman Emperor, with all the prestige it still conveyed, were for the first time for almost two centuries to be lost to the Habsburg family, this would strike a devastating blow at Spain's *reputación*, so essential and apparently so threatened; and such a loss was conceivable, for in 1616–18 there were negotiations between the Palatinate and Bavaria for the possible election as the next emperor of the Bavarian ruler, Duke Maximilian. Moreover, Spain would soon have to face the agonizingly difficult question of whether to begin again the war in the Netherlands when the twelve-year truce with the Dutch ended in 1621. Another effort to recover the lost provinces would make it essential to have full control of the vital route from northern Italy to the southern Netherlands. Alsace, a vital part of this 'Spanish Road', and the Tyrol, which offered an alternative way from the duchy of Milan across the Alps, were both possessions of the Austrian Habsburgs. If, in return for Spanish support, a future Habsburg emperor could be persuaded to place them in Spanish hands, Philip III and his government would have won a great strategic success and reasserted Spain's leading position among the states of Europe. There were unsuccessful negotiations to this end in 1614; but in 1617 it seemed that the goal had been achieved. In that year Oñate, the very

4. B. Chudoba, *Spain and the Empire, 1519–1643* (Chicago, 1952), pp. 190, 202–3.

forceful Spanish ambassador in Vienna, signed with the Archduke Ferdinand, who had ruled Inner Austria since 1596, a secret treaty which provided that Philip III was to abandon any claims of his own to the imperial dignity (through his mother he was a grandson of Maximilian II), which was to go to Ferdinand when the ill and childless Emperor Matthias, who had succeeded his brother Rudolf II in 1612, should die. In return Alsace and the Tyrol were to become Spanish possessions in full sovereignty, while Ferdinand also promised to support Spain in Lombardy if necessary. In the same year the archduke was also elected as the next king of Bohemia, which since 1526 had been part of the Habsburg assembly of central European territories.

Spanish diplomacy had apparently won a brilliant success. It seemed to have consolidated Spain's strategic position and, even more important, secured the imminent succession of a militantly Catholic and reliably pro-Spanish emperor. But the situation in the central European territories of the Habsburgs was extremely strained and unstable. Religious tensions there had now reached a dangerous pitch. In the middle decades of the sixteenth century Protestantism in various forms – Lutheranism, later Calvinism, the indigenous Bohemian Brethren and smaller and more extreme groups such as Anabaptists and Unitarians – seemed to be carrying all before it in central Europe. Not until the end of the century could Catholicism make much effective response. From the 1590s onwards, however, a powerful counter-offensive got under way. In Inner Austria the Archduke Ferdinand began a determined attack on Protestantism: it was his uncompromising Catholicism most of all that made him acceptable to Spain as emperor-to-be. In Moravia Franz Dietrichstein, who became Bishop of Olmütz in 1598, did the same, while a year or two later Zdenek Lobkowitz, the Chancellor of Bohemia, persuaded Rudolf II to dismiss his Protestant advisers and launch an offensive against the Bohemian Brethren.[5] The scene was now set for the last of the series of great religious struggles, with powerful political overtones, that had afflicted much of Europe for almost three generations.

In this the Protestant forces won at first some notable successes. In January 1608 the Hungarian diet forced the Archduke Matthias (who was to become emperor four years later), as a condition of being elected king of Hungary, to concede the right of universal Protestant

---

5. R.J.W. Evans, *The Making of the Habsburg Monarchy, 1550–1700: An Interpretation* (Oxford, 1979), ch. 2, gives a good account of this Catholic revival.

worship and agree to expel the Jesuits from the kingdom. In the following year in Bohemia the more and more ineffective Rudolf II was forced to agree to the Letter of Majesty, in which he promised complete redress of Protestant grievances. But the Protestants lacked the unity of their Catholic opponents: division into competing sects, and often bitter doctrinal disputes, severely weakened them. The Letter of Majesty was never fully applied in practice; and in 1618 a final crisis emerged over the refusal of Catholic religious authorities to allow the building of Protestant churches in two towns, Braunau and Klostergrab. On 23 May a crowd of Protestant delegates, who had been called to meet in Prague, invaded the Hradshin palace there, seized two Catholic ministers of the Emperor Matthias, Martinitz and Slawata, both of whom had refused to sign the Letter of Majesty, and threw them from a window. They were unhurt; but this famous incident marked a final and irrevocable breach and the beginning of a Protestant revolt.

A provisional government was set up, the Jesuits were expelled from Bohemia and efforts were made to raise an army. But the new regime suffered from the outset from crippling weaknesses. It was poorly led and undermined by personal and social divisions, while its newly recruited army was a broken reed. None the less a clear and serious challenge had been offered to Habsburg power, particularly since what had happened offered opportunities for ambitious outsiders to fish in these troubled waters. Charles Emmanuel of Savoy provided a force of mercenaries to support the revolt and dreamed of himself becoming king of Bohemia and perhaps even Holy Roman Emperor when Matthias died. In this situation what was Spain to do? The Spanish government was taken completely by surprise by the sudden outbreak of the Bohemian revolt and deeply divided over how to respond. It was now 'caught up in a situation where all decisions would be wrong'.[6] There were strong arguments in favour of caution and influential advisers to voice them: Philip III's confessor, Fray Luis de Aliaga, strongly opposed intervention. The financial position was more difficult than ever, for in 1617 the government had been forced to make a new issue of debased copper coinage, while a big and expensive expedition against the Barbary corsairs of Algiers was already under serious consideration. On the other hand Spain was still the standard-bearer of Catholicism (though the religious argument was not explicitly made in these discussions), and not merely prestige but also important material considerations pointed towards

6. P. Brightwell, 'The Spanish system and the Twelve Years Truce', *English Historical Review* LXXXIX (1974), 270.

intervention. At the end of April 1619 the Bohemian rebels invaded Moravia and set up a provisional government there, while the estates of Silesia came out in their support and there were signs of sympathy for them in the Austrian duchies. By early June their poorly organized army was at the gates of Vienna. In August the Bohemian estates chose the Elector Palatine Frederick V, the most actively Protestant of the German princes, as king; and if they lost Bohemia, could the Austrian Habsburgs survive as a significant political or military force? If their power collapsed might not the vital 'Spanish Road' be very seriously threatened? After all, only two months after the revolt in Bohemia the Protestant party in the Valtelline had seized power and closed the strategic pass, making it impossible for Spanish forces to move through it from Milan to the Tyrol.[7]

Even after Frederick had been foolhardy enough to accept the Bohemian throne it was far from certain that a great European struggle must now break out. The new king could hope for no active support from his father-in-law, James I. Nor did the other Protestant princes of Germany do anything effective to help him. France, however strong her underlying rivalry with Spain, remained for the time being on the sidelines. Charles Emmanuel of Savoy was too weak to count for much by himself. The crushing defeat of the Bohemian rebels at the White Mountain just outside Prague in November 1620, by an army of the Catholic League provided by Maximilian of Bavaria, might conceivably have ended the crisis which had begun with the defenestration of 1618. But Frederick V, even as a fugitive, refused to make any formal submission to the newly elected (August 1619) Emperor Ferdinand II. More important, the war party, led by Zuñiga (a veteran of the armada of 1588), was now in the ascendant in Madrid. In November 1620 7,000 Spanish troops from Italy entered Innsbruck and large-scale Spanish intervention became an accomplished fact. The Archduke Albert, who had argued strongly with the support of Spinola for a renewal of the truce with the Dutch, died in 1621. He lived just long enough to see the renewal of war with the rebel provinces when the twelve-year truce ended in April, while in September Spinola invaded and easily occupied the Palatinate. Spain had now embarked on a last effort, prolonged, heroic but in the end futile, to preserve the greatness she had achieved under Charles V and Philip II. Germany was to become the prey of ambitious native princes and

---

7. The debate in Madrid is well discussed in two articles by P. Brightwell, 'The Spanish origins of the Thirty Years War', *European Studies Review* 9 (1979), 409–31, and 'Spain and Bohemia: the decision to intervene, 1619', *European Studies Review* 12 (1982), 117–40.

foreign rulers and their brutally destructive mercenary armies. The war that was now beginning, prolonged and incoherent, a series of separate conflicts rather than any single struggle, was to have results quite impossible to foresee in 1618–21 and to mark the beginning of a new age in international relations in Europe.

CHAPTER NINE

The Ottomans and Europe

From the standpoint of international relations in a strict sense it may seem unnecessary to give the Ottoman Empire separate discussion in the history of the sixteenth century. As earlier chapters have shown, it was always a very important factor, potential if not always active, in the relations between the monarchies of Europe. The rulers of France from the 1520s, the Dutch rebels intermittently from the 1560s, Elizabeth and her ministers in the 1580s, all hoped to use the Ottomans as a weapon against Habsburg Spain. The frightening Ottoman conquests in south-eastern Europe and the Danube valley became the greatest military preoccupation of the Austrian Habsburgs and had significant implications for the progress of the Reformation in Germany with all its international repercussions. Yet it is difficult, and would be misleading, to treat the Ottoman Empire as an international player quite like France, Spain or England. Its view of the world and the assumptions on which it was based, both the strengths and weaknesses of its government, the fact that it was an Asiatic power to which Irak, Azerbaijan and the Caucasus were at least as important as the Balkans or the Danube valley, even its size and heterogeneity, all marked it out clearly as unique. It was a great force in international relations, but one with its own peculiar character. It therefore demands at least some degree of separate treatment.

The threat from the east

The later decades of the fifteenth century saw the Turkish advance in the Balkans and eastern Mediterranean become, in the eyes of European observers, extremely menacing. The fall of Constantinople in 1453 to the great Sultan Mehmed II produced widespread dismay.

To many contemporaries the loss of the great city, now far gone in decay but for more than eight centuries a bulwark against the Muslim world, seemed the end of an age, a portent full of threat for the future. It also made clear, with more humiliating clarity than any previous Turkish success, the power of the expanding Ottoman Empire and the impotence of Christian Europe in face of it.[1] The years that followed fully confirmed these forebodings. The remaining small Christian-ruled principalities in Greece, those in Athens and the Morea, fell in 1458–60, while the 'empire' of Trebizond, on the north coast of Asia Minor, the last feeble remnant of Byzantine greatness, was overrun in 1461. Bosnia came under Turkish rule in 1463–64, while in 1475 the Tatar khanate of the Crimea became a vassal-state of the sultan. Simultaneously Mehmed achieved his most important success of all when he conquered the rival Turkish principality of Karaman in Anatolia, which had for many years been a powerful and dangerous rival on his eastern frontier. By 1476 the inability of the Holy Roman Emperor Frederick III to protect his Austrian lands against destructive Turkish raids had led to serious peasant unrest there. These impressive Turkish successes were indeed mingled with some failures. Belgrade withstood a determined attack in 1458. So in 1480 did the island of Rhodes, which in the hands of the Knights of St John was the main centre of Christian raiding and piracy in the eastern Mediterranean. Yet when Mehmed died in 1481 he had justified all too well the title of 'The Conqueror' with which Turkish tradition endowed him and earned the admiration, however reluctant, of many Christian observers.

Moreover the tide of Ottoman victory continued to flow during the genesis and first stages of the Italian wars. In 1480 a Turkish seizure of Otranto in southern Italy, extremely brutal though short-lived (12,000 of the inhabitants were said to have been slaughtered), seemed a terrifying indication of what might be in store for the peninsula: the pope thought of fleeing to the safety of his French territory of Avignon. In 1492, as a new world was being opened to European conquest across the Atlantic, there was a series of very destructive raids into Croatia, Styria, Carniola, Carinthia and Hungary: the Emperor Maximilian I, in his only campaign against the Turks in 1493, could do nothing to stop their attacks. In 1499 another marauding onslaught penetrated Venetian territory as far as Vicenza.

The Italian struggles that began in 1494 therefore took place in a

---

1. These reactions are illustrated in R. Schwoebel, *The Shadow of the Crescent: The Renaissance Image of the Turk (1453–1517)* (Nieukoop, 1967), ch. 1.

world in which the Ottoman Empire was increasingly feared and respected; and much of what happened during the century that followed intensified these feelings. Conquering Egypt, capturing Rhodes, overrunning much of Hungary, becoming a great naval power in the Mediterranean, bringing most of the north African coastline under at least their formal control, the Turks seemed more than any state of Christian Europe with the possible exception of Spain to embody military and political power and a menacing capacity for territorial expansion. By the end of the sixteenth century this feeling was little if at all less than it had been 100 years before. 'Should we then be contemptuous of the Turk', wrote Giovanni Botero, the best-known political commentator of the age of Philip II,

> who has taken so many fortresses, cities, kingdoms and empires from us? Who is master of Africa, who is lord of Asia, who holds more countries in Europe than do the Catholic rulers? Who has so thrived upon our disagreements that for three hundred years he has held sway upon the land and has no rival upon the sea? An enemy, who in peace is better prepared for war than we in time of war, an enemy whose treasury is unlimited, whose armies are without number, whose supplies have no end, an enemy who in the day of battle covers the plains with his cavalry, and when he lays siege to a city throws up whole mountains of earth with spades?[2]

This note of unwilling admiration sounds through a great deal of European comment, little changed from generation to generation. It was realized that the military resources at the disposal of an Ottoman sultan were very great and that his armies could be very large. Often indeed these resources were exaggerated, sometimes grossly so, as when a Venetian observer estimated the Turkish force that threatened Vienna in 1529 at the impossible figure of 305,000.[3] But more impressive than the mere size of these armies was their quality and above all their discipline. Ghiselin de Busbecq, the imperial ambassador to the great Sultan Suleiman in 1554–62, who left the best-known eye-witness account of the Ottoman Empire, was deeply impressed by the silence and good order of a Turkish army, by its cleanliness and the absence in it of drinking, gambling and swearing. All this to him contrasted forcibly and painfully with the dirt, noise and general disorder of its Christian counterparts.[4] Other western diplomats made the same uncomfortable comparison. The Venetian representatives

2. G. Botero, *The Reason of State*, trans. P.J. and D.P. Waley (London, 1956), p. 222.
3. A.H. Lybyer, *The Government of the Ottoman Empire in the Time of Suleiman the Magnificent* (Cambridge, Mass., 1913), p. 107fn.
4. *The Turkish Letters of Ogier Ghiselin de Busbecq*, trans. E.S. Forster (Oxford, 1927), p. 150.

in Constantinople, perhaps the best-informed observers of all, were almost without exception struck by the rarity of desertion and insubordination in a Turkish army. 'In truth', reported one in 1585, 'discipline could not be better, nor the obedience greater.'[5] Forces of such size and quality meant that most of the cities of the Ottoman Empire, notably Constantinople itself, could be left unfortified, another depressing contrast with much of Christian Europe; and there was a widespread belief that any sultan could command great financial resources as well as a highly efficient administrative machine which allowed him to mobilize effectively all the productive powers of a great empire. This belief was considerably exaggerated; but it seemed to be supported by evidence, notably by the very marked growth of Constantinople under Turkish rule. From a population of less than 100,000 when it fell in 1453 it had expanded to five or six times as much by the end of the sixteenth century – larger than any city of Christian Europe.

It is not surprising, therefore, to find throughout the century a constant stream of dire warnings and gloomy predictions in western comment on the Ottoman Empire. One Venetian representative in 1522, when the Turkish offensive was approaching its height, thought that the sultan 'holds in his hands the keys to all Christendom, such that he could easily penetrate the Christians' entrails', and that 'henceforth all Christendom should fear incurring a great extermination'. A few years later Luther had no doubt that the vast resources of the Turks made them a far more menacing enemy than any Christian state could ever be. Busbecq in his turn compared the Turkish armies to 'mighty rivers swollen with rain, which, if they can trickle through at any point in the banks which restrain them, spread through the breach and cause infinite destruction', while in 1573 another Venetian (even though he wrote in the immediate aftermath of the great Christian naval victory at Lepanto) wrote that 'This most powerful emperor's forces are of two kinds, those of the sea and those of the land, and both are terrifying'.[6] Apart from the Holy Roman Empire the Ottoman polity was in the sixteenth century the only one to be formally referred to as an empire.

This fear and admiration of Ottoman strength had much justification. But military strength was far from being the whole explanation of the empire's success. When Botero in 1589 complained that the

---

5. Lucette Valensi, *The Birth of the Despot: Venice and the Sublime Porte* (Ithaca, NY/London, 1993), p. 46; Lybyer, *The Government of the Ottoman Empire*, p. 109.

6. Valensi, *The Birth of the Despot*, p. 28; *Turkish Letters*, p. 15; Dorothy M. Vaughan, *Europe and the Turk: A Pattern of Alliances, 1350–1700* (Liverpool, 1954), p. 13.

Turks had 'thrived upon our disagreements' he identified one of the most important explanations of their overrunning of the Balkans and penetration into east-central Europe. Popes might call for unity among Christian rulers in a crusade to drive the infidel from the Christian lands he had conquered; but this had little effect on monarchs willing to use, or at least attempt to use, Ottoman power as a weapon in their own quarrels. The efforts of Francis I and Henry II to cooperate with the Turks in their struggles with the Habsburgs, the willingness of William the Silent, Elizabeth and the French Huguenots to play the Ottoman card against Philip II, have already been mentioned.[7] In Constantinople, moreover, there was a full awareness of these divisions, from which the empire might hope to benefit. French representatives in Constantinople enjoyed for much of the sixteenth century a privileged status as those of a traditional friend, and often received unusual marks of favour. The new ambassador who arrived in 1572, for example, was met by the grand vizier (the sultan's chief minister) in person, bearing rich presents, at the head of a great cavalcade of 2,000 horsemen.[8] The Reformation added another layer of Christian division which, combined with the existing rivalries between rulers, made still more unlikely any effective cooperation to stem the Turkish advance. Luther, who had at first seen it as a divine punishment for Christian shortcomings, was fairly soon forced to agree that it was legitimate for Germans to defend themselves against the threat from the east. In 1529, the year that saw Suleiman's army at the gates of Vienna, he made this clear in his *Dialogus de bello contra Turcos* and, in German, in his *Heerespredigt widder den Turcken*. But he was always determined that resistance to the Turks should not, by taking the form of a successful crusade, strengthen the papacy.

On a different and perhaps deeper level the Turkish conquests were often helped by the very sharp social divisions of the Christian lands they overran. Such conquests might well mean an improvement in the lot of most of those concerned. The last Christian ruler of an independent Bosnia, for example, can be found in 1464 complaining to Pope Pius II that the Turks were winning over the Bosnian peasants by promising them a freedom they did not enjoy under Christian rule. Of the significance of social factors of this kind, however, Hungary is the outstanding example. The catastrophic defeat of 1526 and the establishment of Turkish rule over much of the kingdom in the years that followed were preceded and in part made

7. See above, pp. 96, 98, 104–7, 111, 115–16, 152, 157, 176, 247.

8 A. Degert, 'Une ambassade périlleuse de François de Noailles en Turquie', *Revue Historique* 159 (1928), 235.

possible by a spectacular worsening of the position of the Hungarian peasantry. The 1490s had seen efforts by the diet to restrict the freedom of movement of the peasant; and in 1504 he lost his remaining hunting and fowling rights, a deprivation of symbolic as well as practical significance. Ten years later a savage peasant revolt was suppressed with great brutality; and this was followed by the diet placing all land in the hands of the nobility alone and condemning the peasants, apart from those of the royal free towns, to 'real and perpetual servitude'. This, coupled with the widespread and bitter resentment of German influences, meant that Hungary was now a deeply divided society in which the ability to resist foreign conquest was correspondingly weakened. The storm of 1526 therefore burst upon a country in which the bulk of the population had little to lose by a change of masters.

Moreover as the Reformation in different forms, notably the Calvinist one in Transylvania, struck deep roots this added a new and powerful element of division. For a Hungarian Protestant Turkish rule was usually preferable to that of the Catholic Habsburgs; indeed it can be argued that the growing identification in the later sixteenth century of Habsburg authority with an intolerant Catholicism did more than anything else to give Turkish rule in Hungary another hundred years of life. By contrast the relative (though far from complete) tolerance of much of Ottoman society allowed it to absorb and make use, particularly in the fifteenth century, of considerable numbers of Muslim converts of Christian origin. Thus one of the sons of the last Christian ruler of Herzegovina married a granddaughter of Mehmed II and was four times grand vizier, while Otranto, when it was taken in 1480, was placed under a governor who was Greek by birth. By the end of the fifteenth century a *gazi* ideology, which stressed that continual if not always active hostility to the non-Muslim world was a religious obligation for all true believers, was gaining ground in the empire; and this inevitably tended to sharpen dividing-lines between Islam and other forms of belief, which had hitherto been considerably less clear-cut. None the less, Christian religious intolerance, when it had to compete with a more tolerant Ottoman alternative, certainly weakened resistance to Turkish conquest of the Balkans and still more Hungary.

A colossus with feet of clay

But though there were serious weaknesses on the side of Christian Europe there were others at least as great on that of the Ottoman

Empire. Its advance in the Balkans and Hungary, so impressive to contemporaries, was at the expense of parts of Europe which were economically backward and for the most part lacking in strong political institutions. Once the Turks were faced, as they were by the 1530s and 1540s, with the resistance of the Austrian Habsburgs in central Europe and the Spanish ones in the Mediterranean, their advance slowed, except to some extent in north Africa, and came to a halt. Christian Europe, it must be remembered, was not the only enemy and often not the most serious one. In Safavid Persia the Ottoman Empire had from the beginning of the sixteenth century an opponent on its eastern frontier at least as dangerous as any it had to face in the west. The *Safawiyya*, a religious order which the Ottoman government, rigid in its Sunni Muslim orthodoxy, detested as heretical, had been growing in strength in Anatolia and Azerbaijan for several generations. In 1499 its leader, Sheikh Ismail, began a series of campaigns that made him ruler of Persia within a few years. The fact that sympathy with the *Safawiyya* was strong in eastern Anatolia, where a serious revolt against Ottoman rule broke out in 1514, made the new regime not merely a religious challenge but a political threat. For well over 100 years from this time onwards there was to be no lasting peace between the two Muslim states. Throughout the sixteenth century, therefore, Persia was always a potentially very serious distraction of Ottoman energies away from the western frontiers of the empire. Thus in 1533 and again in 1546 Sultan Suleiman I (Suleiman the Magnificent), the most famous and admired of all Ottoman rulers, was forced to make a truce with the Habsburgs so that he could fight in Azerbaijan against his Safavid rival. On both occasions, and again in 1553, he was away from Constantinople for eighteen months or more: for him and for every other sultan of this period the enemy in the east was at least as great a threat as that in the west. The great Ottoman–Persian struggle of 1578–90[9] was merely the most prolonged and serious of such distractions. The European opponents of the sultans were aware that Safavid Persia might therefore well become a very useful ally against Ottoman power. In 1509 Persian envoys reached Venice in search of supplies of European artillery and probably also some alliance against the Ottomans. In 1518, and again in 1529, Charles V sent envoys to Shah Ismail in the hope that some anti-Ottoman cooperation might be possible; and the dream of joint action of this kind was to recur periodically for decades to come. These hopes, however, were quite unrealistic. Distance and difficulty

9. See below, p. 244.

of communication, quite apart from the very different outlooks and ambitions of the potential partners, meant that it was never possible for Safavid Persia and Christian Europe to work together.

Though Ottoman government in the empire's great days seemed to many western obervers a model of efficiency they were often struck by one characteristic which marked it as profoundly un-European and seemed an important potential source of weakness. This was the lack of any law governing the succession to the throne, the complete absence of the primogeniture accepted everywhere in western Europe. This meant that it was seldom clear which of a sultan's sons would succeed him, and that his death was often followed, or even preceded, by bitter struggles between rival claimants to the throne and the killing of the defeated ones. The sons of Mehmed II fought over the succession in 1481–83, as did those of Bayezid II in his last years in 1509–12, while Suleiman himself was able to ensure the succession of Selim II in 1566 only by having two other sons put to death in 1553 and 1561. Moreover by the time of Mehmed II it was a well-established rule that a sultan, once in power, should secure his position by disposing of any possible rivals (normally his brothers and their sons): the extreme example of this was Mehmed III who, on coming to power in 1595, had nineteen of his brothers and 30 of his sisters executed.

Whether this tradition, however bloodthirsty and temporarily disruptive, seriously weakened the Ottoman Empire is very doubtful. Its destabilizing effect was limited: the average length of reign of sixteenth-century sultans was little if at all less than that of contemporary monarchs in western Europe. Nor was there ever any possibility of the empire being divided between rival claimants: this was suggested only once, in the succession struggles after the death of Mehmed II. Only once, moreover, was there any chance of an unsuccessful contender for the throne becoming a tool of the empire's Christian enemies. In 1482 Djem, one of the sons of Mehmed II, fled to the Knights of St John in Rhodes after his bid for the succession had failed. The knights at once sent him to France; and in 1489 he was handed over to the pope, Innocent VIII, who from 1490 received a pension from Bayezid II in return for keeping his brother in safe confinement. So long as he lived Djem was a potential threat to the sultan and did something to inhibit his freedom of action: in 1494 it seemed that Charles VIII of France might make use of him in the attack on the Ottoman Empire of which he dreamed. But he died early in 1495; and no other succession struggle offered the Christian powers an opportunity of this kind.

The peculiar character of the Ottoman dynasty was therefore not in itself an important source of weakness. But the empire it ruled had other defects, some of them much more serious. The impressive picture of military strength drawn by many western observers, though it contained much truth, was not the whole truth. Discipline in the army was a good deal less perfect than many of these accounts suggested. The janissaries, the privileged infantry force recruited by a forced levy of Christian children who were then converted to Islam, were particularly demanding and difficult to control. They expected a special gift of money on the accession of a new sultan. They might well plunder a captured city in flagrant disregard of any terms of capitulation agreed with its defenders: Rhodes suffered in this way in 1522 in spite of an agreement with the Knights of St John that this should not happen, and Buda met with the same treatment in 1526. They were likely to grow restive when faced with any long period of peace and demand a new war which would give them the activity and opportunities for plunder they wanted. In 1525 three years of peace led to serious rioting by the janissaries in Constantinople to which even Suleiman I had to give way.

Moreover by the 1530s and 1540s any further advance into central Europe was being made more difficult by the physical factors of distance and poor communications. Any large-scale campaign, as distinct from the incessant border raiding which was the essence of day-to-day *gazi* warfare, was led by the sultan in person; and from the time he left Constantinople in the spring it was about three months before the army had reached Hungary. The organization of such a campaign was impressively thorough, almost certainly superior to anything of the kind any European state could have achieved. Preparations for the spring start began in the previous autumn: stocks of grain and livestock were assembled by requisitioning, supply depots were set up along the route to be followed, notably at Belgrade and Buda, transport vessels were collected on the Danube and if necessary new ones built.[10] But the Danube, undredged and unembanked, was difficult to use as an artery of communication, while bad weather, primitive and washed-out roads and broken bridges, meant that movement was painfully slow. By mid-September it was necessary to prepare for withdrawal: to campaign on a large scale throughout the year was impossible and the janissaries were likely to become restive if kept in the field longer than they thought justified. The result was

10. See the interesting details in G. Veinstein, 'Some views on provisioning in the Hungarian campaigns of Suleiman the Magnificent', in his *Etat et Société dans l'Empire Ottoman, XVIe–XVIIIe siècles* (Aldershot/Brookfield, Vt, 1994).

that the time available for serious fighting, and therefore what could be accomplished in a military sense, was very limited. In 1529, for example, Suleiman left his capital on 10 May; but it was the middle of July before he reached Belgrade and it was only on 27 September, too late for any prolonged siege, that he could begin his unsuccessful attack on Vienna.

Moreover however large the Ottoman armies, however good, at least in comparative terms, their discipline, in terms of technology they lagged behind the best European practice. The role played in the casting and use of artillery by experts from the west, very often converts to Islam, was very important during the great period of conquest in the fifteenth and early sixteenth centuries. The artillery of Mehmed II was created and controlled by Germans, Italians and Bosnians rather than by Turks, while before and in the early stages of the great siege of Rhodes in 1522 Suleiman I made much use of a German renegade, George Frapan ('Master George'), who had a high reputation as an artillery expert and military engineer. The capture of the Spanish-held Peñon of Algiers in 1529 by the great corsair leader Khair-ed-din Barbarossa, again, was made possible partly by the use of French-produced cannon. It is also possible that some at least of the artillery used by the Turks may have been technically inferior to that available in western Europe. The Genoese admiral Andrea Doria, when he captured the Turkish fortress of Patras in 1532, reported that some of its guns must be modernized, recast 'à la moderne', to make them fit for use. At sea a similar situation can be seen in a more pronounced form. Mehmed II began the creation of a Turkish fleet, an entirely new departure; but he did this, inevitably in the circumstances, by drawing on European experts and knowledge and acquiring 'a naval technology that was largely Italian'.[11] Such influences remained important in the growth of Ottoman seapower for decades to come. Under Bayezid II in the early years of the sixteenth century an Italian shipbuilder, Andrea Dere, played a significant role in the growth of the still somewhat embryonic fleet. The ships built at Suez in 1537 and used in the following year in the capture of Aden and an unsuccessful attack on Diu, on the west coast of India, were manned in part by Venetian sailors pressed into service in Alexandria.

By then Ottoman naval power, combined with that of north Africa and its corsairs,[12] had grown to a point at which it could dominate the eastern Mediterranean and threaten the coasts of Italy and even Spain.

11. A.C. Hess, 'The evolution of the Ottoman seaborne empire in the age of the oceanic discoveries, 1453–1525', *American Historical Review* LXXV (1969–70), 1901.
12. See below, pp. 232–3.

Its organization and resources were to be shown by its remarkable recovery after the crushing disaster of Lepanto. Yet by the end of the century it was becoming clear that though it might still hold its own in galley warfare it had nothing to match the warships now being produced on the Atlantic seaboard. The ship that brought an English ambassador to Constantinople in 1593 seemed to a Turkish eye-witness 'a wonder of the age, the like of which has not been seen or recorded'.[13]

It would be unfair to make too much of these western influences. After the early decades of the sixteenth century dependence on foreign expertise of this kind became less marked, certainly so far as the navy was concerned; and after all France, Spain and England also made use of German gun-founders and Italian military engineers. Yet it is significant that in the Ottoman Empire it remained so much easier to hire foreign technologists than to produce native Turkish ones in an environment so completely controlled by Muslim tradition and orthodoxy.

In fundamental ways the Ottoman Empire was falling behind Europe and becoming dependent on her for new knowledge. The most striking and far-reaching example of this is the failure of printing, with all the intellectual potentialities it embodied, to take effective root in it. Jewish refugees from Spain who arrived in the last years of the fifteenth century brought printing-presses with them and were allowed to print books in Constantinople and some other cities, while similar permission was later given to Greek and Armenian Christians. But none of this printing was to be in Arabic characters: Muslims were to be protected against the dangerous influences the new technique might bring with it. There was no printing in Arabic characters until well into the eighteenth century, and only a very limited amount then. The retarding influence of such a prohibition is impossible to measure; but it was clearly immense.

The Turk as outsider

Neither by the European states nor by the Turks themselves was the Ottoman Empire seen as part of the state system that was slowly and almost unconsciously coming into existence. On both sides religion was an insurmountable barrier to any feeling of kinship. To Europeans a Turk was a different animal, a member of a separate and

---

13. Palmira Brummett, *Ottoman Seapower and Levantine Diplomacy in the Age of Discovery* (Albany, NY, 1994), p. 93; B. Lewis, *Cultures in Conflict: Christians, Muslims and Jews in the Age of Discovery* (New York/Oxford, 1995), p. 22.

quite distinct species whose essential nature permanently excluded him from membership of the European family of states.[14] By the early seventeenth century it is possible to find some theorists, at least in Protestant Europe, arguing that so long as the Turks remained at peace with their neighbours the Ottoman Empire had the same right to exist as any Christian state and that to make war on it purely for religious reasons was unjustified. But throughout this period it was universally assumed that at bottom relations with it must be those of hostility. The crusading ideal was not yet dead: nothing, after all, could give greater personal prestige to any ruler than to lead a successful crusade. The first decades of the seventeenth century even saw a considerable revival, notably in France, of the dream of joint action to drive the infidel from Europe. Crusading impulses of this kind were strong in the circle around Cardinal Richelieu, the great French minister, from the 1620s onwards, while in England in 1617 and 1622 Francis Bacon drew up schemes for an Anglo-Spanish alliance which might provide the basis for such an effort. Ingrained religious hostility was at least as strong on the Ottoman side. The whole non-Muslim world was the House of War (*Dar al-Harb*), with which the only possible relations were those of active or potential hostility. To it a pious Muslim could travel, in strict theory, only to ransom fellow-Muslims held prisoner there. With infidels no real peace was possible and even truces should not last for longer than ten years.

But there was a fundamentally important difference between the European and Ottoman attitudes. In Europe there was an active and growing interest in the Ottoman Empire and the Muslim world generally. The Turks, by contrast, were profoundly uninterested in Europe, and except for some specific and limited (usually military) purposes indifferent to the achievements of a Christian world which to them seemed fundamentally and irredeemably inferior. The contrast was sharp and can be seen in many ways. Considerable numbers of Europeans travelled in the Ottoman Empire, not merely from piety (though a good many visited the Holy Land) but from genuine intellectual curiosity and a taste for the exotic. Even the Austrian Habsburg territories, from the 1520s the main target of Turkish expansionism in Europe, provided many such.[15] Comparable Turkish travellers in Europe, in contrast, are simply unknown. Even so great a transformation as the discovery and settlement of America aroused,

14. F.L. Baumer, 'England, the Turk and the common corps of Christendom', *American Historical Review* L (1944–5), 27.

15. See the detailed account in R.J.W. Evans, 'Bohemia, the Emperor and the Porte, 1550–1600', *Oxford Slavonic Papers*, N.S. iii (1970), 85–106.

after a little initial curiosity, hardly any interest in the Ottoman Empire. A Turkish account of the West Indies was written in the mid-sixteenth century; but it was not published until 1729. There was considerable interest in Europe in the study of Arabic, and to a lesser extent of Turkish and Persian, in the sixteenth and early seventeenth centuries: the first Latin treatise on Arabic grammar was published in 1538. Yet by contrast 'we know of no Muslim scholar or man of letters before the eighteenth century who sought to learn a western language, still less of any attempt to produce grammars, dictionaries, or other language tools'.[16] A Latin translation of the Koran was published in Basle in 1543, with another edition seven years later: Luther himself urged the Basle magistrates to allow its appearance.[17] But though Mehmed II asked a Greek of Trebizond to make an Arabic translation of the Bible, this was merely an isolated gesture by a sultan with remarkably wide-ranging intellectual tastes. There was some Turkish interest in the Protestants of Europe as the Reformation developed; but this was merely because they seemed a useful distraction of Catholic, above all Spanish, power to Germany, France and the Netherlands, not for their own sake or even because they might possibly become political allies of the Ottoman Empire.

This indifference to and even contempt for Europe's achievements and potentialities meant that diplomatic relations with the European states were in Turkish eyes of very little importance. Moreover the successes of the Ottoman Empire seemed to show that it need fear no foe, or even any hostile coalition, on its western frontiers. With Venice, the Austrian Habsburgs and possibly Poland contact might at least from time to time be needed: with other states it seemed unnecessary if not undesirable. The result was that the Turks had no approach to a diplomatic service, even of the rudimentary kind now coming into existence in Europe. Occasional Turkish envoys were sent to the west; but these were rare and often sent only for ceremonial or quasi-religious purposes. One who went to France in 1581, for example, brought an invitation from Murad III to Henry III to attend the circumcision of one of the sultan's sons, while the first Turkish mission to the new Dutch Republic was sent merely to negotiate the release of a number of captives taken at sea in the Mediterranean. Foreign representatives in Constantinople were not as a rule welcome. Their presence there was seen as a privilege extended to Christian states; and any idea of diplomatic immunity of the kind

---

16. B. Lewis, *The Muslim Discovery of Europe* (London, 1982), p. 81.
17. J. Pannier, 'Calvin et les Turcs', *Revue Historique* CLXXX (1937), 279–80.

now emerging in Europe[18] was unknown. An unlucky foreign envoy might suffer severely when he or the ruler he represented incurred the sultan's anger. An imperial ambassador was imprisoned in 1541; and his successor, Busbecq, suffered the same fate some years later.

The relations of Christian Europe with this strange and deeply foreign power in the east thus presented a markedly unbalanced and lop-sided picture. On the one hand was respect, even admiration, coupled with interest, curiosity and slowly growing knowledge. On the other was a self-confidence amounting to contempt accompanied by massive indifference. It was to be a very long time before the Ottoman Empire became a normal and recognized part of the European system of international relations. Yet its expansion was one of the major themes of sixteenth-century history. Both the fear and the curiosity it aroused were well justified.

The growing threat, 1494–1529

So long as Djem was alive as a refugee in western Europe Bayezid II, who had succeeded Mehmed II in 1481, was hardly able to commit himself to a full-scale war on either his western or eastern frontier. Very destructive raiding into Croatia, Hungary and even the Austrian duchies and northern Italy continued; but new permanent conquests were difficult to achieve while was any chance that the fugitive prince might become the tool of the Christian states in a counter–offensive against the Ottoman Empire. With Djem's death in January 1495 the sultan recovered his freedom of action; and of this Venice became the first victim. Mehmed II had fought a long war with the republic in 1463–79, in which there were no large-scale or decisive battles; yet when it ended the Turks had won important successes. The superiority of the Venetian navy to the still embryonic Ottoman one was clear. A Venetian merchant in Constantinople in 1466 claimed, probably with justification, that the Turks felt they needed a numerical superiority of four or five to one before they could engage Venetian galleys.[19] Nevertheless when peace came in 1479 it saw them make important strategic gains. The Greek island of Negroponte (Euboea) fell to them in 1470; and by capturing Croia and Scutari in 1478–79 they greatly strengthened their position on the Adriatic, hitherto almost a Venetian lake.

18. See above, pp. 63–4.
19. J.H. Pryor, *Geography, Technology and War: Studies in the Maritime History of the Mediterranean, 649–1571* (Cambridge, 1988), p. 176.

These successes were essentially the result of Ottoman strength on land: at sea the Venetians did not suffer a single defeat. Yet the galleys with which naval wars in the Mediterranean were fought, with their limited range of action and heavy dependence on shore bases for supplies (particularly the water their large crews needed which was difficult for such ships to carry in adequate quantities), could be used to full effect only if their action were coordinated with that of armies on land. The Turks, with their superior military resources, had now embarked on a long and ultimately successful struggle to gain possession of the islands and coastal fortresses that were to give their still undeveloped naval strength control of the whole eastern Mediterranean. The peace of 1479 left Venice still with a strong grip on the coasts of Albania and Dalmatia; but the new struggle which broke out in the summer of 1499, and in which the republic was supported, though ineffectively, by Hungary, saw this seriously threatened. The war, the outcome of much raiding and small-scale fighting in the previous few years, showed how markedly Ottoman strength at sea had grown over the last two decades. In the unsuccessful attack on Rhodes in 1480 about 100 Turkish warships had been employed; but in two naval battles in 1499 and 1500 the empire was able to use 260 and 230 respectively. At least equally serious, more Venetian strongholds in Greece were lost – Lepanto in August 1499, Modon, Coron and Navarino in the following year, Durazzo a year later still. Venice was still a formidable antagonist: in December 1500, with Spanish help, she captured the island of Cephalonia. But the Ottoman Empire, already so powerful on land, was now on the way to becoming a substantial naval power as well. The peace terms agreed in December 1502 thus marked for it an important success.

As yet it had hardly been seen in the western Mediterranean as a seapower; but by the first years of the sixteenth century there were ominous signs of a growth there of Muslim activity. In 1508 a Turkish corsair raided the Ligurian coast, while two years later 1,000 people were carried off from Corsica as slaves and a landing was made near Marseilles. It was an index of the changing situation that Pope Alexander VI began in 1500 to create a small fleet of his own for defensive purposes. Even more ominous was the fact that much of this raiding of Christian shipping and coasts was the work, particularly in Spain, not of Ottomans but of Muslims from north Africa, who in 1505 burnt the suburbs of Alicante and a number of ships at Malaga.[20]

20. There is much detail on Muslim corsair activity in the period in A. Tenenti, 'I corsari in Mediterraneo all'inizio del Cinquecento', *Rivista Storica Italiana* LXXII (1960), 234–87.

These years also saw a Spanish effort, which was to continue for decades, to control much of the north African coastline. Melilla was captured in 1497, Mers-el-Kebir (Oran) in 1505, Bougie and Tripoli in 1510. The intention of this was essentially defensive: possession of these strongpoints, particularly if it could be combined with good relations with the tribes in their hinterland, would protect Spain's own territory and trade. There was no effort to extend her conquests far from the coastline. But her position in north Africa was never at bottom very strong. Service in an area so barren, inhospitable and unglamorous was never popular and was seen as a punishment rather than an honour. The north African *presidios* were therefore often starved of men and resources, while as the population around them acquired gunpowder weapons their situation became increasingly vulnerable.

A crucial moment in the north African struggle came in 1516, when two corsair leaders, Muslims but of Greek origin, Aruj and Khair-ed-din Barbarossa, established themselves in Algiers. Aruj was killed in battle in 1518; and for over a decade Spain's possession of the Peñon, the fortified rock at the entrance to its harbour, impeded free use of the port. Nevertheless Algiers now rapidly became the leading centre of corsair activity. Moreover Khair-ed-din soon began to look to Constantinople for support against his Christian antagonists and to regard himself, at least in form and for tactical reasons, as a vassal of the sultan. At some time after 1517 (the exact date is not known) he acknowledged this allegiance in the traditional way, by having the sultan's head put on the coinage issued at Algiers and his name mentioned in the Friday prayers in its mosques. By the 1520s, therefore, the Ottoman Empire, either directly through its own strength or indirectly through its north African vassal, had become a powerful and threatening force at sea in the Mediterranean.

On land the first two decades of the sixteenth century saw, in spite of endless frontier raiding, a lull in the Turkish advance into Europe. After the end of the war with Venice in 1502 Bayezid II followed a generally pacific policy on his European frontier (and thus lost support among the more warlike and aggressively Muslim elements in Ottoman society). The rise of a powerful Safavid rival in Persia was a very important distraction; and the sultan's last years were marked by a violent struggle over the succession between his three sons. This ended in April 1512 with his own deposition and the assumption of power by Selim, the youngest and most warlike of the three. He was to prove, in his short reign, the most formidable of all warrior-sultans; but his energies were spent on a spectacular expansion of his empire in Asia and Africa which left him, until just before his death in September 1520, unable to wage war in Europe. In the east his achievements were remarkable. In August 1514 he decisively defeated the Safavid ruler Shah Ismail at Chaldiran, north-east of Lake Van in eastern Anatolia. This was a victory won largely by the Ottoman artillery, which the Persians could not match, and the superior discipline of the janissaries. It was followed by the capture of Tabriz and the consolidation of Selim's hold on eastern Anatolia and Kurdistan.

His success had aroused the fear and jealousy of the other great Muslim state of the Near East, Mamluk Egypt (which included Syria and Palestine). There now seemed a real possibility of an alliance of Mamluks and Safavids to resist and turn back the Ottoman advance. That the Mamluks might act as a restraint on the growing power of the Ottomans had not escaped attention in Europe. As early as 1489 Ferdinand of Aragon had thought of sending military help to the regime in Cairo; while in 1501–02 there was a Spanish embassy there attempting to create some kind of common front against the sultan in Constantinople. But the Mamluks were badly placed to hold their own against Selim. Their army was hopelessly inferior in artillery and gunpowder weapons; and Mamluk government was bitterly unpopular with its Egyptian and Syrian subjects. In August 1516, therefore, the Mamluk sultan, Kansuh al-Gauri, was completely defeated and killed near Aleppo. By the end of January 1517 Cairo was in Selim's hands. The gain to the Ottoman Empire was not merely territorial, important though that was. The conquest also brought a great increase in the prestige of the Ottoman dynasty, for with the acquisition of Egypt the sultan became the recognized guardian and servitor of the holy places of Medina and Mecca: this gave him a status among Muslim rulers that no other could match.

If Selim had lived a little longer he would certainly have launched a new offensive in Europe. In 1515 he had begun the building of a great arsenal in Constantinople; and from 1518 onwards he set in train the creation of a new and more powerful fleet. In Europe there was some realization that the conquest of Syria and Egypt had meant a great and menacing accretion of strength to the sultan. There was a brief revival of interest in a new crusade: it was discussed at some length when the imperial diet met in Augsburg in 1518, though almost inevitably without result. It is one of the more remarkable coincidences of history that the year that saw Selim bring about the enforced unity of much of the Muslim world also saw Luther begin an unparalleled division of the Christian one. The sultan's death in September 1520 did little to free Europe from the approaching threat: his son and successor, Suleiman, was to be the most famous of all Ottoman rulers and the most feared by the Christian states on his borders.

The new sultan was quick to show his intentions. In August 1521 came the fall of the great fortress of Belgrade, which had successfully resisted Mehmed the Conqueror more than two generations earlier. This was followed in the next year by the capture of Rhodes, for so long a thorn in Ottoman flesh because of the continual war carried on by the Knights of St John, its rulers, against Muslim shipping. This too was a Christian stronghold which had held out against Mehmed in the siege of 1480: its fall seemed a correspondingly ominous portent. A great Turkish fleet arrived in the island in June 1522; and though the fortress was heroically defended and did not fall until six months later (a good illustration of the length and cost of many sieges in this age), it was taken in the end. Neither the Hungarians and their Serb mercenaries who defended Belgrade nor the knights in Rhodes received any help from the states of western Europe. The Venetian fleet indeed put to sea in 1522; but once it was sure that the Venetian-ruled island of Cyprus was not Suleiman's objective it returned to port. These Ottoman conquests were followed by three years of peace, probably because of continuing unrest in Syria and Egypt, where memories of independence were still fresh; but in 1526 the offensive in the Danube valley began once more. In April of that year Suleiman set out from Constantinople for the conquest of Hungary.

The kingdom was in no state to face the storm that was about to break over it. Royal authority there was now very weak. In the later fifteenth century an able and energetic ruler, Matthias Corvinus, had done a good deal to create a relatively efficient administration backed by a mercenary army, and to check with the help of the minor nobility the disruptive power of the great magnates who dominated so much of the country's life. But he had been more interested in the affairs of the Holy Roman Empire than in relations with the Turks; and his death in 1490 and the accession of Ladislas II, already King of Bohemia, meant a decline in royal authority, a weakening of the army and a recovery of power by the magnates. The worsening of the position of the peasants which has already been mentioned was perhaps an even more fundamental weakness of this ramshackle state; and well before the catastrophe of 1526 it had become clear that Hungary could expect little or no effective help from the west.

As the threat of Turkish attack became more obvious the Archduke Ferdinand, to whom Charles V had transferred control of his

Austrian duchies in 1521–22, increasingly pressed his brother for support, as did the young Louis II of Hungary, who had married Charles's sister Mary. After his victory at Pavia the emperor briefly thought of providing this. But neither the pleas of his brother, nor a suggestion from Pope Adrian VI that a two-year truce in the Franco-Habsburg struggle be negotiated to free resources for effective resistance to a Turkish attack, had any practical result. The war in Italy went on, with the French trying to use the Turks as a weapon in it. The formation of the League of Cognac meant that the emperor's resources were still tied down there: almost to the moment of Turkish victory Charles, far from helping his brother, was pressing him to send forces to support the Habsburg cause in the peninsula. Ferdinand's efforts to raise men and money in Germany achieved little more: there the Turks seemed still a distant threat. In the autumn of 1524 the imperial diet agreed to provide a mere 4,000 men, against the 24,000 that Louis II and his ministers had asked for; and very soon the Lutheran princes, seeing how Turkish pressure strengthened their hand, began to demand religious concessions as the price of any help they might give. Early in 1526 Charles V agreed to negotiate with the pope about the possible calling of a council of the church, that panacea which for decades was to inspire so many hopes of restoring lost religious unity; and Ferdinand promised that one would meet within eighteen months. The diet then agreed to provide the 24,000 men; but by then it was too late for this to have any influence on events. Even among those most directly affected by the Turkish offensive there was deep disunity. The estates of Croatia, seeing that they could hope for no protection from Hungary, refused to contribute anything to her defence, while among the Hungarians resentment of the German influences and advisers around the young king was now very strong.

All this meant catastrophic defeat. On 29 August 1526 at Mohacs the Hungarian army was shattered by a larger Turkish one. The king and many nobles died on the battlefield; and a few days later Suleiman entered Buda, the Hungarian capital. Mohacs meant that the Austrian Habsburgs were now the main bulwark of Europe against the Turkish threat: not for almost two and a half centuries, until the emergence of Russia as the main anti-Turkish power in the later eighteenth century, were they to lose this often unwelcome distinction. The Archduke Ferdinand's position, however, was far from easy. He could still hope for little help from his brother or the German princes; and though he had married Anna, the sister of the dead Louis II, and had inherited from him claims to both the Hungarian and Bohemian thrones, he faced serious opposition in Hungary. In October he was proclaimed king of Bohemia; and two months later he was chosen as their ruler by most of the Hungarian nobility. But he had at once to face a dangerous rival in John Zapolya, *voevode* (governor) of Transylvania, who was himself elected as king in November by the anti-German party. (He could point to the fact that in 1505, on his own proposal, the Hungarian diet had passed legislation barring the succession to the throne of any foreigner.) This began a division of Hungary into three parts which had become complete by the early 1540s. In the north and west Ferdinand ruled a strip bordering his Austrian territories, while Zapolya held Transylvania and Suleiman controlled the remaining and major part of the kingdom; and the rivalry of the two Christian claimants to the throne could only strengthen the position of the Turkish conqueror. When in 1527 Ferdinand's forces defeated Zapolya and forced him to take refuge in Poland (Sigismund I of Poland was his brother-in-law) it was almost inevitable that he should look to Constantinople for help.

To Suleiman a vassal-prince through whom he could rule Hungary indirectly was welcome. He already had similar indirect control of Moldavia and Wallachia, the two principalities on the lower Danube which well over three centuries later were to become the nucleus of the modern Romania. Such control of these frontier areas was less costly and difficult than direct rule and their total incorporation into his empire. He therefore gave his backing to Zapolya, recognized him as king of Hungary and in 1529 launched a new campaign aimed at the capture of Vienna itself. This was a failure. The Turkish army did not reach the city until the last days of September; and bad weather on the long march from Constantinople, shortage of food, determined resistance by the garrison and the need to begin the return march before the onset of winter meant that the siege was abandoned after little more than a fortnight. The Ottoman advance had now reached its limit; but this was far from clear to an alarmed and often defeatist Europe.

These dramatic struggles of the 1520s were of much more than local or even regional significance. They brought Ottoman power closer than ever before to the heart of Europe and completed a structure of Turkish territorial and military strength in the south-east of the continent which was not to be shaken until the 1680s and 1690s. For what was soon to become the distinct Austrian branch of the Habsburgs these years brought even greater changes. Hitherto their power had rested upon essentially German foundations. Now with the acquisition after 1526 of part of Hungary and, more important, the Bohemian crown, their territorial base was becoming much more central European, Danubian and multilingual. This was a change with great and lasting implications.

The threat at its height, 1529–66

The failure before Vienna, whatever its symbolic significance, brought no slackening in the struggle for Hungary. Ferdinand still claimed the whole kingdom, while Zapolya, backed by the sultan, stood by his claims. In 1532 Suleiman launched another great offensive but again failed to strike effectively at the heart of Austrian Habsburg power. The small fortified town of Güns, about 60 miles south-east of Vienna, held out heroically for three weeks against enormously superior forces and did not fall until the end of August. The unexpected delay forced the sultan to abandon any idea of another siege of Vienna, though his cavalry raided far into Austria and even seemed to threaten south Germany, while the army as a whole devastated much of Slavonia. The situation in 1532 had seemed very serious. This was the only occasion on which Charles V sent some of his Spanish veterans to fight against the Turks in central Europe, and also the only one on which he himself visited Vienna (though he spent only eleven days there). But the difficulty of any new and permanent Turkish conquest was becoming clear; and in June 1533 Suleiman made a truce with Ferdinand which left the archduke still in control of the strip of Hungarian territory he had gained in 1526. In 1534–35 the sultan was once more deeply engaged in a struggle with the Safavid ruler of Persia, Shah Tamasp. In this he had considerable success. Tabriz was captured, though it could not be held; and the conquest of Irak meant that Ottoman power had now reached the head of the Persian Gulf. Once more, however, it had been shown that the military power of the empire, though great, could be exerted fully in only one direction at any time. Full-scale war on both the eastern and western frontiers simultaneously was not a practical proposition.

But if the 1530s saw some slackening of Ottoman pressure in the Danube valley they also saw the situation in the Mediterranean become more threatening from the Christian standpoint. In 1534 Barbarossa was appointed Kapudan Pasha, commander of the Ottoman fleet; and in the years that followed Muslim naval activity reached a new pitch of effectiveness and menace. In 1532 Andrea Doria, the veteran Genoese naval commander, took from the Turks with Spanish and papal help the former Venetian fortress of Coron in the Morea; but this limited success was soon more than counter-balanced by a series of Ottoman victories. Coron was recovered in 1534; and in the late summer of 1537 a new struggle between Venice and the Ottoman Empire broke out. For Christian Europe this was, on balance, a failure. Venice was still a significant power at sea; and in the spring of 1538 she signed an alliance with Charles V and the pope. But the allies never cooperated effectively; and the republic was seriously handicapped by the fact that she depended heavily for supplies of grain, the basic foodstuff, on areas in the Balkans and the Black Sea littoral which were under Turkish control. At the end of September 1538, at Prevesa in the Gulf of Arta, Barbarossa defeated the Christian forces ranged against him: though the battle involved little fighting and few losses it was none the less a menacing portent. An Ottoman force had now more than held its own against the com-bined strength of the most important Christian naval powers. By 1539 Venice was suffering severely from a food shortage caused by the war. In October 1540 she was forced to sign a peace treaty which marked another step in her slow but inexorable decline and cost her her remaining bases in the Aegean and the Morea.

In the same years it became clear that the coasts of much of the Christian Mediterranean must now expect to face Muslim raids on a scale not seen before. In spite of Charles V's capture of Tunis in 1535 Barbarossa, driven from the town, was able only a few months later to raid the Balearic islands and the Spanish coast. In 1537 a force led by him attacked Otranto and devastated the surrounding area: such was the alarm in Rome that many people left the city and Pope Paul III made preparations for its defence against Ottoman attack. The fol-lowing year saw the beginning of coastal defence works in southern Italy and Sicily designed to give some protection against attacks of this kind; and such fortifications were soon to be seen also on the Spanish coast and particularly in the Balearic islands, a favourite tar-get of raids from north Africa. This did not prevent the danger from becoming more obvious and acute. In 1543 Barbarossa ravaged the coasts of Sicily and Naples, captured Reggio di Calabria and again spread alarm in Rome. It was not altogether certain that the great corsair would remain firm in his Ottoman allegiance, always to him a matter of convenience as much as conviction. In the later 1530s Charles V negotiated with him in the hope that he might bring his galleys over to the Christian side and perhaps even destroy a part of the Ottoman fleet in the process; but the price of such a volte-face, the handing over of Tunis and adjacent areas to be held by him as a Spanish vassal, was high; and nothing came of these contacts.

In spite of the truce of 1533 incessant border warfare, sometimes on a considerable scale, raid and counter-raid with occasional genuine battles, continued along the Christian–Muslim frontier in Hungary and Croatia. A new outbreak of open war could hardly be more than a matter of time. In 1538 Zapolya and the Archduke Ferdinand came to an agreement which seemed to offer some hope of a solution to their competing claims. Each was to keep the title of king and the territory he controlled; but when Zapolya died his share of Hungary was to pass to Ferdinand, though if before his death he married again (he was in 1538 unmarried and childless) and had issue, his wife and children were to be provided for. In the following year he did in fact marry a Polish princess; and at his death in July 1540 she had just given birth to a son. It at once became clear that the agreement of 1538 would be very difficult to enforce. There was still a strong faction among the Hungarian nobility that was deeply opposed to German influence in the country and therefore to Habsburg rule; and it immediately proclaimed as king Zapolya's baby son, John Sigismund. Its leader, George Martinuzzi, Bishop of Grosswardein (the present-day Oradea, now part of Romania), appealed to Suleiman for support; and in the summer of 1541 the sultan once more moved into Hungary at the head of a large army. He had now decided that direct rule from Constantinople was unavoidable: it was out of the question to set up the baby John Sigismund as a puppet king, as Suleiman had hoped to do with his father.

The years 1543 and 1544 saw considerable Turkish successes; and the situation was now being further complicated and resistance further weakened by the progress of the Reformation in Hungary. The identification of the Habsburgs with Catholicism meant that to Hungarian Protestants rule from Constantinople seemed clearly preferable to dominance from Vienna with the persecution it was likely to involve. In 1545 one of them described the Turkish conquest of most of the kingdom as an act of divine mercy because of the religious toleration it brought. It is significant that Ferdinand pressed his brother strongly though unsuccessfully to take a more accommodating line towards the Lutherans in Germany, in the hope that this might strengthen his own position in Hungary. For generations to come Catholic intolerance and the fears it generated were to hamper any recovery of what had been lost in 1526 and the following years. In 1545 Ferdinand negotiated another truce, while two years later peace terms to last for five years were agreed. The archduke retained the territory still under his control; but he had to agree, as a condition of holding it, to send to Constantinople an annual sum of 30,000 Hungarian ducats. Though this humiliating payment was officially described as a present, it was in fact a kind of tribute and an index of Ottoman power and Habsburg relative weakness.

By 1551 Suleiman and Ferdinand were once more at war. In that year Martinuzzi, still the leading figure in Transylvania, forced Zapolya's widow, Isabella of Poland, to recognize the archduke as ruler of Hungary. In return she received a sum in cash, estates in Silesia and a promise of protection against the Turks. But the ambitious bishop had now overreached himself. His efforts to safeguard his position by mediating between Ferdinand and Suleiman led only to his murder, with the consent of the archduke, in December of the same year. The war dragged on for more than a decade: peace was not made until 1562. Yet neither side could achieve much. Ferdinand was still too weak, and support for him from either his brother or the German princes too lacking, for the Ottoman tide to be rolled back. Suleiman for his part was distracted by a new war with Persia, to which he led another great army in 1553, and by a serious struggle over the succession between two of his sons, Selim and Bayezid, which culminated in open war between them in 1558 and the execution of Bayezid in September 1561 (another son, Mustafa, had already been put to death in 1553). On both sides there was now increasingly a tacit acceptance of stalemate in the Danube valley. Raids and skirmishes, sometimes still on a considerable scale, continued. On both sides they were now well established as an integral part of life on this still very poorly defined frontier. On both sides this vague boundary was more and more strengthened by primitive but effective fortifications, forts of earth and timber, palisades and, in the more important centres, fortresses of a more elaborate kind. On the Habsburg side Ferdinand had considerable success in improving these defensive arrangements. A strip of territory along the border with a special status had now developed. Even before the end of the fifteenth century Matthias Corvinus had given land to refugees, normally Greek Orthodox ones, who had fled from the Turkish advance in the Balkans, in return for their serving as frontier guards. The idea had little practical effect in his lifetime; but a military border of this kind was by the 1550s a reality. In 1553 it was given a unified command under a 'Colonel of the Border' who could override the civilian authorities in the area: the border thus became a check on the Croat and Hungarian magnates as well as a defence against the Turks. In 1556 a *Hofkriegsrat* (Court War Council) was created in Vienna; and though the estates of the various Austrian duchies still provided the money for defence against the Turks and therefore inevitably had much influence, this was the first effort to give some unified direction to the military affairs of the Habsburg lands in central Europe.

At sea in the 1550s and 1560s the Ottoman advance seemed more active and threatening than on land. Barbarossa had died in 1546; but he had able successors, notably another great corsair leader, Dragut (Torghud Reis). In 1551 he recaptured from the Knights of St John Tripoli in north Africa, while in the following years seizures of Christian shipping and raids on the coasts of Italy and Spain became more threatening and disruptive than ever. In 1552 a landing at Gaeta led to a new wave of fears of an attack on Rome itself. In 1560 a Spanish counter-attack was a disastrous failure. An attempt to take the island of Djerba off the coast of Tunisia ended with the defeat of a Spanish fleet by an Ottoman one under Piali Pasha and the surrender of the military force it had landed. The years 1560–65 saw the Barbary corsairs at the height of their success and able to raid even the coasts of Languedoc and Provence, at the extreme effective range of galleys based in north Africa. It was fortunate for the Christian states of the western Mediterranean that none of its islands fell into Ottoman or corsair hands during these years. If in particular the attack launched by Piali Pasha on the Balearics in 1558 had succeeded in establishing a base there the results for Spain might have been very serious.[21] The year 1565 saw the climax of the struggle at sea, with a great Turkish attack on Malta. It failed. The Knights of St John, established in the island since 1530, made a very gallant defence until, after a siege of several months which ranks as one of the greatest in European history, the arrival in September of Spanish reinforcements forced the invaders to withdraw with heavy losses.[22]

In the following year Suleiman died. The death two years earlier of the Archduke Ferdinand (since 1556 Holy Roman Emperor in succession to Charles V) had meant that the peace of 1562 ended with him; and the sultan, in defence of what he saw as the rights of John Sigismund, Zapolya's son, led his army north once more in 1566. He died just before the Hungarian fortress of Szigetvar was stormed by his troops. The forward movement of Ottoman territorial conquest in Europe had reached its effective limit, however, two decades earlier. Distance, the distraction offered by Safavid Persia, increasingly effective Habsburg resistance, were now making any further advance

21. On this see Pryor, *Geography, Technology and War*, pp. 195–6.
22. There is a good account of this famous episode in J.F. Guilmartin, *Gunpowder and Galleys: Changing Technology and Mediterranean Warfare at Sea in the Sixteenth Century* (Cambridge, 1974), pp. 176–93.

impracticable. Some observers had already grasped this fact. Busbecq wrote in one of his more optimistic moments:

> But what has he achieved by his mighty army, his countless hosts? He has with difficulty clung to the portion of Hungary which he had already captured. He who used to make an end of mighty kingdoms in a single campaign, has won, as the reward of his expeditions, some scarcely fortified citadels and unimportant towns and has paid dearly for the fragment which he has gradually torn away from the vast mass of Hungary. He has once looked upon Vienna, it is true, but it was for the first and last time.[23]

This was too grudging an estimate of the greatest of Ottoman sultans. The empire could still at least hold its own with any Christian opponent. It was to remain for generations to come a great, though deeply foreign, element in the life of Europe. But the days of crushing victories and easy conquests were now in the past.

The beginnings of Ottoman decline

The later decades of the sixteenth century saw a marked falling-off in the efficiency of the Ottoman regime and in the respect given it by European and even Turkish observers. The Venetian representatives in Constantinople now much more than in earlier decades voiced serious criticisms – of growing disorder, of the decline of the strict army discipline which had formerly been so impressive, of the personal qualities of the sultans. More and more it seemed that the Turks suffered from an apparently inherent inability to keep pace with the European world as it grew and developed. Some Turkish onlookers echoed these complaints, pointing to increasing corruption and disregard of the law, growing indiscipline among the janissaries, the ineffectiveness of formerly effective institutions and a tendency for excessive power now to be wielded by women and favourites. By the 1580s inflation and debasement of the currency were generating serious tension and discontent: these and other factors underlay an outbreak of rebellion over much of Asia Minor for more than a decade after 1596.

None of this meant that the Ottoman Empire had ceased to be a very great power. It seemed as necessary as ever to strengthen against it the Habsburg frontier in the Danube valley. In 1576–80 the military border was further reorganized, while in 1578 a new *Hofkriegsrat* was

23. *Turkish Letters*, p. 21.

set up in Graz, closer to the frontier than Vienna. It was still possible also for an Ottoman government to dream of further large-scale territorial expansion. In 1569 an unsuccessful campaign was launched in south Russia in an effort to take Astrakhan on the Caspian, at the mouth of the Volga. Underlying this was the idea of building a canal that would link the Volga and the Don and thus create a new northern route for use in any future attack on Persia. Moreover, possession of Astrakhan would make easier Ottoman relations across the Caspian with the Uzbek rulers of central Asia, who were hostile to the Safavids and possible allies against them. It might also perhaps foster Ottoman trade with much of Asia, which had now been effectively blocked by Portuguese naval dominance of the Red Sea and Persian Gulf.[24] The attempt was a failure; but the mere fact of its being made showed that expansion, even of a very ambitious kind, was still the driving force behind Ottoman policy. Stephen Bathory, who ruled Poland with remarkable success in the years 1575–86, seems even to have feared a Turkish conquest of Russia which would, he thought, make the position of the empire in Europe completely impregnable. Popes continued, almost as much as in the past, to hope for a crusade to expel the infidel from Europe. Gregory XII in the 1580s envisaged such a success, and sent envoys to Persia and Ethiopia in the hope of anti-Ottoman alliances with both the Safavids and the Coptic Christian rulers in east Africa.[25] A few years later, in 1592 and again in 1594, Clement VIII wrote to the Safavid ruler Shah Abbas offering co-operation against their mutual enemy, and in particular to send him skilled workmen to help in such an enterprise. But though the Ottoman Empire in the later sixteenth century was still emphatically a great power, as it was to show in the long struggle with the Habsburgs which began in 1593, it was no longer the menacingly expansionist force it had been in the days of Suleiman. From 1578 most of its energies were absorbed in a long and exhausting new struggle with Persia which did not end until 1590. This war, fought in very difficult physical conditions in Azerbaijan, Kurdistan and the Caucasus and complicated by bitter dynastic and factional conflicts within Persia, ended in victory for the Ottomans. The peace of 1590 gave them Tabriz and important gains in Azerbaijan and Georgia. But the struggle meant great costs and losses for both combatants. While it continued no significant Turkish initiative in Europe was possible.

24. C.M. Kortepeter, *Ottoman Imperialism during the Reformation: Europe and the Caucasus* (London/New York, 1973), pp. 28–9.

25. P. Pierling, *La Russie et le Saint-Siège: Etudes Diplomatiques* (Paris, 1896–1912), ii, pp. 287, 248.

In the Mediterranean also the picture is of continuing and even increasing Ottoman activity until the mid-1570s, followed by its rapid decline. By the summer of 1570 the Turks were once more at war with Venice in an effort to conquer Cyprus, which was not merely the greatest Venetian colonial possession but also a base for Christian corsair attacks on Ottoman shipping. In July a Turkish army landed in the island and in September took Nicosia; while an alliance of Venice, Spain and the papacy was with difficulty constructed. The allies were never united. Venice, intent on holding as much as possible of her position in the eastern Mediterranean, had a strong inducement to make peace if she could do so on reasonable terms and a reputation for selfishness in the exclusive pursuit of her own objectives. Spain, inevitably, was more interested in controlling the western half of the sea and protecting her coasts against raids from north Africa: Philip II had responded to the defeat at Djerba in 1560 with a substantial programme of galley-building in Barcelona, Naples and Messina. Not until May 1571 did the three powers, largely at the urging of the pope, Pius V, sign a formal alliance. Five months later, at Lepanto in the Gulf of Patras in western Greece, their combined fleets won over the Ottoman one the most crushing naval victory of the century: the vanquished lost perhaps 30,000 men.

This triumph had deep symbolic and psychological significance for Christian Europe. The greatest artists of the later Renaissance – Titian, Tintoretto, Veronese – all painted pictures to celebrate it. In 1571 alone fifteen different accounts of the battle were published in France. Queen Elizabeth sent her congratulations not only to Venice but also to the pope, who a year earlier had excommunicated her and declared her deposed. But its practical results were small. Famagusta, the last Venetian stronghold in Cyprus, had fallen before the battle was fought: the island was now irrevocably lost. Moreover the victory was not pressed home. The French ambassador in Constantinople believed that if it had been followed by an attack on the city its Christian population would have risen in revolt and the Ottoman capital would have been taken;[26] but there was never any question of this very optimistic estimate being put to the test. Instead the huge losses at Lepanto were rapidly made good by a great programme of new naval building, so that within a year of the battle the sultan could put to sea a new fleet of 220 ships with a fire-power greater than that of the one that had been defeated. The French ambassador, deeply impressed, told Charles IX that 'I should never have

26. Degert, 'Une ambassade périlleuse', 237.

believed the greatness of this monarchy, had I not seen it with my own eyes'.[27]

The Christian powers by contrast achieved nothing in 1572; and by the autumn Venice was already negotiating for peace. In March 1573 she obtained it; but the terms were severe. She had to surrender Cyprus as well as some territory in Albania, pay a heavy war indemnity and limit her navy to 60 galleys. The war had meant great sacrifices for her and marked a further stage in her decline. Economically she was still flourishing. The population of the city was at its height (it was estimated at 168,000 in 1563). But it was increasingly obvious that she did not have the resources to maintain her position in a Europe more and more dominated by a small number of great powers. The Ottoman Empire, however, had also suffered considerably. One grand vizier in the 1570s claimed that merely keeping a single galley in service for a year, without allowing for repairs and maintenance, cost 5,000 ducats; and the rebuilding of the fleet after Lepanto, though it was a truly remarkable achievement, was hugely expensive.

Spain also had incurred heavy expenses. Her share in the Holy League of 1571–73 had cost her seven million escudos; and she had good reason to feel that Venice had deserted her allies by making peace. She now concentrated her efforts on securing her position in north Africa where, it must be remembered, to her and her Italian possessions the situation was more important than almost any Ottoman victory in the Balkans. But here also her achievements were in the end disappointing. Don John of Austria, the half-brother of Philip II who had commanded at Lepanto, captured Tunis in October 1573 and once more appeared to many observers, not least himself, as the champion of Christendom against Islam; but less than a year later the city was retaken by a great Ottoman expedition under Uluj Ali Pasha. This victory was another impressive demonstration of Ottoman power. It may well have involved a force of 100,000 men and was probably the greatest effort of the kind made by any state during the sixteenth century. It was the last major initiative in north Africa undertaken by either Turks or Spaniards, and also the last great success won anywhere by a force of oared galleys. When Uluj Ali returned to the Ottoman capital late in 1574 this was the last triumphal entry a Turkish fleet would ever make to Constantinople. By the

27. F. Braudel, *The Mediterranean and the Mediterranean World in the Age of Philip II* (London, 1972), ii, p. 1120; Degert, 'Une ambassade périlleuse', 237; for a balanced estimate of the limited effects of the battle see A. Hess, 'The battle of Lepanto and its place in Mediterranean history', *Past and Present* 57 (1972), 53–73. The quotation is from N. Housley, *The Later Crusades, 1274–1580: From Lyons to Alcazar* (Oxford, 1992), p. 143.

later 1570s both Spain and the Ottoman Empire had sacrificed much in the struggle and were deeply preoccupied elsewhere. Philip II, in addition to his heavy commitment in the Netherlands, now had his eyes fixed on the Portuguese succession and the opportunities it offered him. Moreover, though so deeply Catholic, he was notably lacking in the crusading zeal that his father had undoubtedly felt. In Constantinople the demands of the new war with Persia were paramount. Rivalry in the Mediterranean was by no means at an end. But on both sides it was becoming of secondary importance; and though religious prejudice on both sides made a lasting peace impossible, by early 1580 a truce had come into existence.[28] It was achieved only after prolonged negotiation, for there had been tentative and intermittent contacts between the two sides for a decade or more. But once achieved it marked a dividing-line in the history of international relations in the Mediterranean.

Spanish–Ottoman hostility, grounded in two generations of struggle, was inevitably slow to die. A Turkish attack sacked Reggio di Calabria in 1594, while in the first years of the seventeenth century Philip III encouraged and supported revolts against Ottoman rule in the Peloponnese and Syria.[29] Philip II's enemies continued to hope for help from Constantinople, especially after the end of the Persian war in 1590 freed resources once more for use on the empire's western frontiers. In the 1590s both the French ambassador in Constantinople and the newly established English one (the first had appeared in 1583) urged Turkish attacks on Apulia and Sicily, now only lightly defended. But such hopes and plans had no practical result. The great moments of the Mediterranean struggle – Charles V's capture of Tunis and failure at Algiers, the Ottoman victory at Djerba, failure at Malta, defeat at Lepanto and success at Tunis – were not to be repeated. Some important and painful decisions had been taken. It was now clear that the Spanish effort to control the north African coastline which had begun under Ferdinand of Aragon had ended, in spite of much effort and sacrifice, in failure. It was equally clear that though the eastern half of the Mediterranean might be under Muslim control its western half would remain, in spite of much raiding and damage to commerce, in Christian hands.

---

28. See above, p. 170.
29. K.M. Setton, *Venice, Austria and the Turks in the Seventeenth Century* (Philadelphia, Pa., 1991), p. 2.

Corsairs in the Mediterranean, stalemate on the Danube

In the last decades of the sixteenth century and the first of the seventeenth north Africa, most of all Algiers, remained a base for corsairs who preyed on merchant shipping throughout the western Mediterranean and increasingly outside it. By the early seventeenth century some of the Moroccan ports had emerged as centres of this sort of activity to supplement Algiers and Tunis. But the situation had changed very significantly from the days of Barbarossa. Ottoman authority in north Africa anywhere west of the Nile delta had never been very effective or the loyalty of the empire's satellites there altogether to be relied on. After the disaster at Lepanto the corsairs of Algiers asked for French protection against Spain; and Charles IX even suggested that his younger brother, the Duc d'Anjou, should rule there (though he was to pay the usual tribute to the sultan). After the truce of 1580 with Spain Ottoman control declined still further. The corsairs became steadily less obedient to instructions or influence from Constantinople and the janissaries in the north African ports more liable to mutiny: those in Tripoli, for example, seized the provincial treasury there in 1587.

Also the nature of corsair activity was by the 1580s changing in several ways. Christian pirates were now more prominent than before. The Knights of St John from their stronghold in Malta became in the decades after Lepanto even more active in their attacks on Muslim shipping; and they were now seconded by the newly founded Tuscan Knights of St Stephen, who from Leghorn waged a similar guerilla war at sea. By the later years of the century the Spanish viceroys in both Naples and Sicily were fitting out ships of their own for what was in effect licensed piracy. On the Muslim side the final expulsion of the Moriscos from Spain in 1609–13 meant that the Barbary corsairs were reinforced by numbers of embittered refugees and stimulated to greater activity. In many respects, therefore, the situation in the Mediterranean was more lawless and chaotic than it had been in the days of Charles V and Barbarossa. In the middle decades of the century it had been possible to think of corsair activity primarily in terms of Muslim raiders from north Africa. By its end the situation had become a good deal more complex.

Important technical changes were also taking place. The galley, with its light construction and few guns, limited range and heavy dependence on shore bases, was rapidly giving way to the sailing ship, more strongly built and heavily armed, more seaworthy and able to operate over much longer distances. Moreover, these sailing ships were very often English or Dutch: from the 1580s onwards growing numbers of English corsairs were using the north African ports, and also Italian ones such as Leghorn and Villafranca, as bases from which they preyed indiscriminately on shipping throughout the Mediterranean. Of the growing damage to the trade of many states there is no doubt. As England's Mediterranean commerce grew there can be found by the early seventeenth century the first hints that she also might become a significant actor in this increasingly complex situation. James I hoped for a time for a joint English–Dutch–Spanish expedition against the Barbary ports; and in 1620–21 an English naval force, with Spain offering the use of her harbours, was sent against Algiers, though quite ineffectively. (Its main achievement was to bring back to England a new variety of apricot.) The greatest sufferer from this free-for-all was once more Venice. What one writer has called a 'pirate offensive' in the decade 1595–1605[30] sharply hastened the decline of her once-great merchant marine and ended any pretensions she might have to be a major commercial power. Now the still considerable energies of her ruling class were to be channelled more and more into finance and landownership. The Ottoman Empire remained a great commercial force in the Mediterranean. It has been estimated (though this can be little more than an intelligent guess) that in the later sixteenth century its merchant marine had perhaps a total tonnage of about 80,000 – double that of Venice and 20,000 more than that of the Mediterranean coast of Spain.[31] But its dominance of the inland sea, which had seemed a real possibility until the checks at Malta and Lepanto, was now no longer even a remote one.

On land, however, it could still more than hold its own, though with growing difficulty, against the Austrian Habsburgs. The uneasy and insecure truce between them had done nothing to end constant border warfare in Croatia and Hungary; and in the 1580s this became more serious and a new large-scale conflict more likely. It is likely also that the need to keep the army and particularly the janissaries occupied, and thus avoid the destabilizing effect in Constantinople of a long period of peace, had some influence. The Venetian *bailo* reported in the early 1590s that 'many here think that the Sultan's anxiety for war is caused by the dread of a rising among the troops which have just come home from the Persian war'.[32] In the summer

30. A. Tenenti, *Piracy and the Decline of Venice, 1580–1615* (London, 1967), p. 98.
31. Braudel, *The Mediterranean*, i, p. 446.
32. Setton, *Venice, Austria and the Turks*, p. 8.

of 1593 open conflict broke out: it was to last for thirteen years. In Christian Europe the new struggle aroused widespread interest and even produced a certain amount of practical help. A considerable number of volunteers from the west, some of them Protestant, served in the Habsburg armies. Pope Clement VIII provided substantial amounts of money; and in 1594 he made serious efforts to construct an anti-Ottoman alliance between Rudolf II and Philip II which he hoped the rulers of Poland and Russia might join.

Yet to inflict any decisive defeat on the Ottoman army was still beyond Hábsburg power. Christian technical superiority in terms of weapons was now beginning to show itself; and in 1594 the Turks suffered a serious setback when the three semi-autonomous principalities of Transylvania, Wallachia and Moldavia renounced their allegiance to the sultan and went over to the Habsburg side. But complex rivalries between the rulers of the three, which also involved the Habsburgs and Poland, made any united anti-Ottoman front impossible. The one important battle of the war, at Mezo-Keresztes in October 1596, was a conclusive Turkish success: the victors saw it as comparable in importance to those at Chaldiran and Mohacs. After this the war became one of sieges, slow, laborious and demanding in terms of resources. As in the past, the Habsburg effort was hampered by religious prejudice, while the Turks benefited from showing themselves much more tolerant than their opponents of Protestantism in Hungary. The Habsburg general Giorgio Basta became particularly noted for the violently Catholicizing policies he carried out in Hungary and Transylvania; and the result was to strengthen both national and anti-Habsburg feeling. In 1604 a revolt made Stephen Bockskay, a local noble, effective ruler of Transylvania; and in June 1606 the Archduke Matthias, acting for the insane and ineffective Rudolf II, was forced to make an agreement which recognized him as such and also conceded limited religious toleration in the principality.

This serious setback for the Habsburgs was followed by a peace treaty, signed in November 1606 at Sitva-Torok. For the Ottoman Empire its terms were virtually a recognition that the war had ended in failure. To the territory it had held in 1593 it added two fortresses, Erlau and Kanisza. But the sultan had now, for the first time, to accept the Holy Roman Emperor as a ruler equal in status: henceforth he was to be referred to in negotiation and official communications by all his titles. The imperial ambassador who went to Constantinople after the signature of the treaty brought with him a gift of 200,000 florins; but it was made clear that such a gesture was never to be repeated. The payment during earlier decades of what was in effect a tribute, though it had been a humiliation rather than a serious handicap, was now at an end. Moreover this peace, unlike its predecessors, was destined to be lasting. Not for two generations was there to be a renewal of serious conflict; and this when it came began the process which, by the nineteenth century, had made the Ottoman Empire in Europe largely dependent on the rivalries of the Christian powers for its continued existence.

CHAPTER TEN

Eastern and Northern Europe: The Russian Advance

A new power takes shape

By the end of the fifteenth century a potentially great state, whose rise had profound implications for all of eastern and northern Europe, was emerging in the plains and forests of north-central Russia. Around the central nucleus of Moscow was now crystallizing, as the result of war and diplomacy, helped sometimes by duplicity and luck, a new political unit with immense possibilities of territorial expansion. This process had begun more than a century earlier; but the reign of the Great Prince (*Velikii Knyaz*) Ivan III of Moscow (1462–1505) saw it at its most rapid and successful. At his accession the hegemony of Moscow over the other Russian principalities was already in large part an established fact. But there were still many that were formally independent. Ryazan, Rostov, Tver and Yaroslavl, with the city republics of Pskov and Novgorod, though they were all threatened by the expansion of Moscow, owed it no formal allegiance. It was the essential achievement of Ivan, the most shadowy of all the major figures of the later Middle Ages, to bring most of these permanently under his control. In 1463 he began the absorption of Yaroslavl, a process that was completed over the following decade. In 1471 he set about the final destruction of the independence of Novgorod, with its enormous undeveloped territory stretching across north Russia as far as the Ural mountains. In that year he forced its ruling merchant oligarchy to agree to have no dealings with his enemies and (of great symbolic importance) that its archbishop should henceforth be consecrated in Moscow. Seven years later the city republic came under his direct control. Already in 1474 the ruler of Rostov had sold to Ivan his rights over the principality, while Tver was annexed in 1485. His son and heir, Vasily III, continued the process by ending the independence of Pskov in 1509 and of Ryazan around 1520.

All this meant the creation of a state, of however undeveloped and embryonic a kind, that might hope to advance in several possible directions: eastwards against the decaying Tatar khanates of the Volga basin; southwards towards the Black Sea at the expense of the still menacing khanate of the Crimea; or westwards against Lithuania and Poland. The 'Tatar Yoke', under which so much of Russia had lived since the overrunning of most of the country from the 1220s onwards by the heirs of Ghengis Khan, was now at an end. By the early fifteenth century the Great Horde or Golden Horde, formerly so formidable, had become merely a ramshackle and unstable principality based on the lower Volga valley; and by the end of the 1450s it had split into three distinct parts – the khanates of Kazan and Astrakhan on the middle and lower Volga and the much more powerful khanate of the Crimea. A Tatar invasion of Moscow's territory in 1480 was a complete failure. Though there was very little fighting a prolonged confrontation of the opposing armies on the river Ugra ended in a Tatar retreat: henceforth the generations-old payment of tribute by the great princes to the former conquerors was at an end. With military success and territorial gain came a heightened sense of status and touchiness about its symbols. When he negotiated a peace agreement with Lithuania in 1494 Ivan III successfully demanded that he be referred to in it by the new title of Sovereign (*Gosudar'*) of all Russia.

The Russia that was taking shape in these decades was still poor and weak by comparison with the states of western Europe. She already covered an enormous area, even though all present-day south Russia and the Volga valley lay outside her boundaries. But this huge country had a scanty population and was for the most part completely undeveloped. Primitive agriculture, little industry, few towns of any size, universities and even schools conspicuous by their absence: all this meant a lack, which was to dog her for centuries to come, of strong and creative institutions – guilds, municipalities, religious orders, corporate life of all kinds of the sort that meant so much in central and western Europe. None the less Ivan III and his son did much to give the state they were welding together at least some degree of political and military cohesion. The absorption by Moscow of almost all the other principalities meant that it was no longer possible, as in the past, for a discontented noble to move from the service of one prince to that of another, perhaps a rival. Now Ivan and his successors had become the sole legitimate focus of secular loyalties at the highest level. Moreover the *pomestie* system, by which land was granted by the ruler on a life tenure in return for service performed for him by the grantee, was now for the first time becoming general. The older *vochina* system, under which land was owned in absolute property, without any formal obligation to serve as a condition of holding it, did not disappear; but from now on it rapidly became less important. In this way again the position of the ruler was reinforced and his claim to the active support of the landholding class strengthened. Ivan III distributed on service tenure large amounts of confiscated land in the principalities he annexed, particularly in the huge territories of Novgorod, to his supporters in his own territory of Moscow and the surrounding areas.

He was not able to end completely the traditional practice of creating appanages, great territorial aggregations placed under the control of younger sons of the ruler. But he disliked the practice, which had for long been a source of weakness and division in all the Russian principalities; and he was able to bring the appanages inherited by his younger brothers under his own effective control. At his death he left two-thirds of all his lands to be ruled directly by his son Vasily; and though the remaining third was divided among four other sons their authority was strictly limited: they were in particular forbidden to mint their own coinage or to have any relations with foreign powers. The embryonic Russian state that was emerging at the end of the fifteenth century therefore showed many of the characteristics that were to mark it for generations, even centuries, to come – an effort to concentrate power in the hands of an autocrat very jealous of his own authority and sensitive to any threat to it, coupled with a strong though intermittent drive towards territorial expansion.

This Russia, however remote and backward, was slowly expanding its contacts, cultural, diplomatic and economic, with western Europe and experiencing west European influences that were, with occasional setbacks, henceforth to strengthen and deepen. Almost all Russians were still virtually untouched by western influences of any kind. Distance, difficulties of communication, the pervasive and deep-rooted conservatism of the Orthodox Church and its instinctive hostility to new ideas and practices, especially if they came from countries not themselves Orthodox, saw to that. There were some signs that a slow influx of influences from abroad was beginning. Ivan III married as his second wife Sofia Paleologa, of the family of the last Byzantine emperors; and when he did so it was an Italian, Giambattista della Volpe, whom he sent to Rome to ask for her hand. In 1494 his daughter Elena married Alexander, Grand Duke of Lithuania. This was an even more striking indication of slowly changing attitudes, for it was the first time since the thirteenth century that there had been any dynastic link between a Catholic family and the ruler of any Russian principality (though Ivan was careful to stipulate that Elena must be free to continue in the practice of the Orthodox faith). By his last years he was thinking in terms of foreign brides for his sons and trying to obtain information about possible ones. New buildings in the Kremlin were designed by Italian architects, Fioravanti degli Alberti and Alevisio Novi; and Ivan seems to have demanded that they be modelled on existing ones in Milan and Bologna which he had heard much praised. These, however, were no more than faint foreshadowings of what were later to become more important developments: conservatism and xenophobia were still immensely strong. When Sofia Paleologa reached Moscow, after she had been formally betrothed to Ivan in Rome in June 1472, the Metropolitan Philip, as head of the Orthodox Church in Russia, threatened to leave the city if the papal legate who accompanied her entered it preceded, as he proposed, by a Latin cross. Ivan himself was determinedly anti-Catholic, an attitude which helped to cut Russia off from the outside world and deprive her of intellectual and cultural stimuli from which she would otherwise have benefited.

Diplomatic contacts between Russia and western Europe, virtually unknown for centuries, began to develop as the power of the new state grew. As early as 1474 Christian I of Denmark had dreamed, as part of his efforts to encircle and defeat Sten Sture the Elder, the rebellious regent in Sweden, of a grand anti-Swedish alliance of which Ivan III, as well as the rulers of Poland and Scotland, would be part, though nothing came of this. In 1493, however, Ivan made with Denmark against the Swedish regent what has been called 'the first west-European alliance of Russia';[1] and there were very frequent Danish embassies to Moscow in the first two decades of the sixteenth century. Already in 1471 a Venetian envoy had appeared there, meaning to go on to the Tatars on the Volga to explore the possibility of an alliance with them against the Turks. An imperial ambassador, Nicholas Poppel or Popplau, reached Moscow in 1486, to be followed by another in 1490. Very occasional Russian envoys also began to be seen in other countries. One visited Constantinople in 1496–97, though he was concerned entirely with protecting Russian merchants trading in the Ottoman Empire, of whom there must have been very

---

1. W. Kirchner, 'Russia and Europe in the age of the Reformation', *Archiv für Reformationsgeschichte* XLIII (1952), 174.

few. Another, who visited the court of Selim I in 1514, brought with him on his return the first Ottoman representative to reach the Russian capital.

These early diplomatic contacts are of historical interest; but they had no practical results. Western rulers sometimes hoped to use Russia as a weapon in their own quarrels. But these hopes were often very exaggerated and unrealistic, as when Jörg von Thurn, the envoy sent by the Emperor Frederick III in 1490, suggested that Russian forces might be sent to serve in Flanders in the struggles of the Austrian Habsburgs with the French. In particular the belief that Russia might become an ally against the menacing advance of the Ottoman Empire, an idea that was to recur for generations to come, proved no more than a dream. A certain tradition of good relations between the Grand Prince Vasily and the Emperor Maximilian built up in the early sixteenth century, mainly because both were opposed to the ambitions of the Jagellon dynasty, then ruling both Poland and Hungary; but this also had little practical importance, given the unreliability of Maximilian and his continual policy fluctuations. The crusading ideal, still not dead in western Europe, never aroused a significant response from any Russian ruler or from the ordinary Russian.

Ignorance of Russia and of the most basic facts about it was still deep and widespread everywhere in the west. Poppel in his mission to Russia, for example, had as one of his tasks to discover whether Ivan III was in fact, as was apparently widely believed, a vassal of the king of Poland. Indeed that his territories, or at least most of them, were really part of Europe at all would have seemed to many contemporaries a very strange assertion. The fourteenth century, with Russia still under the suzerainty of Asiatic conquerors, had seen a growing tendency to identify Europe not merely with Christendom but very often merely with the Catholic part of it. This made it easy to think of a country so remote, so little known and still so barbaric, as not European at all but rather part of Asia. During the sixteenth and seventeenth centuries geographers proposed a number of different eastern boundaries for Europe; but some continued throughout these generations to exclude the whole of Russia as Asiatic.[2] These boundaries between the two continents were always defined in terms of great rivers: the Ural mountains, conventionally accepted today as marking the dividing-line between them, were never mentioned in such discussions. Occasionally the Volga was taken as marking the eastern

2. W. Parker, 'Europe how far?', *Geographical Journal* 126, Pt. 3 (Sept. 1960), 282 Fig. 4, 284.

boundary of Europe (though so little was known of the geography of Russia that it was sometimes believed to flow into the Black Sea rather than the Caspian). The most generally accepted line of division, however, was that constituted by the River Don; and this implied that most of Russia was not in Europe. Moscow itself seemed barely, if at all, a European city. Sigismund von Herberstein, the imperial ambassador who first visited it in 1517–18 and who later produced the most important of all accounts of sixteenth-century Russia in his *Rerum Moscovitarum commentarii* (1549), thought that 'though not in Asia, the place is hard upon its borders'.[3]

That Russia was outside Europe in more than a merely geographical sense seemed to be proved by many aspects of its life and government. Already by the early sixteenth century there can be heard a chorus of criticism and condemnation on this score that was to grow in volume and severity as time went on. Ivan III and Vasily III seemed to the western diplomats sent to their courts to personify autocracy and arbitrary power with a completeness not possible, even in that age of monarchy, in western Europe. Herberstein, for example, was unpleasantly impressed by the arbitrary government of Vasily, the methods by which he seized the lands of the surviving appanage princes and the fact that he normally confiscated for himself presents given to Russian diplomats by the foreign rulers to whom they were sent.[4] Moreover this extreme autocracy went hand in hand with a sensitivity on points of protocol, on precedence, titles and diplomatic etiquette generally which seemed excessive even in that prestige-obsessed age. Allied with this was a deep distrust of foreign diplomats and continual suspicion of their activities and motives. Everywhere in that age it was easy to see the diplomat as a kind of licensed spy; but in Russia this was carried to lengths unequalled anywhere else. Thus when Poppel visited the country as imperial envoy in 1486 he found that his knowledge of Polish and Czech (he had been born in Breslau) intensified the distrust with which he was regarded and seemed to mark him out as a dangerous agent of the Polish government.[5]

Indeed, were the Russians even Christians in any real sense at all? As Russo-Polish rivalry and hostility grew during the sixteenth century, Polish writers in particular often answered this question in the negative. The more conflict between Russia and Poland–Lithuania

3. S. von Herberstein, *Description of Moscow and Muscovy, 1557*, ed. B. Picard, trans. J.C.B. Grundy (London, 1969), p. 20. This is an abridged version of Herberstein's famous work.

4. Ibid., pp. 44–6, 48.

5. H. Uebersberger, *Oesterreich und Russland seit dem Ende des 15. Jahrhunderts.* i, *1488–1605* (Vienna/Leipzig, 1906), pp. 4–5.

became something to be taken for granted, almost a law of nature (the two fought each other for 45 of the 100 years from 1492 onwards), the more propagandists spread the idea of Poland as a bulwark of Christendom and a defence not merely against the infidel Turks but just as much against the equally un-European, schismatic Russians. Such feelings were not confined to Poland and outlived the sixteenth century. In 1518 Sten Sture the Younger, the Swedish regent, described the Russians as schismatics and enemies of the Christian name (*schismatici et Christiani nominis inimici*), while a century later an academic thesis presented at the University of Uppsala and defended there in the presence of the king himself had still as its subject the question 'Are the Muscovites Christians?'.[6] The very names often used, at least in the early sixteenth century, when referring to the inhabitants of Russia and drawn from a remote Greco-Roman past – Scythians, or more rarely Roxolani – carried a strong implication that they were irremediably exotic, Asiatic, non-Christian, in no way European.

The last years of the fifteenth century and the first ones of the sixteenth therefore saw the first steps in the long process of making the huge and mysterious new state in the east part of the European state system. But they were tiny and faltering steps, marked on both sides by doubt and hesitation.

The new state advances

The Russia now taking shape was strongly expansionist; and this drive towards territorial growth was focused most of all on its western frontier, where it was confronted by the huge but incoherent bulk of Poland–Lithuania. Stretching from the Baltic almost to the Black Sea and from the Carpathians far into Belorussia, the kingdom of Poland and the grand duchy of Lithuania, very loosely united since 1336 under the rule of the Jagellon dynasty, made up what was geographically by far the largest element in the European political picture. Its economic resources, though largely undeveloped, were very considerable: it was soon to become, with the possible exception of Sicily, the most important grain-exporting area of the continent. Its military strength seemed impressive; and it was clearly marked out for a signi-

6. J. Tazbir, 'Poland and the concept of Europe in the sixteenth–eighteenth centuries', *European Studies Review* 7 (1977), 30; E. Klug, 'Das asiatische Russland: Über die Entstehung eines europäischen Vorurteils', *Historische Zeitschrift* 245 (1987), 275, 284; A. Lortholary, *Le mirage russe en France au XVIIIe siècle* (Paris,? 1954), p. 16.

ficant role in resisting any expansion northwards of Ottoman power from its Danubian vassal-states of Moldavia and Wallachia into Podolia and the Ukraine. Its last Jagellon rulers, Sigismund I (1506–48) and Sigismund Augustus (1548–72), were competent and ambitious. Though the influence on it of the Renaissance had not been deep or widespread the union was predominantly Catholic (though with a large Orthodox population in Lithuania) and in a real sense part of Europe. To an observer in the early sixteenth century Poland–Lithuania must have seemed a greater force and destined for greater future importance than remote and un-European Muscovy.

Yet there were already deep and growing internal weaknesses which were eventually to doom it to be overshadowed and in the end largely absorbed by its great eastern neighbour. The connection between Poland and Lithuania was purely dynastic: it was only with the Union of Lublin in 1569 that the link between the two became formal and to some extent institutional. More serious, the last Jagellon rulers could not resist a slow but persistent sapping of their authority which was to gather strength under their successors. In sixteenth-century Europe a strong monarch wielding power which could when necessary crush rebellion and override any sectional interest that challenged it was essential for the success, even the safety, of any state. Particularly in one covering a great geographical area such a ruler was the best, very often the only, guarantor of internal peace and stability and the indispensable mainspring of successful action abroad. Poland–Lithuania was now to provide, at first slowly and then at an accelerating pace, the most striking and painful proof of this fundamental truth.

During the fifteenth century the *szlachta* (minor nobles and squires) acquired fairly rapidly an influence over such central government as there was which increasingly challenged that of the ruler. By the early sixteenth century it was becoming more and more difficult for the king of Poland to take any important initiative without the consent of the national *seym*, a quasi-representative body dominated by representatives of the nobility sent to it by district *seyms*. In 1505 a statute usually known as *Nihil novi* provided that he should introduce no change affecting 'the general law and public liberty' without the consent of 'the council and delegates of the lords'; and in the later 1530s Sigismund I, in spite of his own authoritarian tendencies, had to make a similar concession.

The power of the *szlachta* grew in part at the expense of the magnates, the relatively small group of great families who monopolized the main court and government offices. It also increased at the expense of the towns, always less important in Poland–Lithuania than in most parts of western Europe. But most of all it was the great peasant majority that lost as a result of this process. From the 1490s onwards legislation progressively deprived the peasant of his right of free movement: more and more it became difficult or impossible for him to leave the land he worked without the consent of his lord, while at the same time he lost the right to appeal to the royal courts of law against the lord's patrimonial jurisdiction. The peasant was losing his freedom, which even in the fifteenth century had been a reality, and sinking into serfdom.

A similar process was under way in Russia. But there was a crucial difference between the two countries in this respect. In Russia the privileged landowning class, the *dvoryane*, which gained by the loss of peasant freedom and rights, was becoming one of state servants, the essential foundation on which the power of future autocratic tsars was to rest. On the degradation of the peasant were erected the administration and army that were eventually to make Russia a great power. In Poland by contrast peasant unfreedom went hand in hand with a weakening of royal authority and the eventually fatal enfeeblement of the country as a force in international relations. Russia and Poland–Lithuania were now set on paths that diverged radically.

This was all the more serious because the Polish–Lithuanian union included in Belorussia and the Ukraine great areas that had formerly been under Russian rule. Kiev, the greatest city of early mediaeval Russia, and other important centres such as Smolensk and Polotsk, were certain to become a focus for the ambitions of the increasingly powerful autocracy centred on Moscow. To recover the huge lost territories in the west was the overriding foreign policy objective of both Ivan III and Vasily III. Ivan had no doubt of the justification of his claims. To him 'the Russian land which is in the hands of Lithuania – Kiev, Smolensk and other towns' was 'the patrimony of St. Vladimir', historically and rightfully Russian. He was now beginning a process of westward expansion that was not to be halted until the partitions of Poland in the later eighteenth century.

On her western frontier Russia confronted not merely Poland–Lithuania but what was to become an equally important antagonist, the emerging kingdom of Sweden. In the early sixteenth century Sweden was only coming into existence as a truly independent factor in international relations. Since the end of the fourteenth century she had been part of a Scandinavian union led and dominated by Denmark; and though she had enjoyed *de facto* a high degree of autonomy it was only in 1521 that a national rising threw off the rule of the Danish

King Christian II and established Sweden once more as an independent kingdom. Its leader, Gustavus Vasa, was elected king in 1523 and thus began one of the longest-lived of all European ruling dynasties. As yet Sweden was no more than a minor force. Her population was scanty and her economy little developed. Towns, even Stockholm itself, were small and weak and her commercial life still largely controlled by Lübeck, the greatest of the Hanse cities, in a way that made her almost a colony. Bitter hostility between Sweden and Denmark had now taken root and was to be one of the most lasting of such antagonisms in the history of modern Europe. Nevertheless by the 1530s Gustavus Vasa had built up a small but efficient navy; and when in 1532 war broke out with Lübeck this gave a good account of itself and helped to force the Hanse city to end the struggle in November of the following year. By the 1540s Gustavus had begun a series of reforms in recruiting which gave Sweden, alone among the states of Europe, a native standing army, though mercenaries continued to be as important here as in most other parts of the continent. Already she had felt the pressure from the east: there was a considerable history of small-scale fighting on her Finnish frontier with Russia. This meant that Gustavus Vasa at his accession inherited a tradition of relatively good Swedish relations with Poland–Lithuania based on the fear inspired in both by their resurgent eastern neighbour.

In the south the Tatar khanate of the Crimea, since 1475 a vassal-state of the Ottoman Empire, could be a dangerous and very destructive enemy of Russia. Its cavalry forces, mobile and quick-moving, could raid over long distances with devastating effect. In 1482, in alliance with Ivan III, they inflicted a severe defeat on Poland–Lithuania by taking and sacking Kiev. In 1521 another great raid reached the outskirts of Moscow and did much damage. Fifty years later, in 1571, the Crimean Tatars took and burnt the city; and even twenty years later they were able seriously to threaten it once again. The hope that the Ottoman government might exert some control over these unruly subordinates was the main reason why Russian rulers usually wished to keep on good terms with the sultan in Constantinople. Yet in the south the keynote was always defence. It was in the west that territorial gains were sought, often at great cost.

The attack that Ivan III launched against Lithuania in 1500 began under favourable auspices. When Casimir IV of Poland–Lithuania died in 1492 one of his sons, Jan Olbracht (John Albert), inherited the Polish throne while the grand duchy of Lithuania fell to another, Alexander. The insecure Polish-Lithuanian union had for the time being ceased to exist. More important, Ivan was on good terms with

Mengli-Girey, the khan of the Crimea, and could thus feel that his southern frontiers were reasonably secure; while the Orthodox faith of much of the population of Lithuania, and even of some of its greatest nobles, meant that they often felt an instinctive sympathy with their Russian co-religionists. Ivan indeed justified the outbreak of war by pointing to Alexander's efforts to support the union of the Catholic and Greek Orthodox Churches, something deeply repugnant to every pious adherent of the latter. At the same time the pope, Alexander VI, still saw Russia, very mistakenly, as a potential ally of the west European states in a crusade against the Turks and turned down pleas for the issuing of a bull for a Catholic crusade against her.

The Russians won an important victory over the Lithuanians in July 1500; and when the Livonian Order (Knights of the Sword, since 1237 a branch of the Teutonic Order which had its centre in Prussia), the German religious–military order that controlled much of what is now Estonia and Latvia, intervened in support of the Grand Duke Alexander its forces were in turn badly beaten in the autumn of 1501. But Ivan's main objective, the city of Smolensk, escaped him in spite of a long siege in 1502: in the following year he made a truce, to last six years, with Alexander, who had become king of Poland on his brother's death in 1501. This temporary peace brought Ivan considerable territorial gains; and it was clear that Smolensk and even Kiev, the capital of the Ukraine and a city with much greater significance than Moscow in the early history of Russia, were now under threat. In 1507 Vasily III resumed his father's offensive; and a treaty signed in the autumn of 1508 with the new ruler of Poland–Lithuania, Sigismund I, recognized almost all Ivan's earlier conquests as Russian possessions. But this did not halt the Russian advance. Late in 1512 the attack was renewed, with Smolensk once more as the objective; and after two efforts to take the city had failed a third was successful in the summer of 1514, though in September of the same year the Russians were badly defeated at Orsha, almost 100 miles to the west. Vasily hoped for further conquests and for effective allies against the Poles. In 1514 he signed a treaty with the Emperor Maximilian; and three years later he made an alliance with the Grand Master of the Livonian Order, who had for several years been embroiled in a series of complex disputes with Sigismund I. But Maximilian was too untrustworthy, too weak and too preoccupied by other issues to be of any use, while the decaying Livonian Order was ceasing to be an effective military force. The result, after years of bitter and destructive fighting, was another truce signed in 1522: it was initially to last for five years but was later prolonged until 1534. Vasily had thus failed to realize all his hopes. But the capture of Smolensk was an important victory. It strengthened Russia's defences in the west and could become a springboard for further advances. Not for almost a century was Poland to recover it.

Vasily's sudden death in 1533 left as his successor a three- year-old child and began more than a decade of intense personal and factional struggles for power in Moscow. The dead grand prince's brothers, whom he had rigorously excluded from all real authority, his widow until her death in 1538, and the boyars (the high-ranking nobles who were the traditional dominant group in Muscovite society) contended for control of the government as plots and coups d'état followed each other in rapid succession. The young heir, Ivan IV, was marked for life by this exceptionally difficult childhood. It was only in the summer of 1547, after his coronation, that his effective rule began. There were already signs that expansionist ambitions were still at work. The coronation ceremony was closely modelled on that of the Byzantine empire in its later years; and the young ruler assumed the new title of tsar (a russified form of the Latin *caesar*): it is as Tsar Ivan IV that he is known to history. Yet the first years of his reign were a period of internal change and reform, in many ways constructive. They saw improvement, largely by introducing greater uniformity, in what was still a chaotic and inefficient system of administration. The arbitrary powers of provincial governors were curbed, new organs of central government created, an important new law-code promulgated in 1550. Side by side with this, however, went important expansionist moves and a strengthening of Russia's military forces. In 1552 the khanate of Kazan, weakened by decades of internal feuding (Russian suzerainty had been intermittently recognized since 1487 and it had six different rulers in its last six years of quasi-independence), was conquered. Four years later the even weaker khanate of Astrakhan also fell under rule from Moscow: the whole length of the great river Volga was now in Russian hands. In the west these conquests, in areas remote, barbaric and almost unknown, attracted little attention. They were nevertheless of great importance. Hitherto the emerging Russian state had been, apart from unimportant indigenous tribes in the far north, homogeneous in speech and religion. It was now absorbing a large population with a distinct culture of its own. Though still poor and in many ways primitive, it had taken the first crucial step on the road to becoming a great multinational empire. Russian expansion eastward would henceforth face no significant barriers except physical and climatic ones until the Pacific was reached in the 1630s. Simultaneously the creation of the *streltsy* (literally 'shooters'), a force of infantry armed with muskets, equipped Russia with her first regular standing military force. Possibly based on Ottoman practice, it was henceforth, in conjunction with the cavalry provided by the landholding service class, to provide the backbone of the country's army. By the end of the century there were probably about 25,000 *streltsy*, roughly a quarter of the total force of 110,000 men or so on which the ruler could count.

Though the first decade of Ivan's effective reign therefore saw no effort at westward expansion of the kind his father and grandfather had attempted, the strengthening of the state and the increase in its military power which must underpin such territorial growth were very much still under way. After the subjection of Kazan and Astrakhan it might have seemed logical to continue what could be presented as a kind of crusade against Islam by attacking its much more formidable political and military embodiment in the Crimean khanate. Its ruler, Devlet-Girey, had tried unsuccessfully to help Kazan in the last moments of its independence in 1552; and though the Crimean Tatars were never strong enough to contemplate any permanent conquest of Russian territory they could and did raid far into it with devastating results. But Ivan, though many of his closest associates were in favour of such an attack, decided to remain on the defensive in the south: it is one of the more surprising facts of Russian history that no conquest of the Crimea was attempted until the 1680s. Nor did he follow in the footsteps of his father and grandfather by attempting conquests on his western borders, in White Russia and the Ukraine. Poland–Lithuania was still a formidable power; and its two component parts were soon to be more closely united in 1569. Instead the tsar attempted expansion in what seemed an easier direction. In January 1558 he began an effort to conquer Livonia, and thus set in motion a bitter and complex struggle that was to last for a quarter of a century and strain to the utmost Russia's still limited resources.

The struggle for Livonia

It seemed that the conquest of Livonia would not be difficult to achieve, and that once achieved it would yield great benefits. The Livonian Order had now lost most of its earlier military effectiveness, and its master, Wilhelm von Fürstenberg, was willing to make some agreement with Ivan. The rule of the knights was not popular with their subjects; they were divided between pro- and anti-Polish factions; and they were on bad terms with the independent ecclesiastical lands, the archbishopric of Riga and the bishoprics of Osel, Courland and Dorpat, which covered much of Livonia. The peasants, as several observers noted, hated their German masters more than they did the invading Russians, so that the nobility were reluctant to arm their tenants in case the arms might be used against themselves. By gaining control of the area the tsar would give Russia for the first time a secure foothold on the Baltic, and with it much freer contact with western Europe. This would act as a stimulus to her trade and allow her to import from the west the arms and equipment needed by her growing army. Only a few years earlier, in 1553, a small group of Englishmen had reached the White Sea coast of Russia and from there Moscow, where they were well received by Ivan. The formation in 1555 of the Muscovy Company began the development of a significant English trade with Russia, so that by the 1570s a German mercenary soldier with long experience of the country could refer to the route from the White Sea coast to Moscow as 'the English route'.[7] This new trading outlet probably did something to strengthen the country in a military sense: the initial successes in Livonia of Ivan IV were widely believed to have been helped by supplies of war material from England. But the control of Livonian ports, cities such as Narva, Reval and above all Riga, would do far more.

At first the invasion went well. In 1558–59 eastern Estonia and northern Latvia were overrun; and the capture of Narva in May 1558 gave Russia for the first time a usable port of her own on the Baltic. The ineffectiveness of the Livonian Order was now unmistakable in spite of frantic but fruitless efforts to obtain outside assistance from the Emperor Ferdinand and the cities of the Hanseatic League, while some nobles even urged Henry II to send an expedition to conquer the area for France. But the scale of the Russian advance very soon began to arouse more effective opposition. Poland–Lithuania was bound to see it as a threat to its northern borders, while both Sweden and Denmark had interests and ambitions of their own in the area. In November 1561 the new master of the Livonian Order, Gotthard Kettler, ceded its territories to Poland–Lithuania: with this secularization a German crusading effort on the southern shores of the Baltic which had begun in the twelfth century came to an end. In the same year a Swedish army occupied a strip of northern Estonia and the port of Reval accepted Swedish protection, while a Danish force took

7. H. von Staden, *The Land and Government of Muscovy* (Stanford, Ca., 1967), p. 65.

control of the lands of the Bishop of Osel in the north-west of the country. The original Russian invasion had produced a complicated four-cornered struggle for Livonia, often waged with great brutality, that was to occupy the next two decades.

Ivan's position was now very difficult. The involvement of Poland–Lithuania in particular meant that the geographical scope of the war had been greatly extended. Instead of a merely Livonian struggle he was now facing one all along his western frontier. Moreover Sweden, Denmark and Poland–Lithuania could all count, in different ways and to different extents, on some degree of local support in Livonia. This Russia could not do. Her Orthodoxy struck no responsive chord in an area where Protestantism was becoming increasingly dominant; her autocratic government was in direct conflict with the corporate rights that counted for so much in the towns; and Ivan's growing reputation for extreme cruelty became yet another obstacle in the way of making Russian rule acceptable. In 1564 his armies were badly beaten by the Lithuanians at Ulla and Orsha, while Prince Kurbskii, one of his commanders and a personal friend, deserted to Poland. Ivan's paranoiac suspicions now overwhelmed him. For the next decade Russia was divided into two parts. The *oprichnina*, sections of the country (eventually about half, concentrated in the central and more productive areas) which remained under the direct control of the tsar and were administered by followers sworn to unquestioning loyalty, now existed side by side with the *zemshchina*, the remainder of Russia, which was administered as before with its own army, legal system and council. The exact significance of this remarkable change and the intentions behind it are still much debated. But it was accompanied by an unprecedented reign of terror in which much of the old boyar class was destroyed and an all-pervasive atmosphere of fear and insecurity created. While this situation continued it was hard to mount any large-scale offensive in Livonia; and territorial ambitions for the time being receded into the background.

It was also true, however, that Russia's rivals were very far from united. In 1546 Christian III of Denmark showed that claims to suzerainty over Sweden were not yet dead by incorporating the Swedish arms with the Danish ones – a good example of the importance of such symbols and the feeling they could arouse. The two countries were also divided by Baltic trade issues, by Denmark's control of the Sound and the dues she levied on ships passing through it, and by Sweden's ambition to monopolize the trade of the Livonian ports. The result was a war, in which Denmark was supported by Lübeck, still the greatest trading power of the Baltic, as well as by Poland–

Lithuania, which broke out in 1563 and lasted for seven years. This allowed Ivan to hope for a time for an alliance with Sweden, with which he made a seven-year truce in 1564; but these hopes collapsed in 1568 when Erik XIV of Sweden, now insane, was deposed and replaced by his half-brother John, who had Catholic and Polish sympathies and began an exchange of mutually insulting letters with the tsar. Instead Ivan now looked for a time to Denmark as an ally. Magnus, younger brother of the Danish king Frederick II, became the tsar's vassal as 'king' of Livonia, was promised the hand of a member of Ivan's family and commanded the Russian army in a long and eventually unsuccessful siege of Reval, held by the Swedes, in 1570–71. The tsar even proposed in 1567, of course unsuccessfully, an offensive and defensive alliance with England.

This tangled series of conflicts entered a new phase in the mid–1570s. By then the seven-year struggle between Sweden and Denmark was over, ended in 1570 by a peace congress which met at Stettin with the kings of France and Poland and the elector of Saxony acting as mediators and was one of the most large-scale diplomatic gatherings of the century. More important, however, was the election at the end of 1575 of Stephen Bathory, prince of Transylvania, as king of Poland. (Ivan unsuccessfully put forward both himself and his son Fyodor as candidates, and received some support in Lithuania, notably from the great Radziwill and Chodkiewicz families and from the argument that the choice of a Russian ruler would end the incessant struggles between the two countries.) Within a year the new king had established control of his huge and unruly territories; and he struggled to provide them with a more up-to-date and effective military organization. In 1578 an effort was made to form a new infantry force from the peasants of the royal domains, though mercenaries, mainly German and Hungarian, remained essential. The Polish artillery was improved and considerable use was made of Tatar and Cossack irregular cavalry. All this, coupled with the growing exhaustion of Russia, paved the way for victory in the apparently endless Livonian struggle.

In the months that followed Bathory's accession, while the new king was preoccupied by a rebellion in Danzig, Ivan IV made his last throw. Most of Livonia was once more overrun by a Russian army, though the ports of Reval and Riga held out. But this apparently easy success was short-lived. Poland–Lithuania was now supported by Sweden, which hoped to control the northern coastline of Estonia and thus the whole Gulf of Finland. In October 1578 they inflicted a severe defeat on the Russians at Wenden, a battle which can be seen as the turning-point in the war. In 1579 the Poles recaptured the strategically important town of Polotsk, which had been in Russian hands for the last sixteen years. In the following year Bathory took the equally strategic Velikie Luki and thus threatened an invasion of Russia that would isolate Ivan's remaining forces in Livonia. In 1581 a Polish army laid siege, though unsuccessfully, to Pskov, deep in Russian territory. In the same year the Swedes took Narva, a final blow to hopes of a Russian Baltic outlet. The importance that Ivan attached to the city is clear. At its capture early in the war he had granted its merchants the right to trade freely throughout Russia and had promised that it should never have troops quartered in it. Its loss was a correspondingly heavy blow. More than two decades of hopes and efforts had ended in disastrous failure.

Such was Ivan's desperation that an emissary was sent to Rome early in 1581 to ask for papal mediation and to hint that to obtain it the tsar might even be willing to become a Catholic and help forward the conversion of Russia. An Italian Jesuit, Antonio Possevino, therefore left Rome at the end of March with very ambitious instructions to make peace between Russia and Poland–Lithuania, end the schism between the Catholic and Orthodox Churches and lay the foundations for a new crusade against the Turks. In December peace talks began at the ruined village of Yam Zapolskii, midway between Velikie Luki and Pskov. The negotiations were not easy. Inevitably, given the tsar's intense preoccupation with his titles, extreme even for that day, there were difficulties of protocol. His demand to be designated 'tsar of Kazan and Astrakhan' in all official communications played an important role in the early stages of the discussions.[8] But though Ivan won some concessions of this formal kind he could not avoid a disastrous material setback. The peace with Poland–Lithuania in January 1582 meant the abandonment of all his claims in Livonia as well as of Polotsk. Bathory, however, gave up only Velikie Luki. When peace was made with Sweden in the following year it was at the price of further Russian concessions. Most of Estonia was now Swedish territory and was to remain so for well over a century. Russia's foothold on the Baltic, sought at such cost, was now only a short and almost useless stretch of coastline on both sides of the River Neva: her direct contact with western Europe was still restricted to the difficult and dangerous sea route around the North Cape to the White Sea.

Contacts with the west slowly expanding

Ivan's reign saw a growth in contacts of all kinds between Russia and the west and some dispelling of the thick veil of ignorance and prejudice through which each still saw the other. When he died, in 1584, the land he ruled was a little less of an enigma to Europeans than it had been half a century earlier. But this was, almost as much as in the past, a slow and difficult process. War led in Russia to some demand for western technicians who could make her a more effective military power. In 1547 a German in Ivan's service, Hans Schlitte, was sent to his homeland to recruit others, while five years later a foreign engineer helped in the capture of Kazan. Sixty Scots mercenaries, formerly in Swedish service, entered that of Russia in 1574; and they were followed a few years later by 85 others who had been taken prisoner in Livonia. The opening by the English of the White Sea route meant some growth of trade, in which the tsar took a personal interest. Osip Nepea, the first Russian ambassador to England who reached London in February 1557, was himself a merchant and was accompanied by two others, while ten more used his embassy to send goods to England. A decade later there was a Russian merchant in Antwerp and another in England trading on Ivan's behalf; while he placed the houses of English merchants in Russia within the *oprichnina* and hence under his personal protection and control. English recognition of the possibilities of the new market that was now opening is reflected in the fact that Nepea, on his formal entry into London, was escorted by 140 merchants. The foundation two years earlier of the Muscovy Company was another indication of this; and Anglo-Russian trade, though never large, soon became significant. In 1570 thirteen English ships went to Narva, then in Russian hands; and in the later decades of the century an average of ten or twelve seems to have gone each year to the White Sea. By 1587, on the eve of the armada, more than a quarter of the expenses of the English navy were for imported Russian ropes and cables.[9] A few years earlier, in 1577 or 1578, the first Dutch ship had also reached north Russia; and from 1584 onwards Dutchmen were prominent in the growth of the new port of Archangel.

Commercial contacts of this kind were of some value in beginning the process of bringing Russia into Europe; but they were markedly

9. S.H. Baron, 'Osip Nepea and the opening of Anglo-Russian commercial relations', *Oxford Slavonic Papers*, NS 11 (1978), 42, 47, 51, 60; M.S. Anderson, *Britain's Discovery of Russia, 1553–1815* (London, 1958), p. 5.

one-sided. In them the Russian role was almost entirely a passive one. Some English and later Dutch merchants became established in Russia and stayed there for quite long periods; but there was no corresponding settlement of Russians in England or The Netherlands and no effort to develop a Russian merchant marine except on the most limited scale and for purely local trade.

It was only very slowly, moreover, that contacts of this utilitarian kind did much to make each side better informed about the other or more willing to tolerate its apparent defects. In Russia foreign diplomats continued to be seen as potentially dangerous spies to be carefully watched and given little or no freedom of action. Frequent long delays before they were allowed to enter the capital and have an audience with the tsar, and surveillance so close that they were often virtual prisoners in their own houses, produced a litany of complaints from the representatives of foreign rulers. Possevino spoke for many when he complained that on his first visit to Moscow, in 1581, he was constantly surrounded by a guard of 60 men who prevented his going out, meeting anyone or even buying food, and that prison in Poland was preferable to this sort of freedom in Russia.[10] Political contacts so intermittent and restricted inevitably meant that each side remained surprisingly ignorant of the most basic facts about the other. When the Russian government sent an envoy to the papacy in 1581 it was apparently under the impression that the Venetian republic was part of the papal state; but ignorance on the western side was equally striking. Possevino, when he reached Moscow in the same year, brought presents for the Tsaritsa Anastasia, the first wife of Ivan IV, who had died in 1560.[11] Underlying all this ignorance and misunderstanding was the fact that Russia was still seen in the west as fundamentally foreign, essentially Asiatic. Her military strength might be increasing; her territories might be impressively large; the market she offered to foreign traders might be tempting. But she was still only beginning to be part of the European state system or of the growing network of more or less permanent diplomatic contacts that was its outward expression. Even her status as a Christian country could still be explicitly denied: a German observer in the 1570s (admittedly a hostile one) could still refer to the Russians as 'those non-Christians'.[12]

---

10. Pierling, *La Russie et le Saint-Siège*, ii, p. 68; for similar complaints from English diplomats see Anderson, *Britain's Discovery*, pp. 13–15.
11. Pierling, *La Russie et le Saint-Siège*, ii, p. 85.
12. Von Staden, *The Land and Government of Muscovy*, p. 97.

Exhaustion and collapse in Russia

Ivan IV left to his successor, his son Fyodor, a country and society badly weakened. The chaos of the *oprichnina* years and the unsuccessful Livonian war had made heavy and damaging demands. Peasant flight from the central parts of the country to border areas where the grip of the government was less effective, depopulation and abandoned villages, were now frequently commented on by foreign observers. Russia, in the past expanding, often aggressive and threatening, now seemed rather the potential victim of stronger neighbours. Of these the most menacing was Poland–Lithuania. Stephen Bathory, before his sudden death in December 1586, played seriously with the idea of a conquest of the country, which he claimed could be achieved in three years, and of using this as the basis for a new effort to drive the Turks from Europe. The idea was quite visionary. Bathory's continual shortage of money (though Pope Gregory XIII reluctantly gave him some financial help) and the disunity and turbulence of his own dominions made it completely impracticable. But it was an index of how far the pendulum had now swung since the beginning of the Livonian struggle.

After Bathory's death the Russian government proposed Tsar Fyodor as a candidate to succeed him in Poland–Lithuania and a union of both states under his rule, which would have created an enormous aggregation of territories stretching from the Volga to Silesia. But this also had no prospect of realization. Instead in 1587 Sigismund, son of John III of Sweden and a Polish mother of the former ruling house of Jagellon, was chosen. Simultaneously a rival candidate, the Archduke Maximilian, was elected by a competing noble faction; but he was defeated outside Cracow in November, driven across the frontier into Silesia, and there once more defeated and taken prisoner in January 1588. This opened the prospect of a union of Sweden and Poland–Lithuania under a single ruler, something that could only increase the threat to Russia on her western borders. In fact this union never came about. Sigismund III was devoutly Catholic and under considerable Jesuit influence; as such he was unacceptable in a Sweden more and more solidly Lutheran. Moreover Sweden had no intention of giving up her recently gained foothold in Estonia which many Poles, including Sigismund himself, wished to annex. The result was that the death of John III in 1592 was followed by a struggle between the supporters of Sigismund, who was crowned as king of Sweden in 1594, and his rival Charles, Duke of Södermanland, another member of the Vasa family. By 1600 Charles, a strong

Lutheran, had gained the upper hand and become King Charles IX. Swedish–Polish relations henceforth were to be consistently hostile; and Charles, once established on the throne, immediately launched an invasion of Polish Livonia and began a new struggle which dragged on until 1629. Russia need no longer fear a dangerously threatening combination of her western neighbours.

However, when a new Russo-Swedish struggle broke out in 1590 it still seemed that Sweden was to be joined in a dynastic union with Poland–Lithuania; and though her military effort had little success this prospect strengthened her hand diplomatically. Russia in the early 1590s made some gains along the shores of the Gulf of Finland, though she failed to recover Narva, and also in Karelia, the area in south-east Finland bordering Russian territory. But when peace was made at Teusina in 1595 the result was a compromise. Russia retained the conquered territory; but Sweden obtained a promise that her merchants should be able to trade throughout Russian territory without paying duties and that Russian exports should still flow through Swedish-held ports, above all Narva, and hence be a source of profit to the Swedish government.

This relatively minor conflict, however, was overshadowed by the more and more unstable and difficult situation within Russia. Fyodor was not an effective ruler and he was the last of his line. With him ended the six-centuries-old Rurikid dynasty. His death in 1598 therefore opened up a vista of new and dangerous possibilities. He was succeeded, after frantic political manoeuvring, by his brother-in-law, the boyar Boris Godunov, a much abler man who had for years been the dominant force in Russian political life; but whatever his abilities Godunov could not claim the authority and the right to command obedience which legitimate hereditary right alone could convey. He showed himself more anxious than any earlier ruler for closer relations with western Europe and more conscious of the benefits these might bring to Russia. A widening of trade contacts which reduced her commercial dependence on the English, Dutch and Swedes would strengthen her position; and such considerations probably underlay his effort in 1603 to establish trading relations with the grand duchy of Tuscany. The sending of young Russians to study abroad might provide the country with a valuable nucleus of men trained in western techniques which would accelerate her development. (The policy was not entirely new: it seems that some had been sent abroad for study even in the mid-sixteenth century under Ivan IV.[13]) Young men

13. S.F. Platonov, *Russia and the West*, trans. and ed. J.L. Wiecznski (Hattiesburg, Miss., 1972), p. 27.

were therefore sent to England, Germany and perhaps also France, though without the hoped-for result. None returned to Russia; and not for over a century was this policy taken up once more, with greater success, by Peter the Great.

Most striking of all were the new tsar's repeated efforts to forge a dynastic union between his family and one of the major ruling houses of Europe. On his accession he had hoped to consolidate his position in Russia by marrying his daughter, Kseniya, to a Habsburg archduke. When this failed Prince Gustav of Sweden and Duke John of Holstein, son of the king of Denmark, were envisaged as possible bridegrooms, while there were long negotiations for the marriage of both his daughter and his son, Fyodor, to members of the English royal family or at least someone related to it.[14] Nothing came of all these approaches. But that they should have been made and pressed so seriously was a sign of a new attitude. No previous ruler of Russia had made such persistent efforts; and not for more than a century were they to be repeated. But however much historians may approve the attempts of Boris to speed up the 'europeanization' of Russia, such efforts did nothing to strengthen his position or make his rule more popular. A devastating famine, the worst in the country's history, struck in 1601–03 and heightened the atmosphere of strain and failure, the fear of conspiracies and persecution of possible opponents, which marked his last years.

His death in April 1605, followed by the murder of his young son Fyodor who briefly succeeded him, began a period of unprecedented chaos and collapse in Russia. Dmitry, the young son of Ivan IV and half-brother of Tsar Fyodor, had died in 1591, almost certainly as the result of an accident. But the belief that he had survived an attempt to murder him, or perhaps had even arisen miraculously from the dead, soon began to spread: the veneration surrounding the tsardom and the general temper of a fervently religious, not to say superstitious, people, favoured such beliefs. The result was the emergence in 1604 of a 'False Dmitry' backed by a number of Polish nobles, though not by Sigismund III himself, who rapidly gained widespread acceptance and entered Moscow in triumph in June 1605. A month later he was crowned as tsar. His origins are still mysterious; but he showed during his brief reign some personal ability and a willingness to pursue relatively liberal policies. A French soldier of fortune then serving in Russia thought him 'wise, having understanding to serve as

14. N.E. Evans, 'The Anglo-Russian royal marriage negotiations, 1600–1603', *Slavonic and East European Review* 61 (1983), 363–87.

schoolteacher to all his council'.[15] However he was never able to shake off the accusation that he was the tool of Poland, now seen by all Russians as the quintessential hereditary enemy. Most damaging of all, though he seems to have had no very strong religious beliefs of his own he could easily be seen as the representative of Catholicism. In Poland he had held out hopes, in his efforts to mobilize support, of a union of the Orthodox and Catholic Churches and had himself become a Catholic, while the new pope, Paul V, urged that he be given more active Polish backing. The result was a rising in Moscow in May 1606, in which he was overthrown and murdered. The *coup* was carried out in the name of Orthodoxy and the need to defend it against a foreign threat. In it perhaps 2,000 people, most of them Poles, were killed; and the already powerful anti-Polish feeling in Russia can now be seen acquiring a more distinctively religious tone than in the past.

A member of one of the greatest boyar families, Vasily Shuiskii, was now proclaimed tsar; but disorder and disunity were growing uncontrollably. A Cossack and peasant revolt led by Ivan Bolotnikov, a former serf, and joined by several discontented nobles set the southern half of Russia ablaze and was checked at the end of 1606 and then suppressed only after it had reached almost to the gates of Moscow. In 1607 a second False Dmitry emerged, again with Polish backing, and by the summer of 1608 was established with his followers at Tushino, only a few miles north-west of Moscow. It is not surprising that Charles IX of Sweden complained that 'The Russians change their rulers as often as hares their colour; in summer they are grey, in winter white'.

The growing weakness and prostration of Russia, which has been only briefly summarized here, had international significance because it opened the way for foreign intervention on an unprecedented scale. In 1607 the more and more desperate Shuiskii made an agreement with Sigismund III, who promised to recall the Poles then supporting the second False Dmitry, an undertaking he almost certainly could never have kept; but in the following year the hard-pressed tsar changed course and instead came to terms with the Swedes in February 1609. The agreement was onerous from the Russian point of view. In return for the help of 5,000 Swedish troops Shuiskii had to give up the Karelian territory gained in 1595, once more abandon all claims in Livonia and agree to become the permanent ally of Sweden

---

15. J. Margeret, *The Russian Empire and Grand Duchy of Muscovy*, trans. and ed. C.S.L. Dunning (Pittsburg, Pa., 1983), p. 70; the French original appeared in 1607.

against Poland–Lithuania. But this was certain to provoke a Polish re-action. Sweden and Poland were still at war, still struggling for con-trol of an increasingly devastated and impoverished Livonia (its population was now a third or less of what it had been at the original Russian invasion of 1558). Neither could devote its full energies to ac-tion in Russia. But equally neither could ignore any advantage gained there by the other. The appearance of Swedish forces there-fore produced the first formal Polish intervention (as distinct from the unofficial backing given to the two False Dmitrys). In September 1609 a Polish army laid siege to Smolensk, threatening to undo Rus-sia's most important gain of the last century on her western frontiers.

Sigismund III had very ambitious plans. Sweden's objectives in Russia were relatively specific and realistic: she wished to gain terri-tory in the north-west of the country and to establish in Moscow a regime that was reliably anti-Polish. Sigismund by contrast aimed at nothing less than making his eldest son, Vladislav, tsar, or perhaps even becoming tsar himself. There was no chance of such plans suc-ceeding. It was almost impossible to reconcile territorial expansion, the forcible recovery for Poland of lands previously lost to Russia, such as Smolensk, with the simultaneous establishment of Vladislav as ruler in Moscow. More fundamental, to have the faintest chance of general acceptance Vladislav must accept the Orthodox faith. In February 1610 some of Shuiskii's rivals, notably the Romanov family and their relations, agreed to accept the Polish prince as ruler if he embraced Orthodoxy and promised to respect Russian political traditions and the position of the leading Muscovite noble families. But the obstacles in the way of this were great. The Catholic Church was an indispensable supporter of Sigismund's rule in Poland itself and was certain to oppose his son's conversion, while the king still dreamed of ruling Russia himself and using his authority to make her Catholic. Underlying the whole situation, moreover, was the intensity of anti-Polish feeling in Russia, the fact that 'the struggle against Po-land was seen by the Muscovites as a question of life and death'.[16]

Late in 1610 the Patriarch Hermogen, head of the Orthodox Church in Russia and an unyielding religious conservative, began to call for national unity to resist the prospect of a Catholic ruler: more than ever this became the rallying-cry of opposition to Sigismund and Poland. But in 1611 the situation seemed more hopeless than ever. In June of that year Smolensk fell to the Poles, while in the fol-lowing month the Swedes occupied Novgorod. It seemed that Russia

16. W. Leitsch, *Moskau und die Politik des Kaiserhofes im XVII Jahrhundert*, i, *1604–1654* (Graz/Köln, 1960), p. 24.

might be on the point of partition by her western neighbours. It escaped this fate because of the rapid growth in 1611 and early 1612 of a powerful resistance movement with widespread popular support. From Yaroslavl, its temporary headquarters, forces were mobilized for an attack on Moscow, now occupied by a Polish garrison. At the same time efforts were made to weaken the Polish position by diplomatic means. Prince Dmitry Pozharskii, the most important leader of the national resurgence, told an Austrian agent returning through Russia from a mission to Persia that a Habsburg archduke would be welcomed as tsar, though this can hardly have been more than a bait thrown out to attract foreign support. Much more important was the need to ensure that the Swedes would remain neutral while the Poles were expelled. This was achieved by promises to support the candidature for the tsardom of Prince Charles Philip, the brother of the new Swedish king, Gustavus Adolphus; but though Pozharskii himself favoured such a Swedish candidacy there was never any chance of its succeeding. Once more religion was the insurmountable stumbling-block. Without his conversion to Orthodoxy, of which there was never any likelihood, Charles Philip had no hope of becoming tsar.

The Polish garrison in Moscow, after a desperate resistance, surrendered in October 1612. Russia had begun to free herself from foreign invaders, though the process was still far from complete; and early in 1613 a *Zemskii Sobor* (Assembly of the Land, a quasi-representative body very roughly analogous to the estates of west and central Europe) met. Very little is known about its proceedings; but in February it elected as tsar Mikhail Romanov, a member of an important boyar family but a boy of sixteen and of mediocre abilities. His coronation in July gave Russia a new dynasty which was to rule for over three centuries. It is difficult to see this as a triumph of national feeling of a modern and secular kind. Some of the leading families, such as the Mstislavskiis, were willing even now to accept Vladislav as ruler, while Pozharskii still led the Swedish party favouring Charles Philip. It seems that the Cossacks played an important role as strong opponents of any foreign candidate, and that they were largely responsible for the eventual choice of Romanov, while in Sweden there was no strong backing for Charles Philip, who was himself understandably reluctant to accept so onerous and even dangerous a role as that of tsar. Moreover in the spring of 1611 Christian IV of Denmark declared war on Sweden. This new struggle was opposed by powerful forces in both countries and was the work of the ambitious and aggressive Danish king on the one hand and the obstinate and narrow-minded Charles IX on the other. Nor did it last very long. It was ended, on terms very unfavourable to Sweden, by the peace treaty of Knared two years later. But while it lasted it was out of the question for the young Gustavus Adolphus, who succeeded Charles IX in October 1611 (and who himself briefly agreed to become a candidate for the tsardom), to embark on a full-scale military effort in Russia. She had now surmounted a supreme crisis. She was ceasing to be a mere object, an almost helpless victim, in international relations, and was once more becoming an active agent with policies and objectives of her own.

Peace with Sweden was made at Stolbovo in February 1617, a treaty mediated, with some unwelcome Dutch assistance, by Sir John Meyrick (Merrick), a leading figure in the Muscovy Company and perhaps the outstanding west European expert on Russia of that age. Though her representatives were very obstinate and uncooperative in the negotiations, which began in September 1615, for Russia the terms were severe. The cession to Sweden of the part of Karelia given up in 1607 was confirmed. Russia also lost the very narrow foothold on the Baltic that she had retained in the Teusino peace of 1595. Her drive to the west, after so many efforts and vicissitudes, had for the time being ended in failure. Any lasting settlement with Poland was even more difficult to achieve. For a time the Austrian Habsburg court in Vienna, which envisaged Polish support in an attack on the Ottoman Empire, hoped to mediate between the two antagonists; and an imperial envoy made serious efforts of this kind in 1615–16, but with no result. Any possibility of Vladislav ruling in Moscow, if it had ever existed, had now vanished. But the Poles were still unwilling to face this fact; and Russian demands for their recognition of Mikhail Romanov as tsar meant that the 1615–16 negotiations inevitably petered out. In fact no genuine Russo-Polish peace was possible. The best that could be hoped for was an armistice; and one was finally achieved at Devlino in December 1618. In some ways this also was unfavourable to Russia. The Poles still refused to recognize the new tsar; and the fact that the agreement was signed at a place far within Russian territory conveyed, in that status-sensitive age, a flavour of defeat and inferiority. Of more practical significance was the fact that Smolensk, the most important material point at issue, remained in Polish hands together with other important Russian territories, the districts of Starodub, Chernigov and Novgorod-Seversk. Already, however, the powers of Europe had begun to recognize Mikhail as tsar. The Emperor Matthias decided formally to accept him as such in January 1617, though typically he hedged his bets by assuring Sigismund III that this would not prejudice the rights of his son, and thus succeeded in annoying both the Russians and the Poles. In any case Vladislav continued to call himself Grand Prince of Moscow: while he did so and Smolensk remained in Polish hands no lasting Russo-Polish settlement was possible.

Russia's fortunes in 1618 were still at a very low ebb. She was exhausted by years of anarchy, civil war and foreign invasion: the 'Time of Troubles' of 1605–13 is said, though any accurate figure is unattainable, to have cost her two and a half million lives. Her great enemy Poland–Lithuania, by contrast, though the internal weaknesses which were soon to ruin her were already clearly to be seen, now covered a greater extent of territory than at any time in her history. Yet something had been achieved. Russia was still, so far as the major powers of western Europe were concerned, only on the periphery of the continent's political life. Spain had never, by the end of this period, sent any diplomatic representative to Moscow. France sent none until 1586 (and he was a mere merchant of Dieppe sent for commercial purposes), while the first Russian ambassador appeared in Paris only in 1615. But there had been progress, however slow and incomplete. Russia on the eve of the Thirty Years War, in which it can be argued she played a significant indirect role,[17] was less unknown, less totally foreign, more in the minds of European statesmen, than at the beginning of the Italian wars. Her emergence as a great power was to be delayed for another century. But though still often neglected and ignored except by her immediate neighbours she was now more clearly a part of Europe, more a state of which others had to take account, than when Ivan III launched her on the path that was eventually to make her the greatest of all European powers.

17. B.F. Porshnev, *Muscovy and Sweden in the Thirty Years War, 1630–1635*, ed. P. Dukes, trans. B. Pearce (Cambridge, 1995).

Chronology

1477	Defeat and death of Charles the Bold at Nancy. Marriage of Mary of Burgundy and Archduke Maximilian.
1478	Novgorod falls under direct control of Moscow.
1479	End of Turkish–Venetian war begun in 1463. Ferdinand II becomes king of Aragon.
1480	Turks capture Otranto.
1481	Death of Sultan Mehmed II.
1482	Treaty of Arras: duchy of Burgundy becomes part of kingdom of France.
1483	Accession of Charles VIII in France.
1492	Fall of Granada: end of Moorish power in Spain.
1493	Treaty of Senlis: Artois and Franche-Comté given up by Charles VIII. Treaty of Barcelona: Roussillon and Cerdagne given up by Charles VIII.
1494	Charles VIII invades Italy.
1495	Anti-French alliance of the papacy, Ferdinand, Maximilian, Milan and Venice: battle of Fornovo.
1496	French driven from Naples.
1498	Accession of Louis XII.
1499	First conquest of Milan by Louis XII.
1499–1502	War between Venice and Ottoman Empire.
1500	Second French conquest of Milan. Agreement for partition of kingdom of Naples between France and Aragon. Ivan III attacks Lithuania.
1503	Gonsalvo de Cordoba defeats French at Cerignola and on river Garigliano.
1504	Death of Isabella of Castile.
1508	League of Cambrai (papacy, France, Maximilian) formed against Venice.
1509	Battle of Agnadello; Venetians defeated by French.

1510	Pope Julius II makes peace with Venice; break-up of League of Cambrai.
1512	Accession of Sultan Selim I.
	French victory at Ravenna.
	Swiss conquest of Milan.
1513	Death of Julius II, accession of Leo X.
	French defeated at Novara.
	English capture Tournai and Thérouanne.
1514	Poles take Smolensk from Russians.
	Selim I defeats Persians at Chaldiran.
1515	Death of Louis XII, accession of Francis I.
	Battle of Marignano, French recover Milan.
	Infante Charles (future Charles V) takes over government of The Netherlands.
1516	Death of Ferdinand II of Aragon.
	Treaty of Noyon; peace between Charles and Francis I.
	Barbarossa brothers gain possession of Algiers.
1516–17	Selim I conquers Syria and Egypt.
1519	Death of Emperor Maximilian, election of Charles V as Holy Roman Emperor.
1520	Francis I and Henry VIII meet at Field of the Cloth of Gold.
	Death of Selim I, accession of Suleiman I (the Magnificent).
1521	Anti-Danish rising for Swedish independence led by Gustavus Vasa.
	New Valois–Habsburg struggle begins in Italy.
1522	Turks capture Rhodes.
1523	Gustavus Vasa becomes king of Sweden.
	Constable of Bourbon defects to the imperialist side.
1525	Defeat of Francis I at Pavia.
1526	Treaty of Madrid.
	League of Cognac formed against Charles V.
	Battle of Mohacs.
	Archduke Ferdinand elected king of Bohemia and Hungary.
1527	Sack of Rome by forces of Charles V.
	New French invasion of Italy.
1528	Andrea Doria defects to the imperialist side.
1529	Peace of Cambrai.
	Unsuccessful Turkish siege of Vienna.
1530	Charles V crowned emperor by Pope Clement VII.
	Diet of Augsburg and Augsburg Confession.

1531	Archduke Ferdinand elected King of the Romans. Schmalkaldic League formed.
1532	Turkish attack on Vienna fails.
1533	Accession of Ivan IV in Russia.
1534	Duke Ulrich recovers Württemberg.
1535	Charles V takes Tunis. Death of Francesco Sforza, Duke of Milan.
1536	French occupy Savoy-Piedmont; war with Charles V, who invades Provence. French Capitulations with Ottoman Empire.
1537–40	War between Venice and Ottoman Empire.
1538	Truce between Charles V and Francis I. Death of Duke of Guelders.
1540	Death of John Zapolya.
1541	Turks capture Buda. Charles V fails to take Algiers.
1542	Renewed war between Charles V and Francis I.
1543–44	Barbarossa at Toulon.
1543	Charles V defeats Duke of Cleves.
1544	Treaty of Crépy between Charles V and Francis I.
1546	Peace between France and England. War between Charles V and Schmalkaldic League.
1547	Deaths of Francis I and Henry VIII. Victory of Charles V at Mühlberg.
1549–50	Renewed Anglo-French war; France recovers Boulogne.
1551	Habsburg family compact for division of the empire of Charles V.
1552	Treaty of Chambord between Henry II and German Protestant princes; France occupies bishoprics of Metz, Toul and Verdun. Maurice of Saxony forces flight of Charles V. Charles V fails to take Metz. Ivan IV takes Kazan.
1553	English contact with Russia via White Sea begins.
1554	Marriage of Prince Philip, son of Charles V, and Mary Tudor.
1555	Religious Peace of Augsburg in Germany. Siena captured by Spanish forces. Charles V abdicates at Brussels.
1556	Truce of Vaucelles. War in Italy between Pope Paul IV, with French support, and Philip II.

1557	England declares war on France; battle of St Quentin.
1558	French capture Calais.
	French defeated at Gravelines.
	Death of Mary Tudor.
	Russian invasion of Livonia.
1559	Treaty of Cateau-Cambrésis: peace between Henry II and Philip II.
	Death of Henry II.
1560	Death of Gustavus Vasa.
	Treaty of Edinburgh: defeat of French influence in Scotland.
	Spain defeated at Djerba.
1561	Sweden and Denmark intervene in the Livonian war.
1562–63	First 'war of religion' in France; English support for Huguenots.
1563–70	War between Sweden and combination of Denmark, Poland–Lithuania and Lübeck.
1564	Death of Ferdinand I; Maximilian II becomes Holy Roman Emperor.
1565	Failure of Turkish siege of Malta.
1566	Death of Suleiman the Magnificent, accession of Selim II.
	Outbreak of image-breaking in the Netherlands.
1567	Arrival of Alba in the Netherlands; 'Council of Blood' begins to function.
1567–68	Second religious war in France; John Casimir of the Palatinate supports the Huguenots.
1568	Netherlands rebels defeated at Jemmingen.
1568–71	Morisco revolt in Spain.
1569	Union of Lublin between Poland and grand duchy of Lithuania.
1569–70	Third religious war in France.
1570–73	War between Venice and Ottoman Empire.
1571	Alliance of Spain, Venice and the papacy against the Ottoman Empire; battle of Lepanto.
1572	Massacre of St Bartholomew; fourth religious war in France.
	Sea Beggars seize Brill; William of Orange again invades the Netherlands.
1573	Election of Duc d'Anjou as king of Poland.
	Alba recalled from the Netherlands.
	Venice makes peace with the Ottoman Empire and cedes Cyprus.
	Don John of Austria takes Tunis.

1574	Renewed religious war in France.
	Unsuccessful Spanish siege of Leyden.
1575	Stephen Bathory elected king of Poland.
	Bankruptcy of Philip II.
1576	'Peace of Monsieur' in France.
	'Spanish Fury' in Antwerp and Pacification of Ghent.
	Don John of Austria becomes governor-general of the Netherlands.
1577	Renewed religious war in France.
1578	Duke of Parma becomes governor-general of the Netherlands.
	King Sebastian of Portugal defeated and killed in battle of Alcazar-el-Kebir.
	War breaks out between Ottoman Empire and Persia.
1579	Union of Utrecht between rebel Netherlands provinces.
1580	Death of King Henry of Portugal; Spanish invasion led by Alba.
	Renewed religious war in France.
	Truce between Spain and the Ottoman Empire.
1581	Rebel Netherlands provinces renounce allegiance to Philip II.
	Swedes take Narva from Russians.
1582	Peace of Yam Zapolskii between Russia and Poland–Lithuania.
1583	Duc d'Anjou attempts to seize Antwerp.
	Crisis in archbishopric of Cologne when Archbishop Truchsess becomes a Protestant.
1584	Assassination of William of Orange.
	Death of Ivan IV.
1585	Treaty of Joinville between Philip II and Catholic League in France.
1585–86	Drake raids Spanish settlements in the West Indies.
1585–87	Leicester in the Netherlands.
1586	Death of Stephen Bathory.
	Regime of the Sixteen established in Paris.
1587	Execution of Mary, Queen of Scots.
	Drake raids Cadiz.
1588	Henry III driven from Paris after 'Day of Barricades'.
	Defeat of Spanish armada.
	Assassination of Duc de Guise.
	Duke of Savoy seizes marquisate of Saluzzo.

1589	Assassination of Henry III; war between Henry IV and Catholic League.
	Unsuccessful expedition of Drake and Norris to Portugal.
1590	War between Ottoman Empire and Persia ends.
1590–95	War between Russia and Sweden.
1592	Death of Duke of Parma.
1593	Conversion of Henry IV to Catholicism.
	War breaks out between Austrian Habsburgs and Ottoman Empire.
1594	Henry IV regains control of Paris.
1595	Henry IV granted absolution by the pope; Franco-Spanish war begins.
1596	Alliance of England, France and United Provinces against Spain.
	Second Spanish expedition against England defeated by bad weather.
	Bankruptcy of Philip II.
	Turkish victory at Mezo-Keresztes over the Austrian Habsburgs.
1597	Henry IV takes Amiens.
	Failure of third Spanish expedition against England.
1598	Treaty of Vervins: peace between France and Spain.
	Death of Philip II; accession of Philip III.
1600	War between France and Duke of Savoy.
	Charles IX becomes king of Sweden.
1602–03	Suppression of Tyrone's rebellion in Ireland.
1603	Death of Elizabeth, accession of James I.
1604	Treaty of London: peace between England and Spain.
1605	Stephen Bockskay elected king of Hungary.
	'Time of Troubles' in Russia begins.
1606	Treaty of Sitva-Torok: peace between Ottomans and Austrian Habsburgs.
1607–08	Religious–political conflict at Donauwörth.
1609	Death of Duke of Jülich-Cleves.
	Catholic Union in Germany formed.
	Swedish and Polish intervention in Russia begins.
	Twelve Years Truce between Spain and United Provinces.
	'Letter of Majesty' in Bohemia issued by Rudolf II.
	Expulsion of Moriscos from Spain begins.
1610	Assassination of Henry IV.

1611–13	War between Denmark and Sweden.
1612	Death of Rudolf II.
1614	Treaty of Xanten: Jülich-Cleves duchies divided between Brandenburg and Neuburg claimants.
1617	Treaty of Stolbovo between Russia and Sweden.
1618	Russo-Polish armistice at Devlino. Revolt in Bohemia begins Thirty Years War.
1619	Death of Emperor Matthias; election of Ferdinand II. Frederick V, Elector Palatine, elected king of Bohemia.
1620	Defeat of Bohemian rebels at battle of the White Hill.
1621	War between Spain and United Provinces recommences. Death of Philip III; accession of Philip IV.

For Further Reading

This list of further reading inevitably omits many books and articles relevant to the history of international relations during this period. It concentrates in the main on works in English likely to be of use to students, though a small number in other languages have been included.

General

Treatments in English of international relations in Europe as a whole during the early modern period are few. The best substitute is probably the relevant chapters in the volumes of the *New Cambridge Modern History*: i, *The Renaissance, 1493–1520*, ed. G.R. Potter (Cambridge, 1957); ii, *The Reformation, 1520–1559*, ed. G.R. Elton (Cambridge, 1958; 2nd ed, 1990); iii, *The Counter-Reformation and Price Revolution, 1559–1610*, ed. R.B. Wernham (Cambridge, 1968). In French two useful though somewhat summary treatments are H. Lapeyre, *Les monarchies européennes du XVIe siècle: Les relations internationales* (Paris, 1967), and G. Zeller, *Les temps modernes: De Christophe Colomb à Cromwell* (vol. ii of the series *Histoire des relations internationales*, ed. P. Renouvin, Paris, 1953). In German E. Fueter, *Geschichte des europaïschen Staatensystems von 1492–1559* (Munich, 1919), has still much to offer in spite of its age. It is not, in the main, a narrative of events but rather a state-by-state analytical treatment which throws much light on the realities that underlay these events. There are few general works covering the foreign policies of individual countries; but for England R.B. Wernham, *Before the Armada: The Growth of English Foreign Policy, 1485–1588* (London, 1966), provides a substantial and balanced narrative covering most of this period. Of the many wide-ranging studies of it not focused on international relations the most recent is R. Bonney's useful *The European Dynastic States, 1494–1660* (Oxford, 1991).

Chapter One

The best overall discussion of war and its significance is J.R. Hale, *War and Society in Renaissance Europe, 1450–1620* (London, 1985), while important articles by the same author are 'War and public opinion in the fifteenth and sixteenth centuries', *Past and Present* 22 (1962); 'Gunpowder and the Renaissance: An essay in the history of ideas', in *From the Renaissance to the Counter-Reformation: Essays in Honour of Garrett Mattingly*, ed. C.H. Carter (London, 1966); and 'Sixteenth-century explanations of war and violence', *Past and Present* 51 (1971). A short general study is H. Lapeyre, 'L'art de la guerre au temps de Charles Quint', in the collection *Charles Quint et son temps* (Paris, 1959). F. Tallett, *War and Society in Early Modern Europe, 1494–1715* (London, 1992), is based on a very wide range of printed materials and excellent on every aspect of armies and their problems though less full on the wider social and political background. The outstanding work on a single country is *Histoire militaire de la France*, i, ed. P. Contamine (Paris, 1992), part of a series with this title whose general editor is A. Corvisier. The individual chapters are by experts and the whole is finely illustrated. M.E. Mallett and J.R. Hale, *The Military Organization of a Renaissance State: Venice c.1400 to 1617* (Cambridge, 1984), is equally good in a rather different way, and I.A.A. Thompson, *War and Government in Habsburg Spain, 1560–1620* (London, 1976), is an important and impressively thorough study of its subject. For England there are two useful detailed studies by C.G. Cruickshank: *Army Royal: Henry VIII's Invasion of France, 1513* (Oxford, 1969) and *Elizabeth's Army* (Oxford, 1946), while H. Lloyd, *The Rouen Campaign, 1590–1592* (Oxford, 1973), covers an unsuccessful English military enterprise. The stage for the Italian wars is set in M.E. Mallett, 'Diplomacy and war in fifteenth-century Italy', in *Art and Politics in Renaissance Italy*, ed. G. Holmes (Oxford, 1993). On the wars themselves the old and short F.L. Taylor, *The Art of War in Italy, 1494–1529* (Cambridge, 1921), is still useful; but the basic more recent treatment is in Italian, in P. Pieri, *Il Rinascimento e la crisi militare italiana* (Turin, 1952). The increasingly diluted and often debased chivalric traditions which still carried weight in the sixteenth century are illustrated by M. Vale, *War and Chivalry: Warfare and Aristocratic Culture in England, France and Burgundy at the End of the Middle Ages* (London, 1981), and the essays in *Chivalry in the Renaissance*, ed. S. Anglo (Woodbridge, 1990). The technology of the sieges that dominated so much of the fighting of the period is covered in C. Duffy, *Siege War-*

fare: The Fortress in the Early Modern World, 1494–1660 (London, 1979). S. Pepper and N. Adams, *Firearms and Fortifications: Military Architecture and Siege Warfare in Sixteenth-Century Siena* (Chicago, 1986), is an excellent specialized study, while Judith Hook, 'Fortifications and the end of the Sienese state', *History* 62 (1977), deals with an aspect of the same subject. On naval warfare in the Mediterranean there is an important and illuminating book by J.F. Guilmartin, *Gunpowder and Galleys: Changing Technology and Mediterranean Warfare at Sea in the Sixteenth Century* (Cambridge, 1974), while on the embryonic French navy the *Histoire militaire de la France* mentioned above is useful. On the English navy the best general treatment is D. Loades, *The Tudor Navy: An Administrative, Political and Military History* (London, 1992), while the English war effort in the last years of the century is covered in R.B. Wernham, *After the Armada: Elizabethan England and the Struggle for Western Europe, 1588–1595* (Oxford, 1984) and *The Return of the Armadas: The Last Years of the Elizabethan War against Spain, 1595–1603* (Oxford, 1994). G. Scammell, 'The sinews of war: manning and provisioning English fighting ships, c.1550–1650', *Mariner's Mirror* 73 (1987), is a useful article, as is P. Pierson, 'The development of Spanish naval strategy and tactics in the sixteenth century', in *Politics, Religion and Diplomacy in Early Modern Europe: Essays in Honor of De Lamar Jensen*, ed. M.R. Thorp and A.J. Slavin (Kirksville, Mo., 1994), while D. Goodman, *Spanish Naval Power, 1589–1665: Reconstruction and Defeat* (Cambridge, 1996), is a work of impeccable scholarship.

Chapter Two

The influence of the greatest international finance house of the first half of the sixteenth century is brought out in R. Ehrenberg, *Capital and Finance in the Age of the Renaissance: A Study of the Fuggers and their Connections* (London, 1928), which is a shortened version of a German original first published in 1896, and L.Schick, *Un grand homme d'affaires au début du XVIe siècle: Jacob Fugger* (Paris, 1957). The borrowing which was so essential to ambitious but impoverished monarchs is illustrated in a number of articles: for Charles V, F. Braudel, 'Les emprunts de Charles-Quint sur la place d'Anvers', in *Charles-Quint et son Temps* (Paris, 1959); for France, R. Doucet, 'Le grand parti de Lyon au XVIe siècle', *Revue Historique* CLXXI (1933); and for Spain, A. Castillo, 'Dette flottante et dette consolidée en Espagne de 1557 à 1600', *Annales: Histoire, Sciences, Sociétés* 18, ii (1963); D.O. Flynn, 'Fiscal crisis and the decline of Spain (Castile)', *Journal of Economic*

History 42 (1982); and A. Lovett, 'The General Settlement of 1577: an aspect of Spanish finance in the early modern period', *Historical Journal* XXV (1982). The critical importance of money in waging war is brought out in F. Gilbert, *The Pope, his Banker and Venice* (Cambridge, Mass., 1980), and Melissa M. Bullard, *Filippo Strozzi and the Medici: Favour and Finance in Sixteenth-Century Florence and Rome* (Cambridge, 1980). L. Stone, *An Elizabethan: Sir Horatio Palavicino* (Oxford, 1956), throws light on the interrelations of international finance and politics, while G.D. Ramsay, *The City of London in International Affairs at the Accession of Elizabeth Tudor* (Manchester, 1975), is essentially a detailed work of economic history. The efforts at effective economic warfare that marked the later years of the sixteenth century are discussed in J.I. Israel, 'Spain, the Spanish embargoes, and the struggle for mastery of world trade, 1585–1660', in his *Empire and Entrepots: The Dutch, the Spanish Monarchy and the Jews, 1585–1713* (London/Ronceverte, 1990), and Pauline Croft, 'Trading with the enemy, 1585–1604', *Historical Journal* XXXII (1989). The first part of J.I. Israel, *Dutch Primacy in World Trade, 1585–1740* (Oxford, 1989), gives the best account of the meteoric rise of the new force which transformed international economic relationships in the last years of this period. *Economic Systems and State Finance*, ed. R. Bonney (Oxford, 1995), brings together much information on public finance during this period, though it is not much concerned with the impact on it of war expenditures and demands.

Chapter Three

The best book on the growth of quasi-modern diplomatic contacts between the states of Europe during this period is G. Mattingly, *Renaissance Diplomacy* (London, 1955), which is both learned and well written. The first chapter of M.S. Anderson, *The Rise of Modern Diplomacy, 1450–1919* (London, 1993) provides a more summary account of the same developments. The early part of the first volume of *Les Affaires Etrangères et le corps diplomatique français*, ed. J. Baillou (2 vols, Paris, 1984), provides a detailed account of French diplomatic organization for which there is no parallel for any other state. The mediaeval origins of the diplomatic system that was now taking shape are well discussed in D.E. Queller, *The Office of Ambassador in the Middle Ages* (Princeton, NJ, 1967); while M.A.R. de Maulde-la-Clavière, *La diplomatie au temps de Machiavel* (3 vols, Paris, 1892–93) remains a remarkable work of scholarship based on a wide range of primary sources. I.

Bernays, 'Die Diplomatie um 1500', *Historische Zeitschrift* CXXXVIII (1928), summarizes some characteristics of the emerging diplomatic system at the beginning of the sixteenth century, while E. Grisaille, 'Un manuel du parfait diplomate au dix-septième siècle', *Revue d'Histoire Diplomatique* (1915), discusses a typical example of the descriptions of the ideal diplomat which became numerous during this period.

Chapter Four

A detailed narrative of many aspects of the Italian wars in their first stages can be found in vols. ii–iv of J.S.C. Bridge, *A History of France from the Death of Louis XI* (5 vols, Oxford, 1921–36), while I. Cloulas, *Charles VIII et le mirage italien* (Paris, 1986), and B. Quilliet, *Louis XII* (Paris, 1986), are substantial studies of rulers who played a leading role in them. The Emperor Maximilian is less well served, though R.W. Seton-Watson, *Maximilian I, Holy Roman Emperor* (Oxford, 1902), in spite of its age and slightness, is still of use. The policies of Ferdinand of Aragon, a very different personality, can be followed in F. Fernandez-Armesto, *Ferdinand and Isabella* (London, 1975), and more satisfactorily in the last chapters of J.N. Hillgarth, *The Spanish Kingdoms, 1250–1516*, ii, *Castilian Hegemony* (Oxford, 1978). J. Jacquart, *Bayard* (Paris, 1987), a biography of the most famous French soldier of the early sixteenth century, is in large part a narrative of the Italian wars down to Bayard's death in 1524, while the most belligerent pope of the period is covered in Christine Shaw, *Julius II: The Warrior Pope* (Oxford, 1993). Of several good treatments of sixteenth-century Spain the most recent is A.W. Lovett, *Early Habsburg Spain, 1517–1598* (Oxford, 1986), which is short, clear and balanced. Also useful are two well-known books: J.H. Elliott, *Imperial Spain, 1469–1714* (London, 1963), and J. Lynch, *Spain under the Habsburgs*, i, *Empire and Absolutism, 1516–1598* (Oxford, 1964): new editions of this book were published in 1981 and, under the title *Spain 1516–1598: From Nation State to World Empire*, in 1991. On Charles V the basic large-scale work in English remains K. Brandi, *The Emperor Charles V*, trans. C.V. Wedgwood (London, 1939). M.F. Alvarez, *Charles V, Elected Emperor and Hereditary Ruler* (London, 1975), is more cursory, as is the older R. Tyler, *The Emperor Charles V* (London, 1956). Some of the assumptions that influenced the emperor can be followed in Frances Yates, 'Charles V and the idea of the Empire', in her *Astraea: The Imperial Theme in the Sixteenth Century* (London, 1975). The policies of Charles's greatest opponent are well covered in R.J. Knecht, *Francis I* (Cambridge, 1982) (there is a revised edition of this book, *Renaissance Warrior and Patron: The Reign of Francis I* (Cambridge, 1994)), and in French in J. Jacquart, *François Ier* (Paris, 1981). On one of the most important aspects of French foreign policy there is the still useful J. Ursu, *La politique orientale de Francois Ier* (Paris, 1908). The classic contemporary account of the Italian wars can be found in F. Guicciardini, *The History of Italy*, trans. S. Alexander (New York, 1969).

Chapter Five

The relations between Spain and central Europe and between the two branches of the Habsburg family can be followed in B. Chudoba, *Spain and the Empire, 1519–1643* (Chicago, 1952), which, with some faults, includes information not easily found elsewhere. The difficulties and complications of the Austrian Habsburg position are brought out in Paula S. Fichtner, *Ferdinand I of Austria: The Politics of Dynasticism in the Age of Reformation* (Boulder, Col., 1982), which, though somewhat pedestrian, is based on thorough research and the only work in English on its subject. Some of the factors that impeded the policies of both Charles V and his brother in the German world are brought out in S.A. Fischer-Galati, *Ottoman Imperialism and German Protestantism, 1521–1555* (Cambridge, Mass., 1959). On Italy after the most critical period of the struggles there the best recent work in English is E. Cochrane, *Italy, 1530–1630*, ed. J. Kirshner (London/New York, 1988). On Henry II, an important and until recently rather underestimated figure, there is the large-scale biography of I. Cloulas, *Henri II* (Paris, 1985), and the thorough and useful F.J. Baumgartner, *Henry II, King of France, 1547–1559* (Durham, NC/London, 1988). On the Franco-Habsburg struggles of the later 1540s and 1550s there is still much to be learned from the remarkable work of L. Romier, *Les origines politiques des Guerres de Religion* (2 vols, Paris, 1913–14), and important special aspects of this rivalry are covered in D. Potter, 'Foreign policy in the age of the Reformation: French involvement in the Schmalkaldic War, 1544–1547', *Historical Journal* XX (1977), and the early chapters of G. Zeller, *La Réunion de Metz à la France (1552–1648)* (Paris, 1926), vol. i. The outstanding recent book, however, is M.J. Rodriguez-Salgado, *The Changing Face of Empire: Charles V, Philip II and Habsburg Authority, 1551–1559* (Cambridge, 1988). The efforts of the competing powers to dominate English policy are well discussed in E.H. Harbison, *Rival Ambassadors at the Court of Queen Mary* (Princeton, NJ/London, 1940); and D. Loades, *The Reign of Mary Tudor: Politics, Government and Religion in England, 1553–1558* (London, 1977), contains much on foreign policy from a more general point of view.

Chapter Six

Philip II is the subject of two short and useful biographies: P. Pearson, *Philip II of Spain* (London, 1975), and G. Parker, *Philip II* (London, 1979); while H.G. Koenigsberger, 'The statecraft of Philip II', *European Studies Review* I (1971), is a penetrating brief survey by a leading authority. G. Parker, 'David or Goliath? Philip II and his world in the 1580s', in *Spain, Europe and the Atlantic World: Essays in Honour of John H. Elliott*, ed. R.L. Kagan and G. Parker (Cambridge, 1996), throws light on the king's difficulties in his later years. D. Goodman, *Power and Penury: Government, Technology and Science in Philip II's Spain* (Cambridge, 1988), is interesting on the realities underlying the imposing structure of Spanish power. An important but often neglected aspect of Spanish imperialism is covered in A. Hess, *The Forgotten Frontier: A History of the Sixteenth-Century Ibero–African Frontier* (Chicago/London, 1978); while a famous work, F. Braudel, *The Mediterranean and the Mediterranean World in the Age of Philip II* (2 vols, London, 1972), illuminates many aspects, including international ones, of this period. Some of the complexities of England's important but difficult international position in the first years of Elizabeth's reign are elucidated in C.G. Bayne, *Anglo-Roman Relations, 1558–1565* (Oxford, 1913); and various relevant topics are well covered in the essays in Nicola M. Sutherland, *Princes, Politics and Religion, 1547– 1589* (London, 1984). On the Netherlands revolt the best general account is G. Parker, *The Dutch Revolt*, i (London, 1977). The same author has produced an important collection of essays, *Spain and the Netherlands, 1559–1659* (London, 1979); and his 'Spain, her enemies and the revolt of the Netherlands, 1559–1648', *Past and Present* 49 (1970), does much to put the revolt in its international context. Professor Parker has also written a path-breaking book on the military aspects of the long Spanish struggle to subdue the Netherlands rebels in his *The Army of Flanders and the Spanish Road, 1567–1659: The Logistics of Spanish Victory and Defeat in the Low Countries Wars* (Cambridge, 1972), while its naval aspects are covered in R.A. Stradling, *The Armada of Flanders: Spanish Maritime Policy and European War,*

1568–1668 (Cambridge, 1992). C. Wilson, *Queen Elizabeth and the Revolt of the Netherlands* (London, 1970), gives an appropriately critical account of the queen's hesitant and ambivalent attitude, while F.G. Oosterhoff, *Leicester and the Netherlands, 1585–1587* (Utrecht, 1988), covers in detail the unsuccessful English intervention of these years. W.S. Maltby, *Alba: A Biograpy of Fernando Alvarez de Toledo, Third Duke of Alba, 1507–1582* (Berkeley/Los Angeles/London, 1983), is an excellent biography of the most famous of Spanish governors in the Netherlands. On the wars of religion in France there is the short but useful recent work of M. Holt, *The French Wars of Religion, 1562–1629* (Cambridge, 1995), and the same author's *The Duke of Anjou and the Politique Struggle during the Wars of Religion* (Cambridge, 1986); while A. Soman, ed., *The Massacre of St. Bartholomew: Reappraisals and Documents* (The Hague, 1974), deals with the most notorious episode of these struggles.

Chapter Seven

The complexities of the situation in France in the later 1580s and early 1590s and its relationship to events in Europe generally are brought out in De Lamar Jensen, *Diplomacy and Dogmatism: Bernardino de Mendoza and the French Catholic League* (Cambridge, Mass., 1964). The Spanish armada of 1588 is well placed in its European context in G. Mattingly, *The Defeat of the Spanish Armada* (London, 1959). The tercentenary of the armada's sailing produced several discussions of its fate. Of these *Armada 1588–1988* (London, 1988), an illustrated exhibition catalogue, gives the most penetrating account of these dramatic events; much the greater part of the text is the work of M.J. Rodriguez-Salgado. The same author, together with S. Adams, edited *England, Spain and the Gran Armada, 1585–1604* (Edinburgh, 1991), which contains several valuable specialized articles. C. Martin and G. Parker, *The Spanish Armada* (London, 1988), is a short and well-illustrated narrative account: F. Fernandez-Armesto, *The Spanish Armada: The Experience of War in 1588* (Oxford, 1988), though readable, is also narrative and descriptive. The long Anglo-Spanish struggle after 1588 is covered from the English standpoint in the works of R.B. Wernham, *After the Armada* and *The Return of the Armadas*, mentioned above. There is an account of the last stages of the religious wars in France in D.J. Buisseret, *Henry IV* (London, 1984), while the king's often difficult relations with England are covered in the old work of J.B. Black, *Elizabeth and Henry IV* (London, 1914), and M. Lee, *James I and Henri IV* (Urbana, Ill., 1970). J.M. Hayden, 'Continuity in the France of Henry IV and Louis XIII: French foreign policy, 1598–1611', *Journal of Modern History* XXXV (1973), is a useful article.

Chapter Eight

There is an excellent account of the German situation in the first two decades of the seventeenth century and its European ramifications in the first chapter of G. Parker *et al.*, *The Thirty Years War* (London, 1984), while Nicola M. Sutherland, 'The origins of the Thirty Years War and the structure of European politics', *English Historical Review* CVII (1992), is an important and wide-ranging article. The murder of Henry IV and its effects on the Cleves-Jülich crisis and international relations generally can be followed in R. Mousnier, *The Assassination of Henry IV* (London, 1973). The growing pessimism and sense of failure in Spain during these years is well discussed in J.H. Elliott, 'Self-perception and decline in early seventeenth-century Spain', in his *Spain and its World, 1500–1700* (Princeton, NJ, 1988). Many aspects of the situation just before and in the first moments of the Thirty Years War are best covered in a series of articles by P. Brightwell, 'The Spanish system and the Twelve Years Truce', *English Historical Review* LXXXIX (1974); 'The Spanish origins of the Thirty Years War', *European Studies Review* 9 (1977); and 'Spain and Bohemia: the decision to intervene, 1619', *European Studies Review* 12 (1982). G.V. Polisensky, *The Thirty Years War* (London, 1971), is a translation of a book first published in Czech which gives much attention to the Bohemian situation.

Chapter Nine

The growing European preoccupation with Ottoman power in the early part of this period is discussed in considerable detail in R. Schwoebel, *The Shadow of the Crescent: The Renaissance Image of the Turk (1453–1517)* (Nieukoop, 1967). N. Houseley, *The Later Crusades, 1274–1580: From Lyons to Alcazar* (Oxford, 1992), stresses the continuing though declining importance of the crusading ideal. The intellectual and cultural aspects of European–Ottoman relations are well treated in two books by B. Lewis, *The Muslim Discovery of Europe* (New York, 1982) and *Cultures in Conflict: Christians, Muslims and Jews in the Age of Discovery* (Oxford, 1995). The outstanding Christian account of the Ottoman Empire is most conveniently accessible in *The Turkish Letters of Ogier Ghiselin de Busbecq*, trans. E.S. Forster (Oxford, 1927); and F.L. Baumer, 'England, the Turk and the Common Corps of Christendom', *American Historical Review* l (1944), shows that even the Reformation did not destroy the sense of some essential European unity in face of this threat. Ottoman strengths and weaknesses as seen by the best- informed European diplomats can be followed in Lucette Valensi, *The Birth of the Despot: Venice and the Sublime Porte* (Ithaca, NY/London, 1995). The most useful general narrative account of Ottoman expansion and the European response to it is in the relevant chapters of vols i–iii of the *New Cambridge Modern History;* S.N. Fisher, *The Foreign Relations of Turkey, 1481–1512* (Urbana, Ill., 1948), is short and rather mechanical, and Dorothy Vaughan, *Europe and the Turk: A Pattern of Alliances, 1350–1700* (Liverpool, 1954), is pedestrian but brings together a large amount of information. The most famous sultan of the period is still best studied in R.B. Merriman, *Suleiman the Magnificent, 1520–1566* (Cambridge, Mass., 1944). The more recent A. Clot, *Suleiman the Magnificent: The Man, His Life, His Epoch* (n.p., 1993), is less satisfactory, while A.H. Lybyer, *The Government of the Ottoman Empire in the Time of Suleiman the Magnificent* (Cambridge, Mass., 1913), is essentially an administrative study. Aspects of the long struggle of the Ottomans with Christian Europe are summarized in J.F. Guilmartin, 'Ideology and conflict: the wars of the Ottoman Empire, 1453–1606', in R.I. Rotberg and T.K. Rabb, eds, *The Origin and Prevention of Major Wars* (Cambridge, 1989); and the most spectacular Christian success in these wars is re-evaluated in A.C. Hess, 'The battle of Lepanto and its place in Mediterranean history', *Past and Present* 57 (1972). Another special aspect of them is the subject of G.E. Rothenberg, *The Austrian Military Border in Croatia, 1522–1747* (Urbana, Ill., 1960), while a striking episode is covered in A.N. Kurat, 'The Turkish expedition to Astrakhan in 1569 and the problem of the Don-Volga canal', *Slavonic and East European Review* 40 (1961–2). C.M. Kortepeter, *Ottoman Imperialism during the Reformation: Europe and the Caucasus* (London/New York, 1973), illuminates some of the more obscure aspects of international relations in the Near East during the later sixteenth century; and the chaotic maritime situation in the Mediterranean at the end of this period is well brought out in A. Tenenti, *Piracy and the Decline of Venice, 1580–1615* (Berkeley, Ca., 1967).

Chapter Ten

The most useful short general history of Russia in this period is R. Crummey, *The Formation of Muscovy, 1304–1613* (London, 1987), while a more detailed discussion can be found in G. Vernadsky, *Russia at the Dawn of the Modern Age* (New Haven, Conn., 1959) and *The Tsardom of Moscow, 1547–1682*, Pt. i (New Haven, Conn., 1969). Ivan III, a shadowy figure in spite of his importance, is best covered by J.L. Fennell, *Ivan the Great of Moscow* (London, 1961); I. Grey, *Ivan III and the Unification of Russia* (London, 1964), is more popular in its treatment. Ivan IV has, understandably, attracted many biographers, but no book on him in English is really satisfactory. Possibly the best is still K. Waliszewski, *Ivan the Terrible* (London, 1904), while I. Grey, *Ivan the Terrible* (London, 1964), is relatively short and draws heavily on basic Russian printed materials. The first stage of the long and complex struggles for Livonia can be followed in the final pages of E. Christiansen, *The Northern Crusades: The Baltic and the Catholic Frontier, 1100–1525* (London, 1980), and briefly in T. Esper, 'Russia and the Baltic, 1494–1558', *Slavic Review* XXV (1966). Their later developments are discussed in the relevant chapters of D. Kirby, *Northern Europe in the Early Modern Period: The Baltic World, 1492–1772* (London, 1990), and S.P. Oakley, *War and Peace in the Baltic, 1560–1790* (London, 1992), and best of all in M. Roberts, *The Early Vasas: A History of Sweden, 1523–1611* (Cambridge, 1968). The growth of a west European belief in the essential backwardness and even barbarism of Russia is briefly but effectively covered in E. Klug, 'Das "asiatische" Russland. Über die Entstehung eines europäischen Vorurteils', *Historische Zeitschrift* 245 (1987). The growth from the 1550s onwards of trading and diplomatic relations between England and Russia has attracted a good deal of attention from historians: S.H. Baron, 'Osip Nepea and the opening of Anglo-Russian commercial relations', *Oxford Slavonic Papers*, New Series, ii (1978), is the most significant of a number of articles. Two old but still very informative large-scale works are H. Uebersberger, *Oesterreich und Russland seit dem Ende des 15. Jahrhunderts*, i (Vienna/Leipzig, 1906), and P. Pierling, *La Russie et le Saint-Siège*, i–ii (Paris, 1896–7). The Time of Troubles is briefly covered by S.F. Platonov, *The Time of Troubles*, trans. J. Alexander (Lawrence, Kan., 1970), while P.L. Barbour, *Dimitry, called the Pretender, Tsar and Great Prince of all Russia* (London, 1967), though popular in tone and written in a sometimes irritating style, is based on a wide range of printed sources. The most famous of all foreign descriptions of Russia can be read in an abridged form in S. von Herberstein, *Description of Moscow and Muscovy, 1557*, ed. B. Picard, trans. J.C.B. Grundy (London, 1969); and *Rude and Barbarous Kingdom: Russia in the Accounts of Sixteenth-Century English Voyagers*, ed. L.E. Berry and R.O. Crummey (Madison/Milwaukee/London, 1968), provides a well-edited selection of equally important English ones.

Maps

Map 1   *Europe in 1519*

Boundary of Holy Roman Empire

Habsburg territories

RUSSIA

Königsberg
Teutonic Order

L I T H U A N I A
P O L A N D

ndenburg

Saxony

Prague

Bohemia

Budapest

Moldavia

Austria

HUNGARY

Styria

Wallachia

Belgrade

Dalmatia

OTTOMAN

Constantinople

Kingdom of
Naples

Naples

EMPIRE

Malta

Rhodes   Cyprus

Crete

0   500 mls

0   500 km

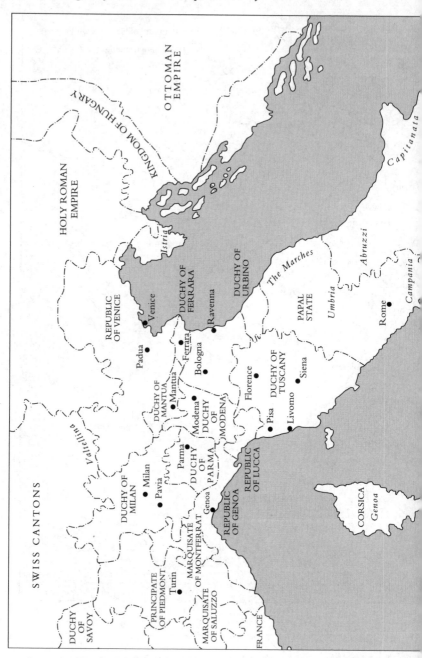

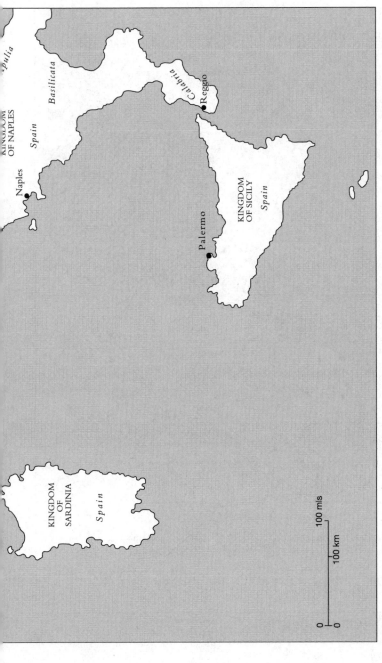

Map 2. *Italy in 1559*

Map 3.   *The Netherlands in 1609*

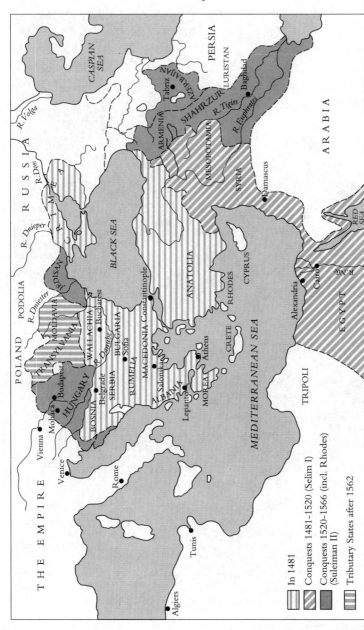

Map 4. *The Ottoman Empire, 1481–1566*

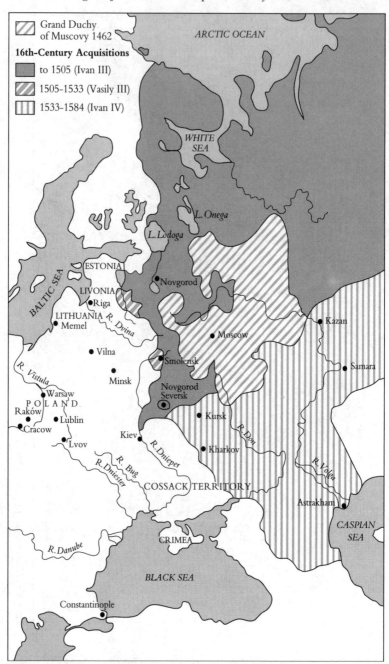

Map 5.   *Russian and eastern Europe, 1462–1584*

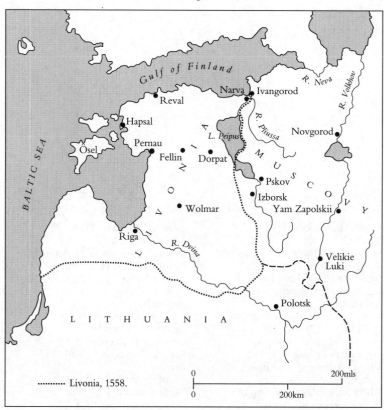

Map 6. *Livonia, 1558–83*

Index